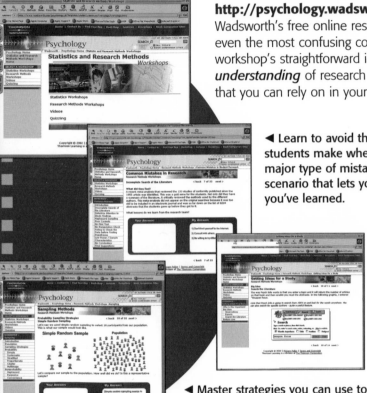

www.wadsworth.com

www.wadsworth.com is the World Wide Web site for Thomson Wadsworth and is your direct source to dozens of online resources.

At *www.wadsworth.com* you can find out about supplements, demonstration software, and student resources. You can also send email to many of our authors and preview new publications and exciting new technologies.

www.wadsworth.com
Changing the way the world learns®

ABOUT THE AUTHORS

Bill Lammers, Ph.D.
I received my B.A. degree in Psychology from San Diego State University (1985) and my Master of Arts (1987) and Doctor of Philosophy (1989) degrees in Experimental Psychology from Bowling Green State University. As an undergraduate student, I conducted research with Dr. R. H. Defran, using operant conditioning techniques to assess the hearing abilities of South American parrots. As a graduate student, I conducted research with Dr. Pietro Badia, using psychophysiological techniques to assess hearing during sleep, memory during sleep, olfaction during sleep, behavioral responding during sleep, habituation during waking, and classical conditioning during waking.

Since 1990, I have been a professor at the University of Central Arkansas. I continue to teach General Psychology, Psychological Statistics, Experimental Psychology, Experimental Psychology Laboratory, and Physiological Psychology. My current research interests include the role of technology in teaching, the types of teaching techniques used in the university classroom, the quality of various teaching techniques, and the factors that most influence student learning. In 2001, I was awarded the University of Central Arkansas Teaching Excellence Award. My homepage (including my vita) can be found at http://faculty.uca.edu/~billl/main.htm.

Pietro Badia, Ph.D.
I received my Bachelor's and Master's degrees from Kent State University and my Doctor of Philosophy degree (Ph.D.) in Experimental Psychology from Adelphi University. I have been teaching at Bowling Green State University since 1963. In 1988 the Board of Trustees of Bowling Green State University awarded me the title of Distinguished University Professor, the highest honor our university can offer a faculty member. I was awarded emeritus status in 1998. I have published more than 100 research articles in scientific journals and have given more than 100 presentations at scholarly meetings. My major research interests have been teaching techniques and factors that affect learning, research methodology, psychophysiology, and the psychology of sleep. My teaching efforts have focused mostly on graduate and undergraduate courses in research methods.

FUNDAMENTALS OF BEHAVIORAL RESEARCH

WILLIAM J. LAMMERS
University of Central Arkansas

PIETRO BADIA
Bowling Green State University

THOMSON
™
WADSWORTH

Australia • Canada • Mexico • Singapore • Spain • United Kingdom • United States

THOMSON
WADSWORTH

Publisher: *Vicki Knight*
Assistant Editor: *Jennifer Keever*
Editorial Assistant: *Monica Sarmiento*
Technology Project Manager: *Erik Fortier*
Marketing Manager: *Dory Schaeffer*
Marketing Assistant: *Nicole Morinon*
Advertising Project Manager: *Brian Chaffee*
Project Manager, Editorial Production: *Jennie Redwitz*
Art Director: *Vernon Boes*
Print/Media Buyer: *Emma Claydon*

Permissions Editor: *Kiely Sexton*
Production Service: *Scratchgravel Publishing Services*
Text Designer: *Delgado and Company*
Copy Editor: *Margaret C. Tropp*
Illustrator: *Richard Sheppard*
Cover Designer: *Lisa Berman*
Cover Image: *Tom Erikson*
Compositor: *Scratchgravel Publishing Services*
Text and Cover Printer: *Phoenix Color Corp*

Library of Congress Control Number: 2004109300

ISBN 0-534-63069-3

Thomson Wadsworth
10 Davis Drive
Belmont, CA 94002-3098
USA

Asia
Thomson Learning
5 Shenton Way #01-01
UIC Building
Singapore 068808

Australia/New Zealand
Thomson Learning
102 Dodds Street
Southbank, Victoria 3006
Australia

Canada
Nelson
1120 Birchmount Road
Toronto, Ontario M1K 5G4
Canada

Europe/Middle East/Africa
Thomson Learning
High Holborn House
50/51 Bedford Row
London WC1R 4LR
United Kingdom

Latin America
Thomson Learning
Seneca, 53
Colonia Polanco
11560 Mexico D.F.
Mexico

Spain/Portugal
Paraninfo
Calle Magallanes, 25
28015 Madrid, Spain

We dedicate this book to our families, especially to Christina and Rita,
and to all of those pursuing the goal of scholarship

BRIEF CONTENTS

CONTENTS

PREFACE

Welcome to the world of behavioral research. We have tried to provide you with a textbook that is clearly written, logically organized, engaging, and designed with a variety of features to enhance your learning.

Organization

The first chapter in the book is designed to provide you with the big picture of behavioral research. It begins with a description of an event experienced by one of your authors (Lammers) that conveys the excitement of doing research. Next, we discuss the skills to be learned in the book. These include the actual skills associated with doing behavioral research as well as the skills of being a critical consumer of research-related information in the media. Following this, we discuss what it means for the field of psychology to be a science. Finally, Chapter 1 provides a broad overview of the research process, including types of research questions, ways of answering those questions, and ways of making the answers public.

Chapter 2 is devoted to ethical considerations. This decision was carefully considered and deliberately made. It is an affirmation that although science is dedicated to advancing knowledge, its primary mission is to serve humanity. You should be aware that ethical concerns are not tangential matters that are given consideration only after "more important" aspects of research design have been resolved. Rather, we are asserting the primacy of ethical concerns. They are as much a part of designing research as the selection of the variables and measures to be used. To this end, we begin the book with ethical issues involving both human (adults, children) and nonhuman participants. In addition, we discuss the controversial issues surrounding the use of deception. Information on these ethical issues is important for all students taking research courses, but it is especially so for those who undertake individual research projects and for those assisting faculty in their professional research efforts.

We also give prominence to ethical issues for another reason. Many people have expressed strong reservations about research done on living organisms. These reservations are based on what are perceived as past and present insensitivities on the part of researchers regarding the welfare of their participants. Unfortunately, examples of insensitivities can be pointed to in the use of both human and nonhuman participants. These occurrences have led to the formation of lobby organizations seeking legislation that places constraints on research beyond the ethical guidelines imposed by professional and governmental agencies. We feel that additional constraints are unnecessary and that full awareness along with strict adherence to current ethical guidelines will lessen future problems considerably. Addressing ethical issues at the beginning of the book is one way of giving prominence to ethical concerns and indicating to others that behavioral scientists are not only fully committed to these concerns in their research but also fully committed to teaching them.

Following this discussion of ethical considerations, Chapter 3 introduces the fundamentals of the scientific approach and clearly differentiates this approach from other ways that we acquire information about our world. Then, in Chapter 4, we explore the development of research questions, including the formulation of testable hypotheses and the identification of the critical variables in an experiment. Chapters 5 and 6 focus on the measurement of these variables and methods of observation. These issues are particularly interesting for the field of psychology because we often deal with important concepts like attitudes, emotions, and cognitions. Though certainly important, these concepts are also challenging to define and measure. Chapter 7 describes the various ways to obtain samples of participants. Chapter 8 discusses the many potential pitfalls that await the researcher and that impair her ability to draw confident conclusions. In Chapter 9, we identify a variety of experimental techniques that can be used to avoid the pitfalls and to increase our confidence that we have truly learned something new from a research study. In Chapter 10, we provide an overview of how data that have been collected can be described and interpreted using a variety of statistical methods.

After the research question has been formed and we understand the basics of avoiding pitfalls and analyzing data, we then must decide on a particular approach to use in answering the research question. As we will see, there are many different approaches. Therefore, it will be important to understand the advantages and limitations of each. Chapters 11–14 describe variations of true experimental designs. These experimental designs provide high levels of control by the experimenter and powerful cause–effect conclusions. For a variety of reasons, however, many important research questions cannot be answered using true experimental designs. Chapter 15 summarizes nonexperimental designs and the types of questions that they are designed to answer.

After the study has been carried out and the data interpreted, the findings should be reported to the scientific community. Chapter 16 describes the fundamentals of writing a manuscript for publication, making an oral presentation, and creating a poster presentation. Finally, Chapter 17 summarizes the important points made in preceding chapters and attempts to bring all the parts together into a coherent purpose.

Pedagogical Features

The chapters of the book have a set of common features that are designed to assist you with learning. These features include the following:

- Chapter outlines provide an overview of the topics. Be sure to review these topics and consider their place in the overall picture of research.
- Key terms that are critical to the understanding of research are bold in the text, listed at the end of each chapter, and defined in the glossary at the back of the book.
- Numerous examples are used to illustrate concepts. These examples are drawn from a wide range of areas within the field of psychology.
- A box approximately midway into each chapter, labeled "Thinking Critically About Everyday Information," describes a report in the public media and asks you to apply the concepts learned so far. These boxes are designed to review concepts, apply concepts, and help you become a better consumer of information.

- A case study toward the end of each chapter presents a research scenario that requires critical evaluation using the concepts in the chapter. These research scenarios provide a valuable teaching tool for integration and application of new concepts.
- Each chapter has two summaries. The General Summary highlights the main points of the chapter and provides a preview of the next chapter. The Detailed Summary provides a more detailed listing of the main ideas of the chapter and serves as a useful study guide.
- A set of review questions and exercises is provided for each chapter. Several review exercises refer the student to InfoTrac College Edition®, an online database of continuously updated, full-length articles from hundreds of journals and periodicals. Students automatically receive four months of free access with each new copy of this book.
- A number of chapters also suggest laboratory research projects from the supplementary book *Research Methods Laboratory Manual for Psychology* by W. Langston.
- Each chapter ends with a reminder to visit the course Web site to:
  - Review chapter summaries, review key terms, and answer practice test questions.
  - Consider Internet links that provide more in-depth information related to a particular topic.
  - Take online quizzes. These quizzes provide an opportunity for you to self-test your knowledge of the concepts presented in each chapter.
  - Engage in online workshops for research design concepts and statistics concepts. These interactive workshops will help you to understand main concepts through examples, graphs, and explanations.

Acknowledgments

We want to thank the excellent publishing team of Thomson Wadsworth, especially Vicki Knight. We are also very appreciative of the numerous reviewers who provided feedback on drafts. These reviewers include Jim Byrd, University of Wisconsin–Stout; Frances Conners, University of Alabama; Julie Evey, University of Southern Indiana; Steve Hoekstra, Kansas Wesleyan University; Donna Stuber-McEwen, Friends University; Tom Mitchell, University of Baltimore; Rachel Thames, University of Southern Mississippi; Paula Waddill, Murray State University; and Jennifer Welbourne, University of North Carolina at Charlotte.

We also acknowledge that inspiration and portions of text for this book are based on a textbook of the same title, published in 1982, by Pietro Badia and Richard P. Runyon.

FUNDAMENTALS OF BEHAVIORAL RESEARCH

OVERVIEW OF BEHAVIORAL RESEARCH

The Excitement of Behavioral Research

It happened in a stairwell closet on a summer's day in 1984. The closet was located in the main building of Hubb's Sea World Research Institute in San Diego, California, and it was the only available location for conducting research that was relatively free from distracting light and sound. As the hungry Blue-fronted Amazon parrot turned in the modified Skinner box toward the front wall, I instantly pressed a button that I held in my nervous hand. A food tray immediately became available, and the hungry parrot quickly grabbed a small nut in his beak before the tray swung away. I continued to reward the parrot first for facing and then for moving closer to a small circular disk on the front wall of the box. On this occasion the desired outcome was to get the parrot to press the disk with his beak in order to close an electric microswitch that would automatically raise the food tray. I experienced momentary setbacks (at one point the parrot began turning circles!), and I knew that motivation (hunger level) of the parrot was diminishing. But the magical moment did arrive. The parrot touched the disk with his beak, and I immediately pressed the button in my now sweaty hand. A few trials later, the parrot was pressing the disk to receive food. Yes!!! I had done it!

That day in the closet was one of the most influential moments for an undergraduate student who is now one of the authors of your textbook (Lammers). Both a parrot and a career as a behavioral researcher were shaped that day. The story illustrates both the excitement and the challenge of conducting behavioral research. The challenge can only be met by understanding the concepts of research methodology and how best to use research design strategies to answer questions about behavior. We hope that our textbook provides you with both the spark of enthusiasm and the tools necessary for the systematic exploration of behavior.

Purpose

Knowledge of research design is a universal requirement for students studying in the behavioral sciences. We have written a book that focuses on fundamental research methods and procedures that we believe are common to most courses in research design. Basic principles of research methodology are the core of the book. The particular topic areas within psychology that are used to illustrate these principles vary across different disciplines within psychology. At times, our examples represent basic research in learning, cognition, social behavior, development, and physiology; at other times, they represent applied research in clinical, counseling, industrial/organizational, and human factors psychology. (A more detailed discussion of basic versus applied research is presented in Chapter 3). Our purpose is to walk the learner through the research process, including the development of a research question, collection of data, analysis of data, and report writing. The intention is to provide students with the necessary knowledge to evaluate research, to do research, and to appreciate its importance.

Skills as a Researcher

One purpose of the book is to introduce you to the basic skills necessary for you to conduct quality research. If you pursue a career in an area of research, these basic skills will provide the foundation upon which your future training will be built. You will have the tools needed to explore the mysteries of human behavior and thought. It is likely that most students reading this book are unsure of their future and have given little consideration to the possibility of being a researcher. That's fine. Part of the purpose of this book is to introduce you to this possible career choice. But even if your career choice is not that of a researcher, there are often opportunities to do research. For example, let's assume you get a job as a manager of a department store. You have an idea for a new approach to advertising, an approach that you believe will be more effective than the one that has been used in the past. Rather than making a subjective assessment or simply having faith that your approach will be better, you have a perfect opportunity to make systematic comparisons between the two approaches, collect data (such as sales), and analyze the results. These types of opportunities to answer real-world questions in an empirical way are used far too infrequently.

Skills as a Consumer of Information

Although there are many opportunities to conduct research, it is entirely possible that you will never do so. However, we are all consumers of information. We are bombarded with information from radio, television, magazines, and the Internet that inform us of this or that new finding. Should we believe it? Should we change our lifestyle because of something we hear? These are decisions that we make every day. One purpose of this book is to help you become a critical consumer of information. For example, while waiting in the doctor's office, you pick up a copy of *Better Homes and Gardens*. This particular issue reports the results of a survey that the magazine conducted to assess attitudes toward the role of women in the workplace. Should you believe the findings? Here's where you need to be critical and ask yourself questions. Who was surveyed—readers of *Better Homes and Gardens*? How were they surveyed? How many were surveyed? How many of those who read the survey completed it and returned it? Could the answers to these questions influence the results?

● Science

Part of the previous example relates to our ability to recognize science when we see it. What makes a discipline scientific? What makes a particular study scientific? Why do we call certain fields *sciences*? Even in the traditional sciences like biology, physics, and chemistry, these questions are often not addressed. There are certain assumptions and methodologies that characterize science, and it is these characteristics that separate scientific knowledge from other forms of knowledge. It is important that we understand these distinctions, whether we want to do research or want to be an intelligent consumer of information.

● Research

Types of Questions

The types of questions that we ask are at the heart of how we gain new knowledge in the behavioral sciences. First and foremost, our questions must be empirical questions. We must be able to answer them by making observations. If you begin to contemplate the various empirical questions that you could ask about human behavior and thought, you begin to realize that the possibilities are nearly infinite. Although our knowledge about behavior has grown enormously over the years, there are many things that we do not yet know.

Some of the questions that we might contemplate relate to the possible effect of one variable on another. For example, we might ask whether sleep deprivation causes memory impairment, whether the drug secretin causes an improvement in autistic children, whether the color of the walls affects worker productivity, or whether violence on television causes more aggressive behavior in children. In other cases, our questions may simply ask whether there is a relationship between two variables. For example, we might ask whether children's intelligence is related to parents' intelligence, whether time spent studying per week is related to a college student's grade point average, whether the attractiveness of an individual is related to the likelihood that someone will help her, or whether a person's personality is related to his likelihood of experiencing cardiovascular disease.

Ways of Answering Questions

Experimental methods are used to answer cause–effect questions, whereas nonexperimental methods are used to answer the relational questions. Experimental methods enable the researcher to control the environment and manipulate the variable of interest. To assess whether sleep deprivation causes memory impairment, the researcher would decide who gets deprived of sleep, when they get deprived of sleep, for how long they are deprived of sleep, and where they get deprived of sleep. The researcher would decide what type of memory test to use, when they receive the memory test, how they receive the memory test, and where they receive the memory test. This extensive level of control is the hallmark of the experimental method and allows the researcher to draw powerful cause–effect conclusions.

Nonexperimental methods are often necessary when the research question does not permit such extensive control or when ethical issues are involved. To understand how personality relates to cardiovascular health, the researcher cannot control or manipulate the personality of an individual (except, perhaps, with the short-term effects of drugs). The researcher can measure both the personality of people and the cardiovascular health of people and determine whether there is a relationship. Assuming there is a relationship, does this imply that personality caused cardiovascular disease? As we will emphasize later in the book, one limitation of nonexperimental methods is that the researcher can conclude that there is a relationship between variables but cannot conclude that one variable caused a change in the other variable.

Ways of Reporting Answers

We have not truly completed the scientific process until we have analyzed, interpreted, and presented our data to the scientific community. How do we know whether our observations support our research hypothesis? We can certainly look at the raw data that have been collected. But there is usually some level of ambiguity. Perhaps some participants clearly show the expected pattern of results, others show no changes, and still others show a pattern opposite of what was expected. How does the researcher arrive at a conclusion that is not inherently subjective? How can the researcher be objective so that other researchers agree with the conclusion?

The field of mathematics provides objectivity. There is no subjectivity in deciding that $2 + 2 = 4$. Therefore, we can apply mathematical principles to the data we have collected to help us arrive at a conclusion with which other scientists would agree. Statistics involve the application of mathematical principles to research data. Descriptive statistics provide ways of describing and summarizing data (often in graphical form) so that the data can talk to us and reveal answers to our research questions. Inferential statistics are then often used to determine whether the patterns we may see are reliable and not simply due to chance.

After we have arrived at our conclusions, we must share the results with the scientific community. There are numerous levels at which this can occur. The researcher can give a talk or present a poster at a scientific conference. The researcher can publish the report in a journal or book. This process is not limited to university professors with PhDs. In fact, no degree is required to do any of the activities just described. Students have the same opportunities to present or publish their research. In fact, there are opportunities specifically designated for students. Most scientific conferences have sessions designated for student research. Some have awards for the best student presentations. There are even conferences just for student research. One example is the Arkansas Symposium for Psychology Students. In this setting, students can present their research findings to a group of fellow students. Finally, several journals restrict their submissions to individuals who have conducted research as undergraduates. Examples of these include the *Psi Chi Journal of Undergraduate Research* and the *Journal of Psychological Inquiry*. All of these provide wonderful opportunities for students to contribute to the field of psychology.

SUMMARY

This chapter provided an overview of the fundamentals of research in the behavioral sciences. The book is organized to provide a logical development of the tools you will need to conduct research. Table 1.1 summarizes the steps in the research process. These steps are elaborated in the chapters that follow. Science provides the framework of methods and assumptions necessary to be confident about the knowledge gained. The methods begin with knowing how to ask effective research questions. After the questions are developed, variables must be defined, observed, and measured in valid and reliable ways. The researcher must be aware of the many unmeasured variables that can influence participant behavior and confuse interpretation of the observations. Awareness of these extraneous variables leads to a decision to use specific re-

search methods to reduce their influence. In some studies, the researcher can conduct true experiments and exert high levels of control, whereas in other studies the researcher must resort to nonexperimental methods. All of the methods involve making observations and interpreting data. Statistics provide a tool to objectively analyze the data and arrive at conclusions. Conclusions are then made public through presentations and publications.

Learning these fundamentals is analogous to taking a hike. Before you set out down the path, it is important to look at a topographical map, to get your bearings, and to see the forest before the trees. It will be much work. There will be peaks and valleys. But in the end there will be a sense of accomplishment. Let's put on our hiking boots and get started.

Table 1.1	Steps in the Research Process

1. Consider what area of psychology fascinates you.
2. Read the literature in this area.
3. Develop a specific and testable research question.
4. Decide who will be the participants.
5. Decide on the most appropriate method to answer the question.
6. Consider ways to reduce the influence of extraneous variables.
7. Consider the ethical issues involved.
8. Obtain ethics approval from a review board.
9. Finalize the specific procedures that will be used.
10. Obtain informed consent from participants.
11. Collect data by making observations.
12. Use descriptive statistics to describe the data.
13. Use inferential statistics to arrive at a conclusion.
14. Consider the implications of your findings.
15. Present your findings to the scientific community.

2

ETHICAL PRINCIPLES OF RESEARCH

● Historical Examples of Research With Ethical Concerns

Tuskegee Syphilis Study

On the afternoon of May 16, 1997, President Clinton made a formal apology to Mr. Shaw, Mr. Pollard, Mr. Howard, Mr. Simmons, Mr. Moss, Mr. Doner, Mr. Hendon, and Mr. Key. These eight African American men were the remaining survivors of a medical research study sponsored by the United States government. In the words of President Clinton, the rights of these citizens and 391 others were "neglected, ignored and betrayed."

Syphilis is a venereal disease caused by the invasion of the body by a spirochete, *Treponema pallidum*. In its early stages, the infection is usually benign. A painless lesion develops at the site of the infection with secondary inflammatory lesions erupting elsewhere as the tissues react to the presence of the spirochetes. If untreated, an early syphilitic infection characteristically undergoes a secondary stage, during which lesions may develop in any organ or tissue throughout the body, although it shows a preference for the skin. Then, in many individuals, the disease goes underground, so to speak. During this latent phase, the spirochete may establish a foothold in an organ, bone, muscle, or any other part of the anatomy. It may be years later before the blight it has inflicted upon the individual becomes evident. If the spirochete settles in the heart, it leads to severe and debilitating cardiovascular disorders. In the spinal cord, it may destroy the ascending sensory neurons. An individual so affected literally loses touch with his or her own legs—all muscle sense is lost—and walking becomes possible only by watching the feet. When the cerebral cortex is attacked, the victim suffers impaired memory, fatigues easily, and undergoes profound and pervasive personality changes. Moreover, many symptoms mimic those of mental disorders.

In 1932, a group of researchers undertook a long-term evaluation of the effects of untreated syphilis. Known as the Tuskegee study on syphilis, it was sponsored by the Venereal Disease Division of the U.S. Public Health Service. The study involved 399 Blacks from Macon County, Alabama. All were 25 years of age or older and were selected because they had the venereal disease of syphilis and had not been treated. There were also two control groups. One consisted of 201 Blacks without syphilis and the other of 275 Blacks previously treated. At the time the study was begun, penicillin was unknown, but less effective treatment compounds were available. The interest in the study was in the natural progression of the disease if left untreated. Earlier observations suggested that some individuals left untreated apparently recovered from the disease spontaneously. Therefore, some physicians felt it might be better not to use drugs known to be hazardous. This was apparently the justification for the study. However, with the advent of penicillin in the early 1940s, an effective cure for syphilis had been found. This cure was withheld from the participants in order to complete the research findings. The public became aware of the study in a story printed by the *New York Times* on July 26, 1972. People were outraged. Four months later, the study was terminated.

Times change, and views are relative. Today scientists do not take pride in this study or those similar to it. They represent research inquiry gone awry. No matter how honorable the underlying motives, the plain truth is that the investigators forgot or ignored their obligation to their participants. Before describing some consequences that followed disclosure of the sort above, we want to describe two additional behavioral studies that have generated considerable controversy.

The Milgram and Zimbardo Studies

Social and behavioral scientists have also had their share of controversy concerning ethical issues in research. Two controversial ones, among others, are Stanley Milgram's studies regarding obedience to authority, and Philip Zimbardo's simulated prison experiment. These studies reveal that difficult to resolve ethical issues often emerge in research. Although important information may have been provided by these studies, the issues raised by them seem to involve a cost/benefit analysis. The studies also reveal that attitudes related to ethical concerns sometimes change. Both Milgram and Zimbardo are highly respected, ethical scientists, yet many individuals objected to the methods of their studies when they were published. We would guess that it is unlikely that either of these studies would be undertaken with today's ethical standards. In this context, it is interesting to note that shortly after his initial study was published (1963), Stanley Milgram received the American Association for the Advancement of Science award for social psychology. We will give a brief description of each study and some of the ethical issues raised by them.

Milgram Obedience Study   Milgram's study dealt with obedience to authority, and it was his belief that it would contribute to avoiding another holocaust similar to that which took place in Nazi Germany (Milgram, 1965). However, participants were not told the true purpose of the experiment until it was over. In essence, Milgram told volunteers that they were participating in a learning-memory task that required them (the teacher) to shock another individual (the learner) when the learner made an error. (The learner, a collaborator of the researcher, was out of view in another room.) Unknown to the participants was that no shock was ever presented, even though cries of pain were heard. Thirty switches identifying the level of supposed shock intensity were clearly marked and ranged from 15 to 450 volts (labels ranged from "Slight Shock" to "Danger: Severe Shock"). Participants were instructed to increase the shock intensity one step for each error made. The learner, according to the plan, was to provide periodic wrong answers and, as shock supposedly increased, was to demand that the experiment be stopped, cry out, or moan. The situation was convincing to participants; as shock intensity increased and cries from the adjoining room became louder, some participants wanted to quit the experiment. At this point the researcher simply instructed the participants that they were required to go on. The real purpose of the experiment was to determine how high a shock intensity participants would "deliver" to others on orders from the researcher. Many participants continued in the experiment and "delivered" the highest shock intensity; others defied the experimenter's order to continue. For some participants the experience was a very intense, emotional one, filled with conflict. It should be noted that Milgram took precautions to debrief each participant and to follow up on their well-being after the experiment was concluded. We will discuss the ethical issues below.

Zimbardo Prison Study   Philip Zimbardo was interested in the psychological effects of imprisonment (Zimbardo, 1969). He conducted his research with college students in a setting designed to achieve psychological effects similar to those found in prisons. Newspaper ads were placed asking students to volunteer for a two-week study of prison life at $15 a day. Only emotionally stable volunteers were chosen, and they were randomly assigned to a role of guard or prisoner. The basement of the Stanford University psychology building served as the prison where three small rooms were converted to prison cells with three beds and barred doors. The experiment began without warning when the students were picked up in a surprise mass arrest one Sunday by real police with sirens screeching. They were charged with a felony, searched, handcuffed, given their constitutional rights, and then taken to the police station for booking and fingerprinting. After this they were blindfolded and taken to the Stanford basement prison, where they were stripped, searched again, and given uniforms, bedding, and so on. For purposes of group identity, prisoners wore a white smock, a nylon stocking cap, and a chain around one ankle. Guards wore khaki uniforms, sunglasses with silver reflectors, and carried clubs, whistles, and handcuffs. The reaction to this simulated environment by both prisoners and guards was very strong. In a short time a distorted relationship developed, with the prisoners becoming passive and the guards aggressive, abusive, and authoritarian. The experiment had to be stopped much earlier than planned because of the intensity of the behavior and the consequences that followed. According to Zimbardo, the first of the nine prisoners had to be released by the second day because of crying, fits of rage, and severe depression. Three others developed similar symptoms on the third and fourth days, and a fifth prisoner had to be released because of a rash over his entire body.

Were ethical issues involved in the Milgram and Zimbardo studies? Many researchers feel that there were. Some deceit was involved in both studies, and participants were not fully informed. There was also the possibility of psychological or physical harm to the participants. Behavioral scientists have expressed concern about the possible negative psychological effects that may have resulted as participants learned that they were capable of inhumane behavior toward others. However, we might note in passing that there is no evidence of negative aftereffects in either study and also that a sizable number of Milgram's participants believed that they had benefited from their participation.

Largely as a result of disclosures of the preceding sort, federal and state governments as well as a number of scientific and professional societies have taken a long, hard look at the ethics of research. Included in their scrutiny are such issues as the professional behavior of the researcher, the treatment of human participants, research with children, and research using nonhuman participants. We shall be examining each of these issues in this chapter and attempt to summarize policies that have evolved to date. Before doing so, we want to note that many ethical questions arise in the course of doing research for which answers are not readily available. In this chapter we deliberately stress the rights of participants, but keep in mind that researchers are obligated to push forward the frontiers of science and to provide new knowledge for the citizens of the world. Therefore, while we justifiably show increasing concern for human and animal welfare, the ethical questions are more a risk (cost)/benefit dilemma; that is, the risk (cost) of research in terms of side effects, money, time, inconvenience, and the like, versus the benefits to humankind in the long run. It is appropriate to note at this point that the quality of research in itself can be an ethical issue. Poorly designed and poorly conducted studies do not permit unambiguous conclusions to be drawn. Thus, such studies are also unlikely to provide any benefits. If benefits cannot be derived from the research, then only risk remains in the risk/benefit ratio. It would surely be unethical to ask participants to participate in a study where risk existed without possible benefits.

● Research With Human Participants: Ethical Guidelines

Ethical Principles and Code of Conduct

Studies such as those described above have sensitized researchers and their professional organizations to the need for guidelines regarding the ethics of research with human participants. Although these studies raised clear ethical issues, more subtle concerns are raised every day in behavioral research. Issues such as the use of deception, the induction of anxiety, or minor manipulations that may affect the participant's self-esteem can all create ethical concerns. The American Psychological Association (APA) has been a leader in the establishment of such guidelines. Today, no investigator should undertake research with human participants without intimate familiarity with these guidelines. It should be noted that writing guidelines is a difficult task. They must be written in a manner that places limits or restrictions on certain research activities without stifling the activities. Moreover, they are not fixed and immutable. In fact, they continue to change and evolve, reflecting the current views and experiences of laypersons and professional organizations regarding the freedom to obtain knowledge and the rights of participants.

For psychologists, guidelines can be found in the APA publication *Ethical Principles of Psychologists and Code of Conduct 2002*. These guidelines are readily available at the APA Web site on the Internet (http://www.apa.org) and consist of a preamble, five general principles, and ten ethical standards. The preamble states:

> Psychologists are committed to increasing scientific and professional knowledge of behavior and people's understanding of themselves and others and to the use of such knowledge to improve the condition of individuals, organizations, and society. Psychologists respect and protect civil and human rights and the central importance of freedom of inquiry and expression in research, teaching, and publication. They strive to help the public in developing informed judgments and choices concerning human behavior. In doing so, they perform many roles, such as researcher, educator, diagnostician, therapist, supervisor, consultant, administrator, social interventionist, and expert witness. This Ethics Code provides a common set of principles and standards upon which psychologists build their professional and scientific work.
>
> This Ethics Code is intended to provide specific standards to cover most situations encountered by psychologists. It has as its goals the welfare and protection of the individuals and groups with whom psychologists work and the education of members, students, and the public regarding ethical standards of the discipline.
>
> The development of a dynamic set of ethical standards for psychologists' work-related conduct requires a personal commitment and lifelong effort to act ethically; to encourage ethical behavior by students, supervisees, employees, and colleagues; and to consult with others concerning ethical problems.

As you can see, the preamble represents the broad themes of ethical conduct. It is important to notice, and will become increasingly clear, that ethical conduct is not limited to the interactions with research participants in the laboratory. Ethical conduct applies to all professional activity of the psychologist. A summary of the five principles makes this clear:

Principle A: Beneficence and Nonmaleficence. Psychologists seek to contribute to the welfare of those with whom they interact professionally, including patients, clients, students, supervisees, human research participants, and animal research participants.

Principle B: Fidelity and Responsibility. Psychologists are professionals who uphold standards of conduct, clarify their professional roles and obligations, accept responsibility for their behavior, adapt their methods to the needs of different populations, and concern themselves with the ethical conduct of their colleagues. Psychologists are aware of their responsibility to make public their knowledge of psychology in order to contribute to human welfare.

Principle C: Integrity. Psychologists are honest, fair, and respectful of others. Any use of deception involves the careful analysis of the potential benefits versus the potential harm.

Principle D: Justice. Psychologists understand that everyone should have access to the benefits of psychological practice and research. Psychologists recognize that there are limits to their competence and expertise. They should not go beyond these limits in their teaching, service, or research.

Principle E: Respect for People's Rights and Dignity. Psychologists respect the fundamental rights, dignity, and worth of all people. They respect privacy, confidentiality, self-determination, and are aware of cultural, individual, and role differences.

The specific guidelines are contained in the ten ethical standards. Together, these standards discuss guidelines in 90 specific areas of professional activity. The categories represented by the ten standards are:

1. Resolving Ethical Issues
2. Competence
3. Human Relations
4. Privacy and Confidentiality
5. Advertising and Other Public Statements
6. Record Keeping and Fees
7. Education and Training
8. Research and Publication
9. Assessment
10. Therapy

Sections under Standard 8 are most relevant to those beginning to conduct behavioral research. Those sections, along with the others, can be found at the APA Web site (http://www.apa.org/ethics/code2002.html).

Although these guidelines attempt to safeguard the rights of research participants, the participants must still often rely on the judgments of the researcher. Researchers must remain vigilant and concerned about human rights, the invasion of privacy, and the possibility of physiological and psychological damage.

There is one further legal matter of which you should be aware. Unlike physicians, lawyers, and members of the clergy, researchers are not protected by laws concerning privileged communications. Though highly unlikely, it is possible that participants' admitting to crimes (stealing, using or selling controlled substances) on questionnaires could result in arrest and prosecution. Consequently, it would be a risk for participants to admit to a researcher that they have participated in a crime. When questionnaires are used and such information is required to achieve the goals of the study, it would be wise to avoid the problem completely by omitting all forms of identification from the questionnaire. When mailed questionnaires are used, you can keep track of which participants have participated and still maintain their anonymity by having each one mail in a separate card indicating that the questionnaire has been completed.

Informed Consent: The Right to Know

The ethical principles make it clear that **informed consent** is fundamental (sections 3.10 and 8.02). Participants must be informed of the nature of the experiment, the degree of detail depending upon potentially harmful effects. Participants should never be informed that there are no risks. At a minimum, there are no *anticipated* risks. When the potential for harmful effects is high (such as in drug research when undesirable side effects may occur), the participant is entitled to a particularly detailed assessment of the risks.

As you can see in Figure 2.1, the Sample Consent Form for a Student Research Project, participants agree to participate in an experiment on the basis of a verbal description, but

Figure 2.1	**Sample Consent Form for a Student Research Project**

University of Central Arkansas Informed Consent Agreement Research: Eye-tracking in Infants

You are being asked to participate in a research study. You are eligible to participate as long as you are at least 18 years of age. You were recruited because your psychology instructor permitted us to inform you of this opportunity. Before you give your consent to volunteer, it is important that you read the following information and ask all questions you need answered to be sure you understand what you will be asked to do.

Investigators

The investigators in this study are students in PSYC 3340 – Research Methods Lab. The investigators are affiliated with the Psychology Department at the University of Central Arkansas. The faculty advisor is Dr. Bill Lammers. He can be reached by phone at (501) 450-XXXX or in Mashburn 257.

Purpose of the Research

This research study is designed to investigate how infants track objects with their eyes. The study will also provide experience to students in the Research Methods Laboratory course.

Procedures

If you volunteer to participate in this study, you will be asked to move a stuffed animal in front of the face of an infant. The procedure will take approximately 20 minutes of your time. Some information about the study is being withheld. A full explanation will be provided immediately after testing.

Potential Risks or Discomforts

There are no foreseeable risks associated with this study.

Potential Benefits of the Research

No direct benefits are anticipated with your participation. Your participation will count toward the Enrichment Activities requirement of the General Psychology course.

Confidentiality and Data Storage

The responses you provide will not be associated with your identity in any way. The data collected from this study will be stored in Dr. Lammers' office in Mashburn 257 for three years. Only student researchers and their faculty advisor will have access to the data.

Participation and Withdrawal

Your participation in this research is voluntary. You may refuse to participate without penalty. If you decide to participate, you are free to withdraw at any time without penalty. To withdraw from the study, simply raise your hand and you will be assisted by one of the researchers. However, since the data is not associated with your name, your data may not be withdrawn from the study after it has been collected.

Questions about the Research

If you have any questions about the research, please ask now. If you have questions later, you may contact Dr. Lammers, by phone at (501) 450-XXXX or in Mashburn 257.

This project has been reviewed and approved by the Institutional Review Board for the Protection of Human Subjects at the University of Central Arkansas. If you believe there is any infringement upon your rights as a research subject, you may contact the Research Compliance Coordinator at (501) 450-XXXX.

Participant Agreement:

I have read the information provided above. My signature below indicates my voluntary agreement to participate in this research study. Please return one copy of this consent form and keep one copy for your records.

_____	_____
Participant's Signature	Date
_____	_____
Researcher's Signature	Date

are clearly informed that they may terminate their participation at any time. Then, if the experiment is different from what the participant expected, consent is revoked by merely withdrawing from the experiment. The consent form also informs participants regarding the nature of the study, who is conducting the research, why they were selected, what risks may be involved, what time commitment is required, and whom to contact with questions.

On the Use of Deception

The Sample Consent Form for a Student Research Project does not state the true purpose of the study. The potential participants are being deceived into believing that the purpose of the study is to track eye movements in infants. In actuality, the student researchers were interested in observing whether there would be a gender bias in the type of toy that the participants selected (an infant was never actually used in the study!). Specifically, participants were told that the baby was either a boy or a girl, or were not informed as to the sex of the baby. They were asked to select one of three: a female doll (feminine), a truck (masculine), or a duck (neutral). Was this type of deception ethical?

The APA guidelines make clear that researchers must assume personal responsibility for assuring the moral acceptability of their research. Providing this assurance can create a conflict situation for the experimenter, particularly as it relates to informed consent. Fully informing a participant about the nature of the research may alter the kind of findings a researcher obtains. In some cases, participants who are fully informed of the nature of the experiment, the procedure, and the hypothesis may try either to help or to hinder the research. In other cases, realism can only be achieved by misinforming or misleading the participant. Under these circumstances, the behavioral scientist may be faced with a dilemma. The researcher wants to be open and honest, but to do so may reduce the accuracy of the findings. Some psychologists have resolved this dilemma by misinforming or misleading their participants about the true purposes of the research. This is usually what is meant by the term **deception**. Participants are fully informed of the true purposes only *after* the experiment is completed, in a statement called a **debriefing**. A major problem with this procedure is that it deprives the individuals of information that could influence their decision to participate in the research (that is, the individuals are not fully informed). The use of deception is a very controversial issue, and we will not resolve it here. However, few psychologists believe that deception can be entirely eliminated. The kind and the degree of deception vary greatly across experiments. Some forms of deception are completely harmless (withholding certain information regarding words to be recalled in a memory task) while other forms are potentially harmful (failure to specify the risks of participation when potential risks exist). It is usually the latter that pose significant problems. The researcher must decide when the potentially harmful effects of the experiment are worth the potentially beneficial effects of the knowledge to be gained. Under these circumstances, researchers often consult with those less personally involved (such as colleagues) to evaluate the merits of the research.

Satisfying solutions to the ethical problems created by the use of deception are not yet available, but it is important to express concern about its use. Deception was once routinely accepted—unfortunately, in some cases, even when it was unneeded. Today it is still used, but with greater concern and always accompanied by elaborate justification and careful debriefing. Alternatives to deception have been tried. One is referred to as role playing. With this procedure, participants are fully informed about the nature of the experiment and then asked to play a role. That is, they are instructed to act as if they were actually a participant under the conditions described. In other instances, an experiment is simulated. Participants are asked to imagine certain conditions and then specify how they would perform. For some experiments these techniques have been successful, but for others they have not. Many psychologists believe that these alternatives to deception are too limited to be useful. Others have tried to avoid some of the ethical issues by abandoning laboratory research in favor of research in natural settings. However, as we describe in this chapter, disguised research in a natural setting has its own problems. As we noted earlier, although satisfying solutions to deception are not yet available, efforts to seek them should continue, and a major effort to reduce the use of deception should be made.

Field Research and Ethics

For a variety of reasons that we will examine later, some researchers have become disenchanted with laboratory experiments. Not least among these reasons are the stringent requirements necessary to achieve and maintain ethical standards. Field experimentation is a possible alternative to laboratory methods. Individuals are observed in a natural setting, experimental variables are manipulated, and behavior is recorded without the participant's knowledge. In fact, individuals are not aware that they are serving as participants.

For example, there have been several incidents of college students' being hit by cars on the crosswalks near campus. One possible intervention would be to post signs that read "Crosswalk Ahead—Please Slow Down." Field research could be conducted to assess the effectiveness of this intervention. A researcher with a radar gun could record the speed of automobiles at a crosswalk at various times when the sign is posted and at various times when the sign is removed and then make a comparison. Notice that the behavior of individuals is observed in a natural setting, an experimental variable is manipulated (sign or no sign), and participants are unaware of their participation in the research.

The behavioral measures recorded during field research are referred to as **nonreactive**, or unobtrusive, **measures.** Those who use nonreactive measures believe that the behavior is more natural or representative than when **reactive measures** are used. With reactive measurement, participants are aware that they are being observed and that their behavior is recorded. Some researchers have expressed concern that the very act of observation changes that which is being observed. Instead of behaving as they normally would, individuals may behave in ways considered more socially desirable.

Because most field experiments fall within the public domain (the observations made by the experimenter can be made by anyone, experimenter or not), it has been argued that permission of the participants is not required. Nevertheless, in some instances, there may be considerable intrusions into the private lives of some individuals. Although the many ethical issues involved in field research have yet to be resolved, it would appear undeniable that the public's attitudes toward this research must be taken into account.

Regulation of Human Research

So who decides whether a particular research study is ethical? As it turns out, this decision is often made at several levels. First, the researcher, guided by the ethical principles, must thoughtfully design the study, often after consulting with colleagues. At many universities, a departmental ethics committee then evaluates the research design. At most institutions (research, educational, hospitals, prisons), the research design is evaluated by an **Institutional Review Board (IRB)** that includes faculty from the sciences, faculty from the nonsciences, administrators, and at least one person not affiliated with the institution. Some ethical issues rise to the level of national concern. For behavioral researchers, the American Psychological Association has an Ethics Committee to continually review the ethical guidelines and monitor adherence to them.

Research With Children and the Mentally Challenged: Ethical Guidelines

What if you wanted to conduct research on the effect of television violence on aggressive behavior in children by presenting different types of TV shows to children and observing their behavior? Our examples so far have considered ethical issues when human adults are used as research participants. However, the ethical principles were designed to apply to all research participants, including children and those who are mentally challenged. Although most of the ethical principles are easily applied to these special populations, the issue of informed consent may present an interesting dilemma.

How do you obtain informed consent when the individual may not yet have acquired language ability? Even if the individual is capable of language, how can we be sure that he or she understands the purpose of the study? Will participants understand their right to withdraw from the study at any time? What about occasions when children are unaware of the fact that they are participants, as in research done in nursery school settings when observations are made under natural conditions?

Clearly, special provisions must be made to protect the interests of children and the mentally challenged. The solution is found in the section of ethical standard 3.10 that states, "For persons who are legally incapable of giving informed consent, psychologists nevertheless (1) provide an appropriate explanation, (2) seek the individual's assent (agreement), (3) consider such persons' preferences and best interests, and (4) obtain appropriate permission from a legally authorized person, if such substitute consent is permitted or required by law. When consent by a legally authorized person is not permitted or required by law, psychologists take reasonable steps to protect the individual's rights and welfare." Therefore, it is important that the researcher carefully and fully inform the parent or guardian of the nature of the research—including information about deception if it is to be used.

Although investigators must be concerned with the health and welfare of all research participants, they must be especially concerned and cautious when using children as participants. Only mild forms of arousal or stimulation should be used. Obviously, the experiment should be terminated if signs of distress become apparent. When using children as participants, careful observations of the children must occur at all times.

The box "Thinking Critically About Everyday Information" reviews some of the concepts presented so far.

Research With Nonhumans: Ethical Guidelines

Most people are surprised to learn that only 7–8% of psychological research consists of animal research and that 90% of the animals used are rodents and birds. Even so, psychologists do make use of such diverse organisms as worms, snakes, fish, cockroaches, birds, bees, mice, rats, dogs, cats, sheep, horses, elephants, pigs, and an assortment of nonhuman primates, to name a few. The reasons for selecting nonhuman organisms are as diverse as the organisms selected. Suffice it for the moment to note that we have greater control over

Thinking Critically About Everyday Information

Ethics of Human Research

In 2002, the *Washington Post* newspaper published an article titled "Study Links a Gene to Impact of Child Abuse." Portions of that article are reprinted below:

> Scientists have discovered a gene that appears to help explain why some boys who are abused or mistreated are more likely than others to grow up to be aggressive, antisocial or violent. . . . The finding, which for the first time links a gene and an upbringing to a specific behavior, could help shed light on why some children who suffer trauma never seem to recover, while others are resilient. By showing that a particular environment can have devastating consequences for children with certain genes, the new research might one day identify children at greatest risk and help direct services to them. . . . While the implications for social policy could be profound, researchers warned against assuming that genes alone determine behavior, and said that any effort to peg certain children as potentially violent was simplistic and unethical. Indeed, in the interplay between this particular gene and the environment, researchers found the environment played a dominant role. Absent abuse, the gene, which is involved in regulating brain chemicals, did not help predict whether a boy would grow up to be violent or aggressive. And some boys without the genetic variation became aggressive if they grew up in an abusive setting. . . . The study, published in today's issue of the journal *Science*, was based on 442 boys in New Zealand who were tracked from birth to age 26. The scientists correlated statistics about abuse and mistreatment among the children with variations of a gene that coded for an enzyme called monoamine oxidase A, or MAOA. The enzyme helps regulate the level of chemicals called neurotransmitters, which carry signals in the brain.
>
> Moffitt said that variations in the gene had previously been linked to aggression in mice, and a small 1993 study had showed a rare mutation in the gene across three generations of one family in the Netherlands was linked to violence and mental retardation. Variations in the MAOA gene may give some people certain advantages, even as it causes them risks in the presence of trauma or abuse. This could be similar to African populations, for instance, who have a genetic variation that increases the risk of anemia but protects against malaria.

This study raises several interesting issues, but let's focus on a few ethical issues that arise from the statement in the article about "442 boys in New Zealand who were tracked from birth to age 26. The scientists correlated statistics about abuse and mistreatment among the children with variations of a gene that coded for an enzyme called monoamine oxidase A, or MAOA." Consider the following questions:

- When and from whom should have consent or assent been obtained?

- What aspects of the study involve the issue of confidentiality?

- Obviously, some of the research participants were abused during the course of the study. Do you believe that the researcher had an obligation to report such abuse to authorities when it happened, or would this interfere too much with the goals of the research?

SOURCE: "Study Links a Gene to Impact of Child Abuse," Shankar Vedantam. *The Washington Post*, August 2, 2002, p. A2. Copyright © 2002 *The Washington Post*, reprinted with permission.

nonhuman participants; they are generally available 24 hours a day over days, weeks, months, or years. Moreover, we may subject them to conditions that would be clearly unethical with human participants. Yet these experiments ultimately are important in promoting human welfare. Experiments of this nature must be carefully assessed and evaluated, even though nonhuman animals are used. Important ethical questions are clearly involved.

To address these ethical concerns, guidelines have been established. The APA code of ethics section 8.09 describes the general principles for the care and use of animals in research. These principles include the use of trained supervisors and research assistants, minimization of pain and discomfort, use of pain and discomfort only when it is necessary for research or applied purposes, use of anesthesia during surgery, and use of rapid procedures to terminate life with minimal pain. The Animal Welfare Act also provides for unannounced inspections and requires that every institution conducting animal research have an Institutional Animal Care and Use Committee (IACUC) to review each research proposal. Further guidelines for the care and use of animals are provided by the Association for the Assessment and Accreditation of Laboratory Animal Care (AAALAC).

Even with extensive ethical standards for the use of nonhumans in research, the topic has been and will continue to be controversial. Many people have very strong feelings regarding animal research. These feelings exist on a continuum. Some believe that we should stop all animal research, some believe that the ethical standards should be more stringent, many believe that the current ethical standards are appropriate, and some believe that the ethical standards are too stringent. Let's examine some of the arguments on each side of the issue.

Arguments Against Animal Research   Some individuals hold the philosophical position that nonhuman animals are "equal" to humans and, therefore, humans do not have the right to use them in animal research. After all, nonhuman animals cannot provide informed consent. These people argue that there are viable alternatives such as research on plants, tissue cultures, and computer simulations. Although many of these individuals agree that the pace of scientific progress would slow, they believe that it is a fair price to pay for the elimination of animal research. Some of these people belong to animal rights organizations such as PETA (People for the Ethical Treatment of Animals), PAWS (Progressive Animal Welfare Society), and SPARE (Students Promoting Animal Rights and Emancipation). Actually, most of the efforts of these organizations are not directed toward psychological research. Rather, they have a very broad agenda that includes medical research, cosmetic research, pet ownership, circus animals, fishing and whaling practices, trade in exotic animals, and the fur industry.

Arguments for More Stringent Standards   Some individuals and groups argue for more stringent standards. Many make the same arguments as those opposed to all animal research, but are not willing to eliminate animal research. Many are interested in curtailing animal research that they define as unnecessary. This type of research might include the testing of cosmetic products, studies that attempt to replicate previous findings, research that does not have an immediate application, and research with "higher" animals such as dogs, cats, and primates. The greatest problems are drawing the lines and defining what is unnecessary.

Arguments for Current Ethical Standards   Many researchers and nonresearchers believe that the current standards provide the most appropriate definitions. The current guidelines have evolved from less stringent guidelines and represent the culmination of much discussion and debate. They are extensive, and researchers who use animals in research are held accountable for their treatment. Researchers are also keenly aware of the many benefits that animal research has provided for both humans and nonhumans. They also argue that alternatives (plants, tissue cultures, computer simulations) are often not capable of answering the research questions.

Arguments for Less Stringent Ethical Standards   There may be some persons who believe that the ethical standards for using nonhuman animals in research are too stringent. However, there has been no organized effort in this direction.

There can be no right answer when it comes to the use of animals in research. However, there must be a national policy. This policy has been, and will continue to be, shaped by national debate on the issue. Everyone should be aware of the arguments on all sides in order to participate in an informed and intelligent discussion.

● Professional Behavior of the Investigator

For students relatively new to the area of behavioral research, several issues related to ethical conduct should be emphasized.

Testing Participants

What is wrong with the following scenario?

Fred M. and Margot T. are engaged in a joint research project. Prior to collecting data, they spent many hours together designing the study, gathering and installing the appropriate apparatus, and preparing forms for consent, debriefing, data collection, and IRB approval. In order to familiarize themselves with the experimental procedures, they tested each other as participants. Based on their preliminary findings, they estimated it would take approximately 25 minutes to test each participant. Accordingly, they scheduled their participants to arrive every 30 minutes. Reasoning that some participants might have difficulty remembering their appointment times, they scheduled each participant on the hour and the half-hour.

On the day they were to begin testing participants, they misjudged the time it would take to get from class to their experimental laboratory. Consequently, they arrived 5 minutes late. After apologizing for their tardiness, they proceeded to conduct the experiment. The first participant was somewhat slower than expected. She finished 35 minutes later. As she prepared to leave, she turned to Margot and asked, "Could you tell me what the experiment was about? I found the task very interesting. Did it tell you anything about me?"

Margot noticed that the next participant was already getting a little impatient. He had arrived a few minutes early and had been waiting almost 15 minutes. She turned to her first participant and said, "I'm sorry, there isn't enough time to explain things right now. The next participant is already here, we are running behind, and I'm afraid we may get backlogged. Why don't you look up Fred or me in a week or two?"

Things did not get better. During the briefing period prior to testing , the second participant asked many questions. He wanted to know how the apparatus worked, whether there was any possible danger, what the experimenters hoped to find out, and whether his performance would be kept confidential. He emerged from the laboratory 50 minutes later. By now the waiting room was beginning to look like a medical doctor's office. One participant was visibly upset. "I thought you told me it would only take a half-hour at the most. I've been here that long already. I'm sorry but I've got a class in 30 minutes." With this he turned and departed abruptly.

Many aspects of Fred and Margot's preparation are commendable. They designed this study in advance, prepared data collection forms, checked out the apparatus, and made an effort to estimate how long the experimental sessions would last.

However, they made two big mistakes. They failed to take into account the convenience and comfort of the participants and to schedule sufficient time for the debriefing period at the end of the experiment. It was correct to test each other as experimental participants because it gave them a participant's view of the proceedings, but they should have recognized that they were not typical participants. Presumably they knew what was going on. They were not entering an unfamiliar situation, a cause of apprehension in many participants. Some fear the possibility of physical discomfort (such as electric shock), and others experience threats to their self-esteem (not measuring up to the performance standards of other participants). Because anxiety and tension frequently provoke an outpouring of questions, it may take considerable time to get some participants underway. Moreover, the completion of the experimental session often opens a floodgate of questions. Therefore, it is important to build into the experiment sufficient time for a debriefing period. Such a period is essential to relieve anxiety, for giving as full an account of the purposes of the experiment as permissible, and for answering questions. What was the experiment all about? How did I do? Are you going to publish the results?

If you are conducting a research study, you should schedule adequate time for each participant so that you are not forced to give him or her the bum's rush after each session. Inform the participants as much as possible about the nature of the experiment without compromising it. In some instances, of course, it will not be possible to provide much information until all participants have been tested. If this is the case, participants should be told this, and a mechanism should be set up to provide detailed information at a later date. After you have set up this mechanism, it is imperative that you follow through. Perhaps you could send the participants a preliminary report, a preprint of a publication, or an abstract of the research. Your efforts should be directed to making participation a pleasant educational experience. Research psychologists want to establish a reputation of trust. When this is not achieved, rumors and folklore develop, particularly on college campuses, which tend to establish local reputations of various departments. After such reputations are established, deserved or undeserved, there is a considerable inertia, making it difficult to change them.

Certain behaviors distinguish between an amateur and a professional or between an incompetent and a competent investigator. Competent investigators show up on time, are well prepared, and have checked the equipment beforehand to be sure it is working well. Moreover, they are familiar with the apparatus, with the procedure, and with the instructions. All the necessary secondary equipment is at hand, such as data sheets with names, dates, conditions, experiment number, and biographical sketch. A checklist of necessary steps and equipment should be used if the experiment is complex. By being well prepared and competent, you inspire confidence on the part of participants.

Keep in mind our earlier observation that participants are often nervous or anxious about participating in psychological experiments. Do not forget the amenities—be thoughtful and courteous. Bluntly telling participants to do something may appear as though you are ordering them to do it. They may regard the order as a threat to their personal freedom, and may then assert their freedom by becoming negative or uncooperative. However, a request coupled with words like *please, thank you,* and *you're welcome* is less likely to arouse negative reactions.

One final word is in order. The experimental setting should be used strictly for research purposes. It should not be a hangout for friends or a place for bull sessions. More than one experiment has been compromised by distractions arising from various activities in the waiting room. In closing this section, we should note that how we conduct ourselves as experimenters can influence the participant in significant ways and can introduce unwanted bias into the experiment.

Integrity of the Data

Remember that data gathered in an experiment are confidential. Individuals are sometimes very sensitive about their performance in experimental tasks. It is imperative that you, as the experimenter, refrain from discussing the performance of individual participants with anyone. Where possible, code the data sheets to preserve the anonymity of participants. If follow-up information is not needed, you may be able to eliminate the participant's name entirely from the data sheet.

For most studies, the raw data will be entered into a data file on a computer so that statistical analyses can be performed. At this stage of the research process, you should realize that the data sheets represent the answer to your research question. Therefore, the data should be handled carefully. Data sheets should be kept together in a secure place, and data files on the computer should be saved in several locations.

During data collection or during data input and analysis, it is common for the researcher to question the validity of some data. For example, you may have noticed that a particular participant did not seem to take the experiment seriously. You may notice that a data sheet is suspicious because the participant answered "C" to all 30 multiple-choice questions on your survey. You may notice a data value that is so far out of range that it does not seem realistic. What is the ethical approach to these situations? Can you simply throw out data? The answer is that you can only do so under certain conditions. These conditions require that you have a valid reason for doing so and you report your reasons for doing so in any published report. Before doing so, it is often wise to consult with colleagues who do not have an inherent interest in the research project and can provide an unbiased opinion.

Because the data that are entered into a computer file are often already manipulated in some way, it is very important to retain the original data if there is the possibility that the data will be published in the future. Many investigations into possible ethical violations have been resolved by examining the original data. Remember that your published research findings, which may be read by scientists for years to come, are rooted in the original data.

Plagiarism and Publication

Plagiarism is a serious violation of ethical principles. It can be defined as taking the ideas or words of someone else and representing them as yours. For example, if you are writing a research paper and express an idea that came from another author, you are required to cite that author. Also, you should express the idea in your own words—not the exact words of the author. In rare situations, you may quote, word for word, the statement of another author. When doing so, you are required to cite that author (including the page number) and to place the statement in quotation marks. Under no circumstances should you simply change some of the words from statements made by another author, even if you cite that author.

Let's examine a few examples of appropriate and inappropriate citations by considering the actual text in a student research article (Sheets, 1999):

> The interview is a crucial part of the selection process for employees and graduate students. Employers use interviews to form an impression about possible employees and to determine whether they would be positive additions to their companies. Written applications can reveal only a limited amount about a person; they do not show the personality or character of a person. (p. 7)

The following is the most obvious example of plagiarism because it includes a direct quote without any citation:

> There are many factors that affect impressions during an interview. Employers use interviews to form an impression about possible employees and to determine whether they would be positive additions to their companies.

The following is an example of plagiarism because it includes a direct quote without a page citation:

> There are many factors that affect impressions during an interview. Employers use interviews to form an impression about possible employees and to determine whether they would be positive additions to their companies (Sheets, 1999).

The following is an example of plagiarism because it includes wording that is too similar to the original source:

> There are many factors that affect impressions during an interview. Interviews are used by employers to form an impression about potential workers and to determine whether they would be positive additions to the workplace (Sheets, 1999).

The following is not plagiarism, but is an example of an unnecessary direct quote:

> There are many factors that affect impressions during an interview. "Employers use interviews to form an impression about possible employees and to determine whether they would be positive additions to their companies" (Sheets, 1999, p. 7).

The following is not plagiarism and is a good example of the appropriate use of another author's idea with a proper citation:

> There are many factors that affect impressions during an interview, and the interview is often a critical component of the hiring process (Sheets, 1999).

The process of conducting research to answer questions is an endeavor undertaken by the community of scientists around the world. Research ideas do not come from a vacuum. As you consider a potential research project with hypotheses and methods, those ideas may come from your own personal experience, something you read in a psychology textbook, something you read in a scientific journal, and/or something one of your professors said. Therefore, those sources of information are valuable and should be recognized by you as you develop your own research proposals and report research results.

It is important to realize that research is a public enterprise. One has not completed the scientific process until the results are made public. Other scientists review research reports before a presentation is accepted at a scientific conference, before an article is published in a journal, or before a book chapter is published in a book. Even the research of an undergraduate student is, at the very least, reviewed by the professor. All of these reviewers are knowledgeable in the field and aware of ethical principles. As such, they are very adept at detecting violations.

CASE ANALYSIS

Janet is a senior psychology major interested in conducting a study to examine the effects of TV violence on behavior in children. A friend of Janet's is the director of a day-care facility in town, and Janet decides that this would be a convenient place to make observations. Janet devises a methodology whereby she will assign the children to two groups. All of the children will watch television programs for two hours each day for a total of three weeks. During the programs and for one hour afterward, Janet will record the number of aggressive acts by each child. One group will watch violent programs, and the other group will watch nonviolent programs.

Janet describes the study to her friend, the director of the day-care center. Her friend agrees that Janet can conduct the study. So Janet develops videotapes that have either violent or nonviolent programs and develops data sheets with space for each child's name, group assignment, and number of aggressive acts. She begins the study. After one week, it has become clear that the children watching the violent programs are engaging in very aggressive behaviors and that some of the children in this group are becoming fearful. To protect the integrity of her research design, Janet continues the study for the remaining two weeks. Janet is pleased that the results clearly support her hypothesis that the children who watched the violent TV programs would show more aggressive behavior. She plans to present her findings at a regional psychology conference.

Critical Thinking Questions

1. Which of the five ethical principles has (have) been violated?

2. Within ethics standard 8, which areas have been violated?

3. What should have been done to make this study ethical?

GENERAL SUMMARY

Ethical conduct, for which there are now guidelines, is of primary importance in conducting behavioral research. Had guidelines been in place earlier, research such as the Milgram obedience study and the Zimbardo prison study might not have been conducted. However, specific ethical standards have evolved over the years, and all behavioral research must now be reviewed for compliance to ethical standards. These ethical principles and standards are clearly articulated by the American Psychological Association and include all areas of professional behavior. Issues particularly important for researchers include informed consent, the use of deception, the use of animals in research, treatment of research participants, integrity of data, and reporting results. The scientific methods described in the remainder of this book are only useful if they are used ethically. In the next chapter, we will explore what it means for behavioral research to be scientific.

DETAILED SUMMARY

1. The Tuskegee syphilis study is an example of unethical research in which participants were not fully informed about the research and effective treatments were withheld.

2. The Milgram obedience studies and the Stanford prison study are examples of social psychology research in which participants experienced anxiety and discomfort at levels that would not be permitted under current ethical standards.

3. The American Psychological Association maintains a set of ethical guidelines for both human and animal research that currently includes five general principles and ten ethical standards.

4. Informed consent is required in most research with human participants. It includes a description of the study, potential risks, the freedom to withdraw, and whom to contact with questions.

5. For children and the mentally challenged, informed consent is obtained from a legal guardian.

6. Providing false information to (or withholding information from) participants constitutes deception. Its use is sometimes necessary to answer the research question, but its use should also be carefully weighed against the potential for harm.

7. Informed consent may not be necessary in field research that involves the recording of public behavior.

8. The Institutional Review Board reviews research to determine whether ethical guidelines for human research are being followed.

9. Ethical guidelines for animal research are provided by the American Psychological Association, the Animal Welfare Act, and the Association for the Assessment and Accreditation of Laboratory Animal Care.

10. The use of animals in research is a controversial topic with arguments on both sides of the debate.

11. All researchers, including student researchers, should strive to be competent, courteous, and professional.

12. All researchers, including student researchers, should maintain integrity during the analysis of research data and the presentation of research results.

KEY TERMS

debriefing *(p. 13)*
deception *(p. 13)*
informed consent *(p. 11)*
Institutional Review Board (IRB) *(p. 14)*

nonreactive measures *(p. 14)*
plagiarism *(p. 20)*
reactive measures *(p. 14)*

REVIEW QUESTIONS/EXERCISES

1. We mentioned several studies that involved questionable ethics. Another one is the Willowbrook Hepatitis Project. Conduct an Internet search to learn more about this study, and identify the ethical principles that were violated.

2. Why is the procedure of deception needed in some research? How is the ethical appropriateness of deception determined?

3. In your own words, summarize in just a few sentences what it means to be an ethical psychologist.

4. In terms of ethical procedures, what is the primary difference between research with adult participants and research with children (or the mentally challenged)?

5. The chapter outlined four positions on the use of animals in research. Which position do you take, and why?

 ## WEB RESOURCES TO INCREASE LEARNING

The chapter outline, chapter summaries, key terms and definitions, additional chapter questions/exercises, and links to relevant Web sites are available at the course Web site (http://psychology.wadsworth.com/lammers_badia1e). Explore the interactive workshops titled "Ethical Issues" and "Effective Debriefing."

CHAPTER 3

FUNDAMENTALS OF THE SCIENTIFIC APPROACH

● Approaches to Knowing

Almost every moment of our waking lives we are confronted with situations that require us to make choices. Shall we obey the strident summons of the morning alarm or turn off the infernal machine in favor of another forty winks? Should we go to the aid of a friend who is in the throes of an emotional "down" even though doing so means breaking other commitments we have made? Should we buy the latest recording of our favorite musical group even though it precipitates a temporary financial crisis? How many times a day do questions like this race through our thoughts? How often are we required to assess situations, make decisions, predict actions, and draw conclusions? Some questions lead to emotional issues. How old is the earth? When and how did humans evolve? What curriculum should be taught in public school? What is the basis for observed racial differences?

Whether we are scientists or not, the ways in which we carry out these activities are of profound significance. They determine the quality of our decisions, the accuracy of our understanding, and ultimately, the quality of our lives. In the hustle and bustle of daily living, we are rarely aware of the assumptions we make as we seek solutions to problems. Nor do we take much time to reflect on the variety of approaches we take. At times we are intuitive, relying on a hunch or some vague feeling. At other times we examine questions in a rational manner. On yet other occasions we become empirical, basing our actions on our prior experiences or on the experiences of others. Often we rely on authority, looking toward experts to fill gaps in our own backgrounds. Let's take a closer look at these approaches to knowing.

Let's assume that you believe that watching violence on television leads children to be more violent in their behavior. Where does this belief come from? How did you acquire this knowledge? Perhaps your parents, minister, or teacher told you this. Perhaps when you were younger you noticed that your own behavior and the behavior of children you played with seemed more violent after watching certain TV shows. Perhaps you have reasoned that because part of a person's development is based on learning by watching others, watching others display violent behavior will undoubtedly lead to more frequent violent behavior in the observer. Perhaps you have read about research studies in a textbook or scientific journal that propose such a conclusion. Finally, and perhaps more realistically, your belief may be based on an integration of information from several sources.

The primary goal of science is to acquire new knowledge. In science, we are interested in making new observations, verifying prior observations, discovering laws, deriving predictions, and improving our understanding of ourselves and the world around us. To these ends, we are interested in improving theories that explain and predict behavior, developing better analytical and measurement methods, and providing a broader database (information) for future development. Science is based primarily on an empirical approach to gathering information—an approach that relies on **systematic observation.** Before discussing empiricism, let's examine three other important sources of information in our lives.

Authority

One source of knowledge is that derived from authority figures. Religious leaders, teachers, parents, and judges may dictate the truth as they believe it. Or truth may be found in authoritative works such as the Bible or an encyclopedia. In the case of the Bible, the method of authority is described as dogmatic (fixed and unbending); if knowledge from the source is wrong, then we would be misled and the search for the truth hindered. Likewise, people often view a text like an encyclopedia as the truth when, in fact, some information is likely incorrect (such as historical accounts of events based on biased viewpoints). Although science as a discipline is not based on authority, scientists as people do, on occasion, rely on authority. In the past, some scientists have believed so firmly in their theories that they asserted, dogmatically, that they were true. When false, these beliefs resulted in faulty knowledge and hindered the development of these disciplines.

For example, a Russian geneticist and agronomist by the name of T. D. Lysenko was involved with the science and economics of crop production. Based on faulty research, Lysenko announced that crop characteristics resulting from environmental changes could be transmitted genetically. Because this view of genetics was compatible with the political doctrine of Soviet Russia, his position was forced upon all geneticists conducting research within the Soviet Union. Lysenko's view was later repudiated, but not before it considerably set back the science of agriculture in Russia. Ivan Pavlov also noted that each generation of dogs conditioned faster than the preceding generation. This was also accepted within the Soviet Union as evidence of the genetic transmission of acquired traits—in this case, learning. The truth of the matter is that the dogs were conditioning faster because the researchers were getting better at their trade, so to speak. Improved conditioning techniques and better control over extraneous variables, rather than genetic coding, were responsible for the generational improvement. Thus, Soviet genetic research suffered from several decades of allegiance to an erroneous theory.

The point can be made more clearly by contrasting creationism with science. Creationists argue that creation science is scientific and should be taught in the schools along with evolution. Is it scientific? Let's take a look.

In traditional science, observations, measurement, and discoveries are repeatedly tested before they are accepted as factual. Also, the findings and interpretations are always provisional and contingent upon additional tests. Scientists question their data with a healthy skepticism and are open to accepting changes in their conclusions if warranted by new evidence. They accept change; they encourage creative ideas, with the focus being on a better understanding of nature. Theories and laws that survive repeated testing are retained; those that do not are modified or discarded. For example, theories such as evolution and gravity have withstood repeated testing from many different scientific disciplines. However, even though they are accepted today, they are still undergoing further testing.

In contrast, creationism asks that we believe on faith and not focus on evidence. For creationists, appeals to authority take precedence over evidence. The conclusions of creationism are fixed and do not change when presented with findings contradictory to their tenets. From a creationist perspective, authoritative conclusions come first and then evidence is sought to support them. Obviously their procedures contrast sharply with those of traditional sciences. In science, new ideas are welcomed. They are particularly exciting when they question the validity of current conclusions and theories—especially when they increase the understanding of our world.

Our physical health, our economic health, our environmental health, and future benefits to humankind depend on our scientific progress. They depend on enhancing our understanding of the world in which we live. To date, science has an excellent track record in approaching these ends.

Another point should be made regarding creationism. Many creationists spend time trying to discredit the theory of evolution. Their argument is essentially that evolution theory is wrong (despite the powerful evidence in its favor). They then draw the improper conclusion that because evolution is wrong, creationism must be right.

Personal Experience

Some individuals (such as writers and artists) have insights derived from experiences and observations unique to them. They attempt to communicate their insights and intuitions to others through writing and works of art. They try to communicate, through their work, general truths with which those familiar with their work can identify. To illustrate, who has read Shakespeare's *As You Like It* and failed to respond to the lines, "All the world's a stage, and all the men and women merely players. They have their exits and their entrances; and one man in his time plays many parts"? Though not all of us make our personal insights public, it is certainly true that much of our own knowledge is based on our own experiences. However, we must be careful. Our own experiences can lead to faulty beliefs. For example, you may have an unpleasant experience with a member of an ethnic minority group and conclude that all individuals of that ethnic background have similar flaws. Such overgeneralization is common and can result in faulty beliefs (in this case, prejudice).

Rationalism

In wearing the hat of **rationalism,** we emphasize reasoning and logic rather than experience. Reasoning and logic can be very powerful methods in the search for knowledge and understanding. They play an important role in the formation of theories and the formation of hypotheses to test those theories. For example, a theory of depression proposes that it is related to below-normal activity of a particular brain chemical called serotonin. Reasoning and logic would therefore suggest that a drug that increases serotonin activity might be an effective antidepressant. We now have a hypothesis for an experiment. (In fact, many antidepressant drugs currently on the market, including Paxil, Prozac, and Zoloft, increase the activity of serotonin in the brain.)

Although rationalism can be useful in the advancement of knowledge, it has drawbacks when used in isolation as the only approach. With rationalism, propositions are not empirically tested, but are accepted as self-evident. Thus, if we accept the proposition that males have better math skills than females, it follows that an engineering firm should give preference to hiring male rather than female job applicants. Although the conclusion may be logical, the original proposition may not be based on empirical evidence and may, in fact, be incorrect. The rational approach will often deny the relevance of observation and experience in a search for universal truths, pointing out that our senses are faulty and incomplete.

Empiricism

Unlike rationalism, which tends to seek universal truths, the goals of **empiricism** are more modest. The empiricist stresses the importance of observation as the basis for understanding our past and present and predicting the future. Reasoning, personal experience, and authority are not enough for the empiricist. For empiricists, experiencing events through stimulation of our senses (seeing, hearing, touching) is required. Recognizing the fallibility of experience, the empiricist does not search for universal or absolute truth. Statistics and probability, which are tools for dealing with uncertainty, are key weapons in the arsenal of the scientist.

All four approaches to knowledge are important, and we use them all. Scientists emphasize the rational and empirical approaches, but also make use of authority and personal experience on occasion. Figure 3.1 summarizes the four approaches to knowing.

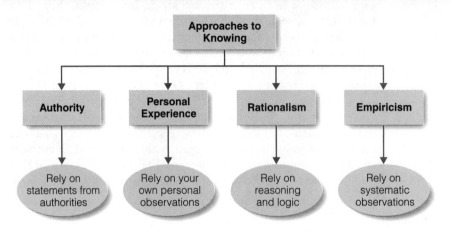

Figure 3.1   Approaches to Knowing

Defining Science

Psychology is a science. But what is science? Most people, including scientists, find it difficult to answer this question because there is no simple, straightforward definition. We might try to break the ice by defining science as an organized body of knowledge that has been collected by use of the scientific method. We should then state what we mean by the scientific method, being careful to state the assumptions and goals fundamental to science. Therefore, to define the term *science* adequately, we must state the goals that are sought, the assumptions that are made, and the characteristics of the method.

Goals of Science

Most scientists, but not all, are interested in three goals: *understanding, prediction,* and *control.* Of these three goals, two of them, understanding and prediction, are sought by all scientists. The third goal, control, is sought only by those scientists who can manipulate the phenomena they study. One of the most rigorous and precise disciplines in terms of prediction is astronomy, but it is unlikely that astronomers will ever acquire sufficient control over their subject matter to manipulate events.

Sometimes *description* and *explanation* are used synonymously with *understanding* when stating the goals of science. Although there is a similarity of meaning among the three concepts, there are also subtle differences. Description of things and events appears first. We must know the "what" of what we are studying. It is important to give an accurate description, identifying the factors and conditions that exist and also the extent to which they exist. As the description becomes more complete—as we identify more factors or conditions affecting the events we are studying—the better our understanding of the event becomes. A complete description of the event would constitute an explanation. We would then be able to state clearly and accurately the conditions under which a phenomenon occurs.

Some have argued that prediction is the ultimate goal that sciences seek. To a degree, we know that we understand (at some level) an event when we can predict the occurrence of that event. Prediction may also permit a substantial amount of control. When events can be predicted accurately, preparation in anticipation of the event can occur. However, we should be careful not to fully equate prediction with understanding. Based on past experience, we may correctly predict that some people with severe depression will evidence a remission of symptoms following electroconvulsive shock. However, we may have little understanding of why this is so.

Considerable research has taken place in countries throughout the world regarding natural disasters such as earthquakes, hurricanes, droughts, and epidemics. Imagine, in terms of human welfare, the impact of acquiring an understanding sufficient to predict these natural disasters. Timely preparation of those threatened could save lives and dramatically reduce injuries and human suffering. But the next step—achieving control of the environmental conditions leading to these events—would permit us to alter the time, place, and intensity of their occurrence or prevent them altogether. The prospect of control over disordered behavior is also exciting to contemplate. When sufficient knowledge is acquired, perhaps we will be able to eliminate or reduce the symptoms of many psychological and physiological disorders, maximize a sense of well-being, enhance memory and learning, or eliminate AIDS.

Ultimately, science seeks to explain, through the development of theory, the phenomena that exist in the universe. Scientists try to arrive at general statements that link together the basic events being studied. If this is accomplished, understanding, prediction, and control follow.

Assumptions of Science

All scientists make two fundamental assumptions. One is **determinism**—the assumption that all events in the universe, including behavior, are lawful or orderly. The second assumption is that this lawfulness is discoverable. Notice that the first assumption does not necessarily imply the second assumption. In other words, we can assume that behavior is lawful without presuming that we will discover this lawfulness.

To say that behavior is lawful is to say that behavior is a function of antecedent events. More loosely, we could say that there is a cause–effect relationship between the past and the present, a continuity between before and after. According to this view, behavior is orderly and lawful; individuals do not behave randomly or capriciously. Even behavior that appears to be random is assumed to follow some underlying lawfulness.

The assumption that behavior is lawful is justified by everyday experiences. Every time we place ourselves behind the steering wheel of a car, we implicitly assume that the behavior of hundreds of other motorists on the road will be orderly. They will not suddenly veer off the road into our path, brake without cause, or try to crash into us. Similarly, when traveling by air, we assume the pilots will take a course that minimizes air turbulence and maximizes the comfort of passengers. We feel assured that they will not commit any act on a whim, such as doing loop-the-loops at 30,000 feet.

The assumption of lawfulness is very important for several reasons. One major reason is that it determines our own behavior as scientists. If we were to assume that behavior is free of causes or determiners, it would not make much sense for us to study it. By definition, if an individual's behavior is free of causes, then there is no lawfulness. There is no pattern to it, no connection with the past. It simply would not make good sense to study a phenomenon assumed to be unlawful. However, even if the assumption of lawfulness is correct, we should not be deluded into believing that it will result in precise predictions of human behavior. We must realize the enormous variability in behavior that results from the enormous number of variables that have affected a person up until a particular moment in life. These variables include genetic composition and every experience that the person has ever had.

Understanding all of these variables and their complex interactions in order to make precise predictions would seem to be an unattainable goal. However, our predictions in the behavioral sciences have certainly become better over the years, and scientists believe that the trend will continue as behavioral science continues to develop.

One effort to better understand the variability in events is chaos theory—a relatively new concept that has been applied to science, including the behavioral sciences. **Chaos theory** is an attempt to understand complex, nonlinear, dynamic systems by using mathematical modeling. The theory attempts to explain the overall behavior of a system without attempting to predict detailed states at any given moment in time. Chaos theory is often misunderstood to imply that there are systems that are not deterministic. This is not true. In fact, the theory assumes determinism but concedes that perfect predictability may not be achievable because of the immense number of variables simultaneously interacting to affect the system. Thus, you can imagine that our behavior and thoughts at this moment are determined by an immense number of natural events, including our genetic makeup, all of our past experiences, our present state of physiology, and the current environmental conditions. Although such determinism is imaginable, it is impossible to imagine a complete understanding of all these variables and their interactions that would lead us to perfect predictions of our behaviors and thoughts. However, we might note that just because something has not yet been done does not mean that it cannot be done.

It is important to note that these assumptions of science are not thought of as true or false, provable or unprovable. As scientists, we make certain assumptions to see where they take us in terms of achieving our goals. If we achieve our goals of prediction, control, and understanding, we feel more confident about the assumptions we have made. But we do not assert that we have proved determinism or that free will does not exist. These assumptions may be thought of as the rules of the games in which scientists engage. We stick by these rules as long as they prove to be useful. When no longer useful, we discard them and adopt others that promise to carry us further in our quest for understanding.

The history of science is replete with instances in which major advances occurred only when one set of assumptions was replaced by a different set. Many refer to this as a paradigm shift. To illustrate, we presently regard astronomy as one of the most accurate sciences. However, a few centuries ago, astronomy was in chaos. Astronomers labored under the assumption that the sun revolves around the earth (Ptolemy). Even though this assumption nicely corresponded with everyday experiences (the sun *does* look as if it revolves around the earth; the earth *does not* appear to be moving), little progress was made in astronomy until it was discarded. Many conflicting observations simply could not be resolved within the Ptolemaic framework. Ironically, astronomy emerged as a vibrant science only when it adopted an assumption that ran counter to casual observation. Copernicus posed the startling hypothesis that the earth revolves around the sun. Only with this assumption did many confusing observations about the behavior of the stars and the planets become coherent. The Copernican assumption ultimately prevailed because it proved more useful in predicting and understanding celestial events.

The Scientific Method

Dreams are a fascinating topic in behavioral science. Some believe, as Sigmund Freud did, that dreams are highly meaningful and full of symbolism that requires interpretation. Others believe that dreams are simply a physiological by-product of the physiological activity of the brain during stage REM sleep. Because of the strong visual content of most dreams, scientists long suspected that the visual centers in the brain would be activated during human dreaming. However, there was no practical method for such localized recording of human brain activity while a person was in a dream state. Thus, the state of technology precluded an answer to the scientific question. However, in more recent years, with the advent of PET scans and functional MRIs, scientists have been able to demonstrate the activity in the visual centers of the brain during dream sleep. Unanswerable questions of yesterday are the facts of today, and the unanswerable questions of today will be the facts of the future.

There are a couple of lessons to be learned from this example. Not all events are subject to scientific inquiry. Some are inaccessible because of technological limitations, as was the case with brain activity during dreaming. Others are inaccessible because there is no **empirical referent** to the presumed event (such as ghosts or evil spirits). By *empirical* we mean that it is capable of being experienced—that the event will stimulate one or more of our many senses. We must be able to feel it, taste it, see it, smell it, or hear it, or we must be able to sense a record it makes. In other words, an event must be observable or measurable, either directly or indirectly. For example, no one has seen a subatomic particle, but some scientists have seen and measured a trace it leaves on a photographic plate. No one has ever seen gravity, but its effects are observable and measurable all around us. Similarly, in psychology the construct of learning is never observed directly, but is measured in terms of its effects on some aspect of behavior.

To say that an event must have an empirical referent implies that the event is a public one, not a private one. It also implies that the observations are objective and not subjective. As noted, there are events that cannot be studied because they do not have an empirical referent. For example, the question "Is there a God?" cannot be answered scientifically. The subject matter is not empirical and therefore cannot be subjected to scientific study. Questions such as this require faith on the part of the believer, and this faith is derived from authority figures and related authoritative texts (such as clergy or the Bible). However, a related question can be asked that would allow us to study religious beliefs. We could ask, "What are the effects of religious beliefs on behavior?" We could study these effects scientifically because the presence or absence of religious beliefs in a person can be determined empirically (through verbal reports or questionnaires, for example), and the effects of these beliefs on behavior can also be determined. Both the beliefs and the behavior are directly or indirectly measurable. They are empirical events.

In addition to the requirement that events must be observable, science also requires that observations be *repeatable* and that science itself be *self-correcting*. The requirement that observations must be repeatable permits one investigator to verify the work of another. Insisting on repeatability allows the self-correcting feature, another essential requirement for science, to operate. The scientific method is perhaps the only one that has a built-in self-correcting procedure. Because events are empirical and repeatable, research conducted in one place can generally be repeated in any other part of the world to either confirm or cast doubt on the reliability of published findings.

Students are sometimes distressed to learn that an event must be repeatable if it is to be studied scientifically. What about unique events? Aren't they as important, and shouldn't they be studied? My birth is unique! My death will be unique! As a person, I am unique! Indeed, all people are unique and important. How can scientists ignore these unique events?

In short, they do not. Scientists are well aware of the problem. The solution is to deal with classes of events. Although your birth is unique, births in general are not. The same is usually true for other unique events. We study the class of events—births, deaths, personality, and so on—and then bring our understanding to bear on particular events. On occasion, however, some important events (such as particular alignments of planets in the solar system) may occur so infrequently that we cannot study a class of these events. There is no happy solution to this problem. Often the best that we can do is to have multiple observers on the scene at the time of occurrence. Although the event itself may not be repeatable, a number of observations can be made independently and the results compared. Fortunately, the rare, important event does not appear with sufficient frequency to pose a serious problem for science.

Distinguishing Observation From Inference

Of the many activities that scientists undertake, two of the most important are making accurate observations of the phenomena under study and drawing inferences from these observations. The activity of drawing inferences includes such things as providing interpretations of the data, explaining the data, theorizing or guessing about the underlying processes responsible for the observations, and creating new concepts to explain the observations. Although both observation and inference are important, the first, accurate observation is critical. Our scientific enterprise begins here. The usefulness or goodness of our interpretation depends on the accuracy of our observations. As we will see in the following chapters, many factors can affect our observations. However, even though we may begin with accurate observations, it does not follow automatically that our interpretations will be correct. They may still be wrong. In other words, the observations that we record may occur for reasons other than the ones we give.

It is important that we distinguish between observing an event and making inferences based on those observations. As the following anecdotes illustrate, the observations may be objective and repeatable, but the inferences can be wrong.

This story, a humorous example of faulty inference or logic, has appeared in many guises. Imagine, if you will, a well-trained cockroach capable of responding to verbal commands. Whenever the trainer said "Jump!" the cockroach immediately did so. A researcher became interested in the behavior of the cockroach and decided to study the jumping behavior. After a few observation sessions, he pulled a leg off the cockroach and gave the command "Jump!" Again the roach jumped. The process of systematically removing legs continued until all legs were removed. Again the researcher gave the command "Jump!" but the roach did not move. The results were written up in an experimental report with the conclusion, "When a cockroach loses all of its legs, it becomes completely deaf."

Consider another humorous example of faulty logic. Imagine a young woman born and raised in a small, isolated community without any form of outside communication. One day, she hears of the wonders of other places and decides to visit them. She travels to one of our large cosmopolitan cities. The sights and sounds of the city fascinate her, but the most fascinating of all are her experiences interacting with people in the ethnic parts of the city. She notes that some people speak very smooth and fluent English, but others have strong accents. She also accurately observes that it is usually the much older members of the community who have these accents. After thinking about this observation for a while, our visitor concludes, "As people grow older, they develop accents."

Systematic Nature of Science

We have noted three major characteristics of the scientific method (empirical referent, repeatability, self-correcting). Another important characteristic distinguishes knowledge gained using the scientific method from that gained through our daily experiences. Science is *systematic*. For example, in psychology, whether scientists or laypeople, we all have some familiarity with the subject matter. We spend major portions of each day of our lives interacting with others, observing others, evaluating people, and considering our own behavior. Everyone has learned something about human behavior without studying it scientifically. Also, philosophers, poets, and literary people often have insights into behavior that exceed those of psychologists. Based on our daily experiences, we arrive at many conclusions. Unfortunately, not all of our conclusions derived from daily experiences are accurate. Many, in fact, are false. To avoid arriving at conclusions that appear intuitively correct but are in fact false, we need a systematic approach to the study of behavior. A systematic approach allows us to collect data under clearly specified and controlled conditions that can be repeated, measured, and evaluated. Considerable emphasis is placed on evaluating and ruling out alternative explanations (hypotheses) for the phenomena being studied. In addition, a special effort is made to identify relations among phenomena. Much of this book is devoted to teaching you how to perform these activities.

Inductive and Deductive Research Strategies

The systematic nature of science involves the use of both inductive and deductive research strategies. **Inductive reasoning** involves the formulation of a general principle or theory based on a set of specific observations. Conversely, **deductive reasoning** involves the formulation of specific observational predictions based on a general principle or theory. Figure 3.2 depicts the direction of reasoning. Notice that with inductive reasoning, multiple observations lead to one theory. With deductive reasoning, one theory leads to multiple predictions.

As an example, let's consider the dopamine hypothesis for schizophrenia. Schizophrenia is a serious mental disorder that may include symptoms such as unreal thoughts, hallucinations, emotional disturbance, and social withdrawal. As you might imagine, one of the first

| Figure 3.2 | The Direction of Reasoning for Inductive and Deductive Research Strategies |

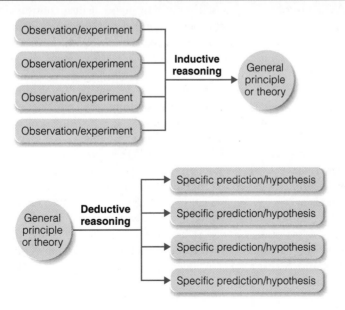

"theories" of the disorder involved possession by evil spirits. During the mid-20th century, a few French psychiatrists administered a new drug for anesthesia (later called chlorpromazine) to a group of mental patients. The schizophrenic patients improved. Other drugs such as amphetamines and cocaine were observed to increase the severity of the symptoms. Animal research showed that chlorpromazine reduced the activity of a certain chemical in the brain (dopamine) and that amphetamines and cocaine increased the activity of dopamine in the brain. Through inductive reasoning, these specific observations, along with others, led to the dopamine hypothesis of schizophrenia. Through deductive reasoning, the theory then predicted that certain other drugs that reduce dopamine activity should be helpful in treating schizophrenia. Many of these drugs have been tested and are now in use.

Role of Theory in Science

So far in this chapter, we have used the term *theory* several times. As we noted, development of theory is one important method we use for making understandable the subject matter that we are studying. Although everyone agrees that theories are important, the question "What is a theory?" is difficult to answer. There is often disagreement about the meaning of the term, and much has been written on the topic. However, some agreement does exist. A **theory** is a system of ideas or a set of principles, often dealing with mechanisms or underlying reasons for behavior, that help us organize and assimilate the empirical relationships (observations) that we discover. This is an important function because without theory to aid us in organizing our observations, we would soon be overwhelmed by the accumulation of huge numbers of isolated facts.

Theories are evaluated through research. There is an interplay between theory and research in that theories guide research and the research findings are then used to revise or modify the theory. The worth of a theory is determined by how well it accounts for the observed relationships, its precision in making predictions, its parsimony (accounting for the largest number of observations with the fewest number of principles), and its internal consistency. Theories, when tested, are not judged to be true or false, proven or unproven. Instead, we describe them as being supported or unsupported, confirmed or unconfirmed.

When testing theories, scientists must guard against confirmation bias. To illustrate confirmation bias, consider the following exercise. We are going to provide you with a series of three numbers. It is your task to discover the rule by which we generated the three numbers. You are to do this in as few trials as possible. We will now give you some numbers generated by our rule—that is, an example of our rule—the series 2, 4, 6. Please generate a further series using what you think our rule is. We will say "yes" if your series agrees with our rule and "no" if it does not. Tell us when you think you know the rule. Begin.

If you behave as most people do, you will say something similar to "8, 10, 12." Our answer is "yes." You may then say "7, 9, 11," and again our answer is "yes." Perhaps you will attempt one more series, such as "14, 16, 18," before you state the rule. Most likely, you have concluded that the rule is "numbers increasing by twos." If so, you are incorrect! You could go on indefinitely generating numbers increasing by twos and never discover that your hypothesis of "two" was incorrect! If you followed a procedure similar to the one described, you were illustrating confirmation bias. You were repeatedly attempting to confirm your hypothesis of "increasing by twos" rather than disconfirming (falsifying, or proving it wrong) it by considering alternative rules. In each case, you gave examples increasing by twos. Thus, **confirmation bias** is a general tendency to emphasize positive confirming outcomes rather than negative or disconfirming ones.

What if your second reply had been "5, 8, 11" and we responded "yes"? At this point, you would have disconfirmed the rule "increasing by twos." You still wouldn't know the rule, but you would have eliminated one hypothesis. Perhaps your next thought is that the rule is "equal intervals between numbers." If you now try 5, 10, 15, you would again receive a "yes," indicating that the series is compatible with our rule, but you would again be illustrating confirmation bias. To test the "equal interval" hypothesis would require that you try to disconfirm (falsify) it by testing "not equal intervals" such as 5, 8, 15. If we say "no," then your hypothesis of equal intervals may be correct. If we say "yes," then you know immediately that it is incorrect, and you go on to another hypothesis, such as "any series of three increasing numbers." The point is that the fastest way to test this hypothesis (identify a false theory) is to try to disconfirm it. To disconfirm the hypothesis, a series of three decreasing numbers might be chosen, such as 8, 5, 2. We would give you a "no," because 8, 5, 2 is not compatible with our rule. This information suggests that your last hypothesis of "three increasing numbers" may be correct. In fact, this was the rule that we wanted you to try to discover.

This example illustrates an important point. We can now return to some points made earlier. Any number of theories or hypotheses can be supported, even if incorrect, by a continuing run of positive instances (successful predictions). You could have continued using inductive reasoning and generalizing the "twos" hypothesis endlessly, thinking it was correct. This strategy is often used by scientists, but as our illustration shows, it has shortcomings of which we should be aware. We can never establish that a theory is correct with this strategy. As the number of positive instances increase (instances of support or confirmation), so does our confidence in the theory. But sometimes this confidence is misplaced.

Summary of the Scientific Method

Let's summarize the characteristics of the scientific method. As we have seen, science cannot be defined simply. An adequate definition requires a statement of the assumptions, goals, and methods. Table 3.1 provides a summary that many, but not all, scientists would agree with. The box "Thinking Critically About Everyday Information" provides an exciting "scientific" claim from the Internet.

Table 3.1	Characteristics of Science
Assumptions of Science	The universe (for psychologists, behavior) is lawful or orderly The lawfulness is discoverable
Goals of Science	Prediction of events in nature Control of events in nature Understanding of events in nature
Characteristics of Methods	Empirical referents (objective, observable, public events) Deals with repeatable events Self-correcting Systematic study Tentative and falsifiable (no appeal to authority)

Thinking Critically About Everyday Information

Human Sex Pheromones

A recent search on the Internet using the search word "pheromone" found this site. The Web site included the following statements:

> Science Has Finally Done It! A men's cologne that contains genuine human sex pheromones. Scientifically designed, tested and proven to Attract Women Like Magic! Now YOU can be more popular with women than you ever thought possible!
>
> Improve your sex appeal 1000% for less than the cost of a good meal! How much is it worth to attract beautiful, sexy women? If you don't try something new—this year won't be any better than last year.
>
> The powerful effects of sex pheromones have been well substantiated. You may have seen stories about human pheromones on *20/20, Dateline NBC, Hard Copy,* or many other television programs. Newspapers from coast to coast, medical journals, and many different magazines have featured stories about the amazing discovery of pheromones.

Wow! That sounds pretty impressive, and it seems to be based on science. Are you convinced? We hope not. We hope that you look at such information with a skeptical eye. Consider the following questions:

- What clues should make you skeptical?
- What "sources of knowing" are used to make the claim?
- How many citations for scientific studies are included?
- How many scientific studies are described?
- How do you believe that they calculated the statistic that your sex appeal will improve 1000%? Empirical data?

Pheromones are chemicals that are released by one animal and detected by another animal. Research shows that pheromones can be a very potent method of communication in many animal species. Human research also supports the existence of pheromones and the vomeronasal organ that detects them. However, no quality studies support the claims made in the preceding advertisement. Much of the research suffers from inadequate research designs that do not account for placebo effects and self-fulfilling prophecies. These issues and the research techniques to control for them are discussed in Chapters 8 and 9. So, let us return to the concepts of the chapter to become more critical consumers of information.

SOURCE: http://androsterone-pheromone-concentrate.com/

Comparisons of Science and Nonscience

One approach to understanding science is to compare it with knowledge that is not based on science. People differ in their views regarding the origins of life on earth. As introduced earlier in this chapter, one set of views has been termed *creationism* or *creation science*; approximately one-third of college students endorse this view. Although some details differ (depending on whether or not one interprets the Bible literally), the basic tenets of this "theory" include the notions that a supernatural force (a God) created the earth and this God is responsible for designing the diversity of life forms on it. Let's examine this "theory" in terms of some of the principles outlined above.

As noted above, one of the hallmarks of scientific theory is that it makes predictions that can be empirically tested. The notion that God created the earth and the life forms on it is not a testable theory. What predictions follow from the theory? How could one make observations in an attempt to falsify the theory? Rather, creationism is not a science but a matter of faith that relies primarily on authority as the source of knowledge.

This debate has been prominent in deciding what is appropriate to teach in public schools. In several instances, the courts have had to intervene and determine whether creationism is a valid scientific theory. For example, in *McLean v. Arkansas Board of Education* (1982), the court determined that "creation science" is not in fact a science and struck down an Arkansas statute that mandated a balanced treatment of "creation-science" and "evolution-science" in the public schools.

A national Harris Poll in 2000 showed that approximately 40% of adults believed in astrology (about the same percentage believed in ghosts). The distinction between astronomy and astrology provides another comparison of science and nonscience. Astronomy is the scientific study of the natural forces that explain planetary phenomena. Astrology is the study of how planetary objects and their alignments affect the behavior of people and the occurrence of events on earth. Theories in astronomy make precise predictions that are testable; theories in astrology typically explain events after the fact or make predictions that are so vague they are not testable. What is very misleading is the current trend by some to label astrology a science. Astrology is not made scientific by its recent use of some principles of astronomy (to better understand alignments) and statistical analyses. There is no scientific evidence to support the basic principles of astrology.

Common Sense and Science

When it comes to human behavior, some have argued that common sense produces the same conclusions that psychological research does. Implied in this comment is that scientific research is a waste of time and effort because common sense would provide the same answers. What is meant by common sense? It is usually taken to mean the accumulation of knowledge through our experiences that allows us to develop generalizations (statements, conclusions, hypotheses) about the world in which we live. These generalizations simplify complex situations by drawing conclusions that are absolute—that is, without qualifications.

It is not unusual for the conclusions of common sense to agree with the findings of science, but the two may also conflict. As already noted, principles derived with the methods of science are based upon careful, systematic observation of empirical events, often in controlled settings. The observations are then evaluated carefully and communicated precisely to others, who can then undertake further evaluation. Usually, the principle (generalization, conclusion) derived from this research predicts behavior consistently. If it does not, further research is undertaken and additional principles are derived. Often the derived principles are stated in a qualified form, such as "Given these conditions, then this behavior is expected to occur." This is not the case with common sense, particularly as found in proverbs of generalized "truths." Proverbs based on common sense often conflict with each other. For example, the proverb "Look before you leap" is contradicted by the proverb "He who hesitates is lost." Yet, given the proper set of circumstances (unspecified by the proverb), both proverbs may be correct. Further examples abound. "Two heads are better than one" is not consistent with "Too many cooks spoil the broth." Is it true that "Absence makes the heart grow fonder," or is it the case that "Out of sight, out of mind"? How often have you heard that you are "Never too old to learn" and also that "You can't teach an old dog new tricks"? Should parents rely on the proverb "Spare the rod and spoil the child" or instead "You catch more flies with honey than with vinegar"?

When stated in absolute terms, as in these examples, the proverbs appear inconsistent and contradictory. It may well be that "Out of sight, out of mind" is an accurate conclusion under certain conditions and that "Absence makes the heart grow fonder" is an accurate conclusion under other conditions, but these conditions remain unspecified. Scientific knowledge improves upon commonsense proverbs by specifying the conditions necessary for the principles to be applied.

We should note that while recognizing the serious weaknesses of a strictly commonsense approach to knowledge, we also recognize the contributions made to our understanding of behavior by nonscientists such as poets, playwrights, novelists, and philosophers. Such individuals can provide us with great insights into human behavior that serve as a creative source for our research.

Molecular to Molar Levels of Analysis and Explanation

The molecular–molar continuum illustrates that the evolution of various disciplines did not occur arbitrarily. Generally, as knowledge accumulated, different questions were asked requiring different units of measurement. Figure 3.3 illustrates the focus of various disciplines and clearly depicts a degree of overlap among them. For example, physicists are generally interested in the level of analysis emphasizing atomic and subatomic particles. This currently is the most molecular level of analysis. Atoms combine and form the basis for molecules, and molecules are the domain of the chemist. The questions usually asked by chemists, therefore, deal with molecules as the unit of analysis. Molecules combine to make up systems such as the circulatory system, glandular system, muscular system, and so on. Physiologists are generally concerned about questions that relate to these systems. These systems combine to give us the next level of analysis, which is the behaving organism. This is the domain of the psychologist. Psychologists are interested in the behavior of individual organisms. Individual organisms combine into groups, and the study of group behavior defines sociology. Groups combine into larger units to make up cultures. The study of cultures defines ethnology. Obviously, these are not competing disciplines; they are usually complementary, each with its own level of analysis.

Figure 3.3 | **The Molecular–Molar Continuum**

The level of analysis is extremely small in nuclear physics (molecular) and extremely large in ethnology (molar). The overlapping boundaries indicate that the various sciences are not rigid and fixed. At times, a psychologist may operate at the level of analysis of a physiologist and, at other times, at the level of a sociologist.

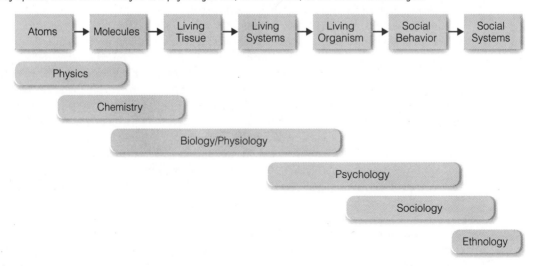

Controversies have arisen from time to time regarding the kind of theory that scientists should develop. At what level should we attempt to theorize about and explain behavior? What would our unit of analysis (level of analysis) be? In psychology, should the unit of analysis be the atom? The molecule? Perhaps it should be a physiological system? What about intact behavior? Could it not also be group behavior or an entire culture?

Some psychologists have argued that the level of analysis and theory construction in our discipline should be at the physiological (molecular) level. Such individuals have been referred to as **reductionists** because they seek to explain complex behaviors in terms of relatively simple structures and functions. Others have argued that the unit of measurement and theory construction should be at the behavioral (molar) level. Obviously, *molecular* and *molar* are relative terms. Psychology, with its emphasis on the physiology of the organism or on the observable behavior of the organism, is molecular relative to sociology, where the emphasis is on group behavior. Yet relative to chemistry, the unit of analysis in psychology is molar.

Most scientists believe that theorizing at different levels is necessary and can be complementary. Perhaps at some future time we may be able to be reductionist (molecular) and interpret the phenomena of all sciences in the language of physics. Clearly, we cannot come close to doing so at this time.

● Importance of Basic Research

Basic research is not easy to define, and unfortunately, it is often unappreciated by those who control considerable sums of money for research. To some, basic research may seem frivolous. Surely, we are indulging scientists by supporting their pet hobbies, such as studies of the sexual behavior of moths, communication among bees, and sexual attractants among insects. But in each instance, as is often the case with basic research, the results of these studies have ultimately had important implications for agricultural practices, the world's food supply system, and the economy. To illustrate, insects cause crop damage in the multimillion dollar range annually, but chemical control of these insects has created its own serious problems. New and safer techniques of biological control have been made possible because of basic research on the behavior and physiology of insects. Nonetheless, such research is often ridiculed or criticized.

One further comment before describing basic research more fully: Political leaders controlling research funds may not appreciate the value of basic research for many reasons. At times they consider it unimportant, but at other times they reject it because of their own bias, prejudice, or moral values rather than on the basis of scientific merit. Whatever their basis for not appreciating its value, the fault, at times, rests with the scientists. Scientists too often consider the value of basic research to be self-evident and have not always made a strong argument in its defense. Thus, scientists and educated laypeople need to devote more care to presenting a defense of basic research.

A Defense of Basic Research

It is often difficult to see the relationship between basic research done years ago and the application of sophisticated technology to current problems. Basic research provides the foundation (database) for the resolution of present and future problems, for the development of technology, and for a better understanding of all aspects of the world in which we live.

Basic research is research directed to the understanding of nature, of all aspects of the universe, of natural processes. It is not research directed toward solving specific social problems. It is not mission oriented; that is, it is not involved in the mission of curing or correcting a specific illness or problem or in developing a specific technology. Basic research has no immediate regard for practical application; paradoxically, however, it is probably the most effective way of solving many of our current and future problems. It has been a critical component in virtually every approach to our major problems. In 1969, the National Science Foundation released the results of a study (TRACES) showing the importance of basic research. They examined technological innovations of wide importance and diverse application, tracing research back to 1850. It was concluded that about 70% of the key and critical events were derived from basic research.

Some examples may provide us with a better appreciation of the virtues of basic research. X-ray photography was not developed by physicians as an aid in the diagnosis of disease. Rather, medical use of X-rays followed the pioneering research of Wilhelm Roentgen who was "only" interested in basic problems dealing with the physics of rays. A few decades ago, poliomyelitis (infantile paralysis) was a dreaded disease that left many of its survivors permanently paralyzed. We are all familiar with the applied research of Drs. Salk and Sabin that culminated in vaccines that immunized against the disease. But how many of us have heard about the basic research of John Enders, who was "merely" interested in studying viruses? To accomplish his goal, he needed to devise a means of growing viruses in cultures. When he finally succeeded, he opened the gates for a veritable flood of practical applications of his techniques. The Salk and Sabin vaccines are but two of many monumental advances that had their underpinnings in the laboratory of John Enders. George Cotzias was not pursuing a treatment for Parkinson's disease, but because of his interest in trace metals and body metabolism, the drug L-Dopa was developed for treating the disease. Similarly, the drug that has nearly eradicated tuberculosis, streptomycin, was discovered by a soil biologist. Most of the treatments now available for AIDS are based on basic research in such areas as molecular virology, immunology, biochemistry, and genetics.

As another example, consider the animal research of behavioral psychologists such as B. F. Skinner. For hours on end, Skinner recorded pigeons pecking at a spot in a cage. Many might ask (and we are sure they did) what pecking pigeons have to do with understanding human behavior. Skinner in fact knew that the basic principles of learning that were being revealed in his research could have far-reaching implications for understanding human learning and that the principles could be used in therapeutic situations to help people with psychological problems and disorders. The present-day widespread use of behavior modification techniques attests to the value of the basic behavioral research that was conducted many years ago and that is still being conducted today.

It is very difficult to appreciate the importance of basic research at the time it is being conducted. How important was the effect of current flow on magnetic needles at the time of Faraday? Today, induction coils in the field of transportation are incredibly important. People interested in transportation didn't discover induction coils (this would have been mission-oriented research). The discovery of induction coils gave rise to a transportation industry. IBM, Control Data, and other computer giants did not set out to discover basic circuits for computers. Physicists in the 1930s interested in nuclear physics discovered them. At the time of Boyle (gas laws), how important were the properties of vacuum tubes? Who could have anticipated transistors, printed circuits, or computer chips? With the discovery of the atom, who could have anticipated the electronics industry?

Basic research continues today to produce exciting and promising findings. Recombinant DNA research has made it possible to produce relatively pure forms of insulin, a marked improvement over the insulin currently derived from animals. The discovery and now production of the substance interferon holds promise for the treatment of certain ailments. A discovery that has excited both scientists and technicians is the identification and production of monoclonal antibodies. This discovery should allow specific antibodies (monoclonal) to be developed that attack specifically targeted bacteria, viruses, or other materials foreign to the body. Important discoveries have also occurred for behavioral scientists. One of these is the use of biofeedback procedures to teach individuals to control their own blood pressure, heart rate, brain waves, and other response systems. In addition, we are now beginning to understand the effects of peptides (compounds formed by groups of amino acids) on social behavior, development, perception of pain, and other human functions.

We could continue with many more examples of this type. Clearly, basic research is important, and its full impact may not be felt for many years. However, we do not mean to suggest that the value of basic research is determined solely by its practical significance. Basic research can be justified on the basis that the production of knowledge is, in itself, of great value. It is our firm belief that knowledge has inherent value—that it is strongly preferred to ignorance. In this sense, practical significance is a bonus.

Two Important Reasons for Supporting Basic Research

After reviewing the history of discovering important events and also observing the problems experienced by each succeeding generation, we conclude that there are two fundamental reasons for fully supporting basic research: (1) We cannot determine today what discoveries will prove important for tomorrow, and (2) we cannot determine today what problems we (the world) will experience tomorrow. In fact, we have not become much better over the years at predicting what important problems we will experience in the future. We do not know today what will be important tomorrow. We must be prepared for any eventuality. Our sights must not be narrow in terms of specific missions or focus solely on today's problems. Change is so incredibly fast that we must be in a position to move in many directions—we must have a solid database in all areas. New problems continue to appear that require more basic knowledge: AIDS, carcinogens, ozone depletion, nutrition and cell health, pollution, energy supplies, and toxic shock syndrome are but a few examples. Others could be the effects of depletion of the rain forest, issues related to biological weapons, ocean warming and melting of glaciers, or new epidemics. The more developed the database of basic research, the better we can deal with these problems.

It is understandable to some extent that some members of society insist that scientists concentrate on more relevant social problems. This emphasis reflects a genuine belief that by addressing the problems directly, we can solve them more quickly. Unfortunately, an excessively focused effort to make science more productive by directing its efforts toward specific unsolved problems may actually make it less productive. The war on cancer may be an example. Nature is not yet ready to reveal its secrets. Scientists within the American Institute for Cancer Research have essentially acknowledged, after years of trying to find cures, that much more basic research on cell physiology is needed before success can be achieved. To insist that scientists solve problems before the basic research data are in may be wasteful of highly trained researchers and other resources in money and personnel.

● Science and Technology

Science is generally thought of as seeking information or discovering basic phenomena in a systematic way and then organizing this information into general explanatory principles. Technology is usually thought of as the application of these scientific discoveries and principles to existing practical problems. As noted earlier, at times scientists discover the basic principles many years before they are applied in the form of technology. Computers are one example; immunization techniques in medicine are another. Before technology develops, the principles must be available; but at times, a technology must be developed before the principles can be applied. Examples of the latter can be related to the space program and to atomic weaponry.

Too frequently, scientists are blamed for the problems created by the technology that follows from scientific discoveries. Although we assert that knowledge in itself is good, the application of that knowledge can be either good or bad. The stereotype of the "mad scientist" might be better applied to the "mad technologist." Again, we use computers as an example. Scientists cannot be blamed for the abuses (invasion of privacy, identity theft) occurring in today's society. Similarly, the automobile is a technical achievement; the problems created by it (pollution) cannot be blamed on scientists. Discoveries related to genetics are leading to technologies of genetic engineering (and even cloning) over which scientists may have little control.

What we are attempting to do here is to urge everyone to think critically about the distinction between science and technology as we ponder the problems besetting society. However, we must also recognize the interplay between science and technology, and that the distinction between them may be blurred. It is unfortunate that scientists are often blamed for problems but not recognized for contributions that benefit society. Technologists, but not scientists, usually get the credit for these contributions. For example, the technology of medicine is based on the sciences of physiology and chemistry; the technology of engineering is based on the science of physics; the technology of education is based on the science of learning. Most people wrongly attribute achievements in medicine, engineering, and education solely to the technologists and not to the scientists. Both groups should receive credit for such achievements.

A final example will illustrate how science and technology can complement one another. Vampire bats are a serious problem in some Latin American countries. At night these bats silently attack sleeping animals by painlessly scooping out a piece of skin and then taking some of their blood. Some cattle receive bites from as many as 15 bats in a single night. Because of an anticoagulant in the bat's saliva, the blood flows freely most of the night. Some of the bitten cattle are infected with rabies carried by the vampire bats. In other cases, the wounds become infected, resulting in lower weight gains and lower milk production. The solution to this problem illustrates the complementary nature of science and technology in solving problems.

Various previous attempts had been made to destroy the vampire bats. These included shooting, netting, and electrocuting bats in flight. A major problem with these procedures was that they killed beneficial insect-eating bats without reducing the loss due to vampires. Biologists from the Denver Wildlife Research Center began working on the problem in 1968. Because only some of these bats attacked cattle, they wanted to devise a method that would control only vampires that attacked farm animals. The biologists brought bats into their Denver laboratories and discovered that the vampires suffered fatal bleeding if an anticoagulant was added to their blood. Question: How do you get additional anticoagulant into free-flying bats? The biologists tried several techniques, unsuccessfully. They then tried injecting the anticoagulant into the first stomach of cattle in doses harmless to the cattle, but not harmless to the vampires attacking cattle. Bats feeding on the blood of treated cattle received sufficient amounts of the anticoagulant to kill them. Cattle could be treated twice a year at 30 or 40 cents per animal. The method resulted in a 91% reduction in vampire bat bites and an increase in milk and beef production (Mitchell, Thompson, & Burns, 1972).

● Science and Public Policy

Sometimes the public is unhappy with the progress that societies make toward the resolution of problems. Science is often implicitly accused. You have heard many times, "If scientists can put a man on the moon, why can't they . . . ?" The implication is that scientists should be able to cure diseases, clear up pollution, end drug and discrimination problems, and eliminate the food supply problem. Some of these problems are technological, some scientific, but all are also philosophical, political, and economic. Problems of society must be dealt with at several levels. In addition to the scientific laws and basic principles, we also need the technology. Equally important, philosophical, political, and economic decisions must be made as to which problems will be addressed, and political support must be given to implement the decisions. We must decide philosophically the priorities of the goals we wish to pursue. Our economic system must be sufficiently robust to provide the necessary wealth. Politically, legislatures must pass legislation and provide funding to implement these goals. Many problems of the world are not scientific or technological, but philosophical, political, and economic.

CASE ANALYSIS

Many individuals claim special abilities, including extrasensory perception (ESP), the ability to predict the future, and the ability to see and hear people who are no longer living. In recent years, a few of the individuals who claim to see and hear the dead have become very well known and financially successful (for example, Sylvia Brown, John Edwards). In his television show *Crossing Over with John Edwards,* Mr. Edwards interacts with people in his audience and relays messages to them from departed friends and family. It is obvious that many people, both in the audience and viewing the TV show at home, believe John Edwards and believe in these special abilities. Let's consider a few important questions.

Critical Thinking Questions

1. First, do you believe the information provided by John Edwards and others like him? Why or why not?
2. For those who do believe this information, what is its source—authority, personal experience, rationalism, or empiricism?
3. Do you believe that this information about our world is scientific? Which of the characteristics of science does this area possess? Which does it not possess?
4. If it is not scientific, is there a way to make it scientific?
5. Even if an area is not scientific, does that necessarily make it wrong or incorrect? Should people believe in knowledge that is not scientific?

GENERAL SUMMARY

Our understanding of the world is based on several factors, including information from authority, personal experience, logical reasoning, and scientific inquiry. Scientific information is based on a set of assumptions, goals, and methods that are designed to provide the most accurate information about our world. By testing ideas through empirical observation and revising theories based on observations, science self-corrects as it reveals the secrets of nature. Although many of these secrets may not have immediate application to practical problems, such basic research increases our foundation of knowledge so that we will be poised to address the issues of the future. To increase this foundation of knowledge, we must be able to ask questions that can be tested empirically. Thus, the next chapter will discuss the formulation of research hypotheses.

DETAILED SUMMARY

1. Four principal means by which we gain knowledge are information from authorities, personal experiences, the logical reasoning of rationalism, and the systematic observations of empiricism.

2. Three primary goals of science are understanding, prediction, and control.

3. Science makes two basic assumptions: first, that events in the universe occur in a lawful and orderly

manner (determinism), and second, that this lawful-ness is discoverable.

4. Chaos theory is an attempt to understand complex, nonlinear, dynamic systems by using mathematical modeling.

5. The scientific method requires empirical referents—observable and measurable phenomena.

6. With science, accurate observations are followed by inferences that reflect the interpretation of and explanation for the observations.

7. The scientific method is characterized by empirical referents, repeatability, self-correction, systematic investigation, and falsifiability.

8. Inductive reasoning involves the formulation of a general principle or theory based on a set of specific observations. Conversely, deductive reasoning involves the formulation of specific observational predictions based on a general principle or theory.

9. Scientific information may or may not match commonsense information. Typically, science provides explanations that are more specific than the generalities of common sense.

10. Disciplines of science exist on a continuum from more molecular levels of analysis to more molar levels of analysis. The same phenomenon can be explained at different levels of analysis.

11. Basic scientific research is very important because we cannot determine today what discoveries will prove important for tomorrow, and we cannot determine today what problems we (the world) will experience tomorrow.

12. It is important to distinguish science from technology. Science is the accumulation of systematic observations and the explanations for those observations; technology is the application of scientific information.

13. Science does not happen in a vacuum. It is influenced by philosophical, political, economic, and technological values and priorities of society.

KEY TERMS

basic research *(p. 39)*
chaos theory *(p. 30)*
confirmation bias *(p. 34)*
deductive reasoning *(p. 33)*
determinism *(p. 29)*
empirical referent *(p. 31)*

empiricism *(p. 27)*
inductive reasoning *(p. 33)*
rationalism *(p. 27)*
reductionist *(p. 39)*
systematic observation *(p. 25)*
theory *(p. 34)*

REVIEW QUESTIONS/EXERCISES

1. Consider several things that you believe to be true in the world. Identify one that is based on authority, one that is based on personal experience, one that is based on rationalism, and one that is based on empiricism.

2. Conduct an Internet search on depression. Find and summarize information for each of the three goals of science—in this case, the scientific study of depression.

3. In your own words, summarize why determinism is a necessary assumption of behavioral science. Do you agree with this assumption? Why or why not? We challenge you to identify a single behavior that is not the result of prior events in the world. Can you do it?

4. Paranormal psychology is a field that investigates phenomena such as extrasensory perception (ESP), astrology, graphology (relating handwriting to personality), ghosts/spirits, and dream analysis. Students who take introductory psychology classes are often disappointed that these topics are not included. The reason is that they are not scientific. You may know that Sigmund Freud emphasized dream analysis. Based on the characteristics of science discussed in this chapter, why is the interpretation of dreams unscientific?

5. Describe how we might study the issue of depression from a very molecular to a very molar level of analysis. Provide several examples of research at various points along this continuum.

6. At a scientific conference that one of your authors recently attended, there were several presentations on the sexual behavior of the Japanese quail. Do you believe that this is worthwhile science? Assume that it is your job to defend this basic research. Write an argument of support. How might such basic research have applicability either now or in the future?

WEB RESOURCES TO INCREASE LEARNING

The chapter outline, chapter summaries, key terms and definitions, additional chapter questions/exercises, and links to relevant Web sites are available at the course Web site (**http://psychology.wadsworth.com/lammers_ badia1e**). Explore the interactive workshop "What Is Science?"

CHAPTER 4

DEVELOPING
RESEARCH QUESTIONS
HYPOTHESES AND VARIABLES

● Common Sources of Research Questions

The first three chapters introduced you to some broad themes in behavioral research, including the purpose of research, types of research, ethical issues, and the nature of science. Beginning with this chapter, we will focus on the details of conducting behavioral research. From a student's perspective, the thought of actually doing behavioral research seems like a daunting task. You are likely to say to yourself, "I couldn't possibly do research. I'm not a behavioral scientist. I don't even know how to get started." Well, we're here to tell you that you can do it, and it is not that difficult to get started.

Have you ever asked yourself, "I wonder why people behave that way?" If so, then you have already begun the research process. Research begins with asking questions. Curiosity about a casual observation that you have made could initiate a series of questions. For example, you may notice that youth spend much time watching television and that many of the television programs include references to sex and/or violence. So you may ask yourself, "Does watching television violence have a negative impact on personality development?" This is the beginning of a good research question. Topics for research questions often begin with your own curiosity. This curiosity may be fueled by your own personal experiences or observations. You may be interested in the topic of memory because you had a grandmother with Alzheimer's disease. You may be interested in people's perceptions of schizophrenics after taking a course in abnormal psychology. Perhaps the latest "reality show" on television stirs questions about why people behave in certain ways when placed in certain conditions. Research is so much more fun when you are pursuing a topic that fascinates you.

For most topics, it is very likely that others have already asked very similar questions and have conducted research in this area. But a good researcher knows that unanswered questions remain in every domain of psychology. So, given an area in which you are interested, what is the next step? A researcher needs to become familiar with the research findings that already exist. These findings are most likely to be reported in books and journal articles. Several strategies for obtaining this information are outlined in the following paragraphs.

Textbooks

Look in the subject index of a textbook in your area of interest. The text will often include the names of researchers and citations of books or articles. For example, look in a Developmental Psychology textbook for "television." You will undoubtedly find a section that discusses the impact of television on development.

Databases

Use keywords to search relevant databases. Several very good electronic databases contain references to journal articles or books. Ask your instructor or a reference librarian for the databases available on your campus. Some databases that are useful for behavioral research include PsycLit, PsycINFO, ProQuest, JSTOR Scholarly Journals, MedLine, Sociological Abstracts, and InfoTrac College Edition (purchase of this textbook provides you access to this last database). After you get access to a database, you can search it for references. You can search by author, year, or other means. Often, you will simply search for some word (or combination of words) that might appear in the title or summary. For example, you could use the PsycINFO database to search journal articles for studies related to the effect of TV violence on children. We did such a search. When we used the keyword "television," the database produced 6,671 hits. No one wants to look through this many titles or abstracts, so we narrowed the search by using the keywords "television violence." This search produced 156 hits, and it would not take too long to skim through those titles. A final search using the keywords "television children" produced a very manageable 17 hits. Thus, if the database finds too many articles for you to examine, narrow the search by entering additional keywords or by trying different combinations of keywords.

Internet

The Internet can be a source of research ideas. However, it takes some skill to search the Internet efficiently. First, much of the information on the Internet has no relation to science, and it can be very difficult to search a topic without hitting these sites. Second, some of the information on the Internet appears to be scientific when it is not. You must critically evaluate each site. For example, is the site located at a university or a known research agency? What are the credentials of the researcher(s)? Are there product advertisements at the site? Also, certain Internet search engines are more focused on scholarly information. As of this writing, two useful search engines are Ingenta (ingenta.com) and Galaxy (galaxy.com).

Professors

Ask the faculty in the psychology department whether they have any information regarding your research question or whether they know of anyone doing research on the topic (this is also a good way to meet the faculty). Often, the research interests of the faculty are listed on a department Web site. Most faculty that we know enjoy discussing possible research topics with students and will often provide suggestions that help to shape and focus the topic. If the topic is of interest to the faculty member, he or she may suggest that you take an independent study course under his or her supervision.

You should also consider professors at other universities. You may encounter these researchers at a scientific conference where you attend their research presentation. Additionally, a search of the literature may reveal a particular researcher who has published several studies related to the topic in which you are interested. You could contact the researcher by e-mail to request a reprint of an article or to ask a few questions.

● Selecting a Research Problem

Scientists select a research problem for any of several reasons. Some studies are undertaken to evaluate or to advance a particular theory. Others may be undertaken for the purpose of comparing the adequacy of two or more theories. The researcher's interest may have nothing to do with solving an existing psychological or sociological problem. As discussed in the previous chapter, terms such as *pure* or *basic research* are often used to describe research when no immediate practical application of the results is intended. In contrast, some research is undertaken because of its applied, practical nature. A social problem exists, and questions related to the problem are in need of answering. Is smoking marijuana a health hazard? Will certain changes in our educational system enhance scores on the American College Test or Student Achievement Test?

Others undertake studies to resolve inconsistencies or contradictory findings. If some research indicated that sleep following learning aids memory (which it does) and other research found that sleep hinders memory (which it doesn't), then the findings would be contradictory. If so, then little could be said regarding sleep and memory without additional research. The additional research would be directed to resolving the inconsistent findings. It would begin with a careful assessment of the two studies to determine in what ways they were similar and in what ways they were different. If important differences in procedure were found between the studies, then the contradictory findings might be due to these differences. In this case, a study could be undertaken to determine whether procedural differences were important.

Some research is conducted to extend the findings of prior research. For example, a study may show a particular effect of TV violence on 10-year-old children. You might ask whether that same effect would be observed in 5-year-old children. Also, you might be interested in extending the conditions that were tested. Perhaps you are interested in testing a type of TV violence that was not tested in another study. At other times, the findings of a particular study may seem implausible. In cases such as these, it is valuable to perform a replication study. In such a study, the method is replicated (duplicated) to determine whether the same results will be found a second time.

Obviously, research questions may be asked for many reasons. Answers to all questions cannot be provided, nor should they be. Clearly, some questions are too trivial and meaningless to bother answering.

● Formulating Hypotheses

After you have reviewed the relevant literature and have a research question, you are prepared to be more specific. You want to make one or more predictions for your study. Such a prediction is called a **hypothesis.** It is an educated guess regarding what should happen in a particular situation under certain conditions. Not all studies require that you test a hypothesis; some may simply involve collecting information regarding an issue. For those that do have a hypothesis, the hypothesis should derive logically from previous findings or the predictions of a particular theory. Hypotheses should not be based simply on what the student believes should happen. A clear rationale is necessary.

An examination of publications by student researchers provides several examples of hypotheses. In a study that examined gender equity in college athletic programs, the authors predicted "female students would have more positive attitudes toward gender equity" (Goon, Teel, Fuller, & Allen, 1998, p. 20). Another study predicted "people would rate representatives of their own culture as more physically attractive than representatives of other cultures" (Khersonskaya & Smith, 1998, p. 40). As a final example, one student predicted "extroverts were more likely to be hired than introverts because of their outgoing and personable behavior" (Sheets, 1999, p. 8). You might be interested in the results of these studies. Goon et al. (1998) found that both male and female students supported gender equity in athletics. Khersonskaya and Smith (1998) did find that attractiveness ratings for American students were higher when made by American participants than by European participants. Sheets (1999) found that college men were more likely to hire extraverts but college women showed no preference.

To provide an example of hypothesis development, let's return to our interest in the effect of TV violence on children. Studies that have been done suggest that children who frequently watch violence on television demonstrate more aggression at school. You wonder whether the effect is the same if the television viewing depicts cartoon/computer-animated characters as opposed to human actors. Based on research that suggests that children over the age of 7 understand that cartoon characters are not real, you hypothesize that the effect

Table 4.1	**Examples of Good and Bad Hypothesis Statements**
GOOD HYPOTHESIS STATEMENT	BAD HYPOTHESIS STATEMENT
In the case of murder, mock juries will be more likely to convict a black defendant than a white defendant.	There is bias in the justice system.
As the number of hours in paid employment increases, the number of hours spent studying for classes will decrease.	College students shouldn't work so much.
Employees will be more productive when working under bright lights than when working under dim lights.	Employees will work differently under different lights.
In detecting enemy aircraft, a fighter pilot will react more quickly to an auditory warning signal than a visual warning signal.	A fighter pilot can be warned with either an auditory signal or a visual signal.

of TV violence on older children's aggressive behavior at school will be less if the characters are not human. Now we have a clear prediction that we can set out to test using the scientific method.

Good hypotheses have several characteristics, including a clear rationale, an if–then format, and a clear description of the relationship between the variables of interest in your study. First, what do we mean by a clear rationale? You want to ask yourself, "Why am I predicting this effect?" It may be that you are replicating a study already reported in the literature. It may be that your prediction is a logical extension of what other researchers have published. Notice that our hypothesis in the previous paragraph was based on existing information. It may be that your prediction follows from a particular theory and provides a test of the theory. For example, one theory in social psychology states that as the number of bystanders increases near a victim, each bystander feels less responsibility to help the victim. Based on this diffusion of responsibility theory, you might predict that if a student drops her books in a crowded student center on campus, then the student will be less likely to receive help than if only a few people are in the student center.

Notice that this hypothesis provides a clear description of the relationship between the first variable (number of bystanders) and the second variable (likelihood of receiving help) and does so using an if–then format. If particular environmental conditions exist, then there will be a particular consequence in terms of human behavior. Table 4.1 provides several more examples of good hypotheses, along with several hypotheses that are not well stated.

● Variables of Interest

When researchers are manipulating an environmental condition to determine its effect on behavior, they use special terms that help describe these activities. A **variable** is any condition that can vary or change in quantity or quality. The **independent variable**, or treatment, is under the control of and administered by the experimenter. The behavior that is potentially affected by the treatment and that we measure is called the **dependent variable**. The dependent variable is always a measure of behavior that we record after first manipulating

Table 4.2	Examples of Qualitative and Quantitative Independent Variables Found in Psychological Research

A quantitative variable involves a single continuum in which different treatment levels or amounts may be administered to participants. Qualitative variables differ in kind rather than in amount.

QUALITATIVE INDEPENDENT VARIABLES

Variable	Example
Teaching method	Lecture vs. discussion
Type of therapy	Psychoanalytic vs. behavioral vs. cognitive
Type of drug	Prozac vs. Zoloft vs. Paxil (antidepressants)
Type of exercise	None vs. walking vs. swimming

QUANTITATIVE INDEPENDENT VARIABLES

Variable	Example
Drug dosage	0 mg caffeine vs. 20 mg caffeine vs. 40 mg caffeine
Level of sleep deprivation	0 hrs vs. 8 hrs vs. 16 hrs vs. 24 hrs
Level of reinforcement	1 food pellet for a correct response vs. 4 food pellets
Size of the group	Group of 2 vs. group of 4 vs. group of 6

the independent variable. It is referred to as *dependent* because changes in it *depend* on the effects of the independent variable. If a systematic relationship is found between the independent and dependent variables, then we have established an empirical or causal relationship. It is also sometimes called a **functional relationship** because changes in the dependent variable are a *function* of values (different amounts) of the independent variable. From these lawful or functional relationships, we can construct theories and make predictions regarding future behavior. As we discuss independent and dependent variables, you will notice that they are always defined in precise and measurable terms. The nature and importance of these operational definitions will be highlighted in the next chapter.

The independent variable may be either qualitative or quantitative. A **qualitative variable** is one that differs in kind rather than in amount. There are different types of violent acts on television, many different kinds of psychotherapy, effects of different drugs on reaction time, and we may receive feedback or fail to receive feedback when learning a psychomotor task. All of these examples involve qualitative variables. In contrast, a **quantitative variable** differs in amount. One could examine different amounts of TV violence to which a child is exposed, different intensities of punishment, the dosage level of a drug, or the number of practice trials. Table 4.2 lists some qualitative and quantitative variables that are used as independent variables in psychological research. It should be clear by now that selecting the independent variable(s) and dependent variable(s) is a very important step in the research process.

Take a look at the box "Thinking Critically About Everyday Information," and consider the different components of the study reported there.

Thinking Critically About Everyday Information

Why We Watch So Much Television

A national news network reported the results of a study with an introduction that stated that researchers "found that switching on the tube helps distract people from their personal failings." The study was published by Moskalenko and Heine (2003) in *Personality and Social Psychology Bulletin*. According to the news report, college students took an intelligence test and received predetermined feedback regarding how well they performed. Half of the students were told that they did well, and half were told that they did poorly. All of the students then had the opportunity to watch television for up to six minutes. Results showed that those students who were told that they had done poorly on the intelligence test watched TV for more minutes and also looked at the TV longer before looking at something else. Students also reported that after watching TV they "perceived less challenge to their chosen self-image." Consider the following questions:

- What was the independent variable in the study? Was it a quantitative variable or a qualitative variable?
- What were the dependent variables in the study?
- Although not mentioned in the description above, what do you suppose was the hypothesis for the study?
- Do you believe that the conclusion as stated in the opening sentence accurately reflects the results of the study? Why or why not?
- Do the results of the study match your own personal experience? Do you believe that your own personal experiences influence whether you believe the results of a scientific study?

SOURCE: Reprinted with permission of *HealthScout News*. "TV soothes low self-esteem," January 23, 2003, *HealthScout News*.

Selecting Levels of an Independent Variable

When we explore completely new areas, little information is available to provide guidelines in selecting the independent variable. When dealing with quantitative independent variables, we are faced with the additional problem of selecting appropriate values of the variable. For example, when testing a new drug, how many milligrams per pound of body weight should be used as the dosage level? This decision is important because too low a dosage may be insufficient to produce an effect, whereas too much may be harmful or even lethal. We must rely on our judgment based upon experience, conversations with our colleagues regarding potential problems, and the information that experts in related areas may be able to provide. In most instances, however, our research builds on previously published research. A rich database is often available to assist in the selection of the appropriate values. In fact, most researchers choose what they consider proper values of a treatment condition based on their own experiments and the published experiments of others.

Some obvious guidelines should be considered when choosing values of an independent variable. As we shall see, a minimum of two groups is necessary to determine whether the independent variable has an effect. One of these groups would receive the treatment (experimental group), and the other group would either not receive the treatment (control group) or receive a different level of the treatment. If you use more than two groups in an effort to ascertain whether increasing levels of the independent variable systematically influence behavior, the choice of values for the independent variable requires more thought.

| Figure 4.1 | Illustration of Various Types of Relationships Between the Independent Variable (IV) and the Dependent Variable (DV) |

Curves A, B, D, and E depict monotonic relationships; C and F show nonmonotonic relationships. In graphing relationships, the horizontal axis (*x*-axis) depicts values for the IV and the vertical axis (*y*-axis) depicts values for the DV.

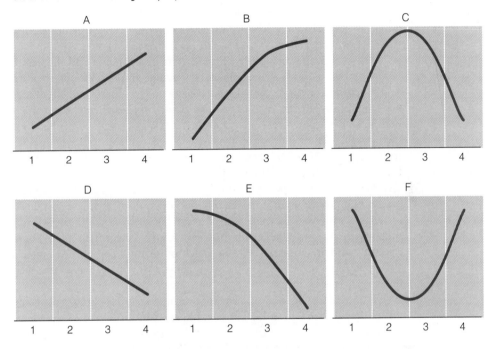

Let's direct our attention to the first of these problems: determining whether an experimental variable has an effect. If we use only two levels (values) of the experimental treatment and they are too similar, what risk do we run? The treatment may not affect behavior differentially, and your efforts to establish a relationship may fail. You would wrongly conclude that the treatment is not worthy of further study. To counter this risk, the first thought that often comes to mind is to select extreme values of the independent variable. The logic is straightforward and simple: The greater the difference in value between the experimental conditions, the greater the probability of showing that the independent variable has an effect. Therefore, choose two points along the continuum that are extreme values. Under certain circumstances, the logic is good and would provide an efficient way of determining whether the independent variable is powerful and worthy of additional investigation. Unfortunately, this simple logic could also result in coming to a wrong conclusion, depending on the relationship between the independent and dependent variable.

The reason for the problem is that a variety of relationships may exist. Some of these are depicted in Figure 4.1. The graphs in Figure 4.1 are constructed so that increasing levels of the independent variable are shown from left to right on the horizontal (*x*) axis and increasing levels of the dependent variable are shown from bottom to top on the vertical (*y*) axis. When the relationship between the dependent and independent variable is **monotonic,** the curve is either continuously rising throughout (A and B in Figure 4.1) or continuously falling throughout (D and E in Figure 4.1). When the relationship is **nonmonotonic,** the curve rises at certain points and falls at other points (C and F in Figure 4.1).

As you might expect, monotonic functions generally do not create difficulties for experiments that use the extreme group approach. With monotonic functions, any two separated values on the horizontal axis could result in finding a difference between groups. Therefore, when the relationship is monotonic, the major limitation of the extreme group approach is that the shape of the relationship or function cannot be established with two groups. Obviously, the effects of intermediate values cannot be determined with only two values of an independent variable.

However, if the relationship between the independent and the dependent variable is nonmonotonic (C and F in Figure 4.1), simply using two groups at extreme points could lead to grossly inaccurate conclusions. For example, an interesting idea that relates effectiveness of performance to level of motivation and task difficulty has come to be called the Yerkes–Dodson Law (Yerkes & Dodson, 1908). The notion described by this "law" is that the optimal level of motivation depends on task difficulty: The more difficult or complex the task, the lower will be the optimal level of motivation needed. According to the law, performance is poor with little motivation; as motivation increases, performance also increases—but only to a point. Beyond that point, depending on the task difficulty, further increases in motivation lead to a deterioration in performance. The so-called Yerkes–Dodson Law has not yet received convincing support, but the idea is intuitively reasonable, and some supportive data are available. On this view, optimal performance does not require the highest levels of motivation; in fact, too much motivation can result in inferior performance. When performance (x-axis) is plotted against motivation (y-axis), the relationship resembles an inverted U.

With this sort of relationship, simply using two groups at extreme points could be quite misleading. If the relationship between the independent and the dependent variable is nonmonotonic (C or F in Figure 4.1), a study using only two groups could easily conclude that the independent variable has no effect on behavior. If values 1 and 4 on the horizontal axis are selected, then both groups would perform in the same manner and no difference would be detected. The same would be the case with values 2 and 3. Finding no difference, the investigator might well conclude that the independent variable has no effect. Some promising research might wind up in the circular file when, in fact, it should be pursued.

The safest way to avoid the problem is to test at least three values of the independent variable. Selecting three points will not necessarily reveal the shape of the relationship, but it will help you to avoid coming to incorrect conclusions in the event that a nonmonotonic relationship exists. The choice between using two values or more than two values often depends on the information available, the importance of the problem, and the cost of doing research.

Selecting a Dependent Variable

The selection of a dependent variable is not in the least a casual matter. Indeed, it is immensely important. It reflects our underlying assumption that the study of behavior is the doorway toward measuring psychological states. Moreover, it is the measure we use to ascertain whether the independent variable has an effect.

Generally, we choose a dependent measure because we judge that it will reveal unobservable but inferable processes that affect it and other behavioral measures. We often assume that our dependent variable reflects some underlying psychological state. For example, emotional processes are often inferred from changes in heart rate, respiration, or sweat gland activity. We might infer stress from ulceration or from adrenal activity. The process of learning is inferred from the elimination of errors, correct anticipation of words, and conditioned responses.

There must be no ambiguity concerning the identification of the dependent variable. Its occurrence or nonoccurrence must be ascertainable according to clearly defined criteria. For example, the dependent measure in an operant conditioning apparatus is any response (usually a lever press or key peck) that closes the microswitch and permits its delivery of reinforcement. Such measures as speed of responding, latency, time to complete a task, eye blinks, errors, heart rate, weight gain, lever press, or key peck can be unambiguously defined and reliably recorded. The reliability of a measure is its ability to give the same result on each occasion. (Note that this is an important concept that will be highlighted in the next chapter.) Such unambiguous measures are not always possible. Some dependent measures require the judgment of observers. What about such measures as self-mutilating behavior in an autistic child, risk taking, aggression, and disruptive classroom behavior? High agreement (reliability) among observers must be achieved before the experiment begins. Special techniques are used to accomplish such reliability. (Chapter 6 will discuss this issue in more detail.)

We should also note that automated responses such as a pigeon key peck or a rat lever press may be unambiguous in terms of a switch closure but ambiguous in terms of what produced the closure. A rat, for example, may produce a switch closure in many ways—with the left paw, the right paw, chin, tail, shoulder, or rump. The experimenter may be interested in the entire class of responses referred to as lever presses, or may be interested only in paw presses.

Characteristics of a Good Dependent Variable

A good dependent variable must be accurately recorded and reliably measured. This is another way of saying it must be *objective* and *quantifiable*. In addition, it must be sufficiently sensitive to detect small changes in the independent variable, yet not so sensitive that it is affected by the slightest uncontrolled factors in the environment.

Further, a good measure should have a "low floor" and a "high ceiling." In other words, the dependent variable should permit a wide range of values or change. Imagine a task so difficult that few individuals are capable of achieving it. For example, in a test of the effectiveness of vitamin supplements on physical strength, the experimenter sets a criterion of bench-pressing 250 pounds or more. In this situation, very few participants would reach criterion even if the supplement actually increased physical strength. The "floor" was simply set too high. In contrast, if the task had been to bench press 10 pounds, the "ceiling" would have been so low that virtually all participants would achieve criterion whether or not the experimental variable affected physical strength.

Floor effects and **ceiling effects** occur sometimes when giving examinations to students. If an exam is so easy that all students correctly answered every test item (all received a score of 100% correct), then the exam may not have discriminated those knowing the material from those not knowing it. In this case, the ceiling was too low. Students "topped out" and could not go higher. On the other hand, if the exam was so difficult that all students answered every test item incorrectly (all received a score of 0% correct), then again the exam did not discriminate those knowing the material from those not knowing. In this case, the floor was too high; everyone "bottomed out" and could not go lower. The sensitivity of the measuring instrument is always reduced when either floor or ceiling effects are prominent.

In the event of too high a floor or too low a ceiling, the range of possible values of the dependent variable is so truncated that it loses its capacity to discriminate among various treatment conditions.

When we observe behavior, human or nonhuman, we find that many different forms of behavior occur—it appears continuous but changing. Even when we observe an organism for a short time, we see different *frequencies* of behaviors such as walking, talking, writing, or grooming. At the same time, physiological changes also occur. The responses that we observe occur for different *durations* with differing *intensities*. Deciding what particular response to measure can be a difficult task. As we noted, selecting an insensitive dependent variable or one unresponsive to the independent variable may cause us to fail in our efforts.

There are several reliable and sensitive measures that you should keep in mind when planning your research. Researchers frequently use these measures because of their sensitivity, reliability, and ease of measurement. They are (1) *accuracy* of responding, (2) *frequency* of responding, (3) *latency* (or speed) of responding, (4) *intensity* of responding, and (5) *duration* of responding. All five of these measures are sometimes taken within a given experiment. Accuracy of responding simply refers to whether the participant is responding correctly. Frequency of responding may refer to the number of times a behavior occurs. Also, a rate of responding measure can be derived if responses per unit of time are recorded. Latency usually refers to the time it takes to initiate a response following the onset of a signal. This measure can be converted to a speed measure by calculating the reciprocal of latency. Intensity of responding, sometimes referred to as amplitude or magnitude of responding, relates to the vigor of the response. Finally, duration or time measures reflect how long a response continues—how long it takes to consume the food, solve the puzzle, or calculate the solution, or how much time is spent in one condition compared to others.

Multiple Dependent Variables

Most experiments record only one dependent variable. One reason for this relates to interpreting what the different measures mean. Does each behavior recorded measure the same thing? That is, does each measure reflect the same inferred or assumed underlying processes? For example, is kicking a vending machine that fails to deliver a candy bar the same inferred underlying measure of frustration as other measures such as cussing at the machine or repeatedly pushing the selector button? A second reason is that when more than one measure is recorded, traditional statistics require a separate statistical analysis for each measure. These multiple analyses, in turn, make it difficult to interpret the true probability (*p*) value for a significant outcome. However, excellent statistical techniques are now available for assessing multiple dependent variables.

Two, three, or more dependent variables are recorded and analyzed in a single procedure referred to as a *multivariate analysis*. Multiple measures may vary together, thus suggesting a common underlying process for all measures. When they do not vary together, different processes are suggested. Both theoretical and practical considerations determine the number of measures used. A discussion of statistical procedures for analyzing concurrently several dependent measures is too advanced for a first course in research methods. Suffice it to say there are advantages to this type of analysis.

Aside from statistical advantages, however, there are other reasons for recording two or more dependent variables. It may be that under the conditions of your experiment, a single dependent measure may not show any systematic relationship to your independent variable. Your measure may be too insensitive or too variable. If you record other, different measures, your chances of finding a systematic relationship may be increased. In addition, recording more than a single dependent variable will allow you to evaluate the relationship among them. You have little to lose and much to gain by recording more than a single dependent variable, unless doing so is inconvenient, time consuming, or expensive.

Response Classes of Dependent Variables

The number of dependent measures recorded by researchers is determined by both theoretical and practical considerations. Investigators studying behavior, whether in a laboratory or an applied setting, generally use three major classes of responses. These three classes of responses are motor responses, physiological measures, and self-report measures. Whatever measure is used, great care must be taken when measuring and recording the response. It is not uncommon for researchers to record different classes of responses within the same experiment. Each has advantages and disadvantages associated with its use.

Motor responses involve the skeletal muscle system in some way. These responses may vary in terms of accuracy, frequency, latency, duration, or intensity. Some examples of motor responses are walking, talking, drinking, eating, crying, fighting, running, smiling, studying, smoking, gambling, freezing, jumping, bar pressing, playing, key pecking, and choosing. When motor responses are automatically recorded, mechanically or electronically, errors due to the human observer are virtually eliminated. However, only some motor responses can be automated; observers must record other responses. Relying on observers to note and record our dependent variables is a serious issue for a considerable amount of research being done in psychology today. The issue is that human observers are not perfectly reliable at the task and thus represent an imperfect measuring instrument. (This issue will be discussed in more detail in Chapter 6.)

Physiological measures can be taken from the surface of the body or from within the body. Measures taken from the surface of the body include brain activity—measured by electroencephalogram, PET (positron emission tomography) scan, or MRI (magnetic resonance imaging)—sweat gland activity, muscle activity, heart rate, blood pressure, blood vessel constriction and dilation, and skin temperature. Measures taken from within the body include activity of neural cells and levels of various substances. The researcher may sample blood, urine, or saliva to determine levels of blood sugar, neurotransmitters, and hormones. Physiological measures generally require more equipment and a degree of technical expertise.

With self-report measures, participants verbalize how they are reacting to the experimental conditions. Participants verbalize whether they are anxious, concerned, aroused, depressed, happy, and so on. Exposure to different conditions presumably has an effect on how the participants react, and they are asked to self-monitor their reactions and then to report them to the investigator. It is obvious that self-report measures are susceptible to distortion on the part of the participant. Further, some researchers believe that the very task of asking participants to monitor and verbalize their reactions may alter the measure; instead of reacting to the independent variable, they may be reacting to instructions. For this reason, some researchers are reluctant to use self-report measures alone; they attempt to correlate self-report measures with physiological responses. Because physiological responses are generally not under voluntary control, they are presumably less susceptible to the criticism directed toward self-report measures.

As we have suggested several times, researchers generally measure several dependent variables in their research. These measures may be within the same class or across classes. It may be especially important to record several dependent measures when your knowledge of the independent variable is limited, when the effects are difficult to predict, or when you are interested in a possible relationship among several dependent variables.

In closing this section, we want to emphasize that whether they are using human or nonhuman participants, experimenters should strive to record dependent measures that are not distressing to their participants. In choosing both dependent and independent variables, researchers should keep careful consideration of ethical principles foremost in mind.

CASE ANALYSIS

A researcher wonders how well the sense of smell functions during sleep. In general, we know that our sensory systems operate at a higher threshold during sleep. That is, a more intense stimulus is required to elicit a response during sleep than during wakefulness. Furthermore, we are less responsive during some stages of sleep than during others. Experiments using sounds suggest that we are less responsive during stages 3 and 4 sleep (deep sleep) than during stages 1, 2, or REM sleep (lighter sleep). Thus, the researcher predicts that research participants will be less responsive to odors during stages 3 and 4 sleep than during the other stages of sleep.

The researcher devises a system for delivering odors while college students sleep in the laboratory. Peppermint fragrance is delivered at specific times through a modified oxygen mask that the students wear while they sleep. Electrodes are attached to each student's scalp, face, and chin to determine sleep staging. Electrodes are also at-

tached to each student's chest to record heart rate. A change in heart rate following presentation of the odor is used to indicate that the participant detected the odor.

Critical Thinking Questions

1. What is the research hypothesis?
2. What is the independent variable?
3. What is the dependent variable?
4. From which response class does the dependent variable come?
5. Is the independent variable a qualitative variable or a quantitative variable? Explain.
6. Why might the researchers want to use multiple dependent variables?
7. Describe one limitation of this study.

GENERAL SUMMARY

We are all amateur researchers in the sense that we ask questions about human behavior and thought. Quality research involves a more systematic approach. A good researcher understands that a research question begins with an idea and is then shaped by information from other professionals and sources. The research question evolves into a more specific research hypothesis that predicts a particular relationship between the independent and de-

pendent variables. The researcher carefully selects appropriate levels of the independent variable and decides on the most appropriate type of dependent variable, whether it be a motor response, physiological response, or self-report. In the next chapter, we will explore all of these variables in more detail, including the development of detailed definitions and strategies for measurement.

DETAILED SUMMARY

1. Research questions are developed by using sources that include curiosity, professors, textbooks, journals, databases, and the Internet.
2. Keywords based on your research topic are used to search the literature for information and prior research on the topic.
3. Research questions can be designed to evaluate a theory, to compare two or more theories, to address a practical problem, to resolve inconsistencies in the literature, to replicate a prior study, or to investigate a particular question that has not yet been studied.
4. Research questions lead to a hypothesis that states the predicted outcome for the study.

5. Good hypotheses have several characteristics, including a clear rationale, an if–then format, and a clear description of the relationship between the variables of interest in the study.
6. The independent variable (treatment) is the variable that is under the control of and manipulated by the experimenter. The behavior that is affected by the treatment and that we measure is called the dependent variable.
7. A qualitative independent variable is one for which the levels represent different and distinct categories. A quantitative independent variable is one for which the levels represent different amounts of that variable.

8. Selection of the levels of a quantitative independent variable depends to a degree on the estimated nature of the functional relationship between the independent and dependent variables. Two levels may be sufficient for some monotonic (single-direction) relationships, but three or more levels may be necessary for nonmonotonic relationships (the curve changes direction).

9. A good dependent variable should be objective, quantifiable, reliable, and sufficiently sensitive to changes in the independent variable.

10. The dependent variable should be selected so as to avoid floor effects and ceiling effects—that is, a limited range of values.

11. Dependent variables often measure accuracy, latency, duration, or intensity of responding. In many situations, multiple dependent variables can be recorded to provide more information about the relationship between the independent and dependent variables.

12. The three major classes of dependent variables are motor responses, physiological responses, and self-report responses. Each has advantages and disadvantages.

KEY TERMS

ceiling effect *(p. 55)*
dependent variable *(p. 50)*
floor effect *(p. 55)*
functional relationship *(p. 51)*
hypothesis *(p. 49)*
independent variable *(p. 50)*

monotonic relationship *(p. 53)*
nonmonotonic relationship *(p. 54)*
qualitative variable *(p. 51)*
quantitative variable *(p. 51)*
variable *(p. 50)*

REVIEW QUESTIONS/EXERCISES

1. Go to a relatively busy area of your college campus and observe some aspect of human behavior. Based on these observations, write a research question that could be tested. Also, write a specific hypothesis that follows the guidelines discussed in this chapter.

2. Consider a research topic in which you are interested, and conduct a database search for journal articles on that topic. Using your InfoTrac College Edition subscription, log on at http://www.infotrac-college.com. Develop a set of keywords that you believe represent your topic. Use these keywords to search the InfoTrac College Edition database. If your search results in more than 20 hits, continue using particular combinations of keywords until your search results in fewer than 20 hits. Review these titles, and select one article to read. Apply the critical thinking questions from the case analysis in this chapter to the article that you have read.

3. Using the same InfoTrac College Edition search or a new search, locate an experiment and print the citation (including the abstract). Identify the independent variable and the dependent variable. Determine whether the independent variable is a qualitative variable or a quantitative variable.

4. Provide a brief description of your own idea for an experiment on the topic of human memory. Write the hypothesis, and identify the independent variable. How many levels will your independent variable have? Specify the levels, and explain why you chose them.

5. Provide a brief description of your own idea for an experiment on the topic of sleep. Write the hypothesis, and identify the dependent variable(s). Is your experiment one in which it could be advantageous to have multiple dependent variables? Explain. Why do you believe that your dependent variable(s) is (are) good? Identify the response class for each dependent variable.

 ## WEB RESOURCES TO INCREASE LEARNING

The chapter outline, chapter summaries, key terms and definitions, additional chapter questions/exercises, and links to relevant Web sites are available at the course Web site (**http://psychology.wadsworth.com/lammers_** badia1e). Explore the interactive workshops "Getting Ideas for a Study" and "Manipulation Checks in Experimental Research."

MEASUREMENT

● <u>Operational Definitions</u>

An essential component of an operational definition is measurement. A simple and accurate definition of **measurement** is the assignment of numbers to a variable in which we are interested. These numbers will provide the raw material for our statistical analysis.

Measurement is so common and taken for granted that we seldom ask why we measure things or worry about the different forms that measurement may take. It is often not sufficient to describe a runner as "fast," a basketball player as "tall," a wrestler as "strong," or a baseball hitter as "good." If coaches recruited potential team members on the basis of these imprecise words, they would have difficulty holding down a job. Coaches want to know how fast the runner runs the 100-yard dash or the mile. They want to know exactly how tall the basketball player is, the strength of the wrestler, the batting average of the hitter. Measurement is a way of refining our ordinary observations so that we can assign numerical values to our observations. It allows us to go beyond simply describing the presence or absence of an event or thing to specifying how much, how long, or how intense it is. With measurement, our observations become more accurate and more reliable.

Precision is important in all areas of our lives, especially in the sciences and technologies, and we look for ways of increasing it. Here is an interesting classroom demonstration of the precision of numbers versus the precision of words. Ask the class members to write down on a piece of paper what number the word "several" represents to them. Gather the responses and then plot them on the board. You will be surprised at the wide range of numbers represented by the word (it usually ranges from 2 to 7).

How often have you been in an argument with a friend, only to find out after much debate that you are using key words in different ways? The argument is one of *semantics* rather than of issues. You defined the word one way, and your friend defined it a different way. This experience is more common among laypersons than among scientists, but it still occurs. Before the merits of an issue or a position can be discussed, there must be agreement about the meaning of the important terms. The same is true in science. If we are to avoid confusion and misinterpretation, we must be able to communicate unambiguously the meaning of such terms as *intelligence, anxiety, altruism, hostility, love, alienation, aggression, guilt, reinforcement, frustration, memory,* and *information.* These terms have all been used scientifically, in very precise ways. Each of these terms could be given a dictionary definition, usually referred to as a literary or conceptual definition. But dictionary definitions are not sufficiently precise for many scientific terms because they are too general and often too ambiguous. When a word is to be used scientifically or technically, its precise meaning must be conveyed—it must be clear and unambiguous. We achieve this clarity of meaning by operationally defining the term. To state the operations for a term means to make the term observable by pointing to how it is measured. An **operational definition,** then, makes the concept observable by stating what the scientist does to measure it.

For example, *anxiety* could be defined in dictionary terms as "a state of being uneasy, apprehensive, or worried." An operational definition of the term could include observable measures such as sweating palms (observable as sweat gland activity), increased heart rate (observable with heartbeat recording), dilated pupils, and other observable physiological changes. It could also be a self-rating scale or a paper-and-pencil questionnaire. We could in each case specify the precise amounts of each measure necessary for our operational definition of anxiety.

As another example, consider the hypothesis that we proposed in the last chapter. We hypothesized that the effect of TV violence on older children's aggressive behavior at school

Table 5.1	**Dictionary and Operational Definitions of Several Terms Commonly Used by Psychologists**	
	For each concept, other operational definitions are possible.	
TERM	**DICTIONARY DEFINITION**	**OPERATIONAL DEFINITION**
Punishment	Harsh or injurious treatment for an offense	Presentation of 3 milliamp shock for .5 second following certain (specified) behavior
Learning	Acquiring knowledge or skill	Change in behavior (specify kind of behavior) as a function of practice
Anxiety	State of being uneasy, apprehensive, or worried	Sweat gland activity (amount), heart rate (amount), physiological changes (specify), self-reported anxiety on a scale of 1 to 7
Intelligence	Ability to learn or understand from experience	Score on the Stanford–Binet Intelligence Test, score on the Wechsler Intelligence Scale for Children
Thirst	Distressful feeling caused by a desire or need for water	Eighteen hours (or other value) without access to water
Sleep	Recurring condition of rest, no conscious thought, eyes closed, etc.	Specific brain wave frequencies (EEG) for different sleep stages
Guilt	A painful feeling of self-reproach	Score on a personality inventory, self-reported guilt on a scale of 1 to 10

will be less if the characters are not human. Although this appears to be a clear statement, more specific operational definitions would be necessary before any research could be undertaken to test the hypothesis. The researcher must make several decisions. What is violence on TV? Certainly, one character killing another character would be considered violence. What about a shove or push? What about a verbal assault? What about when Wile E. Coyote falls off the cliff and is hit in the head with a rock? What constitutes a character that is not human? We could probably agree that Wile E. Coyote fits this category. What about a computer-animated person? How will aggressive behavior at school be defined? Of course, getting into a fight would be aggressive behavior. What about profanity directed toward another student or teacher? What about little Johnny chasing Mary on the playground? Notice that there are no correct answers to these questions. However, the researcher must decide what is going to be meant by each of the variables in a particular study and be able to communicate those operational definitions to those who will be consumers of the research findings.

Table 5.1 contains both dictionary definitions and operational definitions of some common terms. Note that in each case, the operational definition refers to events that are observable or events that can easily be made observable. Note further that the definition is very specific rather than general.

The feature that determines whether a particular definition is more useful than another is whether it allows us to discover meaningful laws about behavior. Some will, and some will not. Those definitions that are helpful to our understanding of behavior will be retained; those that are not will be discarded. The first step in the life of a concept is to define it in clearly unambiguous, observable terms. It then may or may not be useful. If the concept of intelligence were defined as "the distance between the ears," or "the circumference of the head," its meaning would be clear, but it is very doubtful that it would ever become useful.

Let's look at one additional point before leaving the topic of definitions. An operational definition, or any other kind of definition, is not an explanation. When definitions are unintentionally used as explanations, we label them as **tautological** or **circular reasoning**. Circular reasoning has little value. A definition doesn't explain behavior or provide you with information that will, in and of itself, help in understanding behavior. It is a necessary step in discovering lawful relations, but it is only one side of a two-sided law. To explain behavior, two independent (different) types of observation are necessary: One is observations that relate to the independent variable (variable manipulated by the experimenter or "cause"), and the second is observations that relate to the dependent variable (behavior of participant or "effect"). When the relationship between the independent and dependent variables is predictable, we say that we have a lawful relationship. A circular argument uses only one side of the relationship—only one of these observations. For example, suppose we observe two children fighting with each other (body contact with intent to harm). We may be tempted to say they are fighting because they are hostile children, because hostility leads to fighting. To this point, we have not explained anything. All we have is an operational definition of hostility as fighting behavior. Our argument would be a tautology (circular) if we said that the children are fighting because they are hostile and then said that we know that they are hostile because they are fighting. To avoid circularity and to explain the behavior, we would have to define hostility and fighting independently and show that the operations for defining hostility do in fact give rise to fighting.

Tautological reasoning occurs with a higher frequency than it should. For example, it is not uncommon to hear the statement "Individuals who commit suicide are mentally ill." To the question "How do you know they are mentally ill?" the response is often "Because they committed suicide." Another common tautology refers to musical ability. For example, it is said "Individuals who play the piano well do so because they have musical ability." To the question "How do you know they have musical ability?" the response is "Because they play the piano well." Another example is "Individuals drink excessively because they are alcoholics. We know that they are alcoholics because they drink excessively." We repeat, tautological arguments do not advance our knowledge. To avoid circularity in our last example, we would have to define what we mean by "drinks excessively" and then identify the factors that give rise to drinking excessively—for example, genetics, specific early experiences, or stressful events. We then would have an explanation for the drinking.

● Numbers and Precision

As noted earlier, measurement scales are important because they allow us to transform or substitute precise numbers for imprecise words. We are restricted in what we can do with words but less so with numbers. Numbers permit us to perform certain activities and operations that words do not. In many instances, numbers permit us to add, multiply, divide, or subtract. They also permit the use of various statistical procedures. These statistics, in turn, result in greater precision and objectivity in describing behavior or other phenomena. At a minimum, we know that the numbers 1, 2, 3, 4, and so on, when applied to the frequency of occurrence of any event, mean that 4 instances are more than 3, which in turn are more than 2, and so on. Contrast numbers with words such as *frequently, often,* or *many times.* Does an event occurring *frequently* occur a greater or fewer number of times than an event occurring *often*? It may be true that a given individual uses the two terms *frequently* and *often* consistently across situations; another individual may also use the two terms consistently, but in reverse order. The result would be confusion.

The use of numbers rather than words increases our precision in communicating in other ways also. Finer distinctions (discriminations) can often be achieved with numbers if the distinctions can be made reliably. Instead of saying a certain behavior was either present or absent, or occurred with high, medium, or low frequency, numbers permit us to say, more precisely, how frequently the behavior occurred. Words are often too few in number to allow us to express finer distinctions.

Our number system is an abstract system of symbols that has little meaning in and of itself. It becomes meaningful when it becomes involved in measurement. As noted earlier, measurement is the process of assigning numbers to objects and events in accordance with a set of rules. To grasp the full impact of measurement, we need to understand the concept of a measurement scale. There are several different kinds of scales: nominal, ordinal, interval, and ratio. The distinction among scales becomes of particular importance when we conduct statistical analyses of data. Underlying statistical tests are various assumptions, including those relating to the scale of measurement. In other words, the scale of measurement for a variable can determine the most appropriate type of statistical analysis of the data.

● Scales of Measurement

Nominal Scale

There has been some disagreement among experts whether a **nominal scale** should even be described as a scale. Most would agree that it should. The fact is that we do name things, and this naming permits us to do other things as a result. The word *nominal* is derived from the Latin word for *name*. With a nominal scale, numbers are assigned to objects or events simply for identification purposes. For example, participants in various sports have numbers on their jerseys that quickly allow spectators, referees, and commentators to identify them. This identification is the sole purpose of the numbers. Performing arithmetic operations on these numbers, such as addition, subtraction, multiplication, or division, would not make any sense. The numbers do not indicate more or less of any quantity. A baseball player with the number 7 on his back does not necessarily have more of something than a player identified by the number 1. Other examples include your social security number, your driver's license number, or your credit card number. Labeling or naming allows us to make qualitative distinctions or to categorize and then count the frequency of persons, objects, or things in each category. This activity can be very useful. For example, in any given voting year, we could label or name individuals as Democrat or Republican, Liberal or Conservative, and then count frequencies for the purpose of predicting voting outcomes. Other examples of nominal scales used for identifying and categorizing are male–female, violent show–nonviolent show, and punishment–reward. As you will see later, a chi-square statistic is appropriate for data derived from a categorical (nominal) scale.

Ordinal Scale

An **ordinal scale** allows us to rank-order events. Original numbers are assigned to the order, such as first, second, third, and so on. For example, we might determine that runners in a race finished in a particular order, and this order would provide us with useful information. We would know that the runner finishing first (assigned a value of 1) ran the distance faster than the runner finishing second (assigned a value of 2), that the second-place finisher ran faster than the third-place finisher (assigned a value of 3), and so on. However, we would not know how much faster the first runner was than the second-place runner, or the second compared with the third. The difference between the first- and second-place runners may have been a fraction of a second, or it could have been several seconds. Similarly, the difference between the second- and third-place runners could have been very small or very large. An ordinal scale does not convey precise quantitative information. With an ordinal scale, we know the rank order, but we do not have any idea of the distance or interval between the rankings. Some other examples of ordinal scales are grades such as "A," "B," "C," "D," and "F"; scores given in terms of high, medium, and low; birth order in terms of firstborn, second-born, or later-born; a list of examination scores from highest to lowest; a list of job candidates ranked from high to low; and a list of the ten best-dressed persons.

What about the common use of Likert-type scales in behavioral research? For example, a researcher may pose a question to a teacher as follows:

How aggressive has Johnny been in your classroom this week?

Not at all		Somewhat		Very
1	2	3	4	5

Although most psychological scales are probably ordinal, psychologists assume that many of the scales have equal intervals and act accordingly. In other words, the difference in level of aggression between a score of 1 and a score of 2 is about the same as the difference in level of aggression between a score of 2 and a score of 3, and so on. Many researchers believe that these scales do approximate equality of intervals reasonably well, and it is unlikely that this assumption will lead to serious difficulties in interpreting our findings.

Interval Scale

When we can specify both the order of events *and* the distance between events, we have an **interval scale**. The distance between any two intervals on this type of scale is equal throughout the scale. The central shortcoming of an interval scale is its lack of an absolute zero point—a location where the user can say that there is a complete absence of the variable being measured. This type of scale often has an *arbitrary zero point*, sometimes called an *anchor point*. An example may make clear the difference between an arbitrary zero point and an absolute zero point. Scores on intelligence tests are considered to be on an interval scale. With intelligence test scores, the anchor point is set at a mean IQ value of 100 with a standard deviation (SD) of 15. A score of 115 is just as far above the mean (one SD) as a score of 85 is below the mean (one SD). Because we have a relative zero point and not an absolute one, we cannot say that a person with an IQ of 120 is twice as intelligent as a person with an IQ of 60. It is simply not meaningful to do so. Some additional examples of interval scales are both the centigrade and Fahrenheit scales of temperature, altitude (zero is sea level rather than the center of the earth), and scores on a depression scale or an anxiety scale. Students often confuse historical time. Is the year 2000 twice as old as the year 1000? The answer is no. Why?

Ratio Scale

A **ratio scale** has a number of properties that the others do not. With ratio scales, we can identify rank order, equal intervals, *and* equal ratios—two times as much, one-half as much. Ratios can be determined because the zero point is absolute, a true anchor—the complete

Table 5.2	Examples of Variables for Each Scale of Measurement
Nominal Label or category	Type of disorder (schizophrenia, depression, anxiety) Religious affiliation (none, Catholic, Protestant, Jewish, other) Region of the country (Northeast, Midwest, Southwest, etc.) Eye color (blue, brown, hazel, green) Flavor of ice cream (vanilla, chocolate, strawberry) Type of reinforcer (food, water, money, compliment)
Ordinal Rank order	College classification (freshman, sophomore, junior, senior) Grade on a test (A, B, C, D, F) National ranking of a sports team (1st, 2nd, 3rd, 4th, 5th, etc.) Reaction time (fastest, 2nd fastest, 3rd fastest, 4th fastest, etc.) Intensity of light (very bright, bright, dim, none) Age classification (child, teen, young adult, adult, older adult)
Interval Rank order + Equal intervals	Difference between the mean test score and each student's score Score on the Beck Anxiety Scale (scores range from 0 to 44, but note that a score of 0 does not represent a complete absence of anxiety) Score on a Likert-type scale (1, 2, 3, 4, 5, 6, 7) Temperature measured in degrees Celsius or degrees Fahrenheit Weight measured on a scale not calibrated to zero
Ratio Rank order + Equal intervals + Absolute zero	Number of college credits completed Number of correct answers on a test Number of total points scored in a season by a sports team Reaction time measured in milliseconds Intensity of light measured in lumens A person's age measured in years

absence of a property. Zero weight or height means the complete absence of weight or height. A 100-pound person has one-half the weight of a 200-pound person and twice the weight of a 50-pound person. We can say these things because we know that the starting points for these dimensions or measures is 0. It is important to notice that it is not necessary for any research participant to obtain a score of 0, only that it exists on the scale. Obviously no research participant would receive a weight score of 0!

A ratio scale is common when the researcher is counting the number of events. For example, you might measure a child's aggressive behavior by counting the number of times that the child inflicts physical harm on another person during a one-week observation period. Clearly, 10 incidents would be twice as many as 5, and 0 incidents would represent the absence of the variable you are measuring. Frequency counts that represent the number of times that a particular event occurred are a common example of measurement on a ratio scale. But be careful not to confuse this use of *frequency* with the use of *frequency* as a summary statistic for data measured on a nominal scale (how many times observations fit a particular category).

Table 5.2 provides additional examples of each scale of measurement.

| Figure 5.1 | Decision Tree to Determine the Appropriate Scale of Measurement |

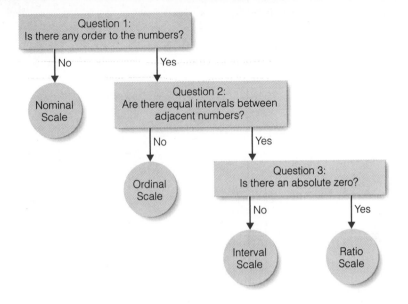

Determining the scale of measurement for a variable is often a challenging task for students learning about behavioral research. One technique that you may find useful is to remember three questions and use the decision tree shown in Figure 5.1.

● Validity of Measurement

Two important concepts relate to the measuring instruments that we use: validity and reliability. In a general sense, **validity** refers to whether the measuring instrument does what it is intended to do, and **reliability** refers to how consistently it does so. It is critical that our measurements of variables be both valid and reliable. If they are not, then we cannot be sure of what we are measuring.

The validity and reliability of a test are established by evidence. Does the SAT (Scholastic Aptitude Test) measure students' ability to do academic work (question of validity), and if so, how consistently does it do so (question of reliability)? Do those students scoring high on the SAT perform predictably better in college than those scoring low (validity)? If a student took the SAT today and then again six months from today, would the score on the two performances be similar (reliability)? We should note that a test may be highly reliable, but if it does not relate to our behavior of interest (validity), it is useless for predicting that behavior. The length of the big toe can be measured with a high degree of consistency, but it is unlikely to be a valid predictor of academic success. We can measure many things very reliably, but unless they enter into meaningful behavioral relationships (lawful relationships), they are not useful. Thus, we can achieve reliability without having validity. However, the reverse is not possible. In order to be valid, a measure must be reliable.

Let us look at five types of validity that are commonly distinguished: content validity, face validity, concurrent validity, predictive validity, and construct validity (see Figure 5.2).

| Figure 5.2 | Ways to Assess Validity |

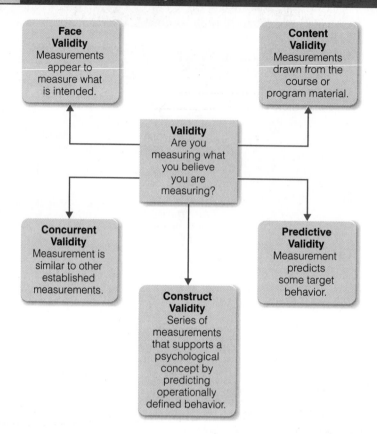

Content validity and face validity relate to tests of current knowledge and skills, whereas predictive validity relates to future performance on a job or task. Concurrent validity assesses similarity to other current measures, and construct validity deals with evaluating theoretical terms.

Content Validity

With **content validity,** we are interested in assessing current performance rather than predicting future performance. A test is constructed to measure whether participants in a program have mastered the contents of the program. Course examinations—whether midterm, finals, or some other kind—deal with content validity. Developers of social programs that require training of personnel are concerned about the effectiveness of the training. Thus, they frequently rely on content validity. *Content validity is achieved by constructing a test drawn directly from material in a program or course.* There can be disagreements regarding the representativeness of the test materials. For example, students taking an exam sometimes complain that it did not cover the material they were required to read. If this were true, the exam would be low in content validity. Although not always possible, we could assure representativeness by constructing a complete list of the content for the program or course and then selecting test items randomly from the material. Thus, content validity is based on prior considerations about what content will be included.

Face Validity

Face validity is similar to content validity, but it is determined *after* the test is constructed. We ask ourselves whether or not the test appears, on the face of it, to measure what we intend it to measure. If the test is known to have content validity, face validity can be assumed. However, it does not work in reverse direction; that is, face validity does not ensure content validity. The face validity of an exam in research methods would be high if the questions appeared to deal with research methods. However, without actual knowledge of the course materials, there would be no assurance that the questions were representative of the actual course material.

Concurrent Validity

Often, we measure psychological constructs for which there is a long history of investigation. Such constructs include intelligence, aggression, fear, attention, depression, anxiety, and many others. One way to assess the validity of our instrument is to determine whether it has concurrent validity—that is, whether it provides measurements that are similar to those provided by other instruments, previously established as valid, designed to measure the same construct. If our new measure of aggression results in scores that are the same as or similar to those found with a traditional measure of aggression, then we can be reasonably confident that we are measuring the same construct. For example, if the authors developed a new Lammers–Badia Depression Scale, we would want individuals to complete our instrument and also to complete an established instrument such as the Beck Depression Inventory (BDI). If our scale in fact measures depression, then individuals who score high (depressed) on our scale ought to score high on the BDI as well.

Predictive Validity

Predictive validity, also called criterion validity, is often used in program evaluation studies and is very suitable for applied research. Essentially, a test is constructed and developed for the purpose of predicting some form of behavior. For example, one's score on the SAT (the predictor) is moderately correlated with academic performance in college (the criterion). Knowing this relationship and an individual's score gives us a better idea of how a student will perform in college than we would have in the absence of this information. The higher the correlation between the criterion and the predictor, the greater the predictive validity. Indeed, if the correlation is perfect (1.00), the prediction is also perfect. However, most of the time correlations are only modest, somewhere between .30 and .60. Nevertheless, they are considered useful. It is very difficult to construct a good predictor measure; it is also very difficult to obtain a good criterion measure.

Construct Validity

Construct validity is one of the most important and also the most difficult to understand. We can only touch upon it here. Construct validity is especially important for the construction of theories. Researchers create theoretical constructs to better understand, explain, and predict behavior. Many hypotheses that are tested in research are derived from constructs, or theories of behavior. The construct or theory predicts how people should behave under certain conditions. The degree to which the results support the theory is a measure of construct validity. Examples of some constructs are frustration, aggression, motivation, learning, fear, hopelessness, creativity, and intelligence. Constructs are created by describing the procedures for measuring them. If the instrument for measuring them assists us in understanding and predicting behavior, they are considered valid. If they do not serve these purposes, their validity is rejected. Notice how constructs are related to the notion of operational definitions discussed at the beginning of this chapter. Constructs are general terms that can be operationally defined in different ways. For example, the construct of aggression could be operationally defined as the number of behaviors that lead to physical harm, or it could be defined as the number of physical and verbal threats. Thus, a construct attempts to summarize or explain a set of operational definitions.

Construct validity asks whether a particular measure actually measures the construct that it is intended to measure. Establishing construct validity involves several steps. Generally, the researcher or theorist designs a test and specifies what it is intended to measure. The test is then tied to, or related to, the relevant theory. Then predictions are made that relate behavior to the test scores. Finally, data are gathered to ascertain whether the predictions are confirmed.

Let's consider two related examples of psychological constructs and how construct validity was assessed. In the late 1960s, Martin Seligman conducted a series of studies with dogs that led him to develop the psychological construct of learned helplessness. He observed that dogs that had been exposed to situations in which they could not avoid an unpleasant event would, in later situations, not even attempt to remove or avoid or escape an unpleasant event even when it was possible (Seligman & Maier, 1967). This finding led to the hypothesis (theory) that early lack of control over environmental events can be debilitating, both cognitively and physiologically. That is, when individuals are subjected to aversive environmental events over which they have no control, the result is learned helplessness, which will be reflected in impaired learning, reduced levels of motivation, poor performance, and physiological deterioration. An extensive series of studies in other animal species (including humans) since the late 1960s supports the notion that the construct of learned helplessness (predictor) does lead to behavioral evidences of impaired learning, motivation, and so on (criterion). This correlation between the predictor and the criterion provides evidence of construct validity. In more recent years, Seligman has developed the related construct of learned optimism (Seligman, 1998) and the Seligman Attributional Style Questionnaire (SASQ) to measure optimism. The construct validity of learned optimism has been demonstrated in numerous studies (reported to be over 500) that show a relationship between optimism scores on the SASQ (predictor) and measures of success, performance, motivation, and physical well-being (criterion variables). Again, such research evidence supports the notion that the psychological construct of optimism is useful in understanding, explaining, and predicting behavior.

What we are suggesting through these examples is that constructs reflect basic behavioral processes. If learned helplessness and learned optimism exist, then certain behaviors should follow. If our expectations are confirmed a number of times in a variety of settings, our construct is useful—that is, valid. Usually, many studies are necessary to demonstrate construct validity. With time and continued research, both the construct and the theory usually undergo a series of modifications and become more refined.

Before turning to the issue of reliability, take a look at the box "Thinking Critically About Everyday Information" and review several concepts presented so far in the chapter.

● Reliability of Measurement

A measuring instrument is reliable if measurements recorded at different times give similar results. Obviously, we would not want to use a measuring instrument if it did not give similar results under similar circumstances. Consistency is imperative if we are to obtain useful data.

Thinking Critically About Everyday Information

Understanding Sleep Apnea

What follows is an article that appeared in the *New York Times* newspaper.

John Holman of St. Paul is a very busy man, and he was not accustomed to having to "let things go" because he was too tired to do them. But tired he was, tired driving to and from work, tired during the day at the warehouse company he runs, too tired some days to play his beloved game of tennis after work, and really tired in the evening—in bed by 8:30 to arise at 6.

But Mr. Holman, an average-size 67-year-old, did nothing about his fatigue until his wife, Marna, threatened to move out of their bedroom because his snoring was keeping her awake. It was she who suggested that he might have sleep apnea. With it, breathing stops, often for a minute or longer, sometimes hundreds of times a night and resumes each time with a loud snort or snore. So at his wife's urging, Mr. Holman spent a night in the sleep laboratory at Abbott Northwestern Hospital in Minneapolis. Her suspicions were confirmed. Mr. Holman now sleeps with a device that assists his breathing, and both he and his wife, who feared he would fall asleep while driving and kill himself or someone else, are feeling a lot better.

The National Institutes of Health estimates that as many as 18 million Americans, 6 percent of the nation, have sleep apnea. After the proliferation of sleep centers around the country and greater awareness of the condition, the diagnosis of sleep apnea increased twelvefold from 1990 to 1998.

Still, experts estimate that fewer than 10 percent of people who have it are aware of it. As a result, they risk their health and their lives and possibly the lives of others.

Sleep apnea is a disorder that occurs only in sleep and more in REM (rapid eye movement) sleep than in the other stages of sleep. When this disorder is present, the individual stops breathing during sleep for 10 seconds or longer but can breathe normally when awake. Cessation of breathing may occur hundreds of times during the night, with no memory of it in the morning. To determine whether the disorder is present requires the individual to spend a night at a sleep disorders clinic where brain waves (EEG) and respiratory activity can be monitored using a polygraph machine. The EEG pattern reveals when the individual is asleep, how long it takes the person to fall asleep, and the various sleep stages that he or she passes through during the night. Measurement of respiration reveals how frequently an individual has stopped breathing and for how long. Respiration is measured in two ways during the night. One is with sensors near the nose and mouth to measure airflow. The second way is with a respiratory belt attached to the diaphragm/chest to measure breathing effort. People with sleep apnea wake up very tired in the morning and are very sleepy all day long. They frequently fall asleep while driving, watching television, reading, or sitting in a meeting. As mentioned, they are unaware that they have sleep apnea, even though they may have awakened hundreds of times during the night. The most prominent symptoms are daytime sleepiness, mood changes, and irritability. If the condition is left untreated, other health problems emerge.

Effective treatments for sleep apnea are available. Any effective treatment would have to address the symptoms noted. One way that sleepiness is measured is with a self-rating scale. Similar rating scales are used for mood changes and irritability. Consider the following questions:

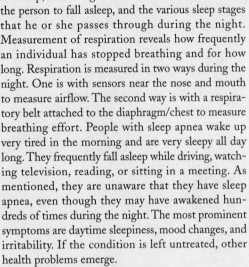

- Is sleep apnea a quantitative or qualitative event?
- What kind of measurement scale would be involved in measuring severity of sleep apnea?
- What measurement scale would be involved if sleepiness, irritability, and mood were each rated on a self-report scale from 1 to 10 (1 = not at all sleepy, 10 = extremely sleepy)?
- In addition to a self-report assessment of sleepiness, can you think of another way to operationally define sleepiness that would be less subjective (perhaps on a ratio scale)?
- How might you show concurrent validity for the psychological construct of sleepiness?
- How might you show predictive validity for the psychological construct of sleepiness?

SOURCE: Jane E. Brody, "Sleep Apnea: A Noisy but Often Invisible Threat," *New York Times*, 17 September 2002, p. F7. Copyright 2002 The New York Times Company. Reprinted with permission.

Figure 5.3   Ways to Assess Reliability

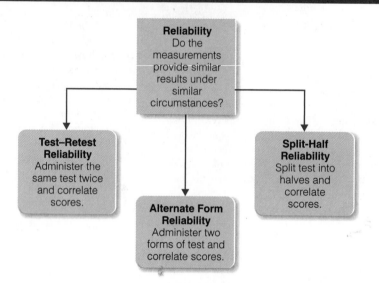

As we have previously noted, reliability is a necessary but not a sufficient condition for validity. Information regarding test reliability should be available for every test or measure. This information should specify the extent of the reliability, including the type of reliability and the conditions under which it was obtained. Reliability estimates are expressed in terms of a correlation coefficient and, therefore, are not all-or-none scores. As we noted, correlations can vary from −1.0 to 1.0, but most reliability coefficients remain in the 0.0 to 1.0 range.

The upper limits of a test of reliability are established by the similarity of items in terms of what they have in common (interitem correlation) and the number of items on the test. As long as the test items provide independent measures of the same construct, the larger the number of items on a test, the more reliable the test will be. This notion is reflected in the way many sports championships are determined (as in baseball, basketball, and hockey), using a series of several games rather than just one. On any given day, a weaker team may defeat a stronger team, but it is unlikely that a weaker team will consistently beat a stronger team. Similarly, witness the Olympic decathlon. It is a contest in which an athlete must take part in ten events. Consider another example. A course in psychology at the end of the term may have available 1,000 questions that could be used on the final exam. The final exam will be constructed by sampling these items. A sample of only 5 items would be too few for reliability purposes. As we added items, our reliability would increase rapidly, but beyond a certain point, reached rather quickly, adding more items would add very little to our reliability. Thus, a 50-item test would be considerably more reliable than a 5-item test.

For those interested in pursuing this notion further, an estimate of reliability that considers both interitem correlation and the number of items on a test is referred to as the *coefficient alpha* or the *Kuder–Richardson Method*. Among other things, this method will allow you to determine the number of items needed to achieve a given value of reliability.

Next, we discuss three specific methods to assess reliability (see Figure 5.3).

Table 5.3	Test–Retest Reliability Coefficients for Two Different Tests			
	TEST A		**TEST B**	
TEST TAKER	**1st Administration**	**2nd Administration**	**1st Administration**	**2nd Administration**
Ryan	76	78	76	87
Beth	84	83	84	92
Brandi	85	85	85	94
Chandler	67	64	67	73
John	86	89	86	98
Mary	92	91	92	100
Casey	71	75	71	84
Nina	58	55	58	64
Amy	63	60	63	69
	$r = 0.98$		$r = 0.98$	

Test–Retest Reliability

One obvious way to determine the reliability of a test is to administer the same test twice to the same individual. To establish **test–retest reliability,** we administer the identical test a second time, usually after a week or two has gone by. We then calculate a correlation coefficient for the first and second test scores. The time interval between the tests must be specified because retest correlations decrease as the time interval between tests increases. Some problems with this procedure relate to possible practice effects. Also, if the interval between the tests is very short, the individual may be able to remember previous answers given the first time, and the scores between the two sets of test scores would not be independent.

Take a look at the scores shown in Table 5.3. These scores represent a test–retest assessment for two different tests. Although high test–retest reliability ($r = 0.98$) suggests that both instruments are relatively free of measurement error, care should be taken in interpreting this coefficient. It is evident in Table 5.3 that high reliability does not mean that an individual's first and second scores are nearly the same; this may or may not be the case. Glancing over the pairs of scores for Test A, you do get the impression that the individuals scored similarly on both test administrations. However, glancing over the pairs of scores for Test B, you can see that the similarity in scores is much less and that, overall, the scores on the second administration are higher. Because test–retest reliability is derived through a correlational analysis, the strength of the relationship depends upon the similarity in rank order on the first and second test distributions—that is, whether the individual was first, second, third, and so on, on the two distributions of test scores. In this regard, test–retest reliability is a relative measure. It is possible to have high test–retest reliability and yet have different absolute scores on the first and second testing. Although this situation is unusual, the occurrence of some significant event between the two test administrations could cause a shift in scores.

We also want to comment on low test–retest reliability. Low reliability does not always suggest a faulty measuring instrument. If a significant event occurs between the two test administrations for some of the test takers but not all, then low test–retest reliability may result. For example, a therapy or training program for a reading disability may take place between the first and second testing periods. If those with the greatest disability showed the greatest improvement, then this would lower test–retest reliability. However, if no deliberate effort to change the condition of individuals was made and only a short period of time intervened between the first and second tests, then low test–retest reliability is most likely due to a faulty measuring instrument.

Alternate Form Reliability

Some of the difficulties with the test–retest procedure can be avoided by using **alternate form reliability**. With this method, an individual is tested on one form of the test (Form A) and then again on a comparable second form (Form B). Again, a correlation coefficient is computed between the scores on Forms A and B. The period of time between the two tests is usually a week or two, although this time varies considerably. Usually, the two forms contain the same number of items and cover similar content. Alternate form reliability is used more frequently than test–retest reliability because it has fewer associated problems, including a substantial reduction in practice effects.

Split-Half Reliability

Only a single test session is involved when using the method of **split-half reliability**. Two scores for each individual are obtained by splitting the test into comparable halves. This is usually achieved by assigning odd-numbered items to one form and even-numbered items to the other (odd–even split). Generally, this method is not preferred over others because the scores on the two halves are not independent. To illustrate, if a test taker is "spaced out" while taking the test, both scores will be depressed. With a sufficient number of instances of this sort, a spuriously high correlation will result, and the reliability will appear to be higher than it really is.

Factors That Affect Reliability

A number of factors can lower the reliability of a test. Within a testing period, individuals may become upset or ill, or they may misread the question, make a clerical error when recording an answer, or guess at the answer. Between testing sessions, an individual may change, there may be differences between the two tests (alternate form), or scoring criteria may change. It is also important to remember that reliability is measured using correlation coefficients. One factor than can reduce correlations is a restricted range of scores on one or both variables. A restricted range of scores can result from a testing instrument that does not allow a variety of possible scores or from testing samples of individuals who all score very similarly on the instrument (either very high or very low). For example, you would not want to assess the reliability of a depression scale by using a sample of suicidal individuals!

Experimental procedures are available to address these factors that affect reliability. In addition to selecting an appropriate sample of research participants, researchers can reduce measurement error and improve reliability by writing the items carefully. They should follow a standardized procedure for giving the test so that testing conditions are very similar. They should state instructions clearly so that they are easily understood. Finally, they should use objective scoring procedures to avoid error due to subjectivity and changing criteria. We should also restate that longer tests (given the same interitem correlation) are more reliable than shorter tests. Obviously, when new tests are being constructed, considerable "pilot testing" (preliminary selection of items, testing, revising) is necessary before a useful instrument can be developed.

Acceptable reliability levels depend on what the test is used for. For basic research purposes, reliabilities of approximately .70 are not uncommon, but correlations of .80 or higher are considered desirable. To obtain higher estimates of reliability requires considerable effort in selecting items, standardizing the procedure, and administering and scoring the test. For applied problems dealing with social issues such as placement in a retraining program or a special class, or for awards, measurement error must be minimized. Under these and similar circumstances, reliability coefficients less than .90 are usually not acceptable.

We should note that this discussion has focused on the reliability of testing instruments. Often in behavioral research, human observers record behavior, and their observations provide the data for analysis. The reliability of researcher observations is also an important issue and involves the degree to which multiple observers record the same observations. This notion of interobserver agreement (interrater reliability) will be discussed in the next chapter, along with other issues of observation.

CASE ANALYSIS

Universities continually examine ways to increase the academic success of their students. One factor may be the level of emphasis on academics in the student's life. Thus, you believe that students who experience an out-of-class living environment that emphasizes academics will be more successful in college. Your university has several housing options for incoming freshmen. You work with the housing office to assign some freshmen to live in off-campus apartments, some freshmen to live in on-campus residence halls, and some freshmen to live in on-campus residence halls called residential colleges. These residential colleges emphasize academics by having faculty live in the residence hall, by holding classes in the residence hall, by creating a peer tutoring system in the residence hall, and by creating a program of activities that revolve around academics. At the end of their freshman year, you assess the students' study skills and grade point average. You assess study skills by asking the students 63 true/false questions related to actions and attitudes toward studying. The study habits score is the number of questions answered positively.

Critical Thinking Questions

1. Identify your independent variable(s).

2. Identify your dependent variable(s).

3. What is your hypothesis?

4. What is your operational definition of academic emphasis?

5. What is your operational definition of success in college?

6. Your independent variable is measured on what scale of measurement?

7. Study skills are measured on what scale of measurement?

8. What criterion could be measured to support the predictive validity of the study habits instrument?

9. How would you test the reliability of the study habits instrument?

GENERAL SUMMARY

Many of the concepts that we study in psychology are subject to different interpretations. Therefore, the researcher must provide operational definitions that define the variables in specific and measurable terms. For the purpose of analysis, the observations that are made must be assigned numerical values. These numbers that result from the measurement process possess particular characteristics defined by the scale of measurement. Numbers on a nominal scale are simply labels with no greater-than or less-than qualities. Numbers on an ordinal scale indicate greater than and less than, but do not tell us how much greater or less. Numbers on an interval scale have equal intervals between adjacent numbers, but the scale has no absolute zero. A ratio scale has order, equal intervals, and an absolute zero.

Quality research involves measurements that are valid and reliable. Validity refers to confidence that you are measuring what you intended to measure, and reliability refers to consistency in your measurements. Validity is composed of content validity, face validity, concurrent validity, predictive validity, and construct validity. Reliability can be assessed with test–retest, alternative forms, and split-half methods. Although all of these concepts may seem a bit tedious, the good researcher knows that attention to them is directly related to confidence that the results will indeed answer the research question.

Now that we understand some of the issues regarding the measurement of variables, the next chapter will focus on the methods we use to collect such data.

DETAILED SUMMARY

1. Measurement is a way of refining our observations so that we can assign numerical values to them. Measurement requires precise definitions of psychological variables such as intelligence, anxiety, altruism, hostility, love, alienation, aggression, guilt, reinforcement, frustration, and memory.

2. Operational definitions provide precision by defining psychological variables in terms of specific operations. For example, hunger could be defined as the number of calories consumed. Operational definitions are useful when they allow us to discover lawful relationships among variables. Operational definitions, by themselves, are not explanations. Using definitions as explanations results in inappropriate tautological reasoning.

3. The conversion of observations to numbers permits the use of mathematical operations to better describe and analyze observations. The numbers that represent observations exist on one of four scales of measurement: nominal, ordinal, interval, or ratio. The scale of measurement is important because it determines the types of mathematical operations and statistical analyses that are appropriate.

4. On a nominal scale of measurement, numbers simply represent labels and have no quantitative meaning (for example, religious affiliation). On an ordinal scale of measurement, numbers represent rank order but without equal intervals between adjacent numbers (for example, letter grade on a test). An interval scale has equal intervals between adjacent numbers but no absolute zero (for example, score on a Likert-type scale). A ratio scale of measurement has equal intervals and an absolute zero (for example, number of correct test questions).

5. Validity refers to whether the instrument measures what it is intended to measure. Validity can be assessed in different ways.

6. Content validity is the degree to which measurement items are drawn from the content of the course or program to be evaluated. Face validity is the degree to which measurement items appear (on the face of it) to accurately represent the content to be evaluated. Concurrent validity is the degree to which measurements correlate with measurements from an established (validated) instrument. Predictive validity is the degree to which measurements predict some target behavior. Construct validity is the degree to which measurements support a psychological concept that helps to explain and predict behavior.

7. In order for measurements to be valid, they must be reliable; that is, they should provide similar results under similar circumstances.

8. Test–retest reliability is the degree to which measurements are similar when the same instrument is administered a second time. Alternate form reliability is the degree to which measurements are similar when a comparable version of the instrument is administered. Split-half reliability is the degree to which measurements are similar when different halves of the same instrument are compared.

9. Factors that can lower the reliability of a test include a restricted range of scores, feeling ill, misreading questions, making clerical errors, guessing at answers, changes in the test takers, differences between two tests (alternate form), or changes in scoring criteria.

KEY TERMS

alternate form reliability (p. 74)
concurrent validity (p. 69)

construct validity (p. 69)
content validity (p. 68)

face validity *(p. 69)*
interval scale *(p. 65)*
measurement *(p. 61)*
nominal scale *(p. 64)*
operational definition *(p. 61)*
ordinal scale *(p. 64)*
predictive validity *(p. 69)*

ratio scale *(p. 65)*
reliability *(p. 67)*
split-half reliability *(p. 74)*
tautological (circular) reasoning *(p. 63)*
test–retest reliability *(p. 73)*
validity *(p. 67)*

REVIEW QUESTIONS/EXERCISES

1. Provide an operational definition for each of the following variables: hunger, reaction time, academic success, college year (such as freshman or sophomore), fear, and type of automobile.

2. For each of the variables in question 1, describe the types of numbers that would be used to measure these variables, and identify the appropriate scale of measurement.

3. Search InfoTrac College Edition for a study that addresses the validity of an instrument or construct. Describe which methods were used to assess validity.

4. Search InfoTrac College Edition for a study that addresses the reliability of an instrument. Describe which methods were used to assess reliability.

5. In your own words, describe why validity and reliability of measurement are important in behavioral research.

 ## WEB RESOURCES TO INCREASE LEARNING

The chapter outline, chapter summaries, key terms and definitions, additional chapter questions/exercises, interactive workshops, and links to relevant Web sites are available at the course Web site (**http://psychology. wadsworth.com/lammers_badia1e**). Explore the interactive workshops "Scale of Measurement," "Reliability and Validity," "Operational Definitions," and "Specifying Constructs."

CHAPTER

6

METHODS OF DATA COLLECTION

Introduction to Methods of Data Collection

By now, it should be abundantly clear that behavioral research involves the collection of data and that there are a variety of ways to do so. For example, if we wanted to measure aggressive behavior in children, we could collect those data by observing children with our eyes, by using equipment to measure the force with which they hit an object, by examining juvenile crime records, by surveying parents and teachers, by interviewing parents and teachers, or by administering an aggression scale to children. This is just a sample of the methods that are possible; we are sure that you could imagine many others. However, these examples do illustrate several distinctly different methods that can be used to collect data. As with most research design techniques, each method has advantages and limitations. Perhaps the most interesting and challenging of these is the method of observation. (In a sense, all of behavioral research is based upon observation. What we describe here is a specific kind of observational procedure.) Historically, behavioral research has relied heavily on this method, and it will undoubtedly continue to be a primary method for gathering behavioral data. Let's begin this chapter by discussing the nature of observations, the ways to make observations, and the reliability of observations. Following this discussion, we will turn to other methods illustrated by the examples above.

The Nature of Observation

Observations involve the use of our sensory systems (including eyes and ears) to record behavior. They require that humans make *judgments* about the occurrence of the behavior, its frequency, its duration, or its latency. These measures are the basic data used to describe naturally occurring behavior or to assess the effects of our independent variable. Therefore, they must be gathered with care. Observations such as these (judgments that behavior has or has not occurred) are inherently more subjective than other data collection procedures. Because judgments are based on our perceptions, the same event occurring in the environment will be perceived differently by different people. We may observe Johnny chasing Mary around the playground and call it aggressive behavior. You may observe the same event and call it play behavior. Certainly, attention is one important factor. I may be attending to the conversation between two people, and you may be attending to the body language exhibited by those two people. As a result, we may interpret our observations similarly or differently.

Behavior measures based upon response categories such as play, aggression, and self-assertion are more complex than specific responses such as talking, walking, or attending. These, in turn, are very different from the lever press, the key peck, heart rate, latency to respond, or eye blink responses. The recording of these behaviors is usually automated, and there is little doubt about the criteria used for their occurrence or nonoccurrence. They do not require the judgment of human observers.

Data derived from human observers are playing an increasingly important role in research, particularly in applied settings. They also play an important role in some laboratory settings. As you know, the interests of psychologists are extremely varied. This broad scope of interest has resulted in studying behavior under a wider variety of conditions than in the past. Some studies involve making unobtrusive observations of animals behaving in their natural settings, including primates and animals lower on the phylogenetic scale. Psychologists often record laboratory observations in addition to the behavior that is automatically recorded. These observations are often interesting behaviors in their own right. Applied psychologists sometimes encounter special problems. For example, behavior modification experts must be adept at recognizing when a given behavior achieves criterion (for example, when the sound made by a mute autistic child is sufficiently close to "mama" to warrant rewarding the child). Moreover, observers must be able to make fine distinctions between behaviors that are closer and more distant approximations to the criterion behavior. Similarly, those studying the effects of psychologically active drugs must attend to a wide variety of both specific responses and broader classes of behavior. Reliable observations are essential in assessing the treatment effects. In many instances, the primary and often the only data are derived from direct observation by the investigators. It is essential that these primary data be accurate, objective, and reliable.

In this chapter, we will discuss some problems associated with using human observers and some factors that decrease the accuracy and reliability of observations. We will also discuss some ways of assessing interobserver reliability. You should be aware that the method of observation does not apply to only some research designs. In fact, all of the research designs discussed in this book, both experimental and nonexperimental, can involve observation. One specific type of nonexperimental design, naturalistic observation, always involves observation; it will be discussed in Chapter 15.

● Ways of Observing

Participant Versus Nonparticipant Observation

There are two broad approaches to observing behavior: **participant observation** and **nonparticipant observation.** Participant observers conduct their observations "from the inside"; that is, the researcher is an integral part of the environment being observed. Nonparticipant observers conduct their observations "from the outside"; the researcher does not interact with those being observed.

The following extract describes the habituating techniques used by Jane Goodall to study the mountain gorilla in its natural habitat:

> My technique of habituating the gorillas was simple but essential, for I could only obtain unbiased data on their behavior if they remained relatively unaffected by my presence. I usually attempted to approach the group undetected to within about 150 feet before climbing slowly and in full view of the animals onto a stump or the low branch of a tree where I settled myself as comfortably as possible without paying obvious attention to them. By choosing a prominent observation post not only was I able to see the gorillas over the screen of herbs, but, reciprocally, they could inspect me clearly, which was the most important single factor in habituating the animals. Under such circumstances they usually remained in the vicinity to watch me, and even approached me to within 5 feet. (Schaller, 1963, p. 22)

This description of Jane Goodall's methodology suggests that she was a nonparticipant observer. However, if you are familiar with her work with gorillas, you know that the gorillas not only habituated to her presence but later began to interact with her. At this point, she became a participant observer.

Let us imagine that we want to observe 9-year-old children on the playground and that we want to record frequency of aggressive behavior. After establishing an operational definition of aggressive behavior, we must decide how the observations will be made. Several options are available. As a participant observer, you could play with the children on the playground and make them aware that you are observing their behavior. Another option as a participant observer is to play with the children on the playground without making them aware that you are observing their behavior. A third option is to be a nonparticipant observer, observing the children "from a distance" and making them aware that you are observing their behavior. A final option is to be a nonparticipant observer, observing the children "from a distance" without their awareness. Note that "from a distance" may refer literally to a geographic distance or may represent a method such as a one-way mirror or a hidden camera. So, which method would you use? If you are already considering the pros and cons of each approach, then you are thinking like a behavioral scientist!

Whether you are observing gorillas in the rainforest or children on the playground, you will probably not be able to observe them continuously. Scheduling observations is therefore an important consideration.

Scheduling Observations

Decisions must be made regarding frequency, duration, and time of day for scheduling observations. These decisions depend upon the purposes to be served by the observations. Researchers may only be interested in a restricted, narrow time period, or they may be interested in a broad, representative time period. If you are interested in a representative description of naturally occurring behavior, it is necessary to observe over many different time periods and across several days. Jane Goodall's description of primate behavior under natural conditions is an excellent example. Laboratory studies, in contrast, often follow a rigid schedule in that the experiment takes place at the same time each day for an hour or more. In this case, the observation period is confined to the laboratory session time. An applied program would follow a different approach. A behavior modification program dealing with disruptive and unruly behavior in social settings would require that observations be made in each setting where the disruptions occur. Whatever the purpose of the observations, individual observation sessions should be sufficiently long to provide an adequate sample of the response of interest. Behaviors that occur with a low frequency may require longer observation periods than high-frequency behaviors. For some purposes, it may be necessary to sample a behavior at different times during the day to determine its range and variability. For most studies, however, observations are made at the same time each day so that observations are made under similar conditions from day to day.

If the occurrence or nonoccurrence of complex behavior is being judged, the criteria for establishing the presence of this behavior must be established. Before the behavior is recorded as present, these criteria must be satisfied. To minimize the observer's drifting away from the originally established criteria, a periodic review should be scheduled during the course of observing. Although **observer drift** has been a problem in some studies, it is usually correctable.

Defining the Behavior to Be Observed

As we have noted, our concern is to make observations that are both objective and reliable. We want to maximize "pure" observations and minimize the degree to which our observations are affected by our own interpretations and inferences. To this end, we attempt to define the dependent variable (behavior) in terms of specific observable responses and to specify clearly the criteria for judging when the behavior has occurred. As discussed in Chapter 5, we need clear operational definitions for behaviors to be observed. This is an important step if we are to ensure that different observers make similar observations. A good response measure will have relatively high interobserver agreement. The more precise we are in specifying our definition of a response or of the behavioral criteria, the higher the interobserver agreement will be. For example, if we were interested in the self-mutilating behavior of an autistic child, it would be unsatisfactory to instruct the observers to record every instance of self-mutilating behavior. The term is too broad, abstract, and undefined to be useful or to assure agreement among observers. However, if we operationally defined self-mutilating behavior as "head banging," "biting one's body," or "beating oneself with fists," we could more easily and reliably measure this class of behavior. Similarly, if observers are instructed to record incidents of children's aggressive behavior on the playground, one observer's perception of aggression could be quite different from another observer's perception of aggression. Again, an operational definition is needed so that we know specifically what is being measured.

Specific Techniques for Recording Behaviors

Consider the following. A research team is interested in observing the self-mutilating behavior of children diagnosed as autistic. Having decided on a satisfactory operational definition of the target behavior, the team must now decide on the observational technique to use. Three choices are commonly available: (1) Count the number of occurrences of self-mutilating behavior during an observational session (frequency method); (2) record the period of time during which the target behavior lasts (duration method); or (3) break the observational sessions into equal time intervals and record the occurrence of self-mutilating behavior within each interval (interval method). Let's take a closer look at each technique.

Frequency Method   The **frequency method of observation** is simple, straightforward, and easily understood. The observer simply counts the number of occurrences of the behavior of interest in a given interval of time. The interval of time is arbitrary; it may be as little as a few minutes or as much as several hours. Further, it may be based on one observation session, or it may run across many sessions over several days. Often, the investigator is only interested in the frequency of the observations in a given session and not in changes that may occur during that session. However, when the interest centers on assessing change or obtaining interobserver agreement within a session, the session may be divided into smaller, equal time intervals. For example, a 60-minute session may be divided into ten 6-minute intervals, and changes in frequency can be observed across this entire interval. Usually, observation periods are of the same duration from day to day. If not, then comparing frequencies based on 15 minutes with those based on 30 minutes would not be appropriate. If different durations are used, it is necessary to convert frequency to response rate. This measure can easily be derived by dividing the frequency of the response by the unit of time—for example, responses per minute. The frequency method of recording observational data is most appropriate with discrete responses that take a relatively constant period of time to complete—for example, number of cigarettes smoked, number of words spoken, or number of headbanging incidents.

Responses occurring over long periods of time would not be appropriate for the frequency method. Responses such as time spent talking, sleeping, eating, or observing would be inappropriate. Counting these observations would be wasteful of information, and counting their frequencies might not be a sensitive way to assess a treatment effect. For these responses, the duration method is more appropriate.

Frequency measures, particularly rate measures, are popular among psychologists interested in the experimental analysis of behavior. In applied settings, attempts are often made to modify both excesses (such as fighting) and deficits of behavior (such as not talking). In these settings, monitoring frequency is obviously important. Moreover, frequency and rate measures have been shown to be sensitive to contingencies of reinforcement.

Duration Method   As we noted, in those instances where response duration is long and/or the occasions of its occurrence relatively infrequent (such as sleep or inactivity), it is usually inappropriate to record frequency. Instead, we want to measure the duration of the response. For example, using the **duration method of observation,** we might measure the duration of time spent either in solitary or in social activity. Using a stopwatch or an event recorder, the observer activates the instrument when the behavior begins and terminates the time recording when the behavior ends. Even though response frequency is not of primary interest, it is possible to obtain a frequency measure by simply counting the number of times the recording instrument was activated. Judging when a response is initiated or terminated can often be difficult. For example, imagine you are studying the talking of an autistic child. There may be many pauses of varying duration, brief interruptions, or changes in the intensity of the behavior that requires a judgment as to whether a different response occurred. It is important that another observer (interobserver agreement) be able to make similar observations. Consequently, the decisions must be made as objective as possible.

Interval Method   The **interval method of observation** is the most flexible and widely used recording method. This method permits the recording of any behavior, whether discrete (head banging) or continuous (sleeping). With this method, the observation period is broken into equal intervals, the size of which varies with the particular observations of interest. Behavior is recorded as occurring (yes) or not occurring (no) in each interval. The interval size may be as short as a few seconds or as long as a few minutes, depending on the behavior under observation. A desirable time interval is long enough to accommodate a single response but not long enough to accommodate more than one response. Research interest is focused on the number of intervals during which the response occurs. For high-rate, short-duration responses, the interval should be short so that no more than one response per interval will occur. If more than a single discrete response can occur per interval, then counting the intervals may underestimate the frequency of the observed behavior. In contrast, if the intervals are so short that a single response can fall into two or more intervals, counting the intervals in which a response occurs may overestimate the frequency of behavior.

Obviously, the criterion for occurrence or nonoccurrence of behavior must be clear so that its occurrence can be quickly and reliably determined. The problem is more difficult than it at first appears because only a portion of the behavior may occur in a given interval. It becomes even more difficult if the observer is recording several different responses concurrently. When this happens, a decision rule is sometimes adopted; if a response fills one-half or more of the interval, it is scored as occurring in that interval. For continuous responses (such as talking), each interval in which talking occurred would be scored as an occurrence. Therefore, the interval scoring method allows the investigator to derive both frequency (discrete responses) and duration (continuous responses) data.

Recording More Than One Response

With the interval method, it is common to score several different responses that occur concurrently in an interval. When this is done, it is essential to reserve time at the end of each interval for recording whether the different behaviors occurred. We will first give an example of scoring one response across different participants. Then, we will give an example of scoring multiple responses.

Let us assume that our observational period will be daily 30-minute sessions and we are interested in the occurrence or nonoccurrence of a single behavior. We decide that an interval size of 30 seconds is appropriate for our response. Therefore, we would divide the

Table 6.1	Interval Scoring Sheet for a Single Response With Three Participants								
Experiment:		Researcher:				Observer:			
Participants:		Location:				Date:			
Time:		Behavior:				Codes:			

	Intervals								
	1	2	3	4	5	6	7		60
Participant 1	+ −	+ −	+ −	+ −	+ −	+ −	+ −	.....	+ −
Participant 2	+ −	+ −	+ −	+ −	+ −	+ −	+ −	.....	+ −
Participant 3	+ −	+ −	+ −	+ −	+ −	+ −	+ −	.....	+ −

30-minute session into 60 30-second intervals. For each of these 30-second intervals, we would record whether or not the behavior occurred. If we were observing three participants, our scoring sheet would look like Table 6.1. Please note the documentation required for each scoring sheet. This is important information that can easily be forgotten if not recorded in permanent form.

Because we are recording only one response or one kind of behavior whenever it occurs during the interval, we can circle the + as soon as it is observed. If, by chance, the response occurs again in that same interval, we would simply ignore it. Finally, we would circle the minus sign if the behavior did not occur during the interval.

When several participants are observed during each session, only a single participant is observed at any given time. Thus, if there were 60 intervals, each participant would be observed independently 60 times. You could start with Interval 1, Participant 1, go to Interval 1, Participant 2, then to Interval 1, Participant 3. Then you could begin the sequence again with Interval 2.

When more than one behavior is being observed and recorded, it may be necessary to reserve a part of the interval for scoring purposes. Otherwise, the time it takes to record the occurrence or nonoccurrence of several responses may interfere with the task of observing. As a result, some responses may be missed. It is not difficult to reserve time for recording purposes. With our 30-second interval, we could designate the first 25 seconds for observing and the last 5 seconds for recording. If we were observing smiling (S), frowning (F), hitting (H), and biting (B), our data sheet might look like Table 6.2. If any of the behaviors occurred during the 25-second observation period, we would record it during the 5-second recording period simply by circling the proper code.

We should note that when short intervals are used, it may be necessary to use a signaling device to identify the beginning and end of each interval. A cassette recorder with an earpiece can fill the bill admirably. The precise time intervals can be recorded prior to making observations, and listening to the tape can pace the observers through the session, telling them exactly when to observe and when to record. With time intervals of 30 seconds, the tape could be arranged to signal the beginning of the observation interval by prerecording "Time Interval 1, Begin" and 25 seconds later "Time Interval 1, Record." Then the tape would identify "Time Interval 2, Begin," and so on. This procedure could be used when there is more than one observer. By coupling the recorder with two or more earpieces, we

Table 6.2	Interval Scoring Sheet for a Single Participant and Four Different Responses				
Experiment:		Researcher:		Observer:	
Participant:		Location:		Date:	
Time:		Behavior: smiling, frowning, hitting, biting		Codes: S, F, H, B	
	Intervals				
	1	2	3		60
Participant	S F H B	S F H B	S F H B	......	S F H B

would have an excellent means of assuring ourselves that the investigators are observing and recording the same time periods. This achievement is particularly important to assess inter-observer agreement.

After the experiment is completed, the interval observations can be converted into percentages. This is done by taking the number of intervals in which the response occurred, dividing it by the total number of intervals, and then multiplying by 100. Thus, if a response was observed during 12 out of 60 observational periods, the percentage would be: $12/60 \times 100 = 20\%$.

Before we consider the issue of reliability of observations, let's think about an MSNBC news report of a study that examined poor posture associated with the use of school backpacks by children (see "Thinking Critically About Everyday Information").

Thinking Critically About Everyday Information

School Backpacks and Posture

A news report by MSNBC describes a study in which children were observed carrying school backpacks. The article states:

> Thirteen children ages 8 and 9 walked about 1,310 feet without a backpack, and wearing packs weighing 9 and 13 pounds, while researchers filmed them with a high-speed camera. . . . The kids did not change their strides, the images showed. Instead, the youngsters bent forward more as they tried to counter the loads on their backs, and the heavier loads made them bend more, the study found. As they grew more tired, their heads went down, Orloff said.

Think about the following questions:

- Would you classify this as participant or nonparticipant observation? With awareness or without awareness?

- Could the answer to the previous question have influenced the children's behavior? If so, in what way?

- How could the dependent variables "stride" and "bend" be defined in terms that would permit quantitative measurement?

- Why do you believe the researcher used a high-speed camera instead of simply having human observers record observations?

SOURCE: Retrieved June 11, 2003, online at http://www.msnbc.com/news/922623.asp?0si=−

● Reliability of Observations

It is important to undertake a periodic check of the accuracy of your recorded observations by having another observer *independently* record his or her observations for the same time periods. These **independent observations** must not be influenced by the original observer's opinions or behavior. To accomplish this objective, it may be necessary to shield the two observers from each other. Even subtle recording movements on the part of one observer may be sufficient to bias the other observer. Having assured ourselves that the observations are independent, we can do a check for interobserver reliability.

Interobserver Agreement

We have noted several times that when different raters, judges, or observers are used to record data, it is important to determine whether the observations are objective and reliable. We try to assure this objectivity by carefully defining the behavior of interest and clearly specifying criteria for the occurrence or nonoccurrence of the behavior. Only when the behavior meets the criteria will it be counted as an observation. However, this procedure is not sufficient in itself. We must have evidence that our observations are objective and reliable, and that we have avoided observer bias, subjectivity, and observer drift. We simply cannot determine the accuracy of our data based upon the observations of a single observer. Therefore, a careful researcher will periodically use two or more observers simultaneously and then calculate a statistical measure to determine the degree of **interobserver agreement.** Several ways of calculating interobserver agreement will be described in the next section.

High interobserver agreement suggests that the behavior being observed is sufficiently well defined that we can generalize the results recorded by one observer to a population of observers. This then makes the behavioral phenomenon more meaningful to the individual investigator and to other investigators as well. Low interobserver reliability can cause problems. It could reduce the likelihood of finding an empirical relationship between the independent and the dependent variable. This would be unfortunate and wasteful of time and energy if, in fact, a relationship did exist. On the other hand, if an empirical relationship is found, low interobserver reliability would most likely diminish the confidence that one has in the firmness of the relationship. If we cannot obtain high interobserver agreement in spite of strong efforts to do so, then little confidence should be placed in the phenomenon because it may be impossible to detect systematic behavior of any kind or to assess the effects of any treatment. Reliability checks are expensive and time-consuming, but essential. Evaluation of interobserver agreement should be undertaken before the experiment begins and periodically thereafter. If agreement is either low or variable, then additional work is needed on defining behaviors, establishing criteria, and training observers. When agreement is low, a discussion should take place immediately after the interobserver agreement check to develop new rules and techniques that might improve reliability.

Let's briefly summarize the steps for maintaining observer reliability.

1. Establish objective criteria (decision rules) for determining whether the behavior did or did not occur.

2. Before you begin collecting data, conduct pilot testing to determine whether interobserver agreement is high with the established criteria.

3. If agreement is low or variable, additional work is needed. Reevaluate definitions or criteria. Behavior may not be well defined. Consider a training program for observers. Videotape can be very helpful.

4. If agreement is high, begin your study, but make periodic checks on observer reliability.

5. Periodic retraining may be necessary to avoid observer drift—that is, drifting away from established criteria or definition. Continue to assess interobserver agreement periodically.

6. If possible, use observers "blind" to the purposes of the study to prevent bias. If this is not possible, attempt to use a "blind" second observer when assessing interobserver agreement.

Measuring the Reliability of Observational Data

As we have seen, the researcher commonly has one of three different recording procedures from which to select: frequency of occurrence of a target behavior, duration of the occurrence of that behavior, and the occurrence versus the nonoccurrence of a behavioral event within a time interval. We will now consider some of the methods that are available to assess the reliability of observational data. More specifically, we will look at measures that involve percentage agreement among observers and correlational procedures modeled on the classical psychometric approach to reliability.

Percentage Agreement Among Observers   Let's suppose we are observing self-mutilating behavior among autistic children, and that we agree upon its definition. Using the occurrence/nonoccurrence procedure, we obtain the data shown in Table 6.3. Note that two different observers have independently recorded the presence or absence of self-mutilating behavior over four different observational intervals and five different sessions.

There are several methods of calculating the **percentage agreement among observers** for these data. One that is direct and easily understood simply involves dividing the session total of the observer with the smaller value by the corresponding session total of the observer with the larger value. Multiplying the resulting proportion by 100 yields a percentage agreement. To illustrate, on Session 1 Observer A's total was 2 and B's total was 4. Dividing 2 by 4 and multiplying by 100 yields a percentage agreement of 50%. Similarly, the percentages for sessions 2, 3, 4, and 5 are, respectively, $3/4 \times 100 = 75\%$, $1/2 \times 100 = 50\%$, $0/1 \times 100 = 0\%$, $3/3 \times 100 = 100\%$. The main limitation of this measure is that it is highly dependent on the rate at which the behavior is occurring during a given session. If the rate is

Table 6.3   Occurrence or Nonoccurrence Data Involving Two Independent Observers, Four Observational Intervals, and Five Sessions

OBSERVATIONAL INTERVAL, OBSERVER A						OBSERVATIONAL INTERVAL, OBSERVER B					
Session	1	2	3	4	Total	Session	1	2	3	4	Total
1	0	1	1	0	2	1	1	1	1	1	4
2	1	1	1	1	4	2	1	1	0	1	3
3	0	1	0	1	2	3	0	0	0	1	1
4	0	0	0	0	0	4	1	0	0	0	1
5	1	1	0	1	3	5	0	1	1	1	3

Table 6.4	Frequency of Agreement by Two Observers				
		OBSERVER A		
	CATEGORY	Nonaggressive	Aggressive	
OBSERVER B	Nonaggressive	$f_O = 50$ $(f_C = 42)$	$f_O = 10$ $(f_C = 18)$	60
	Aggressive	$f_O = 20$ $(f_C = 28)$	$f_O = 20$ $(f_C = 12)$	40
		70	30	$N = 100$

NOTE: f_O = frequency observed; f_C = frequency expected by chance

either high or low, so that the target behavior either occurs or fails to occur during most or all observational intervals, the percentage agreement will be correspondingly high. Under these circumstances, it is also difficult to specify what constitutes chance levels of agreement.

A second percentage agreement statistic focuses on the percentage of session scores for which there is complete agreement between the two observers. Referring back to the total columns in Table 6.3, we see that the two observers have complete agreement only during session 5. Since there are five sessions, the percentage of agreement is $1/5 \times 100 = 20\%$. Because this percentage measure of reliability imposes a strict criterion of agreement (both totals must be identical) and does not utilize much of the data, it is not often used as a measure of interobserver reliability.

At times, your observations will attempt to classify a person into one category or another. For example, you may want to classify a child as aggressive or nonaggressive. Kappa is a statistic that will measure the proportion of agreement between observers and will correct for the level of chance agreement (Cohen, 1960). This is particularly important when one of the categories represents the "typical" behavior and occurs with a higher frequency.

Table 6.4 shows the frequency with which two observers agreed and disagreed across a total of 100 instances of behavior. Notice that in 50 instances both observer A and observer B agreed that the behavior was nonaggressive and that in 20 instances both agreed that the behavior was aggressive. The frequencies expected by chance are calculated by multiplying the frequency for the row times the frequency for the column and dividing by the total number of observations (N).

Kappa is calculated by using f_O and f_C on the diagonal where the categories match. Thus:

$$\kappa = \frac{f_O - f_C}{N - f_C} = \frac{(50+20)-(42+12)}{100-(42+12)} = \frac{70-54}{100-54} = \frac{16}{46} = 0.35$$

Notice that Kappa will equal a value of negative one (−1.0) when there is absolutely no agreement, will equal a value of zero (0) when agreement is at chance level, and will equal a value of one (1.0) when agreement is complete and perfect. The Kappa value that represents acceptable reliability of observations depends on several factors, but researchers generally seek Kappa values greater than 0.75. Therefore, the above example illustrates a situation in

| Table 6.5 | Three Degrees of Correlation Between the Session Totals of Two Observers |

A negative correlation should rarely be found; if obtained, a serious review of observational procedures and recording techniques would be warranted.

	OBSERVER		OBSERVER		OBSERVER	
Session	A	B	A	B	A	B
1	2	4	2	3	2	3
2	4	3	4	4	4	1
3	2	1	2	1	2	1
4	0	1	0	1	0	4
5	3	3	3	3	3	3
	$r = 0.58$		$r = 0.83$		$r = 0.68$	

which either the categories were not well defined or one (or both) of the observers was not doing a good job.

The Reliability Coefficient   The use of a measure of correlation—usually the Pearson product moment coefficient (r)—finds its origin in the psychometric tradition. The reliability of a test is expressed in terms of the size of the correlation coefficient. Although the Pearson r may vary from -1.00 to $+1.00$, it is rare that a negative **reliability coefficient** is found. For all practical purposes, we can assume that reliability coefficients vary between 0.00 and 1.00, with $r = 0.00$ meaning an absence of reliability and 1.00 meaning perfect reliability.

When using correlation to establish the reliability of observers, we regard the session total as a score. If two observers are in complete agreement, their totals for each observational session should be identical. Table 6.5 illustrates three different degrees of relationship between two observers in which N (the number of sessions) is 5. This is shown only for illustrative purposes, since N is not sufficiently large to establish the reliability with any given degree of confidence.

As we indicated, when observers are in complete agreement on their session totals, the correlation is 1.00. Generally, it is reasonable to assume that a high correlation means that both observers made the same or highly similar observations. On occasion, this may not be the case. It is possible to obtain a high or even a perfect correlation and still have observations that are not in agreement. This occurs because the correlation reflects only the relative position of paired observations and not the absolute values of these observations.

Imagine, for example, that two observers were simultaneously but independently rating a number of individuals on a scale of self-assertiveness. They obtain the results shown in Table 6.6.

Note that the ranks of the ratings are in perfect agreement. The individual judged as highest in self-assertiveness by Observer A was also rated highest by Observer B. However, the ratings of Observer B were systematically four units higher than those of Observer A. As noted in Chapter 5, it is important to realize that reliability estimates reflect the relative position (rank order) of individual scores. Interrater reliability may be very high in making

Table 6.6	Hypothetical Data Showing Independent Ratings by Two Observers of Five Participants on Self-Assertiveness			
	OBSERVER A		OBSERVER B	
Participant	Rating	Rank	Rating	Rank
1	18	3	22	3
2	16	4	20	4
3	20	2	24	2
4	24	1	28	1
5	14	5	18	5

observations, yet it is possible for one rater to be consistently higher or lower in the total number of observations that are made. For this reason, measures of central tendency should accompany reliability ratings. If this difference were to go uncorrected and each observer were subsequently assigned to different experimental conditions, this difference between observers would be confounded with the independent variable. It would not be possible to separate the confounded effects of the independent variable from those of the observer. To eliminate this possibility of confounding, each observer should be required to observe an equal number of times under each experimental condition. However, although the confounding would be corrected, the interobserver differences would add to the variability of the dependent measure. Consequently, the ability to detect differences among experimental conditions would be reduced. What this all means is that utmost care must be taken to assure interobserver reliability during all phases of the study.

The preceding example involved reliability of observations when the variable was quantitative in nature. The phi coefficient (Φ) is a correlation coefficient that can be used to measure the relationship when the variable is qualitative in nature—that is, on a nominal scale of measurement. You simply assign values of "0" to one category and values of "1" to the other category and then calculate the phi coefficient in the same manner that you would calculate a Pearson r. Notice that the sign (positive or negative) on the phi coefficient is not relevant because the assignment of 0s and 1s was arbitrary.

Thus, we see that observations are a common method of data collection in behavioral research but that special care is needed to ensure the quality of such observations. Depending on the specific nature of the observations, we can assess interobserver reliability in different ways. In most cases, values for reliability coefficients vary from 0.00 to 1.00, with a higher value indicating greater reliability. There is no set standard for an acceptable level of reliability between observers; what is acceptable will depend to some extent on the variable being observed. Generally speaking, researchers should seek coefficients of .85 and higher.

Recordings by Equipment

Although observational methods of data collection are useful and widespread, it is clear that there can be a degree of subjectivity in the process. It is also evident that some variables cannot be measured or are poorly measured via the human senses and that some form of equipment is needed. For example, most physiological measures (heart rate, blood pressure, sweat gland activity, brain electrical activity, hormone levels, chemical levels) require equipment.

Equipment often increases precision in data collection. However, it is important to check that all equipment is functioning properly and calibrated prior to data collection. If the data collection extends over some period of time, periodic checks of equipment accuracy are important.

● Public Records

A wealth of information regarding human behavior is available in the public domain. This information includes census data, crime statistics, voting patterns, and national survey results. Using such data, a researcher can describe human behavior and can ask questions regarding possible relationships among variables. This research strategy is often referred to as archival research because it relies on existing records. For example, is there a relationship between race and voting patterns? Public polling of people who had just voted in the 2000 national election showed that European Americans were more likely to vote Republican and African Americans were more likely to vote Democratic. As another example, a colleague of one of your authors has been investigating factors that relate to recidivism (repeat offending) in juvenile offenders. She received permission from the Department of Youth Services and the clinical psychologist who works with these juveniles to examine the criminal and psychological records of single offenders and multiple offenders. She is interested in whether juveniles diagnosed with psychological disorders are more likely to commit multiple offenses.

Although public records provide a wealth of information, they also have drawbacks. As a researcher, you did not collect the data. Therefore, you must investigate the methodology used to collect the data. Were sampling procedures involved? If so, were they adequate? Who collected the data? How did they collect the data? How have the data been stored? Can the accuracy of the data be trusted? These questions should be answered before you begin to explore and analyze data from public records.

● Survey Methods

Survey is a broad term that often includes interviews, questionnaires, and instruments or inventories. Let us make a few general comments regarding surveys in the broad sense. Several specific issues, such as the advantages and limitations of sampling techniques, will be detailed in the next chapter.

A survey is an attempt to estimate opinions, attitudes, and characteristics of a large number of individuals based on data collected from some of those individuals. The Kinsey reports in 1948 and 1953 provide well-known examples. Alfred C. Kinsey and his group interviewed more than 10,000 men and women regarding their sexual behavior and attitudes. Unfortunately, participants were not chosen randomly (each individual did not have an equal chance of being chosen). It is therefore debatable whether the findings can be generalized to the general population. Other researchers surveying sexual beliefs and practices have started with a sample of individuals representative of the population. However, only about 20% of those contacted were willing to share their beliefs and practices. Because of this low response rate, the resulting sample can hardly be regarded as representative of the population. Individuals who are willing to divulge intimate information are probably different in important ways from those who are not.

If survey results are to apply to a population, the sample chosen must be representative. When this principle is violated, serious problems can occur, and risk of error is high. For example, in the presidential election of 1936 between Alf Landon and Franklin Roosevelt, the *Literary Digest* conducted a poll concerning voting preferences. Based on the results of their poll, the *Literary Digest* predicted a Landon (Republican) victory. As you know, the outcome of the election was Roosevelt by a landslide. This survey is a classic case of the unrepresentative sample. The magazine polled only those whose names appeared on lists of telephone subscribers and automobile owners. Because 1936 was a depression year, only wealthier people had cars and telephones—hardly a representative group. Affluent people tend to favor more conservative politics. Thus, if only the wealthier citizens had been allowed to vote, the Republican candidate would have won by a landslide.

Surveys, under different guises, have been used to obtain information on political opinions, consumer preferences, health care needs, abortion, and many other questions. The four most familiar are the U.S. Census, the Gallup Poll, the Roper Poll, and the Harris Poll. It is also quite common for news agencies and other organizations to conduct both phone surveys and Internet surveys.

Questionnaires

The **questionnaire** is more than simply a list of questions or forms to be completed. When properly constructed, a questionnaire can be used as a scientific instrument to obtain data from large numbers of individuals. Construction of a useful questionnaire that minimizes interfering problems requires experience, skill, thoughtfulness, and time. A major advantage of the questionnaire is that data can be obtained on large numbers of participants quickly and relatively inexpensively. Further, the sample can be very large and geographically representative. Often, anonymity can be easily maintained; that is, identifying information is not associated with the data. When constructed properly, a questionnaire provides data that can be organized easily, tabulated, and analyzed. Because of these apparent advantages, the use of the questionnaire is a popular method.

There are two broad classes of questionnaires: descriptive and analytical. Descriptive questionnaires are usually restricted to factual information, often biographical, which is usually accessible by other means. Job application forms and U.S. Census questionnaires are typically of this type. Analytical questionnaires deal more with information related to attitudes or opinions.

The results of a questionnaire are about as useful as the care and thought that went into its preparation and dissemination. Just as in normal social intercourse, the way questions are formulated and posed may present problems. They may be ambiguous; they may suggest the answer that the researcher "wants"; they may contain loaded words. Ambiguity is relatively easy to eliminate. A pilot project, limited to a small number of respondents, will usually uncover sources of ambiguity of which the researcher was unaware. These may then be corrected. Table 6.7 illustrates several examples of ambiguous and leading survey questions and also suggests improved versions of the questions.

As much as we might wish it to be, completing questionnaires is not a neutral task, devoid of feelings and emotions. Often respondents are somewhat apprehensive about how they will appear in the researcher's eye. They want to look good and do well. Consequently, their responses may reflect their interpretations of the investigator's desires rather than their own beliefs, feelings, or opinions. This is referred to as demand characteristics. We will say more about this later. Obviously, questions should be stated in a neutral way and not in a

Table 6.7	Examples of Poor Survey Questions and Better Survey Questions
POOR SURVEY QUESTION	**BETTER SURVEY QUESTION**
How religious are you? (vague; not sure what is being asked)	How would you rate your level of spirituality? Not at all spiritual — 0, 1, Somewhat spiritual — 2, 3, Very spiritual — 4
What do you think about smoking on campus? (vague; too many possible answers)	Do you believe that all buildings on campus should be designated as smoke-free? Yes No
How important is spirituality in your life? Not at all — 1, 2, Somewhat — 3, 4, Very much so — 5 (leading; suggests that spirituality is important)	What role does spirituality play in your life? Not important — 1, 2, Somewhat important — 3, 4, Very important — 5
What policy would best deal with the annoying and unhealthy effects of smoking on campus? (a) smoking should be permitted anywhere (b) smoking only in designated areas of buildings (c) smoking only in outdoor areas (d) no smoking on campus (leading; suggests greater restrictions)	With regard to smoking on campus, which policy do you prefer? (a) smoking should be permitted anywhere (b) smoking only in designated areas of buildings (c) smoking only in outdoor areas (d) no smoking on campus

way that suggests a particular response. A fundamental requirement is that the question should be answerable. If respondents are given answers from which to choose, the options should be clear and independent. Also, different results can occur when open-ended or closed-ended questions are used. In some cases, the questionnaire is sensitive to position effects. Respondents are more likely to skip items placed toward the end of a questionnaire, and the answers are also slightly different when answered.

More attention has been given to response bias than to other sources of possible bias and contamination. As we noted earlier, results can be markedly affected by the sample on which they are based. The problem of sampling bias is compounded in mailed surveys because of the low return rates. The actual sample on which the data analyses are based is generally a subsample of the original sample. Low returns make it difficult to assess the representativeness of the final sample. It is safe to assume that it is biased and that those who participated in the survey are different in some way from those who did not. How important is this difference? It may be considerable, or it may be trivial. Because its importance cannot be assessed, any generalizations based on low returns must be restricted. For this reason, it is important to know the return rate on survey research. Unfortunately, some studies fail to provide this information. Other things being equal, the higher the return rate, the better the survey.

A number of factors affect return/response rates. Some are quite costly, so that economic factors must be balanced against the greater generality permitted by higher rates of return. Methods to increase return rate include follow-up contacts, general delivery and pickup, use of closed-ended rather than open-ended questions wherever possible, use of rewards for participation, and limiting the length of time needed to complete the survey.

Instruments and Inventories

Instruments and **inventories** are questionnaires that have stood the test of time. That is, they were designed to measure particular attributes and have been demonstrated to do so with validity and reliability. Examples include personality tests, aptitude tests, and achievement tests. Personality tests measure some state or trait of an individual. Examples include the Minnesota Multiphasic Personality Inventory (MMPI), Beck Depression Inventory (BDI), California Psychological Inventory (CPI), and the Sixteen Personality Factors Questionnaire (16PF). Aptitude tests measure some skill or ability. Examples include the Stanford–Binet Intelligence Scale, the Wechsler Adult Intelligence Scale (WAIS-III), the Wechsler Intelligence Scale for Children (WISC-III), and the Graduate Record Examination (GRE). Achievement tests measure competence in a particular area. Examples include the Stanford Achievement tests that students take as they progress through K–12 grades in school; state licensing exams for teachers, counselors, lawyers, physicians, and other professionals; and the Major Field Achievement Test that psychology majors at some universities take just prior to graduation.

If you consider a research project in which a questionnaire might be used, it would be wise to determine whether an instrument or inventory already exists to measure the variable of interest. Don't reinvent the wheel. If someone else has already invested the time and effort to develop a measure with known validity and reliability, use it. One of the characteristics of science is that we make information public and continue to build upon what others have done.

Interviews

The **interview** may be regarded either as an alternative to other survey methods or as a supplementary source of information. Although it is more costly in both time and money than the questionnaire, it is also more flexible. Additional information over and above initial plans can be readily obtained and ambiguity and misunderstanding eliminated immediately.

One of the greatest strengths of the interview—direct verbal communication—is also a source of weakness because variability is so common in social interactions. For an interview to be successful, rapport is generally required. It is most readily established when the interviewer is nonjudgmental, supportive, and understanding. However, these very characteristics lead to variability in social interaction among those interviewed. We could achieve sufficient control over social interactions so that the interviews are more homogeneous. However, this would inevitably lead to a sterile interview situation. This, in turn, would result in less rapport, which, we have noted, is important for a good interview.

Other problems beset the interview, especially when there is more than one interviewer. Different interviewers may vary in the way they ask questions or interpret responses, or in the way respondents react to them. Interviewer differences are common. How do we assess the comparability of different interviewers? If you reflect a moment, you'll realize that the situation is similar to using several raters in noninterview settings and determining the interrater reliability. In the present case, we are asking whether there is inter-interviewer reliability.

One way to achieve greater inter-interviewer reliability is to standardize the interview procedures. While this standardization increases the interview reliability, it decreases its flexibility. Because of these weaknesses, the interview might best be reserved as an exploratory method to generate ideas and hypotheses that can later be tested by the use of other methods.

Table 6.8 summarizes some general tips for the development of effective surveys.

Table 6.8	Tips for Effective Surveys
1. Avoid ambiguous questions.	
2. Avoid leading questions.	
3. Avoid lengthy surveys or those that require lengthy written responses.	
4. Consider how initial questions might influence answers to subsequent questions.	
5. Think carefully about your sampling technique to avoid a biased sample.	
6. Seek to achieve the highest response rate possible.	
7. Standardize administration procedures.	
8. Guarantee anonymity (or confidentiality at a minimum).	
9. Seek measures of reliability.	
10. Assess validity.	

● Laboratory Versus Field Research

Data can be collected either in the laboratory or in the field. **Laboratory research** takes place in an environment designed by the researcher, whereas **field research** takes place in an environment not designed by the researcher. Most of the experimental and nonexperimental designs that will be discussed in subsequent chapters can be carried out either in the laboratory or in the field. However, it is true that experimental designs are more likely to be implemented in the laboratory and nonexperimental designs are more likely to be implemented in the field.

As we will see, high levels of control characterize experimental designs. The experimenter controls the assignment of participants to conditions, manipulates the levels of the independent variable, and seeks to eliminate extraneous variables that may affect the dependent variable. These objectives are much easier to accomplish in a laboratory environment than in a natural setting. Thus, the researcher is often more confident in drawing strong cause–effect conclusions when the experiment is conducted in the laboratory.

Field research has its own advantages. Research conducted in a natural setting is more likely to involve natural behavior, and thus the findings are more likely to generalize to the "real world." If we are interested in generalizing or applying our experimental findings to practical problems or to social issues, then this external validity is essential. Further, if we are interested in understanding and predicting human or nonhuman behavior in situations other than those studied in the laboratory, then our research methods should be more representative of these situations. Some examples will clarify the distinction between laboratory and field research.

Social psychologists have used field research frequently and successfully; they also, of course, use laboratory research. An excellent film, *Bystander Intervention: When Will People Help?* depicts both types. Bystander intervention is one area in which both field and laboratory experiments have been conducted. In the typical field experiment on bystander intervention, a person suddenly collapses in full view of other pedestrians. The researchers are usually interested in the number of people who come to the aid of the distressed person and how long it takes for the person to receive help. A number of factors, such as age, race, gender, appearance of the individual, location in the city, and time of day, may be systematically varied in order to assess their effects on helping behavior. Observers stationed nearby can unobtrusively collect different kinds of data, such as the proportion who offer aid, the time it takes before aid is offered, who offers aid, and so forth. Follow-up questionnaires or interviews may be used to pinpoint more precisely the differences between those who offered aid and those who did not.

Another example of a field experiment is the "lost letter routine." The investigator writes letters addressed to himself or herself, complete with necessary postage. The letters are then dropped ("lost") at various locations. The dependent variable is the number of letters returned. The independent variable may be any number of different factors. For example, the address could be a political party, a religious group, a political candidate, a government agency, or a particular section of the city. Individuals finding a "lost letter" must decide what to do with it—return it, open it, ignore it, or discard it. Dependent variable measures noted in this and the previous paragraph are referred to as **unobtrusive measures** because individuals are unaware that they are being measured.

During the research design phase, you must consider whether data collection will occur in the laboratory or in the field. In most cases, the research question itself dictates the appropriate setting. The more important point is to be aware of the advantages and limitations of each setting. The laboratory affords a high level of control and leads to more powerful and confident conclusions regarding the relationships among the variables under study. The field affords a natural setting, permits research not possible in the laboratory, and leads to conclusions that are more likely to generalize to the real world.

CASE ANALYSIS

One of your authors, along with several undergraduate research assistants, is interested in the types of teaching techniques that professors use in the classroom. One specific question concerns the prevalence of lecture in the university classroom and whether male and female instructors use this teaching technique to different extents. Rather than rely on self-reports from professors, this study attempts to answer the question by using observational techniques.

Two student researchers randomly sample 20 male and 20 female professors to observe. They inform the professors of the purpose of their study and obtain consent to sit in on one class for each of the professors. The student observers coordinate their schedules and decide on the class to be observed for each professor. For each class, they find two seats near the back of the room and record, at 10-minute intervals, whether the professor is lecturing. If the class begins at 8:00 and ends at 9:15, the student observers record either "yes" or "no" at 8:10, 8:20, 8:30, 8:40, 8:50, 9:00, and 9:10. After observing all 40 professors, they total the number of times that male professors were lecturing and compare that to the number of times that female professors were lecturing.

Critical Thinking Questions

1. Were the two students participant observers or nonparticipant observers? Which technique do you believe would be best in this situation?

2. How did the observers schedule their observations (pick the class, day, time)? Can you think of a better way to do this?

3. Which specific technique was used to record the lecturing behavior? Do you believe that this was the best method to answer the original research question? How would you use the duration method instead?

4. What should the two students do to ensure that their observations are independent?

5. What statistic should they use to measure the reliability of their observations?

6. In what other ways could the design of this research be improved?

GENERAL SUMMARY

Behavioral research often uses dependent variables that rely on identification by the researchers. Several issues must be considered during the design phase of the research. Will the researcher engage in participant or nonparticipant observation? Participant observation occurs when the observer is an integral part of the environment to be observed. This allows the observer to be closer to the behaviors being observed, but may inadvertently affect those behaviors. If this is a serious risk, the researcher should consider nonparticipant observation, remaining "outside" the environment to be observed. After deciding on the type of observation technique, the researcher must also decide on the schedule for observations, the definition of the behavior to be observed, and the aspect of the behavior to be observed. Sometimes it is appropriate to use a frequency method, in which the observer records the number of times that a defined behavior occurs. Sometimes it is appropriate to use a duration method, in which the observer records how long a defined behavior lasts. At other times it is appropriate to use an interval method, in which the observer determines whether or not a particular behavior occurs at specified intervals of time.

Observers rely on sensory systems and perceptual processing to record observations. Psychological research shows that a multitude of factors influence our sensation and perception. This argues for the value of multiple observers. A high measure of reliability across multiple observers enhances the objective nature of our research. A low measure of reliability indicates a degree of idiosyncrasy in the observations and reduces our confidence in the objectivity of our research.

In addition to observations made by researchers, other methods of data collection include recordings by equipment, public records, and survey methods, including questionnaires, instruments/inventories, and interviews. Each method has advantages and disadvantages. Finally, all methods of data collection can occur either in a laboratory or in a field setting. A laboratory affords more control over the environment, and the field affords a more natural setting. Whichever method of data collection is used in whichever setting, the researcher must decide which members of the population will be observed. The next chapter discusses these sampling techniques.

DETAILED SUMMARY

1. Observational procedures represent a methodology that is critical to the field of behavioral science. Observations can be appropriate in natural, applied, and laboratory settings.

2. Because observations are based on our perceptions, the same event occurring in the environment will be perceived differently by different people.

3. It is essential that observations be accurate, objective, and reliable.

4. Participant observers conduct their observations "from the inside"; that is, the researcher is an integral part of the environment being observed. Nonparticipant observers conduct their observations "from the outside"; the researcher does not interact with those being observed.

5. When making observations, investigators must make decisions regarding frequency, duration, and time of day for scheduling observations. These decisions depend on the purposes of the observations.

6. It is important to define the dependent variable (behavior) in terms of specific observable responses and to specify clearly the criteria for judging when the behavior has occurred. This is an important step if we are to ensure that different observers will make similar observations.

7. With the frequency method of observation, the observer simply counts the number of occurrences of the behavior of interest in a given interval of time. With the duration method, the observer records the beginning and the end of a particular behavior. With the interval method, the observation period is broken into equal intervals, the size of which varies with the particular observations of interest. Behavior is recorded as occurring or not occurring in each interval.

8. It is important to assess the reliability of observations by having another observer independently record his or her observations for the same time periods. Depending on the nature of the data, reliability can be measured by percent agreement, a Kappa statistic, a Pearson r statistic, or a phi coefficient.

9. In addition to human observers, we can use equipment, public records, surveys, questionnaires, instruments/inventories, and interviews to collect data. Each method has advantages and disadvantages that should be carefully considered.

10. Data can be collected either in the laboratory or in the field. Laboratory research takes place in an environment designed by the researcher, whereas field research takes place in an environment not designed by the researcher. Laboratory research has the advantage of control, and field research has the advantage of natural, real-world behavior.

KEY TERMS

duration method of observation *(p. 83)*
field research *(p. 95)*
frequency method of observation *(p. 82)*
independent observation *(p. 86)*
instrument *(p. 94)*
interobserver agreement *(p. 86)*
interval method of observation *(p. 83)*
interview *(p. 94)*
inventory *(p. 94)*

laboratory research *(p. 95)*
nonparticipant observation *(p. 80)*
observer drift *(p. 81)*
participant observation *(p. 80)*
percentage agreement among observers *(p. 87)*
questionnaire *(p. 92)*
reliability coefficient *(p. 89)*
survey *(p. 91)*
unobtrusive measures *(p. 96)*

REVIEW QUESTIONS/EXERCISES

Several years ago, a group of students at the University of Central Arkansas conducted a study in which they observed the rate at which cars failed to stop at a campus stop sign and recorded whether the car had a student parking decal or a faculty/staff parking decal. Use the above study to answer questions 1–7.

1. Which method of observation would be best (participant or nonparticipant, aware or unaware)? Justify your answer.

2. How would you schedule observations?

3. Define the categories of behavior that you would observe.

4. Describe how you would optimize and measure the reliability of observations, including the use of independent observers and calculation of interobserver agreement.

5. Describe how you could use equipment for observations rather than human observers. What are the advantages and disadvantages?

6. Describe how you might use public records to answer the same research question. What might be some limitations of this approach?

7. Describe how you might use a survey method to answer the same research question. What might be some limitations of this approach?

LABORATORY EXERCISES

 Some of you taking this course may be using as an accompanying text *Research Methods Laboratory Manual for Psychology* by William Langston (2005). At times throughout the remainder of our textbook, we will suggest particular laboratory exercises from Langston's manual. This is the first instance.

• Chapter 1 in Langston's manual discusses observations of territoriality in parking lots and suggests several related projects. Consider conducting one of these yourself.

• Chapter 2 in Langston's manual discusses the use of survey methods to investigate grade inflation in the college classroom and suggests several related projects. Consider conducting one of these.

 ## WEB RESOURCES TO INCREASE LEARNING

The chapter outline, chapter summaries, key terms and definitions, additional chapter questions/exercises, interactive workshops, and links to relevant Web sites are available at the course Web site (**http://psychology. wadsworth.com/lammers_badia1e**). Explore the interactive workshops "Surveys" and "Designing a Survey."

CHAPTER 7

SAMPLING TECHNIQUES

● Introduction to Sampling

The way in which we select a sample of individuals to be research participants is critical. How we select participants (random sampling) will determine the population to which we may generalize our research findings. The procedure that we use for assigning participants to different treatment conditions (random assignment) will determine whether bias exists in our treatment groups (Are the groups equal on all known and unknown factors?). We address random sampling in this chapter; we will address random assignment later in the book.

If we do a poor job at the sampling stage of the research process, the integrity of the entire project is at risk. If we are interested in the effect of TV violence on children, which children are we going to observe? Where do they come from? How many? How will they be selected? These are important questions. Each of the sampling techniques described in this chapter has advantages and disadvantages.

● Distinguishing Between a Sample and a Population

Before describing sampling procedures, we need to define a few key terms. The term **population** means *all* members that meet a set of specifications or a specified criterion. For example, the population of the United States is defined as all people residing in the United States. The population of New Orleans means all people living within the city's limits or boundary. A population of inanimate objects can also exist, such as all automobiles manufactured in Michigan in the year 2003. A single member of any given population is referred to as an **element**. When only some elements are selected from a population, we refer to that as a **sample**; when all elements are included, we call it a **census**. Let's look at a few examples that will clarify these terms.

Two research psychologists were concerned about the different kinds of training that graduate students in clinical psychology were receiving. They knew that different programs emphasized different things, but they did not know which clinical orientations were most popular. Therefore, they prepared a list of *all* doctoral programs in clinical psychology (in the United States) and sent each of them a questionnaire regarding aspects of their program. The response to the survey was excellent; nearly 95% of the directors of these programs returned the completed questionnaire. The researchers then began analyzing their data and also classifying schools into different clinical orientations: psychoanalytic, behavioristic, humanistic, Rogerian, and so on. When the task was complete, they reported the percentage of schools having these different orientations and described the orientations that were most popular, which were next, and so on. They also described other aspects of their data. The study was written up and submitted for publication to one of the professional journals dealing with matters of clinical psychology. The editor of the journal read the report and then returned it with a letter rejecting the manuscript for publication. In part, the letter noted that the manuscript was not publishable at this time because the proper statistical analyses had not been performed. The editor wanted to know whether the differences in orientation found among the different schools were significant or if they were due to chance.

The researchers were unhappy, and rightly so. They wrote back to the editor, pointing out that their findings were not estimates based on a sample. They had surveyed *all* training programs (that is, the population). In other words, they had obtained a census rather than a sample. Therefore, their data were exhaustive; they included all programs and described what existed in the real world. The editor would be correct only if they had sampled some schools and then wanted to generalize to all schools. The researchers were not asking whether a sample represented the population; they were dealing with the population.

A comparable example would be to count *all students* (the population) enrolled in a particular university and then report the number of male and female students. If we found that 60% of the students were female, and 40% male, it would be improper and irrelevant to ask whether this difference in percentage is significantly different from chance. The fact is that the percentages that exist in the school population are parameters. They are not estimates derived from a sample. Had we taken a small sample of students and found this 60/40 split, it would then be appropriate to ask whether differences this large could have occurred by chance alone.

Data derived from a sample are treated *statistically*. Using sample data, we calculate various statistics, such as the mean and standard deviation. These sample statistics summarize (describe) aspects of the sample data. These data, when treated with other statistical procedures, allow us to make certain inferences. From the sample statistics, we make corresponding estimates of the population. Thus, from the sample mean, we estimate the population mean; from the sample standard deviation, we estimate the population standard deviation.

The above examples illustrate a problem that can occur when the terms *population* and *sample* are confused. The accuracy of our estimates depends on the extent to which the sample is representative of the population to which we wish to generalize.

● Simple Random Sampling

Researchers use two major sampling techniques: probability sampling and nonprobability sampling. With **probability sampling,** a researcher can specify the probability of an element's (participant's) being included in the sample. With **nonprobability sampling,** there is no way of estimating the probability of an element's being included in a sample. If the researcher's interest is in generalizing the findings derived from the sample to the general population, then probability sampling is far more useful and precise. Unfortunately, it is also much more difficult and expensive than nonprobability sampling.

Probability sampling is also referred to as **random sampling** or representative sampling. The word *random* describes the procedure used to select elements (participants, cars, test items) from a population. When random sampling is used, each element in the population has an equal chance of being selected (simple random sampling) or a known probability of being selected (stratified random sampling). The sample is referred to as *representative* because the characteristics of a properly drawn sample represent the parent population in all ways.

One caution before we begin our description of simple random sampling: Random *sampling* is different from random *assignment.* Random assignment describes the process of placing participants into different experimental groups. We will discuss random assignment later in the book.

Step 1. Defining the Population

Before a sample is taken, we must first define the population to which we want to generalize our results. The population of interest may differ for each study we undertake. It could be the population of professional football players in the United States or the registered voters in Bowling Green, Ohio. It could also be all college students at a given university, or all sophomores at that institution. It could be female students, or introductory psychology students, or 10-year-old children in a particular school, or members of the local senior citizens center. The point should be clear; the sample should be drawn from the population to which you want to generalize—the population in which you are interested.

It is unfortunate that many researchers fail to make explicit their population of interest. Many investigators use only college students in their samples, yet their interest is in the adult population of the United States. To a large extent, the generalizability of sample data depends on what is being studied and the inferences that are being made. For example, imagine a study that sampled college juniors at a specific university. Findings showed that a specific chemical compound produced pupil dilation. We would not have serious misgivings about generalizing this finding to all college students, even tentatively to all adults, or perhaps even to some nonhuman organisms. The reason for this is that physiological systems are quite similar from one person to another, and often from one species to another. However, if we find that controlled exposure to unfamiliar political philosophies led to radicalization of the experimental participants, we would be far more reluctant to extend this conclusion to the general population.

Step 2. Constructing a List

Before a sample can be chosen randomly, it is necessary to have a complete list of the population from which to select. In some cases, the logistics and expense of constructing a list of the entire population is simply too great, and an alternative procedure is forced upon the investigator. We could avoid this problem by restricting our population of interest—by defining it narrowly. However, doing so might increase the difficulty of finding or constructing a list from which to make our random selection. For example, you would have no difficulty identifying female students at any given university and then constructing a list of their names from which to draw a random sample. It would be more difficult to identify female students coming from a three-child family, and even more difficult if you narrowed your interest to firstborn females in a three-child family. Moreover, defining a population narrowly also means generalizing results narrowly.

Caution must be exercised in compiling a list or in using one already constructed. The population list from which you intend to sample must be both recent and exhaustive. If not, problems can occur. By an **exhaustive list,** we mean that *all* members of the population must appear on the list. Voter registration lists, telephone directories, homeowner lists, and school directories are sometimes used, but these lists may have limitations. They must be up to date and complete if the samples chosen from them are to be truly representative of the population. In addition, such lists may provide very biased samples for some research questions we ask. For example, a list of homeowners would not be representative of all individuals in a given geographical region because it would exclude transients and renters. On the other hand, a ready-made list is often of better quality and less expensive to obtain than a newly constructed list would be.

Some lists are available from a variety of different sources. Professional organizations, such as the American Psychological Association, the American Medical Association, and the American Dental Association, have directory listings with mailing addresses of members. Keep in mind that these lists do not represent all psychologists, physicians, or dentists. Many individuals do not become members of their professional organizations. Therefore, a generalization would have to be limited to those professionals listed in the directory. In universities and colleges, complete lists of students can be obtained from the registrar.

Let's look at a classic example of poor sampling in the hours prior to a presidential election. Information derived from sampling procedures is often used to predict election outcomes. Individuals in the sample are asked their candidate preferences before the election, and projections are then made regarding the likely winner. More often than not, the polls predict the outcome with considerable accuracy. However, there are notable exceptions, such as the 1936 *Literary Digest* magazine poll that predicted "Landon by a Landslide" over Roosevelt, and predictions in the U.S. presidential election of 1948 that Dewey would defeat Truman.

We have discussed the systematic error of the *Literary Digest* poll. Different reasons resulted in the wrong prediction in the 1948 presidential election between Dewey and Truman. Polls taken in 1948 revealed a large undecided vote. Based partly on this and early returns on the night of the election, the editors of the *Chicago Tribune* printed and distributed their newspaper before the election results were all in. The headline in bold letters indicated that Dewey defeated Truman. Unfortunately for them, they were wrong. Truman won, and the newspaper became a collector's item.

One analysis of why the polls predicted the wrong outcome emphasized the consolidation of opinion for many undecided voters. It was this undecided group that proved the prediction wrong. Pollsters did not anticipate that those who were undecided would vote in large numbers for Truman. Other factors generally operate to reduce the accuracy of political polls. One is that individuals do not always vote the way they say they are going to. Others may intend to do so but change their mind in the voting booth. Also, the proportion of potential voters who actually cast ballots differs depending upon the political party and often upon the candidates who are running. Some political analysts believe (along with politicians) that even the position of the candidate's name on the ballot can affect the outcome (the debate regarding butterfly ballots in Florida during the 2000 presidential election comes to mind).

We will describe the mechanics of random sampling shortly, but we want to note again that in some cases random sampling procedures simply are not possible. This is the case for very large populations. Because random sampling requires a listing of all members of a population, the larger the population the more difficult it becomes.

Step 3. Drawing the Sample

After a list of population members has been constructed, various random sampling options are available. Some common ones include tossing dice, flipping coins, spinning wheels, drawing names out of a rotating drum, using a table of random numbers, and using computer programs. Except for the last two methods, most of the techniques are slow and cumbersome. Tables of random numbers are easy to use, accessible, and truly random. Table A.1 in Appendix A is a table of random numbers.

Let's look at the procedures for using the table. The first step is to assign a number to each individual on the list. If there were 1,000 people in the population, you would number them 0 to 999 and then enter the table of random numbers. Let us assume your sample size will be 100. Starting anywhere in the table, move in any direction you choose, preferably up and down. Since there are 1,000 people on your list (0 through 999) you must give each an equal chance of being selected. To do this, you use three columns of digits from the tables. If the first three-digit number in the table is 218, participant number 218 on the population list is chosen for the sample. If the next three-digit number is 007, the participant assigned number 007 (or 7) is selected. Continue until you have selected all 100 participants for the sample. If the same number comes up more than once, it is simply discarded.

In the preceding fictional population list, the first digit (9) in the total population of 1,000 (0–999) was large. Sometimes the first digit in the population total is small, as with a list of 200 or 2,000. When this happens, many of the random numbers encountered in the table will not be usable and therefore must be passed up. This is very common and does not constitute a sampling problem. Also, tables of random numbers come in different column groupings. Some come in columns of two digits, some three, some four, and so on. These differences have no bearing on randomness. Finally, it is imperative that you not violate the random selection procedure. Once the list has been compiled and the process of selection has begun, the table of random numbers dictates who will be selected. The experimenter should not alter this procedure.

A more recent method of random sampling uses the special functions of computer software. Many population lists are now available as software databases (such as Excel, Quattro Pro, Lotus123) or can be imported to such a database. Many of these database programs have a function for generating a series of random numbers and a function for selecting a random sample from a range of entries in the database. After you learn the particular menu selections to perform these tasks, this method of random sampling is often the simplest.

Step 4. Contacting Members of the Sample

Researchers using random sampling procedures must be prepared to encounter difficulties at several points. As we noted, the starting point is an accurate statement that identifies the population to which we want to generalize. Then we must obtain a listing of the population, accurate and up-to-date, from which to draw our sample. Further, we must decide on the random selection procedure that we wish to use. Finally, we must contact each of those selected for our sample and obtain the information needed. Failing to contact all individuals in the sample can be a problem, and the representativeness of the sample can be lost at this point.

To illustrate what we mean, assume that we are interested in the attitudes of college students at your university. We have a comprehensive list of students and randomly select 100 of them for our sample. We send a survey to the 100 students, but only 80 students return it. We are faced with a dilemma. Is the sample of 80 students who participated representative? Because 20% of our sample was not located, does our sample underrepresent some views? Does it overrepresent other views? In short, can we generalize from our sample to the college population? Ideally, all individuals in a sample should be contacted. As the number contacted decreases, the risk of bias and not being representative increases.

Thus, in our illustration, to generalize to the college population would be to invite risk. Yet we do have data on 80% of our sample. Is it of any value? Other than simply dropping the project or starting a new one, we can consider an alternative that other researchers have used. In preparing our report, we would first clearly acknowledge that not all members of the sample participated and therefore the sample may not be random—that is, representative of the population. Then we would make available to the reader or listener of our report the number of participants initially selected and the final number contacted, the number of participants cooperating, and the number not cooperating. We would attempt to assess the reason or reasons participants could not be contacted and whether differences existed between those for whom there were data and those for whom there were no data. If no obvious differences were found, we could feel a little better about the sample's being representative. However, if any pattern of differences emerged, such as sex, education, or religious beliefs, a judgment would have to be made regarding how seriously the differences could have affected the representativeness of the sample.

Differences on any characteristic between those who participated and those who did not should not automatically suggest that the information they might give would also differ. Individuals can share many common values and beliefs, even though they may differ on characteristics such as sex or education. In situations requiring judgments, such as the one described, the important thing is for the researcher to describe the strengths and weaknesses of the study (especially telling the reader that only 80 of the 100 surveys were returned), along with what might be expected as a result of them. Alert the reader or listener to be cautious in interpreting the data, and provide them with the information necessary to make an informed judgment.

The problem just described may be especially troublesome when surveys or questionnaires deal with matters of a personal nature. Individuals are usually reluctant to provide information on personal matters, such as sexual practices, religious beliefs, or political philosophy. The more personal the question, the fewer the number of people who will respond. With surveys or questionnaires of this nature, a large number of individuals may refuse to cooperate or refuse to provide certain information. Some of these surveys have had return rates as low as 20%. If you are wondering what value publishing such data has when derived from such a low return rate, you are in agreement with us. We, too, wonder why such data are published. Even if we knew the population from which the sample was drawn and if the sample was randomly selected, a return rate as low as 20% is virtually useless in terms of generalizing findings from the sample to the population. Those individuals responding to a survey (20% of the sample) could be radically different from the majority of individuals not responding (80% of the sample).

Let's apply these four steps of random sampling to our TV violence study. Our first step is to define the population. We might begin by considering the population as all children in the United States that are 5–15 years old. Our next step will be to obtain an exhaustive list of these children. Using U. S. Census data would be one approach, although the task would be challenging and the Census does miss many people. The third step is to select a random sample. As noted earlier in the chapter, the simplest technique would be to use a database of the population and instruct the database software to randomly select children from the population. The number to be selected is determined by the researcher and is typically based on the largest number that can be sampled given the logistical resources of the researcher. Of course, the larger the sample, the more accurately it will represent the population. In fact, formulas can be used to determine sample size based on the size of the population, the amount of variability in the population, the estimated size of the effect, and the amount of sampling error that the researcher decides is acceptable (refer to statistics books for specifics). After the sample is selected from the population, the final step is to contact the parents of these children to obtain consent to participate. You will need to make phone calls and send letters. Again, this will be a challenge; you expect that you will be unable to contact a certain percentage, and that a certain percentage will decline to participate. All this effort, and we have not even begun to talk about collecting data from these children.

From this example, it is clear that random sampling can require an incredible amount of financial resources. As noted earlier in the chapter, we have two options. We can define the population more narrowly (perhaps the 5- to 15-year-olds in a particular school district) and conduct random sampling from this population, or we can turn to a sampling technique other than probability sampling. Before we discuss these nonprobability sampling techniques, let's look at one other form of probability sampling.

● Stratified Random Sampling

This procedure known as **stratified random sampling** is also a form of probability sampling. To stratify means to classify or to separate people into groups according to some characteristics, such as position, rank, income, education, sex, or ethnic background. These separate groupings are referred to as *subsets* or *subgroups*. For a stratified random sample, the population is divided into groups or strata. A random sample is selected from each stratum based upon the percentage that each subgroup represents in the population. Stratified random samples are generally more accurate in representing the population than are simple random samples. They also require more effort, and there is a practical limit to the number of strata used. Because participants are to be chosen randomly from each stratum, a complete list of the population within each stratum must be constructed. Stratified sampling is generally used in two different ways. In one, primary interest is in the representativeness of the sample for purposes of commenting on the population. In the other, the focus of interest is comparison between and among the strata.

Let's look first at an example in which the population is of primary interest. Suppose we are interested in the attitudes and opinions of university faculty in a certain state toward faculty unionization. Historically, this issue has been a very controversial one evoking strong emotions on both sides. Assume that there are eight universities in the state, each with a different faculty size (faculty size = 500 + 800 + 900 + 1,000 + 1,400 + 1,600 + 1,800 + 2,000 = 10,000). We could simply take a simple random sample of all 10,000 faculty and send those in the sample a carefully constructed attitude survey concerning unionization. After considering this strategy, we decide against it. Our thought is that universities of different size may have marked differences in their attitudes, and we want to be sure that each university will be represented in the sample in proportion to its representation in the total university population. We know that, on occasion, a simple random sample will not do this. For example, if unionization is a particularly "hot" issue on one campus, we may obtain a disproportionate number of replies from that faculty. Therefore, we would construct a list of the entire faculty for each university and then sample randomly within each university in proportion to its representation in the total faculty of 10,000. For example, the university with 500 faculty members would represent 5% of our sample; assuming a total sample size of 1,000, we would randomly select 50 faculty from this university. The university with 2,000 faculty would represent 20% of our sample; thus, 200 of its faculty would be randomly selected. We would continue until our sample was complete. It would be possible but more costly and time consuming to include other strata of interest—for example, full, associate, and assistant professors. In each case, the faculty in each stratum would be randomly selected.

As previously noted, stratified samples are sometimes used to optimize group comparisons. In this case, we are not concerned about representing the total population. Instead, our focus is on comparisons involving two or more strata. If the groups involved in our comparisons are equally represented in the population, a single random sample could be used. When this is not the case, a different procedure is necessary. For example, if we were interested in making comparisons between whites and blacks, a simple random sample of 100 people might include about 85 to 90 whites and only 10 to 15 blacks. This is hardly a satisfactory sample for making comparisons. With a stratified random sample, we could randomly choose 50 whites and 50 blacks and thus optimize our comparison. Whenever strata rather than the population are our primary interest, we can sample in different proportions from each stratum.

Although random sampling is optimal from a methodological point of view, it is not always possible from a practical point of view. Let's look at the advantages and disadvantages of several other sampling techniques.

● Convenience Sampling

Convenience sampling is used because it is quick, inexpensive, and convenient. Convenience samples are useful for certain purposes, and they require very little planning. Researchers simply use participants who are available at the moment. The procedure is casual and easy, relative to random sampling. Contrast using any available participants with random sampling, where you must (1) have a well-defined population, (2) construct a list of members of the population if one is not available, (3) sample randomly from the list, and (4) contact and use as many individuals from the list as possible. Convenience sampling requires far less effort. However, such convenience comes with potential problems, which we will describe. Convenience samples are nonprobability samples. Therefore, it is not possible to specify the probability of any population element's being selected for the sample. Indeed, it is not possible to specify the population from which the sample was drawn.

A number of examples of convenience sampling can be given. In shopping malls or airports, individuals are selected as they pass a certain location and interviewed concerning issues, candidates, or other matters. Phone surveys may be based on anyone answering the phone between the hours of 9 A.M. and 5 P.M. Politicians use convenience sampling to determine the attitudes of those they represent when they report on the number of letters voluntarily sent to them by their constituents. Statements such as the following are quite common: "My mail is running about 4 to 1 in favor of House Bill 865A. I guess I know how my constituents feel about the issue." Unfortunately, many of these samples are virtually without merit. We do not know what population (whom) they represent.

These and other examples can be used to illustrate the point. Observations at airports may overrepresent high-income groups, whereas observations taken at bus terminals may overrepresent low-income groups. Surveys taken at a rock concert would likely be different from those taken at a symphony concert. In the case of political attitudes, we do know that many special interest groups make it a matter of policy to write letters to their political representatives. A thousand people vitally concerned about an issue may write more letters than a million people who are indifferent. Polls taken on the Internet have become more popular and suffer from the same drawbacks. The point we are making is this: Because the population from which the sample came is unknown, it is unclear to whom the data can be generalized. We can generalize to known populations, but only with some risk. We will have more to say about this below.

The examples used here are extreme and the problems obvious, but there are instances where these problems are not as serious or as apparent. In these instances, some researchers believe that convenience sampling is a good alternative to random sampling.

As noted earlier, most laboratory research in psychology, human and nonhuman, uses a convenience sampling procedure. Some universities require that students taking the introductory psychology course serve as participants in research projects of their choosing. When participants are required to participate in research and are allowed to choose certain experiments over others, then for any given experiment, it is simply impossible to specify the population to which the sample data can be generalized. In other words, to what individuals, other than those of the sample, are the data relevant? We have here a sample in search of a population.

Requiring students to participate in research serves several purposes. It assures that each student has an opportunity to learn firsthand about scientific research. In this regard, an attempt is made to make participation in research a worthwhile educational experience. It also assures that participants are generally available for research, thus serving the purposes of the researcher and that of psychology as a science. The system requiring students to participate in research of their choosing operates in the following manner: Research projects to be undertaken are listed on a bulletin board (or a Web site), with a brief description of the project and a sign-up sheet indicating the time, place, and experimenter. If our earlier description was clear, you will recognize this as a convenience sampling procedure. Although the students are required to participate in research, they choose the particular project in which to participate. If students are available at a given time, and the particular experiment appeals to them, they simply sign their name on the sign-up sheet.

Frequently, the description on the sign-up sheet is neutral, but sometimes it is not. The titles alone—for example, Reaction Time to Electrical Stimulation, Problem Solving and Cognitive Skills, or Personality Assessment—are often threatening to some individuals. Obviously, these are not neutral topics, and you can anticipate what may occur. Participants concerned about the words "electrical stimulation" will avoid that particular experiment. Those concerned about their problem-solving ability may think they are to be evaluated and thus avoid that particular experiment. And so it goes. Although all students may participate in research, certain experiments may attract students with certain characteristics. In principle, students with different characteristics represent different populations. Even experiments with titles and descriptions that appear neutral may attract certain kinds of participants over other kinds. We will restate the point we stated earlier: Students participating in these experiments may be thought of as a sample of students from a population of students with certain characteristics, but a population that we cannot identify. Again, we ask: "To what individuals, other than those in the sample, are the data relevant or generalizable?" More concretely, conclusions drawn from the data of students who signed up for a study using electrical stimulation could be very different than if the data had come from students who avoided the experiment. It would be improper to generalize the findings to all students.

Some researchers using convenience samples are not concerned about the population to which they can properly generalize because their interest is in assessing the relationship between the independent and dependent variables. Their concern is focused on internal validity (minimizing confounding) rather than on external validity (generalizing their findings). Others, however, interested in generalizing from the sample to the population represented by it, argue that there is no good reason for assuming that students making up convenience samples are different from the general population of college students. Therefore, they would be willing to generalize their findings to all college students.

A similar argument is made by researchers using convenience samples of nonhuman participants, such as rats, cats, and dogs. In this case, sample findings are generalized to all rats, cats, or dogs of a given strain. The argument that the sample results are generalizable to all college students or to all animals of a given species and strain may be correct, but the argument is not based on firm theoretical grounds, nor can it seek support from statistical sampling theory. The argument is based more on faith and intuition than on objective argument derived from sampling theory. To what populations can convenience samples be generalized? The population to which it is permissible to generalize is that from which the sample was drawn. Strictly speaking, the population from which the sample was drawn is unknown. Because the sample was not drawn randomly from a list of some well-defined population, the population to which the sample findings can be generalized cannot be identified. A real dilemma exists. We have a sample in search of a population. We want to generalize our results beyond the sample, but to whom? This dilemma is inevitable when convenience sampling is used. Under these circumstances, statements concerning generality should be cautious, conservative, and appropriately qualified.

Had a listing of all introductory psychology students at a given university been available, and an adequate number of participants selected *randomly* from the list for any given experiment, we would not face the dilemma of generalizing our results. If we randomly drew names from this list, our sample would represent the population of introductory psychology students at the university. However, generalizing from our sample to introductory students at other universities would entail some risk. Our sample may not be representative of the population of introductory psychology students at other universities.

Quota Sampling

In many large-scale applications of sampling procedures, it is not always possible or desirable to list all members of the population and randomly select elements from that list. The reasons for using any alternative procedures include cost, timeliness, and convenience. One alternative procedure is **quota sampling.**

This technique is often used by market researchers and those taking political polls. Usually, when this technique is used, the population of interest is large and there are no ready-made lists of names available from which to sample randomly. The Gallup Poll is one of the best-known and well-conducted polls to use quota sampling. This poll frequently reports on major public issues and on presidential elections. The results of the poll are syndicated for a fee that supports it. In this quota sampling procedure, localities are selected and interviewers are assigned a starting point, a specified direction, and a goal of trying to meet quotas for subsets (ethnic origins, political affiliations, and so on) selected from the population. Although some notable exceptions have occurred, predictions of national elections over the past few years have been relatively accurate—certainly, much more so than guesswork.

With the quota sampling procedure, we first decide which subgroups of the population interest us. This, in turn, is dictated by the nature of the problem being investigated (the question being asked). For issues of national interest (such as abortion, drug use, or political preference), frequently used subsets are age, race, sex, socioeconomic level, and religion. The intent is to select a sample whose frequency distribution of characteristics reflects that of the population of interest. Obviously, it is necessary to know the percentage of individuals making up each subset of the population if we are to match these percentages in the sample. For example, if you were interested in ethnic groups such as Italians, Germans, Russians, and so on, and knew their population percentages, you would select your sample so as to obtain these percentages.

Within each subset, participants are *not* chosen randomly. This is simply because there are usually no ready-made lists from which the researcher can select randomly. Often individuals are selected in the sample on the basis of availability. For this reason, quota sampling is less expensive. It would not be so if lists of the population of interest had to be constructed. However, if exhaustive ready-made lists were conveniently available for the population of interest, then choosing participants randomly would be possible and preferable. In the absence of such lists, it is much more convenient to select quotas by knocking on doors, telephoning numbers, or sending mailings until the sample percentages for subsets match those of the population. Obviously, even though the quotas may be achieved and the sample may match the population percentages in terms of subsets, the sample may still not represent (reflect) the population to which we wish to generalize.

Often interviewers, for sampling purposes, concentrate on areas where large numbers of people are likely to be. This could bias the findings. As we noted earlier, samples taken in airports may overrepresent high-income groups, whereas those at bus or rail depots may overrepresent low-income groups. Samples at either place may underrepresent those who seldom travel. Also, people who are home during the day, and are therefore available for house-to-house interviews or telephone calls, may be quite different in important ways from those who are not home. In this respect, quota sampling and convenience sampling are similar. In spite of these difficulties, the quota system is widely used and will unquestionably continue to be so for economic and logistic reasons.

We have just reviewed four sampling techniques: simple random sampling, stratified random sampling, convenience sampling, and quota sampling. Table 7.1 presents one more example of each technique as it relates to our TV violence study, noting the advantages and

Table 7.1	Examples, Advantages, and Limitations of the Four Sampling Techniques		
SAMPLING TECHNIQUE	EXAMPLE	ADVANTAGES	LIMITATIONS
Simple random sampling	The names of all 1,000 children are placed into a computer database. The computer is then instructed to randomly select 100 names. These children and their parents are then contacted.	Representative of the population	May be difficult to obtain the list May be more expensive
Stratified random sampling	The names of all 1,000 children are placed into a computer database and organized by grade (sixth, seventh, eighth). The computer is then instructed to randomly select 35 names from each of the three grades. These children and their parents are then contacted.	Representative of the population	May be difficult to obtain the list May be more expensive
Convenience sampling	The researcher knows one of the middle-school teachers, and the teacher volunteers her 35 students for the study. These children and their parents are then contacted.	Simple Easy Convenient No complete member list needed	May not be representative of the population
Quota sampling	Using the middle-school directory, the researcher selects the first 20 sixth-grade boys, the first 20 sixth-grade girls, the first 20 seventh-grade boys, the first 20 seventh-grade girls, the first 20 eighth-grade boys, and the first 20 eighth-grade girls. These children and their parents are then contacted.	Simple Easy Convenient No complete member list needed	May not be representative of the population

limitations of each. For the purposes of these examples, we will define the population as all middle-school children in the Conway, Arkansas, school district (approximately 1,000 children).

As we have seen, the method of sampling is an important issue in research. See "Thinking Critically About Everyday Information" for a news report in which the method of sampling may be problematic.

● Sample Size

We briefly mentioned the issue of sample size earlier when we discussed random sampling for our TV violence study. We are always confronted with the question of how large a sample should be drawn. The size of the sample depends on various considerations, including population variability, statistical issues, economic factors, availability of participants, and the importance of the problem.

In inferential statistics, the sample size required depends on how big a difference between two groups you want to be able to detect. With large sample sizes, small differences can be detected. If the sample size is sufficiently large, virtually any population difference

Thinking Critically About Everyday Information

Can Cheating Make Your Marriage Stronger?

The following report of a study in Italy was obtained from the online edition of *Weekly World News*. The title of the report is "New Study Reveals ... Cheating Makes Your Marriage Stronger." A portion of the report reads:

> "I started the analysis project to discover how damaging infidelity was to marriages," says Dr. Ostertag. "I was as surprised as everyone when the numbers proved that cheating on your spouse is actually good for your marriage." According to the scientific survey, the more extramarital flings a couple enjoys, the more likely they are to remain together and the happier they will be. "Some of the strongest unions I studied included spouses who each were involved in repeated extramarital affairs throughout the relationship," explains Dr. Ostertag. "My findings have turned our preconceived notion of the strength of monogamy on its head."

Carefully consider the following questions:

- Although the article does not provide methodological details (a shortcoming of many media reports), of the sampling techniques discussed in this chapter, which comes closest to the type that was probably used for this study?

- Think about how the researcher might have sampled married couples. How could biased sampling explain the pattern of results?

- What would be the most effective (accurate) method of sampling in order to answer the research question?

SOURCE: "New Study Reveals ... Cheating Makes Your Marriage Stronger," November 5, 2002, *Weekly World News*, American Media, Inc. Reprinted with permission.

will result in statistical significance. On the other hand, the smaller the sample size, the larger must be the population differences to achieve statistical significance. Stated another way, other things being equal, the greater the sample size, the less is the probability of drawing a conclusion that is in error. In carefully conducted survey research, the sample size determines how closely the sample values approximate the population values. Assuming valid sampling procedures, the larger the sample, the more closely (on average) will the sample values approximate the population values. However, the relationship between sample size and sensitivity is a curve of diminishing returns. Beyond a certain point, the cost and effort required to achieve greater sensitivity becomes disproportionately large.

There is generally a trade-off between the accuracy of the sample in representing population values and the costs associated with sample size. The larger the sample, the more confident we can be that it accurately reflects what exists in the population, but large samples can be extremely expensive and time consuming. A small sample is less expensive and time consuming, but it is not as accurate. Therefore, in situations requiring minimal error and maximum accuracy of prediction of population values, large samples will be required. In cases where more error can be tolerated, small samples will do. It is not unusual to use relatively small samples to generalize to millions of individuals. For example, a dramatic difference in size between the sample and the population to which the results are generalized is found in the Nielsen ratings. The Nielsen organization surveys the television viewing habits of about 5,000 households (13,000 persons) each week. From this survey, they make estimates concerning the viewing habits of around *250 million* individuals watching television in the United States. This amounts to sampling about 1 in every 20,000 viewers. Even so, apparently the Nielsen estimates are sufficiently accurate to satisfy the competitive TV networks. This survey again illustrates that useful estimates of population values can be made using a small number of observations. The key factor in this case is the representativeness of the sample.

If an entire population were surveyed, then we could specify the makeup of that population—number of Democrats, Republicans, Independents, income, sex, and so on. However, to do this for the entire population of the United States would cost hundreds of millions of dollars. Once every ten years, the U.S. Census is taken. The cost of the last Census (2000) has been estimated at more than $7 billion. For different purposes, far more limited than the U.S. Census, we could obtain a very good idea of some U.S. population characteristics from a relatively small representative sample of 2,000 to 3,000 people. That is, with a sample of this size, we could generalize our results to the entire population. In fact, some have argued that sample surveys can produce more accurate results regarding a given population than can a census. A census requires skilled interviewers in greater numbers than available. It also requires that *all* members of a population be reached. This does not always happen, and considerable unhappiness resulted in recent censuses because of what many viewed as an undercount of some segments of the population. Some cities were especially unhappy with the undercount because important funding decisions were tied to the census. A good sampling procedure might have been both less expensive and more accurate.

Other factors that help determine what is considered an adequate sample size are diversity of the population concerning the factors of interest and the number of factors. The greater the diversity among individuals and the greater the number of factors present, the larger the sample that is required to achieve representativeness.

Members of any population vary among themselves in many ways. In some instances, this variability may be small; in other instances, it may be quite large. To illustrate, say that we are interested in selecting a representative sample for height of individuals in a given population. If everyone in the given population were identical in height—say, 6 feet tall— then a sample with one individual would be representative of the population. Even if our population varied slightly, say from 5 feet 11 inches to 6 feet 1 inch, a very small sample could be taken whose average would be representative of the population average. In fact, a sample with one individual, in this case, would not seriously misrepresent the population value. However, if the height of individuals in the population varied from 4 feet to 7 feet, our sample would have to be relatively large to obtain an average that was representative of the population average. In this instance, a small sample could seriously misrepresent the population average.

● Sampling Error

Error can occur during the sampling process. **Sampling error** can include both systematic sampling error and random sampling error. **Systematic sampling error** is the fault of the investigation, but **random sampling error** is not. When errors are systematic, they bias the sample in one direction. Under these circumstances, the sample does not truly represent the population of interest. Systematic error occurs when the sample is not drawn properly, as in the poll conducted by *Literary Digest* magazine. It can also occur if names are dropped from the sample list because some individuals were difficult to locate or uncooperative. Individuals dropped from the sample could be different from those retained. Those remaining could quite possibly produce a biased sample. Political polls often have special problems that make prediction difficult.

Random sampling error, as contrasted to systematic sampling error, is often referred to as *chance error*. Purely by chance, samples drawn from the same population will rarely provide identical estimates of the population parameter of interest. These estimates will vary from sample to sample. For example, if you were to flip 100 unbiased coins, you would not be surprised if you obtained 55 heads on one trial, 49 on another, 52 on a third, and so on. Thus, some samples will, by chance, provide better estimates of the parameter than others. In any given sample, some attributes of interest may be overrepresented and some underrepresented. However, this type of error is random. Moreover, it is possible to describe this error statistically and take it into account when drawing inferences. Thus, in sampling voters prior to an election, we can make claims of the following sort: "There is a 95% probability that the proportion of voters who will cast their ballot for Candidate A will fall within the interval from 43% to 47%." Before selecting a sample, researchers usually decide the amount of error they are willing to tolerate and the level of confidence they want to have. This margin of error is expressed in terms of a **confidence interval**—for example, 95% of the time the sample will correctly reflect the population values with a margin of error of plus or minus 4 percentage points.

Sampling error can affect inferences based on sampling in two important situations. In one situation, we may wish to generalize from the sample to a particular population. With a small sampling error, we can feel more confident that our sample is representative of the population. Thus, we can feel reasonably comfortable about generalizing from the sample to the population. Survey research is most concerned about this kind of sampling error. The second situation in which sampling error plays a role is when we wish to determine whether two or more samples were drawn from the same or different populations. In this case, we are asking if two or more samples are sufficiently different to rule out factors due to chance. An example of this situation is when we ask the question "Did the group that received the experimental treatment really differ from the group that did not receive the treatment other than on the basis of chance?"

● Evaluating Information From Samples

The information on sampling presented in this chapter not only guides the beginning researcher, it also guides all of us in being critical consumers of information based on sample data. In recent years, our exposure to sampling and information from samples has grown tremendously, and we need, more than ever, to be able to critically evaluate that information. Through the educational system and the media, we continue to be informed about new research findings from scientists around the world. We can be fairly confident of that information because scientists are trained in proper methodology and findings are generally reviewed by other scientists before the findings become public. Likewise, there are reputable organizations that gather information for the public. For example, the Gallup Organization specializes in conducting polls to assess attitudes. In the months leading to a presidential election, we are inundated on a daily basis with poll numbers that show the public's views on a variety of political issues. Gallup polls are often used because the organization has a solid reputation for its sampling methodology and clearly states the margin of error in its polls. But what about other sources of information that have become more prevalent?

Polling and surveys are now routinely conducted in magazines, on radio talk shows, on Internet sites, and through 900 numbers on television programs. First, it is important to realize that none of these uses random sampling. All of the respondents who provide data self-select themselves. As a result, the sample of respondents often represents a small and narrow segment of the population. For example, the CNN Web site often has an on-going poll regarding some issue in the news. When you view the results of the poll, there is an appropriate warning that reads, "This QuickVote is not scientific and reflects the opinions of only those Internet users who have chosen to participate. The results cannot be assumed to represent the opinions of Internet users in general, nor the public as a whole. The QuickVote sponsor is not responsible for content, functionality or the opinions expressed therein." Unfortunately, many sources of polling do not provide such a warning to the consumer. We must realize that the results of a magazine survey reflect the views of only the individuals who read that type of magazine, have that magazine available to them to buy, actually buy that magazine, are interested enough in the survey to respond, have the time to respond, and take the time to mail their answers. Exactly who are you left with in the sample, and what do the results mean? These are important questions to ask yourself as a consumer.

CASE ANALYSIS

On April 20, 1999, Eric Harris and Dylan Klebold entered Columbine High School and began shooting teachers and students. Thirteen individuals died, and the psychological community was again asked to explain such violent behavior. A psychologist might decide to interview Columbine students to obtain their perspectives on the factors that motivated the two young men to commit such a horrendous act. A group of ten students has already decided to meet and discuss the events of that day. The psychologist asks if it would be all right to attend the meeting and ask them some questions. The students agree, and the psychologist records their thoughts. Based on this information, the psychologist concludes that a primary reason for the violent behavior was the peer dynamics in the school that created groups of outcasts.

Critical Thinking Questions

1. Who appears to constitute the population of interest?

2. Which type of sampling procedure best describes that used by the psychologist?

3. What are the limitations of this sampling method, and in what specific ways could the sampling method have affected the findings?

4. What specific steps would you have taken to obtain a representative sample?

GENERAL SUMMARY

When we conduct research, we are generally interested in drawing some conclusion about a population of individuals that have some common characteristic. However, populations are typically too large to allow observations on all individuals, and we resort to selecting a sample. In order to make inferences about the population, the sample must be representative. Thus, the manner in which the sample is drawn is critical. Probability sampling uses random sampling in which each element in the population (or a subgroup of the population with stratified random sampling) has an equal chance of being selected for the sample. This technique is considered to be the best means of obtaining a representative sample. When probability sampling is not possible, nonprobability sampling must be used. Convenience sampling involves using participants who are readily available (such as introductory psychology students). It is the easiest technique but the poorest from a methodological standpoint. Quota sampling is essentially convenience sampling in which there is an effort to better represent the population by sampling a certain percentage of participants from subgroups that correspond to the prevalence of those subgroups in the population.

By their very nature, samples do not perfectly match the population from which they are drawn. There is always some degree of sampling error, and the degree of error is inversely related to the size of the sample. Larger samples are more likely to accurately represent characteristics of the population, and smaller samples are less likely to accurately represent characteristics of the population. Therefore, researchers strive for samples that are large enough to reduce sampling error to an acceptable level. Even when samples are large enough, it is important to evaluate the specific method by which the sample was drawn. We are increasingly exposed to information obtained from self-selected samples that represent only a very narrow subgroup of individuals. Much of such information is meaningless because the subgroup is difficult to identify.

DETAILED SUMMARY

1. Sampling is the process whereby some elements (individuals) in the population are selected for a research study.

2. The population consists of all individuals with a particular characteristic that is of interest to the researchers. If data are obtained from all members of the population, then we have a census; if data are obtained from some members of the population, then we have a sample.

3. With probability sampling, a researcher can specify the probability of an element's (participant's) being included in the sample. With nonprobability sampling, there is no way of estimating the probability of an element's being included in a sample.

4. Although often more difficult and expensive, probability sampling is a methodologically more precise method to obtain a sample that is representative of the population.

5. With simple random sampling, each individual in the population has an equal chance of being selected for the sample. The four steps of simple random sampling are (1) defining the population, (2) constructing a list of all members, (3) drawing the sample, and (4) contacting the members of the sample.

6. Stratified random sampling is a form of probability sampling in which individuals are randomly selected from specified subgroups (strata) of the population. This method can be used to increase the representativeness of the sample and/or to allow comparisons to be made among individuals in the different strata.

7. Convenience sampling is quick and inexpensive because it involves selecting individuals who are readily available at the time of the study (such as introductory psychology students). The disadvantage is that convenience samples are generally less representative than random samples; therefore, results should be interpreted with caution.

8. Quota sampling involves the selection of a certain percentage of individuals from specified subgroups of the population when the population is large and lists of members are not available. Many polling organizations use this technique.

9. Appropriate sample size depends on various considerations, including population variability, statistical issues, economic factors, and availability of participants. In general, with larger samples you will have a smaller margin of error and you can detect smaller differences.

10. The larger the variability of scores in the population, the larger the sample must be in order to be representative.

11. Sampling error includes systematic error and random error. Systematic error occurs when the sample is not properly drawn (an error of the researcher). Random error is the degree to which the sample is not perfectly representative of the population. Even with the best sampling techniques, some degree of random error is expected.

12. Increasingly, we are exposed to information based on sample data. Understanding the principles of sampling, particularly the limitations of various methods, should make us more critical consumers of such information.

KEY TERMS

census *(p. 100)*
confidence interval *(p. 113)*
convenience sampling *(p. 106)*
element *(p. 100)*
exhaustive list *(p. 102)*
nonprobability sampling *(p. 101)*
population *(p. 100)*
probability sampling *(p. 101)*

quota sampling *(p. 109)*
random sampling *(p. 101)*
random sampling error *(p. 112)*
sample *(p. 100)*
sampling error *(p. 112)*
stratified random sample *(p. 105)*
systematic sampling error *(p. 112)*

REVIEW QUESTIONS/EXERCISES

1. You hypothesize that students in fraternities/sororities on your campus are more extroverted (on an introversion/extroversion scale) than other students. To answer your research question, you need to obtain a sample of "Greek" students and a sample of "independent" students. For each of these two populations of students, how would you obtain simple random samples using the four steps described in this chapter?

2. For the hypothesis in question 1, describe how you would obtain samples using stratified random sampling, with stratification based on the sex of the student. Assume that 60% of the Greeks are women.

3. For the hypothesis in question 1, describe how you would obtain samples using convenience sampling.

4. For the hypothesis in question 1, describe how you would obtain samples using quota sampling based on the sex of the student. Again, assume that 60% of the Greeks are women.

5. For the hypothesis in question 1, describe a poor method of sampling that you believe would result in systematic sampling error and thus bias the research findings. Explain why you believe the sample would be biased.

6. Go to an Internet Web site that has an online poll. (If you are not familiar with such a site, simply conduct a search using the keywords "online poll" or "online survey" and select one of the sites.) Participate in the survey, and view the current results. Describe the nature of the survey and the current results. What method of sampling was used? What characteristics do you believe the members of the sample possess? Do you believe that these characteristics influence the poll results? Would the results be different if the general population of U.S. adults were polled?

 WEB RESOURCES TO INCREASE LEARNING

The chapter outline, chapter summaries, key terms and definitions, chapter questions, additional chapter exercises, and links to relevant Web sites are available at the course Web site (**http://psychology.wadsworth.com/lammers_badia1e**). Explore the interactive workshop "Sampling."

CHAPTER 8

SOURCES OF EXTRANEOUS VARIABILITY

● Understanding Variability

In this chapter, we will deal with three very important concepts: systematic variance (also called between group variance), systematic error (also called confounding), and random error (also called within-group variance or error variance). As a general rule, we want to maximize systematic variance, minimize random error, and eliminate systematic error.

When we make observations and measure dependent variables, there will undoubtedly be variability in the scores that we obtain. That is, not all of the participants' scores will be the same. Let's try to understand the reasons why their scores are not all the same. Assume that we have two groups of children. One group watches a television program without violence, and another group watches a television program with violence. We then allow the children to play on the playground, and we observe the number of aggressive behaviors that each child exhibits. We obtain the data shown in Table 8.1.

Systematic Variance

Clearly, there is variability in these scores. Why didn't each child show the same number of aggressive behaviors? One possible source of variability is the **systematic variance** that results from the treatment effect. This is the variability that we hypothesized would occur as a result of our manipulation of the independent variable (level of TV violence). Systematic variance contributes to and helps explain the difference or variability between participant scores in the two groups, and therefore the difference between the two group means.

Systematic Error (Confounding)

The difference between the two group means could also be due to factors other than the independent variable. These other factors cause **systematic error** and are often referred to as

Table 8.1	Number of Aggressive Behaviors on the Playground	
	CHILDREN WHO WATCHED NONVIOLENT PROGRAM	CHILDREN WHO WATCHED VIOLENT PROGRAM
	4	3
	0	2
	2	0
	2	6
	3	8
	5	1
	1	4
	1	4
	0	5
	4	6
	Mean = 2.2	Mean = 3.9

confounding variables, or **confounds.** Systematic error relates to internal validity, which we discuss at the end of the chapter.

The hallmark of a good experimental method or procedure is that you allow to vary only one factor (IV) at a time and everything else is held constant. Then if you observe a systematic change in behavior, you know that the change is due to your IV. If everything else is held constant, no alternative (rival) explanations are needed for your findings. However, if the method did allow one or more factors to vary along with the IV, then you would not know which factor caused the change in the observed behavior.

Whenever more than one factor at a time varies, you have confounding. For example, if you had asked the group of 20 children for 10 volunteers to watch *Mister Rogers* (nonviolent) and 10 volunteers to watch *Beast Wars* (violent), is it possible that the two groups differed even before you presented the TV program? Is it possible that those children who elected to watch *Beast Wars* were more aggressive to begin with? In this case, it would not be possible to separate the effects of your independent variable from differences in aggression that result from self-selection to the groups. Is it possible that you, the experimenter, were more likely to rate a behavior as aggressive if you knew that the child had just finished watching *Beast Wars*? These issues, along with several others, are discussed in more detail below.

Remember that confounding variables affect the scores in one group differently than the scores in another group. Sources of systematic error affect the variability between the groups. If they increase variability in the same direction as the hypothesized effect of the independent variable, you may falsely conclude that your treatment had an effect when, in fact, the difference was a result of systematic error. If there is an increase in the opposite direction, you may falsely conclude that your treatment had no effect when, in fact, the effect was masked by systematic error.

Random Error

So, confounds result in alternative interpretations (rival hypotheses) of the data and make an unambiguous interpretation of the findings difficult. They can also affect, along with other factors, the variability of scores between the groups. Other extraneous variables affect the variability of scores *within* the groups. Why didn't each child who watched *Mister Rogers* exhibit the same number of aggressive behaviors on the playground? Why didn't each child who watched *Beast Wars* exhibit the same number of aggressive behaviors? Some sources of **random error** are obvious. These are different children with different backgrounds. You expect them to be different. Other factors may not be so obvious. Did some or all of the children know that they were being watched on the playground? Did the level of personality development vary? Age? Number of males and females? The number of siblings each participant had? Each of these factors could have affected behavior—that is, caused behavior to vary from person to person. Is it possible that the experimenter experienced lapses in attention and missed some aggressive behaviors? The fact that these extraneous variables increase the variability of scores within the groups makes it more difficult for the experimenter to discover sources of systematic variance between groups resulting from manipulation of the independent variable.

Thus, behavioral research presents the interesting challenge of attempting to discover sources of systematic variability while simultaneously attempting to eliminate sources of systematic error (confounds) and reduce (minimize) random error. Although there is no perfect experiment, an experiment can be evaluated in terms of how well it answers the questions that are asked. If they can be answered unambiguously, without either qualifying comments or the availability of alternative explanations, the experiment may be considered unusually good. We will now explore extraneous variables in more detail.

● Sources of Extraneous Variability

Extraneous variables should be evaluated both when planning research and when evaluating the results after the data have been collected. Some extraneous variables can be anticipated; others are revealed during the course of the experiment. Those that are anticipated can often be addressed by using specific experimental design techniques (discussed in the next chapter). Those that are revealed during the experiment aid in interpretation of the research findings.

Sources of extraneous variability can be categorized into the areas of research participants, experimenter, and method (experimental design). Table 8.2 provides an overview of the various sources of extraneous variability and includes some of the relevant questions that should be asked during both design and evaluation of research. Note that some of these extraneous variables are more likely to be confounds that contribute to systematic error, whereas others are more likely to contribute to random error. Each should be evaluated on both counts. Also, keep in mind that identifying a possible source of confounding is much more important than labeling or categorizing it. The label itself is unimportant. Indeed, different individuals may place a possible source of confounding in different categories.

Participants as a Source of Extraneous Variability

History   Whenever a measure is taken more than one time in the course of an experiment—that is, pre- and posttest measures—variables related to **history** may play a role. Specific events occurring between the first and second recordings may affect the dependent variable. The longer the time period between the measurement periods and the less control over the participants (degree of isolation) during this period, the greater is the likelihood that these factors will affect the participants.

Let's consider an example involving our TV violence question. On a Tuesday morning, we show the children at a day-care center a TV program with violence and then observe their behavior during playtime. The following Tuesday, we show the same group of children a nonviolent TV program and again observe their behavior during playtime. We find that the children showed fewer aggressive behaviors during the second observation period. We also know that the day after the first observation the day-care center hired a new, and much stricter, director. This new director is a potential confound because this person could have affected the children's behavior in one condition but not the other. We do not know whether the change in children's behavior is due to the independent variable (type of TV program) or this confounding variable (new director).

Maturation   With history, specific events occur that are often external to the participants and are largely accidental. Similar to history are maturational events. However, **maturation** is a developmental process within the individual. Included under maturational events are such factors as growth, fatigue, boredom, and aging. Indeed, almost all biological or psychological processes that vary as a function of time and are independent of specific events may be considered maturational factors. On occasion, it is difficult to determine whether to classify an observation in one category or another. As we noted, this is not a matter of concern. The important thing is to recognize that other factors besides the independent variable may be considered as a rival explanation for behavioral change.

On Tuesday, we show our group of children a two-hour movie that includes violence and then put them in a playroom for two hours for observation of aggressive behavior. We do the same on the following Tuesday but show a two-hour movie that does not include vi-

Table 8.2	Sources of Extraneous Variability	
SOURCE		**RELEVANT QUESTION**
Participants	History	Has some historical event occurred that accompanied one or more of the experimental treatments?
	Maturation	Have some developmental processes paralleled the treatment effects?
	Attrition (loss of research participants)	When participants drop out during the course of the study, is the attrition balanced over the various conditions or confined to selected treatment groups?
	Demand characteristics	Is it possible that some aspects of the experimental setting provide clues that permit participants to speculate about what is demanded (expected) of them in the study?
	Evaluation apprehension	Does the experiment elicit undue concern among the participants regarding the adequacy of their performance?
	Diffusion of treatment	Have initial participants informed later participants about the experiment?
Experimenter	Experimenter characteristics	Is it possible that the gender, attractiveness, or personality of the experimenter has affected the behavior of the participants?
	Experimenter bias	Is it possible that the experimenter's theoretical bias has led to unintentional recording errors? Or caused the experimenter to unintentionally communicate expectations to the participant?
Method	Selection	Could group differences be the result of the way that participants were selected for the study or assigned to the groups?
	Task and instructions	Is the task well defined and the same for participants in all experimental groups?
	Testing	If a pretest is used, is it possible that changes have resulted from the pretest (prior testing)?
	Carryover effects	Could participation in a previous condition influence behavior in a subsequent condition?
	Instrumentation	Have changes in the instrument—human or physical—accompanied variations in the experimental conditions?
	Regression to the mean	Have the participants been preselected so as to represent the extremes on the behavioral dimension of interest?

olence. If these are young children, can we expect all of them to sit still for two hours and watch a movie? If they get distracted after a short period of time, then we are not really manipulating our independent variable. Likewise, during the observation period, will they get bored being in the same playroom with the same toys? Could this boredom affect their level of aggressive behavior? Could this boredom affect one condition more than the other?

Attrition   In Chapter 2, we pointed out that human participants must be permitted to withdraw from an experiment at any time. Some will exercise this option. Some may withdraw for reasons of illness, others because they do not find the research to their liking. In animal studies, some participants may die and others become ill. Some **attrition,** in and of itself, is not serious. However, confounding may occur when the loss of participants in the various comparison groups is different, resulting in the groups' having different characteristics. This type of confound is referred to as *differential participant attrition.*

For example, a group of children, with consent from their parents, take part in a three-month study to assess the effect of TV violence on aggressive behavior. The experimenter randomly assigns half of the children to watch nonviolent TV programs and the other half to watch TV programs that contain some violence. As we will see in the next chapter, by randomly assigning participants to each condition we assume that the groups are equal on all characteristics. Random assignment is the best way that we know of to form equal groups on all known and unknown factors. During the course of the three months, approximately one-fourth of parents whose children have been assigned to watch TV violence reconsider their consent and decide to withdraw their children from the study. During the course of the three months, there is no attrition in the nonviolent group. Clearly, this will reduce the sample size in one of the groups. More important, the differential attrition could be a confound. It is possible that the parents most concerned about the welfare of their child would have children who tend to be less aggressive. Thus, you may not only be losing participants from one of the groups, you may be losing participants with specific characteristics related to the dependent variable. Therefore, what started out as equal groups in the two conditions ends up as two very different groups.

Let's look at another example. Imagine that a research team is interested in comparing the traditional lecture approach to instruction with the Personalized System of Instruction (PSI), in which each student works at his or her own pace. They randomly assign students to lecture or PSI sections. The students assigned to the lecture method will serve as a comparison group for students assigned to the PSI method. A pretest on abilities at the beginning of the school term shows that the characteristics of students in the two instructional conditions are comparable. As is true in all classes, students drop courses for a variety of reasons as the term goes on. At the end of the school term, a common final exam is given to all students in the lecture and PSI sections. It is found that the PSI students do much better than the lecture students. However, the research team kept careful records of those who dropped out of the different instructional sections. It was found that more students of low ability dropped from the PSI than from the lecture sections. Consequently, the comparison between the lecture method and the PSI method was confounded. Not only did the method of instruction differ, but because of differential attrition, the abilities of students also differed. Because of this confounding, the actual differences obtained could be due to differences in instructional methods or to differences between high-ability students in PSI and lower-ability students in the lecture sections.

Particularly vulnerable to the effects of attrition are developmental and follow-up studies. The loss of participants in itself, though unfortunate, does not lead to differential bias or confounding. Confounding occurs when subjects with certain kinds of characteristics tend to be lost in one group but not another. To avoid drawing a faulty conclusion, it is important to keep careful records. It must be possible to document and assess the loss of participants.

Demand Characteristics   Different situations "demand" different behavior patterns. The behavior of people in church is very different from their behavior at a football game, or when they are at their place of employment. Similarly, the behavior of students in classroom situations is typically different from their nonclassroom behavior. These behavior patterns may vary with the size and type of class and characteristics of the instructor. Thus, situations tend to "call out" or "demand" expected behavior patterns. Experimental settings are similar. It is possible that the implicit and explicit cues found in research settings may be responsible for the observed behavior rather than the independent variable. If this is the case, we have compromised the integrity of the study. We must remain aware that the very act of measuring behavior may change the behavior measured.

The implicit and explicit cues surrounding the experiment, referred to as **demand characteristics,** may consist of the instructions given, the questions asked, the apparatus used, the procedures, the behavior of the researcher, and an almost endless variety of other cues. Cues from these various sources allow participants to speculate about the purpose of the experiment and the kind of behavior that is expected of them.

Demand characteristics can have different effects. They may lead participants to form hypotheses—either correct or incorrect—about the nature of the experiment. Some participants may react in a compliant way to "help" the experimenter's efforts, whereas others may react in a defiant way to "hinder" the experimenter's efforts. Still other participants may simply perform in a way they think is expected of them. Whatever the case, demand characteristics can affect the quality of the experiment.

For example, the children in our TV violence study may not behave naturally during the observation period because they know that they are part of a study. As a result, they "perform" for the researchers based on what they believe the researchers expect of them. Some studies actually demonstrate demand characteristics. One such study investigated the acceptance of rape myths (for example, that women have more control in a rape situation than is actually the case) in both men and women (Bryant, Mealey, & Herzog, 2001). The Rape Myth Acceptance Scale was given to young adults at a shopping mall. Half the time the researcher was dressed provocatively, and half the time the researcher was dressed conservatively. Results showed that rape myths were more accepted (by both men and women) when the researcher was dressed conservatively, and the researchers attributed this effect to demand characteristics. Note that such an effect could also be labeled experimenter effects. Again, the particular label is not the critical point.

Before describing how demand characteristics can be detected and their effects minimized, we should note that participants are generally conscientious when participating in research. There is little evidence that most participants are either compliant (giving "right" data) or defiant (giving "wrong" data).

Although we cannot ignore demand characteristics, we should not become unduly concerned about them to the point of pessimism concerning research. Debriefing is one common method used to assess demand characteristics. Debriefing can include a postexperimental questionnaire aimed at discovering how participants interpreted the situation—their perceptions, beliefs, and thoughts of what the experiment was about. This information can reveal whether demand characteristics were operating. The researcher must be careful that the questions do not guide the participant. Otherwise, the answers to the questionnaire are themselves a component of demand characteristics. To obtain useful information, the investigator should use open-ended questions followed up by probing questions.

In the long run, the most valid way of ascertaining whether demand characteristics posed a problem is to evaluate the extent to which the results generalize. If the results generalize to other situations, laboratory or nonlaboratory, then demand characteristics that restrict our conclusions to a specific experimental setting were not operating.

Evaluation Apprehension   Participants entering the laboratory bring with them a variety of concerns and motivations. The laboratory setting, as we have seen, leads to demand characteristics, but it also leads to concern and apprehension about being evaluated. Many participants become particularly concerned about doing well or making a good impression. Under these circumstances, they may become sensitive and eagerly seek out cues from the experimenter. After the experimental session is over, the floodgates are open for a flow of questions: "How did I do?" "Did I pass?" "I didn't make a fool of myself, did I?"

The participant's **evaluation apprehension,** or fear of being judged, leads to several problems. One we have noted already: Participants tend to be especially eager for cues from the experimenter. It is also possible that one treatment, in an experiment having several, may give rise to greater apprehension or concern about being judged than the others. If this happens, we then have the problem of confounding. By differentially arousing suspicion among participants in an experiment, we have, in fact, created different conditions over and above the treatment condition. Anything in an experiment that arouses suspicion that a participant is being judged can create these difficulties.

Diffusion of Treatment   Some of the preceding factors can be magnified if participants learn about details of the experiment before they participate. This can occur inadvertently by overhearing a conversation about the experiment. More often, a friend or college classmate who has already participated informs the future participant. This is particularly problematic when the experiment involves some degree of deception in order to elicit natural behavior. If **diffusion of treatment** is a concern, it is wise to take a minute at the end of each experimental session to request that participants not discuss the experiment with others who might be participants in the future.

Experimenter as a Source of Extraneous Variability

Experimenter Characteristics   The personality and physical characteristics of the experimenter are often overlooked as sources of extraneous variability. Many of the factors just discussed, including attrition, demand characteristics, and evaluation apprehension can be affected by **experimenter characteristics.** The way that the experimenter interacts with the participants can increase or decrease the degree to which these other factors become extraneous variables. It is important for the experimenter to act like a professional. The more serious the experimenter is about the study, the more serious the participants will be. An experimenter who dresses in shabby clothes, appears unprepared, and jokes around with participants runs the risk of increased random error from participants who do not take their role seriously.

There is also evidence that physical characteristics of the experimenter can be an extraneous variable. Think about it. Can your behavior be affected by the gender, attractiveness, age, or race of the person you are interacting with? Of course it can, and the same is true in the experimental situation where the participant interacts with the researcher. We have already mentioned a study in which the dress of the experimenter influenced participant responses on the Rape Myth Acceptance Scale. Other studies have shown that gender (Barnes & Rosenthal, 1985; Friedman, Kurland, & Rosenthal, 1965), attractiveness (Barnes & Rosenthal, 1985; Binder, McConnell, & Sjoholm, 1957), age (Ehrlich & Riesman, 1961), and race of the experimenter (Katz, Robinson, & Epps, 1964) can affect scores on the dependent variable. This is not to say that these factors will serve as extraneous variables in all, or even most, studies. Their possible effect will depend on the particular variables manipulated and measured in the study. The point is that the researcher should consider these as possible sources of extraneous variability in both the design and evaluation phases of research.

Experimenter Bias   One of the great myths about scientists is that they are aloof, objective, unbiased, and disinterested in the outcomes of their research. They are interested in one thing and one thing only—scientific truth. Although objectivity is a goal toward which to strive, in actual fact many if not most scientists fall considerably short of the mark. Indeed, they have made a considerable personal investment in their research and theoretical reflections. They passionately want their theories confirmed in the crucible of laboratory or field research. The very intensity of their desires and expectations makes their research vulnerable to the effects of **experimenter bias.** Two major classes of experimenter bias are (1) errors in recording or computation and (2) experimenter expectancies that are unintentionally communicated to the experimental participants.

Recording and computational errors do not affect the participant's behavior. Generally unintentional, they may occur at any phase of the experiment, such as when making observations, transcribing data, or analyzing results. If the errors are random, then no problem exists. It is when the errors are systematic that real problems develop. We mentioned earlier in this chapter that an experimenter making observations of children may be more likely to record a behavior as aggressive if the experimenter knows that this child just finished watching the TV program with violence.

The second class of experimenter effects do affect the participant's performance. These are often referred to as **experimenter expectancies.** Here, the behavior desired by the experimenter is unintentionally communicated to the participant. Perhaps one of the most interesting illustrations of experimenter expectancy is the story of Clever Hans. Clever Hans was a horse owned by a schoolteacher named von Osten during the 1800s. Clever Hans developed a reputation for solving various mathematical problems. If Clever Hans was asked the product of 3 × 3, he would stomp with one of his hoofs nine times. Similar feats were routinely performed. Interestingly, von Osten believed that Hans actually possessed advanced mathematical ability and invited scientific inquiry into the abilities of the horse. Detailed and painstaking research revealed that Hans was able to perform as billed, but only under specific conditions.

The individual posing the problem had to be visibly present while the answer was being given, and he or she had to know the answer. For example, if the questioner thought that the square root of 9 was 4, Hans would answer "four." You may have guessed that the experimenter (questioner) unintentionally communicated the desirable behavior (correct answer) to the participant (Clever Hans). It was later determined that Clever Hans was a very ordinary horse, but one that had developed an uncanny ability to respond to slight visual cues. It seems that when a question was asked, the questioner tilted his head forward to look at Hans' leg and hoof. When the correct number of stomps occurred, the questioner then looked up. This was a cue to Hans to stop "counting." How the horse learned this difficult discrimination probably relates to operant conditioning and reinforcement principles.

How expectancies may affect behavior in an experimental setting is illustrated in a series of studies that investigated the effect of teacher expectancies on student performance in the classroom. In an early and well-known study, Rosenthal and Jacobson (1968) gave an intelligence test to students in grammar school. They then told the teachers that some of the students were "late bloomers" and that these children would show considerable improvement over the year. In fact, the children described as late bloomers were chosen randomly and were no different from the others. The effect of this label was apparently dramatic. When those identified as late bloomers were later retested, their mean score was much higher than that of other children who were not labeled late bloomers. Although some researchers have been critical of the methodology used in this early study, the basic effect has been supported.

We can speculate how teachers might treat children labeled as "bright" or "slow." Those carrying the bright label might be given more attention, more encouragement, and greater responsibilities. In short, teachers' expectations probably affect the way they interact with students. The quality of this interaction may help or hinder a student, depending on a teacher's expectations. This is one reason why some educators are opposed to systems of education that segregate students on the basis of ability testing. In such systems, educators would have different expectations of students, thereby affecting the way the students are treated and what is expected of them. These expectations might, in turn, affect the students' performance. Some have called this process a self-fulfilling prophecy. Such effects have been demonstrated between teachers and gifted children in the classroom (Kolb & Jussim, 1994), experimenters and participants performing a psychomotor task (Callaway, Nowicki, & Duke, 1980), and coaches and athletes (Solomon, 2002).

To sum up, studies have demonstrated experimenter expectancies in various settings. Although these studies designate experimenter expectancy as an independent variable, the danger is that the behavior of participants in many studies could be unknowingly affected by experimenter expectancies. In such studies, quality is jeopardized. The observed effects represent a confounding of experimenter expectancy and experimental treatment.

Method as a Source of Extraneous Variability

Selection   In a typical experiment, groups are selected to receive different levels of the independent variable. To conclude that this manipulation caused differences in the dependent variable, the researcher must be confident that the groups were not selected in a way that created differences in the dependent variable before the independent variable was even introduced. That is, the researcher must be confident that the groups were equivalent to begin with. A researcher would not want children with aggressive personalities in the group that watches violent TV and children with nonaggressive personalities in the group that watches nonviolent TV (or vice versa). Any differences in behavior between the two groups could be due to either the independent variable (level of TV violence) or the way in which children were assigned to the groups. In other words, **selection** would be a confound. In the next chapter, we will discuss design methods to avoid this problem. There are also statistical methods that can adjust for initial differences between groups.

Task and Instructions   The **task** is what participants have to do so that we can measure our dependent variable. If we are interested in reaction time as a dependent variable, do the participants press a telegraph key, or release it, or do we measure it in some other way? If we are interested in reading rate, what material does the participant read? How is it read? Subvocally? Aloud? If we want to measure aggressive behavior, do we ask children to play on a playground? Play in a room full of toys? In an experimental study, it is essential that participants in all groups perform identical tasks. If we knowingly or unknowingly vary both the independent variable and the task, any observed differences between groups could be due to the independent variable or to the different tasks they performed.

Sometimes task confounding is so obvious that we have no difficulty recognizing it. For example, we would not observe aggressive behavior on the playground for one group and in a room full of toys for the other group. Likewise, we would not compare gasoline consumption of two different makes of automobiles of the same size and power by calculating the miles per gallon of one car on a test track and the other one in real traffic. If we were interested in comparing individuals' ability to track a moving target while experiencing two types of distraction, we would want the target being tracked to move at the same speed for both types. The only thing that should vary is the type of distraction. In these examples, task confounding can be easily seen. However, on some occasions, task confounding is so subtle that it is difficult to recognize. To illustrate, researchers were interested in the effects certain colors have on learning words. They prepared a list of ten five-letter words. Five of the ten words were printed in red, and five were printed in yellow. Twenty students were randomly selected from the college population and given the list of words to learn. All participants learned the same list. The criterion for learning was two perfect recitals of the ten-word list. Results showed that words printed in red were learned more rapidly than those printed in yellow. On the surface, it appears that the speed of learning was a function of the color of the printed words. Before drawing this conclusion, however, we should ask, "Was the task the same for the different colored words?" A few moments' reflection should produce a negative reply. Why? Because different words appeared in the red as opposed to the yellow condition, the tasks were different. This suggests a possible alternative interpretation of the findings—namely, that the five words printed in red were easier words to learn, independent of the color used. This problem could have been avoided by using a different procedure. Instead of all participants' having the same five words printed in red and the other five words printed in yellow, a different set of words could have been randomly chosen for each participant, of which five were printed in red and five in yellow.

The following example describes a case of task confounding so subtle that many experts would miss it. Folklore has it that the more frequently you test students, the more they learn. Imagine that instructors of introductory psychology courses are interested in improving learning in various sections of the course. One obvious possibility is to increase the frequency of testing. Before doing so, however, they must assure themselves that the folklore is correct. Consequently, they design a study to test the "frequency of testing" hypothesis.

Many classes of 40 students each are available for research. Students and instructors are randomly assigned to courses that are to be tested different numbers of times. The researchers decide to give some students nine tests, others six tests, and still others three tests. Only introductory sections are used, with an equal number assigned to each test frequency. The same book and chapter assignments are used. Further, all instructors select test questions from the same source book. All tests contain 50 multiple-choice items. Grades on each exam are based on percentages: more than 90% correct, an A; 80%, a B; 70%, a C; 60%, a D. The results are clear and statistically significant: the more frequent the tests, the better the performance. Are there alternative interpretations to the frequency of testing hypothesis?

If each test contained 50 items, the number of items differed from condition to condition. Thus, the nine-test condition received 450 items during the semester; the six-test condition received 300 items; and the three-test condition received 150 items. In other words, the three conditions varied in the number of items received during a semester as well as in the number of tests. The treatment condition was therefore confounded with task differences. To avoid this problem, the researchers could have limited the number of questions to 180 and then given nine tests each with 20 questions; six tests with 30 questions, and three tests with 60 questions. This way, the total number of items would be constant while allowing frequency of testing to vary. But a problem still remains. If the researchers allow a full hour for each test, then the nine-test groups receiving only 20 questions could spend as much as three minutes per item, the six-test groups with 30 questions about two minutes, and the three-test groups with 60 questions only about one minute. The investigators could give everyone only one minute per test question, giving the nine-, six-, and three-test frequency groups 20, 30, or 60 minutes, respectively. This is somewhat better, but task confounding is still present if fatigue is a factor or warm-up time is necessary. The problems encountered here are excellent examples of the difficulties involved in doing well-controlled research.

When human participants are used, **instructions** in some form are necessary to inform the participants about what the task is. If they are to perform the task in the way that the experimenter wants them to, then the instructions must be clear. If unclear, instructions may result in greater variability in performance among participants, or worse, they may result in participants' performing different tasks. The task would vary depending on the level of understanding of the instructions. It is essential when using complex instructions to evaluate their adequacy before beginning the experiment. It is not unusual for instructions to go through several modifications before they are etched in stone. Even then, the post-experimental interview might reveal that portions of the instructions were unclear for some participants.

Testing Effects   Researchers sometimes find it necessary to give a pretest and a posttest. The pretest is given before and the posttest after the experimental treatment. Presumably, any differences that occur between the pre- and posttests are due to the treatment itself. However, a possible rival explanation is that the pretest accounts for the results; that is, there was something about taking the pretest that affected scores on the posttest. There is a substantial body of evidence showing such **testing effects.** Individuals frequently improve their performance the second time they take a test; on occasion, the opposite may be found. The test may be a comparable test, an alternate form of the same test, or actually the same test. Because these changes in performance occur without any experimental treatment, it is important to assess them and to use the proper controls (these controls will be discussed later in the book). Many researchers have expressed concern that the process of measuring apparently changes that which is measured. We are not yet sufficiently knowledgeable to know the reasons why this may be so. Pretests may sensitize participants to selectively attend to certain aspects of the experiment simply by the nature of the questions asked. Therefore, changes observed on posttests may be largely due to pretests' alerting or guiding the participant.

Carryover Effects   Testing effects can occur when a participant has prior experience with the test. **Carryover effects** involve a more general issue whereby prior experience in an experimental condition (or conditions) affects behavior in a subsequent condition (or conditions). Thus, carryover effects are a concern whenever the research design requires data collection from each participant in two or more sequential conditions. At times, participation in an initial condition will alert the participant to the purposes of the study and, thereby, influence their behavior in later phases of the research. At other times, simple practice with a task leads to better performance in subsequent conditions. A more detailed discussion of carryover effects, including the research design techniques to address them, is presented in Chapter 12.

Instrumentation   The term **instrumentation** encompasses a class of extraneous variables larger than the word implies. It includes not only physical instrumentation (electrical, mechanical, and the like) but also human observers, raters, or scorers. In much research, repeated observations are necessary. Any changes in performance between the first and all following observations may be due to changes in your measuring instrument—physical or human. Raters or observers may become more skillful in identifying certain behaviors, but they may also become fatigued or bored.

As an experimenter, you may be nervous at the beginning of the experiment and much more relaxed after you become accustomed to your participants and procedure. When handling animals, you may be initially timid, tentative, and somewhat uneasy. With experience and familiarity, your handling techniques improve. Grading essay exams poses a problem for instructors at times. The criteria for evaluation may change in a gradual and systematic fashion between the start and completion of the task. Papers read earlier may have either an advantage or disadvantage, depending on the direction in which the criteria change.

Because psychologists must frequently rely on raters or observers, the problem of accurate and reliable measuring techniques is important. Minimizing changes in these measurements requires careful training of observers. As we noted in Chapter 6, some investigators use more than one rater or observer and then calculate, periodically, the extent to which (1) different observers or recorders agree with one another (interobserver or interrecorder reliability) or (2) the same observers or recorders agree with themselves at different times (intraobserver or intrarecorder reliability). Because some shifts are almost inevitable, it is wise to randomly assign the experimental treatment to the available experimental session. For example, if all participants in one condition are seen first, and those in another condition are seen second, the treatment effects are confounded with possible systematic changes in instrumentation.

Regression to the Mean Let us imagine that you have developed a procedure you believe will alleviate chronic depressive disorders. You administer a depression scale to large numbers of people. As your treatment group, you select a group drawn from those who obtained the highest depression scores. Subsequently, you administer the experimental treatment and find a significant improvement in their scores on the depression scale. Can you conclude that the treatment was effective?

This study is typical of many pilot research programs that report exciting initial results that are not substantiated by later, better-designed studies. It suffers from vulnerability to the regression phenomenon: Whenever we select a sample of participants because of their extreme scores on a scale of interest and test them again at a later date, the mean of the sample on these posttest scores typically moves closer to the population mean. This occurs whether the extremes are drawn from the low end or high end of the scale. This movement of the extremes toward the center of the distribution is known as **regression to the mean.** There is nothing mysterious about this phenomenon. Whenever performance is exceptional, a number of factors combine to produce this unusual outcome. Many of these factors are temporary and fleeting. They are what statisticians refer to as chance variables. If these variables combine in such a way as to lower performance at a given time, it is unlikely that they will repeat themselves the next time. Thus, the individual will appear to improve. On the other hand, an exceptionally good performance has enjoyed the confluence of many favorable chance factors. It is unlikely that these will repeat themselves on the next occasion. Thus, the individual will appear to get worse.

In short, regression to the mean is a function of using extreme scores and imperfect measuring instruments. The more extreme the scores and the lower the reliability of the instrument, the greater will be the degree of regression. For example, let's say that we are interested in whether the effect of TV violence depends on the prior level of aggressive behavior in the child. So we want to select one group of children who are nonaggressive and another group of children who are already very aggressive. To do this, we observe a large number of children on the playground and select for the experiment those children who showed no aggressive behavior and those who showed high levels of aggressive behavior. Both groups watch the TV program with violence, and then we observe them again on the playground. We find that the nonaggressive children now show some aggressive behavior and that the aggressive children now show lower levels of aggressive behavior. These may be interesting findings, suggesting that the effect of TV violence depends on the prior aggressive nature of the child; or these findings may simply represent the effect of regression to the mean. Because the two groups were selected for being at the extremes, regression to the mean would predict that their behavior would moderate to the center at a second observation setting.

Regression is a statistical phenomenon and is *not* due to any experimental treatment. Therefore, if we select participants who score extremely low on a pretest and then give them a posttest (same test) without introducing a treatment of any kind, participants would be expected to perform higher on the posttest. The reverse of this is true for extremely high scores; that is, participants should perform lower on the posttest. When a treatment condition is added between the pre- and posttests, investigators often confuse regression to the mean with the treatment effect and wrongly conclude that the treatment was effective.

Let's consider a few more examples. I have just completed grading my midterm exam in my Research Methods course. The results were very disappointing, and I now have to improve the performance of at least some of the students. I am especially concerned with those doing very poorly. During the remainder of the term, I introduce a number of new teaching procedures, carefully keeping a record of each. After the final exam, I immediately compare the midterm and final exam scores of those who were doing very poorly. I find that the mean score of this group has increased. My satisfaction is enormous. This new teaching technique and its accomplishments should be shared with my academic colleagues. Question: Is this enthusiasm justified? Probably not. As the instructor, I might be very unhappy and disappointed if I were to compare the midterm and final grades of those doing extremely well in the course. I would probably find that my most brilliant students did not perform as well on the final as they did on the midterm. Again, regression to the mean rather than the new teaching method may be responsible.

For any given year, we select 50 active baseball players with the poorest hitting records and calculate their mean batting average. In this group of 50 ballplayers, we will have some who are not very good hitters, and they will always remain in this category of poorest hitters. However, there are also those who are much better hitters than the current year's batting averages reflect. They will no doubt improve their hitting the next year. The batting average of these better players may have been reduced because of injury, illness, changing batting stance, dissatisfaction with play, unhappiness with teammates, playing a new position, or other temporary reasons. These factors lead to error variance; that is, they result in an imperfect correlation between their batting record in one year and in the subsequent year. It is this second group of players who will move the mean batting average upward to the mean. The two essentials are present for regression to the mean: extreme scores, and imperfect correlation between pre- and postmeasures due to error factors. Improvements in the overall batting average (regression to the mean) may also be aided by those players who deserve to be in the "poorest hitter" category. If you assume that their average is so low that it cannot go lower (floor effect), then the only way they can change at this extreme is to improve.

Another example from sports also illustrates regression to the mean. Those of you who play golf will appreciate this. The weekend is here and you have a tee time for 18 holes of golf at one of your favorite courses. The day is sunny and warm with no wind to speak of. You had a good night's sleep and are feeling very good. It has not rained for several days, and the fairways are hard and give the ball lots of roll. They have watered the greens so that they are soft and hold well. Your tee shots for the day cut the middle of the fairway and you hit every green with your approach in regulation play. Your putting, like your woods and irons, is as good as it has ever been, and every event that happens seems to go your way. It turns out that your score is the best you have ever had. The question is, How will your golf score compare the next time that you play? Why?

Take a look at the box "Thinking Critically About Everyday Information," and consider the issue of extraneous variables in a news report regarding the link between smoking in films and teenage smoking.

Validity of the Research Design

As we have noted, extraneous variables negatively impact the quality of research. In Chapter 5, we introduced the concept of validity—an assessment as to whether you are studying what you believe you are studying. Several specific types of validity are often used to assess qualities of an experimental design. **Internal validity** considers the degree to which there was an effective manipulation of the independent variable and an effective measurement of the dependent variable, and the degree to which sources of extraneous variability were eliminated or controlled. **External validity** considers the degree to which the results of the study will generalize from the specific sample and conditions of the experiment to the more general population and more general conditions of the real world.

Internal Validity

Extraneous variables that contribute to random error or are confounds and contribute to systematic error are undesirable. Whenever they occur, we compromise the internal validity of the experiment. We cannot be sure whether a lack of significant results is due to no effect of the independent variable, to systematic error, or to too much random error. We cannot be sure that an observed relationship is between our independent and dependent variables, because other factors also varied concurrently with the independent variable. The relationship obtained could be due to confounding variables. As we noted earlier, when confounding occurs, the relationship that we observe is open to alternative interpretations. It is important to note that the mere suspicion of confounding is sufficient to compromise internal validity. The burden of ruling out the possibility of extraneous factors rests with the experimenter. The greater the number of plausible alternative explanations available to account for an observed finding, the poorer is the experiment. Conversely, the fewer the number of plausible alternative explanations available, the better the experiment is. As we shall see, true experiments that are properly executed rule out the greatest number of alternative hypotheses.

External Validity

Another form of validity, referred to as external validity, deals with generalizing our findings. We want to design our research so that our findings can be generalized from a small sample of participants to a population, from a specific experimental setting to a much broader setting, from our specific values of an independent variable to a wider range of values, and finally, from a specific behavioral measure to other behavioral measures. The greater

Thinking Critically About Everyday Information

Smoking in Movies and Smoking by Teenagers

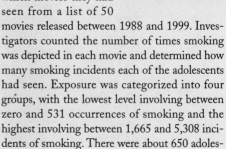

Several news organizations reported the results of a large study that examined the link between cigarette smoking depicted in movies and the number of teenagers who start smoking. Portions of the report that appeared in an Associated Press article are printed below:

Study: Smoking in Movies Encourages Teens

LONDON (AP)—Youngsters who watch movies in which actors smoke a lot are three times more likely to take up the habit than those exposed to less smoking on-screen, a new study of American adolescents suggests. The study, published Tuesday on the Web site of *The Lancet* medical journal, provides the strongest evidence to date that smoking depicted in movies encourages adolescents to start smoking, according to some experts. Others said they remain unconvinced. Many studies have linked smoking in films with increased adolescent smoking, but this is the first to assess children before they start smoking and track them over time. The investigators concluded that 52% of the youngsters in the study who smoked started entirely because of seeing movie stars smoke on screen. . . .

However, Paul Levinson, a media theorist at Fordham University in New York noted there are many reasons people start smoking and the study could not accurately determine how important each factor is. "It's the kind of thing we should be looking at but . . . the fact that two things seem to be intertwined doesn't mean that the first causes the second," said Levinson, who was not involved in the study. "What we really need is some kind of experimental study where there's a controlled group." . . .

The research, conducted by scientists at Dartmouth Medical School, involved 2,603 children from Vermont and New Hampshire schools who were aged between 10 and 14 at the start of the study in 1999 and had never smoked a cigarette at the time they were recruited. The adolescents were asked at the beginning of the study which movies they had seen from a list of 50 movies released between 1988 and 1999. Investigators counted the number of times smoking was depicted in each movie and determined how many smoking incidents each of the adolescents had seen. Exposure was categorized into four groups, with the lowest level involving between zero and 531 occurrences of smoking and the highest involving between 1,665 and 5,308 incidents of smoking. There were about 650 adolescents in each exposure group.

Within two years, 259, or 10%, of the youths reported they had started to smoke or had at least taken a few puffs. Twenty-two of those exposed to the least on-screen smoking took up the habit, compared with 107 in the highest exposure group—a fivefold difference. However, after taking into account factors known to be linked with starting smoking, such as sensation-seeking, rebelliousness or having a friend or relative who smokes, the real effect was reduced to a threefold difference.

Think about the following questions:

- Can you identify possible extraneous variables in this study? Actually, several potential sources of systematic error are mentioned in the report. What are they?

- If people just read the title of the report, would they get the impression that smoking in the movies at least partially causes teenage smoking? Do you believe that this is misleading? Do you agree with the comments of Paul Levinson?

- Can you think of a more accurate title for the article?

SOURCE: "Study: Smoking in Movies Encourages Teens," June 9, 2003, Associated Press. Reprinted with permission of the Associated Press.

the generality of our findings, the greater is the external validity. It should be clear by now that if an experiment does not have internal validity, then it cannot have external validity. Other threats to external validity can include specific characteristics of the laboratory setting and the particular characteristics of the participants used.

The laboratory setting usually involves the research participant in an unfamiliar environment, interacting with unfamiliar people. In some cases, this can lead to observed behaviors that are different from those that would be observed in the real world. Consider little Johnny who is in our TV violence study. Let's assume that we design our study such that Johnny arrives at the university research center along with the other children who were randomly sampled, is randomly assigned to be with a particular group of unfamiliar children who watch an unfamiliar TV program with violence, watches the program in an unfamiliar room, goes to another unfamiliar room to play with the unfamiliar children and the unfamiliar toys that are present, and is observed by an unfamiliar adult. Will we observe natural behavior? Will Johnny behave as if he had just watched the show at home and then gone to his room to play with friends?

Generally, the greater the degree of experimental control, the more concern there must be with external validity. The challenge to the researcher is to maximize the degree of experimental control (internal validity) while designing a testing environment that will result in natural behavior that can be generalized to nonexperimental settings (external validity). However, we should note that some laboratory experiments are interested in testing a specific hypothesis under highly controlled conditions and not too interested in generalizing the data for that study. In this case, internal validity is paramount, and external validity is less of an issue.

External validity is also related to the particular sample of participants used. In the last chapter, we discussed the importance of obtaining a representative sample from a well-defined population. It is important to return to this in our discussion of external validity and to focus on the issues of age, gender, race, and cultural differences. For many years, the typical human participant in behavioral research was a young, white, adult American male. Too often, these research findings were translated into general theories of human behavior without due consideration of the relatively narrow population from which participants were drawn. In more recent years, researchers have examined how these participant characteristics can affect results, and there is an increased emphasis on diversity when selecting participants for a study. However, there continues to be a preponderance of human research in which the participants are white, American college students. Again, it is important for the researcher to realize the population from which participants are sampled and to avoid overgeneralization beyond that population.

Figure 8.1 summarizes the components that determine the validity of a research design.

Figure 8.1   Validity of the Research Design

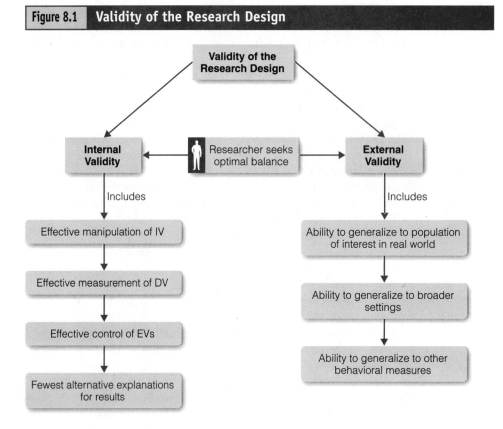

CASE ANALYSIS

"We are inadvertently steering girls away from computer technology. Video games are children's gateways to computers. And ultimately this has ramifications for the kinds of careers people choose." Dr. Sandra Calvert of Georgetown University made this statement at a recent conference of the American Psychological Association.

Carol was concerned about this and developed a computer game that she believed would appeal to girls in their early teens. In addition to some visual/spatial challenges that typify most computer games, Carol included challenges that required verbal reasoning and strategic cooperation among the characters to successfully complete challenges. She then designed a study to verify that girls would be more interested in her game than would boys. She began by posting a request for participants in the eighth-grade classrooms at the local school. Boys and girls signed up for specific test dates and times. Testing took place after school in the school's media room. When each participant arrived, Carol informed the student that she had developed a computer game that she believed would be more appealing to girls than to boys and that she was testing this research question. Carol decided to

measure the participants' interest in the game in two ways. First, she sat adjacent to each participant at the computer and rated, at five-minute intervals, the perceived interest of the participant. Second, she asked each participant, at the end of the session, to rate on a Likert scale their interest in the computer game.

The testing went well except that one-third of the boys had to withdraw from the experiment early to attend football practice. Carol summarized the data and was happy to note that both the experimenter ratings and participant ratings showed that the girls were more interested in the computer game than the boys.

Critical Thinking Questions

1. Describe at least six potential sources of extraneous variability in Carol's study.

2. For each source identified, describe a more effective methodology that would reduce or eliminate that source of extraneous variability.

3. What other aspects of the study could be improved?

GENERAL SUMMARY

The heart of behavioral research design is an understanding of the sources of variability in behavior and an understanding of how to manipulate or control those sources of variability. Systematic variability explains differences in behavior that result from manipulation of the independent variable. The researcher attempts to maximize systematic variability. Extraneous variability represents differences in behavior that result from systematic error (confounds) and random error. The researcher attempts to eliminate systematic error and to minimize random error.

Sources of extraneous variability include participants (history, maturation, attrition, demand characteristics, evaluation apprehension, diffusion of treatment), experimenter (experimenter characteristics, experimenter bias), and method (selection, task and instructions, testing effects, carryover effects, instrumentation, regression to the mean). The degree to which systematic variability is established and extraneous variability (error) is minimized relates directly to the internal validity of the study. Internal validity is necessary but not sufficient to ensure external validity, whereby the researcher can generalize the results to a particular population of individuals. In the next chapter, we will focus on experimental control techniques that are designed to reduce both systematic error and random error and, thus, to increase internal and external validity.

DETAILED SUMMARY

1. Variability in participant scores is often the result of systematic variance, systematic error, and random error. Systematic variance is due to any treatment effect (IV); systematic error is due to extraneous variables (confounds) that affect scores between groups; random error is due to extraneous variables that affect scores within groups.

2. Extraneous variables should be evaluated both when planning research and when evaluating the results after the data have been collected.

3. Sources of extraneous variability can be categorized into the areas of participants, experimenter, and method.

4. Participant sources of extraneous variability include history, maturation, attrition, demand characteristics, evaluation apprehension, and diffusion of treatment.

5. History is the occurrence of an event during the course of the experiment that affects participant behavior. Maturation includes short-term and long-term changes in the state of participants that affect behavior. Attrition is the loss of participants during the course of the study. Demand characteristics are the expectations for certain behaviors that participants experience as a result of the study. Evaluation apprehension is the uncomfortable feeling that participants may experience and that may affect behavior. Diffusion of treatment occurs when initial participants inform later participants about specifics of the study.

6. Experimenter sources of extraneous variability include experimenter characteristics and experimenter bias.

7. Experimenter characteristics are the personality and physical characteristics of the experimenter that affect participant behavior. Experimenter bias includes expectations by the experimenter that influence the recording or scoring of data, as well as the unintended communication of expectancies to participants that may affect their behavior.

8. Method sources of extraneous variability include selection, task and instructions, testing effects, instrumentation, and regression to the mean.

9. Selection is an issue when the groups are selected in a way that creates differences in the dependent variable before the independent variable is even introduced. Task and instructions are issues when participants do not perform identical tasks during measurement of the dependent variable or do not receive identical instructions. Testing is an issue when prior measurements (pretest) influence subsequent measurements (posttest). Carryover effects occur when participation in one condition of the experiment influences behavior in a subsequent condition of the experiment. Instrumentation is an issue when the criteria for measurement by physical instruments or human observers change during the course of the experiment. Regression to the mean is an issue when groups are formed based on extreme scores.

10. The validity of a research design is synonymous with the quality of the study and consists of both internal validity and external validity.

11. Internal validity of a study includes effective manipulation of the independent variable, effective measurement of the dependent variable, effective control of extraneous variables, and the ability to eliminate alternative explanations for the results.

12. External validity of a study includes the ability to generalize from the sample to the population of interest, the ability to generalize to broader settings, and the ability to generalize to other behavioral measures.

KEY TERMS

attrition *(p. 122)*

carryover effects *(p. 128)*

confounding variables (confounds) *(p. 119)*

demand characteristics *(p. 123)*

diffusion of treatment *(p. 124)*

evaluation apprehension *(p. 124)*

experimenter bias *(p. 125)*

experimenter characteristics *(p. 124)*

experimenter expectancies *(p. 125)*

external validity *(p. 131)*

history *(p. 120)*

instructions *(p. 128)*

instrumentation *(p. 128)*

internal validity *(p. 131)*

maturation *(p. 120)*

random error *(p. 119)*

regression to the mean *(p. 129)*

selection *(p. 126)*

systematic error (confounding) *(p. 118)*

systematic variance *(p. 118)*

task *(p. 126)*

testing effects *(p. 128)*

REVIEW QUESTIONS/EXERCISES

A psychology student is interested in whether involvement in aerobic exercise improves mood more than involvement in nonaerobic exercise. He decides to study a group of university students who have enrolled in a bowling course for the fall semester. At the beginning of the semester, he gives them a mood scale to complete. At the end of the semester, he again gives them the mood scale to complete. He asks that all the participants enroll in a jogging course for the spring semester. He gives them the mood scale again at the end of the spring semester.

1. What method of sampling was used?

2. Evaluate the study in terms of each source of extraneous variability listed in Table 8.2. For each source, explain why or why not you believe that it is a design issue. If you believe that it is a design issue, explain whether it is a source of systematic error or random error.

3. How would you rate the internal validity of the study—good, fair, or poor? Explain.

4. How would you rate the external validity of the study—good, fair, or poor? Explain.

 WEB RESOURCES TO INCREASE LEARNING

The chapter outline, chapter summaries, key terms and definitions, additional chapter questions, chapter exercises, and links to relevant Web sites are available at the course Web site (**http://psychology.wadsworth.com/lammers_badia1e**). Explore the interactive workshop "Confounds: Threats to Validity."

CHAPTER 9

USING EXPERIMENTAL CONTROL TO REDUCE EXTRANEOUS VARIABILITY

Introduction to Experimental Control

In the previous chapter, we saw how extraneous variables can contribute to systematic error and to random error. Both sources of error reduce the internal validity (quality) of research and make interpretation of results difficult. As we discussed issues such as demand characteristics, experimenter bias, and testing effects, you likely had some ideas regarding how we might design a study to reduce or eliminate these and other sources of error. Indeed, the researcher has many research design tools that can be used to address these concerns. The good researcher is aware of both the sources of extraneous variability and the research design techniques that can be used to reduce or eliminate extraneous variables.

Characteristics of a True Experiment

In this book, we explore a variety of research methods. In fact, for most areas of research, we have a choice of several research methods. These methods incorporate techniques designed to reduce or eliminate sources of extraneous variability and permit more powerful conclusions. Through the next several chapters, we focus on the most powerful methodology available—the true experiment.

Advantages

The hallmark of the true experiment is control. The experimenter is in control of many facets of the research design. The experimenter controls the way in which a sample of participants is obtained from the population, participants are assigned to different treatment conditions, the environment is organized during testing, instructions are presented to participants, observations are made, and data are collected. As we will see, the purpose of this control is to reduce the influence of extraneous variables so that changes in the dependent variable can be attributed to the independent variable.

In this chapter, we will describe random assignment, the use of control groups, and careful experimental techniques as means of reducing extraneous variability and increasing internal validity. In brief, we will look at how research should be done. Keep this principle in mind: The time to avoid random error (the largest component is individual differences) and confounding (systematic error) is during the design phase. Possible sources of confounding should be anticipated and eliminated before gathering data. After the data have been gathered, it is too late to eliminate any confounding that may exist.

Limitations

Generally speaking, whenever a true experiment can be used to answer a research question, it should be used. However, experiments have their limitations. There are situations in which a true experiment cannot be used because of the nature of the research question or because of ethical issues. As discussed in the previous chapter, a potential limitation of many experiments is the generalizability of the findings from the controlled environment of the laboratory to the real world. That is, can the pattern of results in the experiment be extended to behavior in the real world? To achieve the highest degree of experimental control, most experiments take place in a laboratory setting. To what extent will this artificial environment and the particulars of the setting contribute to the patterns of behavior that are observed? For example, is learning a list of words in a laboratory the same as learning in the classroom?

Some research questions do not lend themselves to the true experiment. The question "Are men more aggressive than women?" cannot be answered using a true experiment because random assignment to the two groups cannot be used. The same issue applies to a host of physical and personality characteristics (for example, anxious versus nonanxious, heavy versus thin, optimist versus pessimist). Consider another example. We might ask whether a change in the level of violence on U.S. television in the past 50 years has corresponded with a change in the level of juvenile delinquency in the United States. This is a valid question, but obviously the events have already occurred (as in our men/women example). We cannot randomly assign participants to treatment conditions and thus cannot achieve the level of control required for a true experiment.

Another example will highlight situations in which ethical concerns are paramount. Let's say that we are interested in whether children who are abused are more likely to grow up to become parents who abuse their own children. This is a very interesting and important question, but not one that can be answered with a true experiment. Can you imagine the following experimental procedures? We go out and sample a group of children to be in our study. We then randomly assign some of them to be physically abused for the next five years, some to be sexually abused for the next five years, some to be neglected for the next five years, and some to be in families with wonderful parents. We then wait for these children to grow up and have their own children, and we observe their parenting behaviors. Might there be an ethical issue here?

Thus, the true experiment cannot be used in every research situation, because of either methodological or ethical issues. We dedicate a chapter toward the end of this book to alternative research designs. But for the moment, we focus our attention on the characteristics of a true experiment and the procedures for conducting a true experiment.

The Notion of Experimental Control

The previous chapter introduced us to the variety of factors that can be sources of extraneous variability. As we noted, the challenge of good research is to develop a research design that will eliminate or reduce sources of systematic error and random error so that systematic variance resulting from manipulation of the independent variable can be revealed. The primary goal is to create a research design that is internally valid. Achieving this goal may seem rather difficult, and it is true that there is no perfect experiment. However, behavioral scientists have a set of methodological tools at their disposal that can be very effective in controlling sources of extraneous variability. The key is to understand what is in the toolbox and when to use it. Figure 9.1 summarizes the control tools available. Let's open this toolbox and take a peek inside.

Control Through Sampling

Methods of sampling, discussed in Chapter 7, can effectively reduce extraneous variability due to selection and regression to the mean. Remember that we want to select a sample of participants that is representative of the population of interest. Also, we need to realize that samples selected for their extreme scores on some variable will likely show a drift in their scores away from the extremes—that is, toward the mean. As discussed previously, random sampling is often the best approach to obtain a representative sample. Random sampling not only controls several extraneous variables, it also allows us to generalize to a given

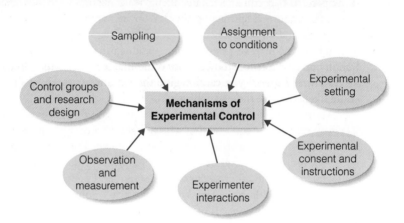

Figure 9.1 Summary of the Research Design Tools That Are Available to Achieve Experimental Control

population (increases external validity). However, as we discussed in Chapter 7, it is often difficult to obtain truly random samples, and the researcher often resorts to the use of convenience sampling (such as using introductory psychology students). Thus, the researcher should consider how the sampling procedure might affect the study's outcome when truly random sampling is not possible.

Control Through Assignment to Conditions *(Independent Samples)*

Although we have not yet discussed specific research designs, it is clear by now that experiments typically involve a comparison of scores obtained under different conditions. Methods for assigning participants to conditions can control a variety of extraneous variables. These methods fall into two categories. The first category involves the creation of groups by random assignment. This technique creates what is termed **independent samples,** and it is the best way that we know to create equality of groups on all known and unknown factors. The second category involves the creation of correlated samples by pairing scores. We provide a brief explanation of each category here; specifics are provided in subsequent chapters.

Independent Samples Design

Random assignment relates directly to internal validity and is concerned with the way in which we assign participants to experimental conditions. It is an essential characteristic of experimentation. The purpose of random assignment is to avoid bias in the composition of the different groups. We want to create groups that are essentially equal so that any differences we subsequently find can be attributed with some confidence to the effects of the treatments themselves, assuming that everything else is held constant. We want to be reasonably sure that the independent variable, and not the method of assigning participants to groups, gave rise to the obtained differences. Random assignment is the best way of doing this. Moreover, random assignment of participants to experimental conditions is a basic assumption of many statistical techniques that we use to make inferences from samples to populations. Satisfaction of this assumption is essential for using these statistical procedures.

With **random assignment,** groups (independent samples) are created such that each participant has an equal chance of being selected for a particular experimental condition. Although random assignment does not guarantee the formation of equal groups, it is the best way that we know to create equality. The value of this technique can be demonstrated by considering the opposite technique—asking for volunteers. If we ask our sample of children in our TV violence study, "Who would like to watch *Beast Wars,* and who would like to watch *Mister Rogers?*" you can imagine the extraneous variables likely to surface, and you would likely observe these variables in the children's response to the question. In response to the request for a *Beast Wars* group, you would likely observe a group of predominantly boys emphatically thrust their hands in the air and yell "Oh, yeah!" Conversely, the volunteers for *Mister Rogers* might meekly raise their hands to half extension and quietly reply "I'd like to." Although this may be a bit of an exaggeration, the point is clear. By not using random assignment, you run the risk of creating groups that are systematically different on a host of variables before the independent variable is even manipulated.

Correlated Samples Design

Control can also be achieved by pairing scores to create **correlated samples.** The paired scores in the groups may represent natural pairs, matched pairs, or repeated measures.

Natural Pairs In a **natural pairs** design, the scores in the groups are paired for some natural reason. Studies using twins provide common examples in the behavioral sciences. One typical source of extraneous variability is that the participants in the comparison groups have different genetic backgrounds, and this factor contributes to the random error in the scores. One solution is to equate the genetic backgrounds by using identical twins. For each pair of twins, one twin is randomly assigned to one condition, and the other twin is assigned to the other condition.

Matched Pairs In a **matched pairs** design, the scores in the groups are paired because the experimenter decides to match them on some variable. In some experiments, the experimenter may decide that there is some extraneous variable so critical to the research that the researcher does not want to rely on random assignment to equate the groups on that variable. For example, if our sample of children for our TV violence study contains children of various ages, we may decide that age is an extraneous variable that must be equated across the groups. Thus, we begin by grouping the children in our sample according to age. We then randomly assign them to the two groups according to age. That is, if we have four 5-year-olds in our sample, two will be randomly assigned to one group and two to the other group. Therefore, when we complete data collection and compare scores in the two groups, we are assured that age is not contributing to the variability in scores between groups.

Repeated Measures In a **repeated measures** design, the scores in the two groups are paired because they come from the same participants. In other words, each participant is tested in each experimental condition. This technique can be an excellent method to reduce random error between groups that is due to individual differences. For our TV violence study, we could test all the children under both conditions. That is, one week the children could be presented with a TV program with violence and their behavior observed, and another week the same children could be presented with a TV program without violence and their behavior observed. However, the method does raise the possibility of carryover effects—an issue that is discussed more fully in Chapter 12.

Control Through Experiment Setting

Experimental control is enhanced by selection of a setting that you can control. That is, you can control the size, temperature, and location of the setting. You control when participants enter the setting, where they stand or sit, what they see, hear, smell, taste, and touch. In other words, you control the environmental stimuli that they experience.

Let's return again to our TV violence example and assume that we are comparing level of aggressive behavior in a group of children who watch a TV program with violence to a group of children who watch a TV program without violence. We can control the experiment setting in a number of ways. We can designate a particular room in the psychology building for testing. We can decide on the size of the room, the color of the walls, the size of the TV, the volume setting on the TV, the type and amount of furniture in the room, the type and number of toys that may be available for the observation period, the number of children in the room during testing, the number of experimenters in the room during testing, the duration of testing, and the time of day of testing. Notice that each of these factors is a potential source of extraneous variability. We want to carefully consider each factor and be sure that both groups of children have the same experimental setting (except for the type of TV show).

In making these decisions, it is important to consider both internal and external validity. In addition to designing an experimental setting that maximizes control of extraneous variables, we also want to design a setting that seems real, so that we will be more confident that our findings will generalize to the real world. Internal validity might be enhanced by testing the children in a room that is completely empty except for a TV, but we would likely sacrifice some degree of external validity.

Meticulous attention to all aspects of our experiment must be pursued right down to the administration of the treatments to the participants. For example, it might be convenient for you to give the treatment to all participants in the experimental group at the same time (all at once) in one session, and to participants in the control group (all at once) in a different session. However, there are risks associated with this procedure. Under these conditions, the individual scores may not be independent. It is possible that any extraneous or unwanted event that occurs during that session could have a marked effect on the performance of one of the groups and not the other.

In essence, we risk confounding the "time and setting" of administering the treatment with the treatment itself. Here are some examples: one very unhappy and uncooperative or unruly participant in one group and not in the other; a hot, noisy room versus a cold, damp room; a knowledgeable, helpful experimenter versus one less knowledgeable and helpful. Some participants may complete the task quickly in one condition and create panic among others in the group who perform more slowly; or the groups may interact differently and ask different questions regarding the task and the instructions, thus resulting in groups very different from what the experimenter envisioned. In short, many things may happen that affect all participants in a particular condition. The scores of individual participants would no longer be independent. Thus, careful thought must be given when choosing between a procedure that administers treatments individually and one using intact groups. Obviously, if intact groups are to be tested, great care must be taken to see that each group is treated as similarly as possible. An alternative to intact groups would be to test several smaller groups under a given condition or to test one individual at a time.

If we decide to test participants one at a time rather than in intact groups, then other considerations arise. To start with, good experiments have, at a minimum, two comparison groups (usually an experimental group and control group) to which participants are randomly assigned and then tested individually (one at a time). There is a proper procedure that should be followed when testing participants one at a time. On any given day, an equal number of participants from each condition (experimental and control groups) should be tested, so that each treatment is represented daily. In an experiment with two conditions, at least two participants (or multiples of two) should be tested on any given day, one from each condition; in an experiment with three conditions, at least three participants (or multiples of three) should be tested on any given day, one from each condition. It is not a proper procedure to administer the treatment to all participants individually in one treatment condition first and then to all participants in another treatment condition. If the latter procedure were used, systematic changes that occur in the separate experimental sessions, or between the time when the first treatment was presented (Time 1) and when the second treatment was presented (Time 2), would be mixed with the effects of the independent variable—that is, confounding. As experimenters become more experienced in dealing with participants, apparatus, instructions, and data recording, they change in some ways. If, in an experiment with two treatment groups, one group was tested first and the other tested second, the experimenter may be naïve for the first group but knowledgeable and sophisticated for the second group. Further, the experimenter may be in a different psychological state (bored) or physical state (ill) for one group. These changes between Time 1 and Time 2 could result in the experimenter's treating the two groups differently.

Other events capable of exerting a systematic effect could occur between Time 1, when the first group is tested, and Time 2, when the second group is tested. Participants in one group may be getting the treatment during midterm or final examinations; the other group, at a different time. Measuring instruments, clocks, and other equipment may become less reliable; observers may change their scoring criteria. The important point is that the procedure of testing one group or treatment condition first, either all at one time or individually, is a faulty one and should be avoided.

The following principle should be kept in mind when planning your experiment: If any extraneous variable with the potential for exerting a systematic effect cannot be eliminated, then it must be held constant for each treatment group—that is, its effects must be distributed to each treatment group as equally as possible. Balancing participants so that each condition is equally represented each day automatically takes into consideration possible variables such as time of year, seasons, and time of school term (such as midterms or finals). When more than one participant is tested each day, balancing for the time of day that they are tested is also necessary. We should note, also, that if more than one experimenter is involved in collecting data, each should test an equal number of participants under each condition.

● Control Through Experiment Consent and Instructions

With human participants, careful consideration of the communications to participants via the consent form and instructions can control for such extraneous variables as demand characteristics, evaluation apprehension, diffusion of treatment, task, and instructions. The language used should be relaxed and professional. Our goal is to observe natural behavior. We want the participants to feel relaxed and not experience apprehension about being evaluated or observed.

Although the consent form should provide sufficient information for informed consent, unnecessary details and specific hypotheses should be avoided. Such details can quickly lead to demand characteristics on the part of participants. If the participants are to be assigned to a particular group, it is often wise to use a **single-blind study** in which participants do not know to which group they have been assigned. Again, knowing which group they are in can create demand characteristics. This can be a particular problem in drug studies, where belief in the efficacy or effects of a drug can cause changes in behavior regardless of the actual effect of the drug. These placebo effects and the use of placebo control groups will be discussed a little later in this chapter.

It is critical that the same instructions be provided to every participant in the study (unless the instructions themselves are the independent variable). This can be accomplished in several ways. Instructions can be read from a script or presented as an audio recording. Participants may read the instructions on a sheet of paper or on a computer screen. If diffusion of treatment is a concern, then it is useful at the end of participation to instruct participants not to discuss the experiment with others who might be future participants.

As we discussed in Chapter 2, the use of deception is sometimes necessary to control demand characteristics so that natural behavior is observed. A good example is the classic study on conformity by Solomon Asch (1956). Asch was interested in whether a participant, judging the length of lines, would provide an incorrect response simply because several others had done so (results showed that they often did). If participants had been informed that this was a study of conformity rather than a study of visual perception, it is unlikely that natural behavior in a situation with social pressure would have been observed.

Let's consider the instructions that might be given to the children in our TV violence study. Of course, it would be important to give both groups of children exactly the same instructions. What would we tell them when they arrived for the experiment? We would probably want to use the single-blind technique and provide general instructions without specifics. For example, we might tell them that they are going to watch a TV program and that when the program is finished, they will be able to play in the room. Notice that the children will not know which group they are in and will not know that aggressive behaviors will be recorded during the play period. We suspect that you would have thought of this. However, have you considered what the experimenter would do if one or more children stopped attending to the TV program, if one or more children wanted to see a parent before the testing was complete, or if one or more children hurt another child? Would you intervene? If so, what would you say? These types of situations are the ones often overlooked during the planning stages of the experiment. The key is to develop a protocol for every possible situation that you can imagine.

Control Through Experimenter Interactions

We have mentioned several ways that the experimenter can be a source of extraneous variability, including experimenter bias in observations, experimenter effects, enhancement of demand characteristics, and enhancement of evaluation apprehension. One additional dimension that deserves attention is the professional demeanor of the experimenter during interactions with the participants. The importance of this factor should not be underestimated. The quality of data obtained from human participants is directly related to the seriousness with which they assume their role as a research participant. If the experimenter is dressed unprofessionally, appears unprepared, or jokes around with participants or other experimenters, then the participants are less likely to take their participation seriously. They are less likely to follow instructions, attend to stimulus presentations, and do their best. All efforts to design a high-quality experiment can be wasted if the experimenter acts unprofessionally.

Control Through Observation and Measurement

Methods of observation and measurement have been discussed in previous chapters. Particular methods can effectively reduce extraneous variability due to demand characteristics, evaluation apprehension, experimenter characteristics, experimenter bias, and instrumentation. Recall that observations can take place with or without the participant's awareness. If observation without awareness is used, demand characteristics and evaluation apprehension are greatly reduced. For example, in some psychological experiments, the critical observations have taken place as participants waited in a waiting room. Similarly, if children are observed without their knowing that they are being observed, more natural behavior is expected.

In the previous examples, participants were unaware that they were being observed. In situations where the participants know that they are being observed but the observer is not physically present, one is more likely to observe natural behavior and to eliminate extraneous variability due to experimenter characteristics. If the experimenter is not present, characteristics of the experimenter (such as gender, age, or attractiveness) cannot affect participant behavior. This can be accomplished, for example, by using one-way mirrors, video recording, or computer-controlled protocols.

We noted earlier in this chapter that participants can be affected by knowing which group they are in and that a single-blind technique can be used to control this problem. Likewise, experimenter observations can be affected by knowing which group a participant is in. In the previous chapter, we referred to this potential confound as experimenter bias. It can be controlled by making the experimenter "blind" to the condition to which the participant was assigned. An experiment in which neither the participant nor the experimenter knows which group the participant is in (at least when the observations are made) is referred to as a **double-blind study**.

Another issue already discussed is the use of specific operational definitions and multiple observers. Both reduce the opportunity for experimenter bias and provide a mechanism for high interobserver agreement. Finally, instrument decay should be avoided by verifying that the actual recording of data has not changed over time or varied with the experimental conditions. This may involve periodic checks on observer performance (observer drift) or periodic calibration of equipment.

Let's consider the information discussed so far in the chapter by applying it to a news report regarding the effect of lead exposure in children (see "Thinking Critically About Everyday Information").

Control Through Use of Control Groups/Research Design

True experiments involve making comparisons between participants' scores in different experimental conditions. Thus, the design of these comparison groups and the way in which participants are assigned to these conditions are critical in determining the integrity of the research design. If comparison conditions are not included in the research design or the

Thinking Critically About Everyday Information

Effects of Exposure to Lead

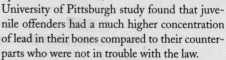

ABC News reported new research on the effects of children's exposure to lead on development. A portion of the report on their Web site follows:

Poisoned Minds: Lead Levels Linked to Lower IQ in Children

. . . The harmful effects of lead poisoning on children are well-documented, but new research suggests that the danger is more widespread than ever imagined, and that exposure to levels currently deemed safe can lower children's IQ scores. . . . A study recently published in the *New England Journal of Medicine* looked at the blood lead levels of 172 children in Rochester, N.Y., ranging in age from six months to 5 years. Researchers tested the children's IQ at ages 3 and 5, and found that those whose blood levels of lead increase from one microgram per deciliter to 10 (the limit under CDC's safety guidelines) experienced an IQ drop of 7.4 points. Children whose blood levels rose from 10 to 30 micrograms per deciliter lost an additional two to three IQ points. But the key point in the research is that even at levels below the limit deemed safe by the CDC, children were losing IQ points. A separate study in the journal from the Environmental Protection Agency found that low levels of lead delay puberty for several months in young girls, especially African-Americans and Latinas. The concern is that the lead is interfering with hormonal processes during development. In addition, a University of Pittsburgh study found that juvenile offenders had a much higher concentration of lead in their bones compared to their counterparts who were not in trouble with the law.

These are important and interesting findings. Now think about how these studies were done. To this point in the chapter, we have discussed characteristics of true experiments and several control techniques that can be used.

- Do the above studies qualify as true experiments? Why or why not?

- Was the setting controlled by the experimenter?

- Was there random assignment to different lead exposure levels?

- Based on your answers to these questions, what can you conclude from the above studies? What can you not conclude?

SOURCE: "Poisoned Minds: Lead Levels Linked to Lower IQ in Children," June 2, 2003. From http://abcnews.go.com/sections/GMA/AmericanFamily/GMA030602Lead_level_research.html. Reprinted with permission.

assignment of participants to conditions does not follow established methodological guidelines, then the extraneous variables discussed in the previous chapter make interpretation of the data impossible.

Primitive Research Designs

To highlight this last point, we will begin by discussing two primitive research designs that do not meet the standards of a true experiment. These two primitive designs give rise to the concept of a control or comparison group. Without proper control conditions, results are generally uninterpretable, and the research is often useless. With a primitive design, it is virtually impossible to determine whether the relationship is between the dependent and independent variables or between the dependent variable and some unwanted variable. With this type of design, it would not matter how carefully the observations were made; the data would remain uninterpretable.

Two primitive designs that are still occasionally used are the one-group posttest design and the one-group pre- and posttest design. These two designs are depicted below.

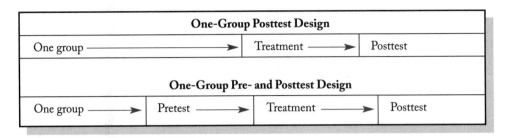

With the one-group posttest design, a single group of participants is selected, a treatment is given, and the behavioral effects of the treatment are measured (posttest). For example, we could sample a group of children, expose them to TV shows with violence for one week, and then measure their level of aggressive behavior the following week. Let's assume that our group of children exhibited a mean of four aggressive behaviors in the 60-minute observation periods. What does this tell us? Did the violence in the TV programs cause these aggressive behaviors? If your answer is "there is no way to know," then you are thinking like a researcher. Of course there is no way to know. The most obvious shortcoming is that there is no comparison condition. There is nothing to compare their aggressiveness to. How aggressive are these children normally? The children may have exhibited the same level of aggression (or even a greater level) without the TV programs. There are various other problems with this design that we will not dwell on. Suffice it to say that it is primitive, lacking many features of better designs.

The one-group pre- and posttest design is an improvement over the first design because it permits us to say at least some things. In this case, we assess the children's level of aggressive behavior before viewing the TV programs and after viewing the programs. In contrast to the one-group posttest design, we now have a standard (pretest) against which to compare any changes in aggression that occur on the posttest. Let's imagine that we find a marked increase in aggression between the pre- and posttest scores. Can we attribute the change to our independent variable—that is, our presentation of the TV programs with violence? Or are alternative accounts also possible? Again, you are thinking like a researcher if you concluded that the second design does not rule out alternative accounts.

Other factors could have occurred during the period when the children watched the TV programs with violence that are fully or partially responsible for the change in aggressive behavior. However, their effects are confounded with the effects of the TV programs. Events at home, at school, or in peer groups could have affected the children's behavior from one week to the next. Also, the natural maturational process could be responsible.

The one-group pre- and posttest design does not provide a way to assess such historical or maturational factors. Indeed, the effects of testing itself may be a factor and should be considered as a possible basis for any change in behavior that is observed. In our example with the children, there is no test per se, but there is an initial observation period that may sensitize the children to being measured and sensitize them to the types of issues involved. These issues are particularly relevant when it comes to an actual test or questionnaire. Students taking the same or similar tests a second time often score differently. The pretest may sensitize them to the kinds of issues involved, and they may react in ways that are unpredictable. Questions on the pretest may make the participants more aware that issues exist. After taking the pretest, they may decide that certain answers are more socially desirable on the posttest. Further, participants may become more cooperative and trustful regarding the questionnaire only after experiencing the pretest. Whether or not these things actually happen is not at issue. The point is that the possibility exists. Consequently, we are unable to untangle the effects of the independent variable from the "spaghetti" of possible alternative explanations.

In some instances, our examples of alternative accounts may be weak and debatable. We do not want you to focus on this point. The important issue is that we cannot assess separately the possible effects of the independent variable and the possible effects of these other factors. Other problems associated with the one-group pre- and posttest design may include such extraneous variables as regression toward the mean, demand characteristics, participant expectancies, and experimenter bias.

A point should be made that some of the criticisms of this design are not valid when the experiment is very short term and takes place under laboratory conditions in which the participant is relatively isolated. In short-term laboratory studies, few events are likely to occur between pre- and posttests, nor are major changes in the participant likely to occur. However, test sensitization and the other factors noted above continue to play an important role.

Importance of Control Groups

A simple addition to the two designs discussed so far would improve the research method considerably. This simple addition would rule out a number of the alternative interpretations that we noted were possible with these designs. Adding a control or comparison group that did not watch TV programs with violence would provide valuable additional information. The comparison group would have to be similar to the treatment group (experimental group) and treated in an identical manner on the pretest and posttest. The only difference is that they would not watch programs with violence. Under these circumstances, we could better isolate the effects of our independent variable. If the groups are assigned randomly and treated properly, we could eliminate most of the alternative accounts noted for the primitive designs.

The use of control groups is important in both laboratory and applied settings. This is particularly the case when new techniques of therapy are being evaluated. Often, when a new medical or psychological therapy is introduced to a group of patients, they show a remarkable recovery. It is tempting to conclude that the improvement is due to the treatment. However, this conclusion cannot be supported without a control group. Recovery from the disorder may not be due to the treatment—medical therapy or psychotherapy—but may arise from other factors. Some individuals may have recovered spontaneously. We are reminded of the frequent observation about the common cold: With the finest of medical treatment, it will be "cured" in a week; otherwise, the patient will require seven days to recover. It is also possible that the simple act of giving attention and showing concern for the well-being of the individual may be the important factor (placebo effect). Participants may expect to get better because experts are attending to them, technology is being used, and gadgets are on display—more placebo effects. Alternatively, experimenter expectancies may operate to the extent that the experimenter sees improvement when there is none. Control groups combined with a single-blind or double-blind procedure would be essential in this situation.

Sometimes data derived from studies without proper control groups are very compelling, even though alternative accounts are plausible. These data do not have to be dismissed. They should serve as a basis for properly designing a study. Let's consider an example dealing with blood dialysis for schizophrenics.

Researchers continue to learn more about the causes of schizophrenia. One view is that the disorder is linked to a chemical imbalance in the brain. About 20 years ago, a controversial study was reported that relates to this biochemical view. A University of Florida professor of medicine, after reviewing the evidence on schizophrenia, believed that a strong case could be made that it was an inherited disorder. He then assumed that it had an organic basis and that it might possibly be related to the individual's blood supply. If this was so, then it might be possible that the material circulating in the blood could be removed by dialysis. Dialysis is a process used to remove waste material from the blood of patients with kidney disorders. The researcher decided to try this "blood cleansing" process on schizophrenics. He selected 16 patients diagnosed as schizophrenic and treated them with dialysis. The dialysis treatment he used was the traditional, well-established procedure (the particulars are unnecessary), and the patients were fully informed of the nature of the treatment. His results were remarkable. Hallucinations and depression disappeared in 14 of the 16 patients. These same patients also showed a considerably improved ability to adapt to normal social situations—often a difficult ordeal for schizophrenics. Could it be that our investigator had discovered a cure for schizophrenia?

Results may have been favorable because patients wanted to believe in the treatment, and in a therapeutic/caring environment their expectations may have been very high. Also, the therapist (researcher) evaluating the subsequent behavior of the schizophrenics was aware that they had undergone dialysis treatment. In this case, the experimenter's expectancies, if any, could be biasing the outcome. The question could also be raised regarding how the patients were treated by others during this period of receiving dialysis. If they were treated in a different way, then this is another form of treatment different from dialysis. The results were very dramatic and certainly suggested that follow-up research on the new technique be undertaken with a much better design.

To rule out expectancy effects, experimenter bias, other forms of inadvertent treatment, and other possibly important factors, a control-group design using random assignment is needed. In contrast to the one-group pre- and posttest design, this design rules out a large number of alternative interpretations.

All schizophrenic patients would first be evaluated (pretested) by a group of independent therapists not involved with the research. The patients would be randomly assigned to the placebo control condition (control for expectancy plus other factors) or to the experimental condition. The patients would be "blind" in the sense that they would not know what condition they were in. Those in the control group would go through a "dummy dialysis" procedure, in which blood would be drawn but not treated. In other words, all patients would be treated exactly alike except for the actual dialysis given the experimental group. Only an attending physician would know who received the treatment. This procedure would assure that the therapists evaluating the subsequent behavior of schizophrenics were also "blind," thus avoiding therapist (experimenter) bias. Because both patients and experimenters would be blind, the study is described as a double-blind one. To avoid changes in our instrumentation, the same therapist would evaluate the patients pre- and posttreatment. At the end of the first phase, all patients would be evaluated and the second, crossover phase begun. In the second phase, the experimental and control participants would have the conditions reversed. Those who were in the experimental treatment would have it withdrawn, and those in the control condition would have the treatment introduced—that is, the groups would cross over to the other condition. No information would be given at this time, and participants would be unaware that a change had taken place. It goes without saying that before the experiment began, all participants would be informed of the two conditions of the experiment and asked to consent to participate.

Soon after the initial report of success with dialysis, Schulz, van Kammen, Balow, Flye, and Bunney (1981) studied eight chronic schizophrenic patients using a double-blind procedure. None of the patients improved with dialysis; in fact, four patients got worse. To this day, dialysis is not considered a treatment for schizophrenia.

Designs With Control Groups

The importance of control groups cannot be exaggerated. When properly used, they allow us to isolate the effects of the independent variable. In doing so, we can distinguish the effects of the independent variable from the effects of other variables that might produce systematic error. The proper control groups allow us to conclude that the observed relationship is between our independent and dependent variables.

As we noted, the primitive research designs lack control groups, and thus the data they provide, though suggestive, are not interpretable. We will now describe two experimental designs that make use of random assignment and control groups. These are powerful designs for isolating the effects of the independent variable. The randomized posttest control-group design and the randomized pre- and posttest control-group design are true experimental designs that use randomization to assign participants to the experimental treatment conditions and to the no-treatment control condition. The only difference between the two designs is the presence or absence of a pretest.

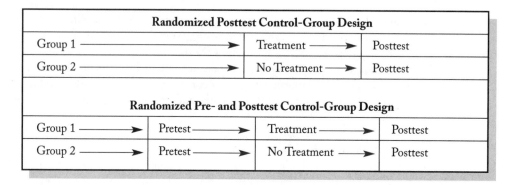

The simplest instance of a control-group procedure can be seen in these two designs. The treatment and no-treatment groups are treated exactly alike except that one receives the independent variable, and the other does not. A comparison (baseline) condition is provided by the no-treatment control group to judge the effects of the treatment condition in the experimental group. We should add that the term *no treatment* should not always be taken literally. It simply means that the experimental treatment was not given to this group. At times, some form of treatment different from the experimental treatment is given. On other occasions, several groups are used, each receiving lesser amounts of the independent variable. Designs involving systematic variations in the amount of a given independent variable, known as parametric designs, will be discussed in Chapter 13.

Experimental designs with control groups are powerful. The addition of a control group combined with random assignment greatly increases our understanding of what is occurring in our experiment. As noted, if a relationship is found, these designs allow us to rule out many competing interpretations. Therefore, with these designs, we can separate the effects of our independent variable from such factors as individual histories, maturation, participant selection, testing effects, participant expectancies, regression effects, and various other possibilities.

Because random assignment is used in these designs, it is likely that the two groups are about equal and that any differences observed on the posttest measure between the two groups are due to the independent variable and not to participant bias. In this regard, the use of a pretest has both positive and negative facets. Researchers sometimes use a pretest measure to assure themselves that the random assignment procedure did, in fact, result in equivalent groups before treatment. This assurance is not usually necessary; most researchers believe that random assignment in itself is sufficient.

Pretests can be useful. A pretest measure makes it easier to assess whether any loss of participants (attrition) during the course of the experiment results in a bias for one group (inequality between groups in terms of participant attributes). Determining whether attrition has biased one of the groups can be done easily with pretest scores by assessing the scores of those remaining in the experiment in the two groups or by comparing those lost from the experiment for the two groups. Pretests also permit us to use a more powerful statistical test such as analysis of covariance, given that the assumptions for its use are met. A covariance analysis is a finely tuned statistical instrument that permits the detection of small treatment effects. Pretests are also useful, sometimes necessary, if you want to assess how effective a treatment is for a specific individual—for example, determining the level of anxiety before therapy and again after therapy.

At times, a pretest measure may not be available, or you may be concerned with the potential problems it might create. Pretest measures require more time, effort, and expense. Moreover, they are often inconvenient for both participant and experimenter. Recall that they may also sensitize the participants, causing some to form hypotheses concerning the experiment (demand characteristics). If the purpose of a pretest is to determine whether random assignment has resulted in equal groups, it can be dispensed with; the design with only a posttest would be as effective. However, if participants cannot be assigned randomly, as in quasi-experimental designs (discussed in Chapter 11), pretest measures are essential. Without these measures, researchers would have little idea about the equivalence or non-equivalence of their groups.

Obviously, these two experimental designs have advantages and disadvantages, depending upon the needs of the experimenter. These relate to the pretest and whether or not it serves some essential function other than assessing the equivalence of groups. We now turn to more detailed discussions of two specific types of control groups: yoked control and placebo control.

Yoked Control Procedure   The **yoked control** procedure allows the researcher to isolate the important effects of the independent variable while holding other possible factors constant. Perhaps you recall reading about the "executive" (experimental) monkeys and the "employee" (control) monkeys described in a study by Brady (1958). Using a yoked control design, Brady placed experimental and control monkeys in identical restraining apparatus where mild shock was periodically delivered. The only difference was that the experimental executive monkeys could avoid shock by responding properly. They learned the task quickly but not perfectly, and on some occasions they received shock. Whenever the executive monkey received shock, the employee monkey, yoked to the executive, also received shock. Both experimental and yoked participants thus received the same number of shocks, the same duration of shocks, and the same temporal distribution of shocks within each experimental session. The only difference between the participants was that for one the response–outcome relationship was dependent (contingent—participant has control) and for the other the relationship was independent (noncontingent—participant has no control).

The executive monkeys, who could control whether or not shock was avoided, all developed serious ulcers, but the employee monkeys did not. Brady concluded that ulceration was a function of the executive role forced upon the monkeys. This conclusion is intuitively satisfying to many people, and belief in the debilitating effects of the executive role is widespread. Yet subsequent studies, such as those of Weiss (1968, 1971a, 1971b, 1971c), report opposite findings. Why the conflict in findings?

A look at Brady's assignment procedure suggests one possible reason. Only four pairs of monkeys were used, and they were assigned to experimental and yoked control conditions on the basis of pretest avoidance scores. The monkeys assigned to the executive condition were those that had the highest rate of avoidance responding. The other four monkeys became the yoked control participants. Unfortunately, rate of avoidance responding and ulceration are positively related. Therefore, those assigned to the executive condition were probably more prone to ulceration than were the controls. Because of this, it is difficult to conclude that having control over aversive environmental events (executives) leads to greater physiological debilitation than not having control (employees). Indeed, the research of Weiss, who used random assignment and the yoked control procedure, supports the opposite conclusion.

Another example of the use of yoked control can be seen in a long series of studies in rats that attempts to understand the detrimental effects of sleep deprivation. Note that the word *detrimental* is appropriate because rats that experience continual and total sleep deprivation die in about 16 days. As you might imagine, the basic design includes a group of rats that are deprived of sleep (experimental group) and a group of rats that are not deprived of sleep (control group). A common method to deprive rats of sleep is to force them to move (using some form of treadmill) when the first sign of sleep appears in their recordings of brain activity. Do you see the potential confound? Not only will the experimental rats be deprived of sleep, they will also engage in much more physical activity. Thus, any observed effects could be due to sleep deprivation or could be due to physical activity.

To eliminate this potential confound, Allen Rechtschaffen, a sleep researcher, devised an experimental methodology that incorporated a yoked control. The experimental apparatus consists of a Plexiglas box with a pool of water at the bottom. Elevated above the pool is a circular disc that can rotate and a wall that separates one half of the box from the other. Two rats are placed on the circular disc, one on each side of the wall. Whenever the experimental rat begins to fall asleep, the circular disc begins to rotate. To avoid hitting the wall and falling into the pool of water (which rats do not like), the experimental rat will awaken and begin walking in the opposite direction. Because the control rat is on the same circular disc, the control rat must engage in the same amount of walking behavior. However, the control rat can sleep anytime that the experimental rat is awake. Thus, the experimental rat is deprived of sleep while the control rat is not (at least to a great extent), and the amount of physical activity is controlled. Even with this elegant design, there are several other potential confounds that the researchers needed to control. Can you identify some of them?

Placebo Control Procedures   The word *placebo* comes from the Latin verb meaning "to please." The evolution of the term from both a research and therapeutic perspective is interesting. Medical historians have noted that almost any kind of treatment used in the early days of medicine seemed to have therapeutic properties. Even though these therapeutic treatments had no obvious direct relationship to the problem being treated, they did, in fact, alleviate distress. Remedies such as lizard blood, bat blood, crocodile dung, frog sperm, putrid meat, hoof of ass, and others were used (Shapiro & Morris, 1978). Often, complex rituals were used, and the ingredients that were given caused bodily discomfort. These rituals and the administration of the "therapy" had the effect of arousing faith and also the expectation that the "therapy" would be effective. Rituals of a different kind are still used by physicians, therapists, and researchers.

Today, physicians and therapists are well aware of the placebo effect and often use it to their advantage. The phenomenon is well documented in medicine and psychotherapy. Interest in understanding more about the placebo is very high, and prominent medical and physiological investigators are giving serious attention to studying it. There is now considerable evidence indicating that the placebo can act like medication and can result in marked physiological changes. Placebos have been shown to actually alter the body chemistry and to mobilize the body's defenses. There is also evidence showing that administering a placebo has an effect on the neurochemistry of the brain. In studies dealing with the experience of pain, placebos have been shown to significantly reduce pain. These studies have shown that placebos trigger the brain to release internal opiates (endorphins), which are known to have a marked effect on the experience of pain. Why and how placebos do this is still a mystery.

The placebo effect is similar to demand characteristics, in that cues or treatment in the situation give rise to expectations on the part of the participant. However, demand characteristics are more idiosyncratic and vary among individual participants, whereas the placebo effect tends to be specifically and directly tied to the treatment condition. The placebo effect in research settings is generally seen in outcome studies where different drug treatments or therapies are being compared. Outcome studies of treatments are different from experimental studies where other kinds of interests are evaluated. In outcome studies comparing different therapies or different drugs, a **placebo control** group is necessary simply to assess the therapeutic effects of believing that one has received a curative treatment.

We can illustrate the need for this type of control. For example, if we were interested in evaluating the effectiveness of a therapeutic drug, we would have to untangle the actual effects of the drug from the expectation that the drug has a therapeutic effect. Simply believing that a drug or a therapeutic treatment has an effect can lead to a consistent and marked change in behavior. In our experiment, we would have two groups. One group would be responding to the drug *and* to whatever placebo effect it might have; the other group would respond to the placebo effect alone. In the latter case, the placebo would be an inert substance or sugar pill that appeared exactly like the drug itself. If differences in behavior followed, then we would attribute these differences to the effects of the drug because we have controlled for the placebo effect by allowing it to occur in both groups. The placebo is used to ensure that participants in both groups have the same expectations and beliefs. As noted, for the placebo to be effective, it must be indistinguishable in appearance from the actual drug. In some cases, it may be necessary to provide side effects similar to those experienced with the actual drug. When using a placebo control procedure, the expectations of participants are distributed equally among the groups used in the experiments.

The placebo control group method for evaluating the effects of the independent variable is a powerful technique, but under some circumstances, its use presents real problems. Both ethical and practical problems can arise when evaluating the effectiveness of clinical-therapeutic procedures, such as psychological or medical treatment. Several recent articles have addressed the use of placebo controls in the development of new drugs to treat Alzheimer's disease (Kawas, Clark, & Farlow, 1999) and schizophrenia (Fleishhacker & Marksteiner, 2000). When evaluating a therapeutic technique, the placebo control method requires that a sample of individuals suffering from an illness or disorder be divided into at least two groups—one that receives the treatment therapy and one that receives the placebo condition. For example, in the case of a drug therapy, the evaluation requires that the drug be given to the treatment group and be withheld from the placebo group—even though the drug might in fact help them. What do you do under these circumstances when, partway through the study, the drug appears to be effective for the treatment group? This becomes an ethical issue. How do you maintain patients for the placebo control condition after information becomes available suggesting that a treatment is effective? This poses a practical problem.

Some alternatives to the placebo control method are available, in addition to the crossover design. One is to use an **active control** procedure. With this procedure, half the patients receive an established treatment whose degree of effectiveness is known; the other half receives the new treatment. Another method is the **historical control** procedure. In this case, the new therapy is compared with clinical records of past patients who were untreated or who received another therapy. In still other instances, if a drug or treatment clearly reduces pain, or lowers blood pressure, or prevents suicide, or *dramatically* reduces any important physical or behavioral problem *consistently*, then a placebo control study may not be necessary. There are also instances in which all participants in a research study receive the treatment but in varying doses. Sometimes, therapies have been adopted on the basis of the therapists' observations rather than controlled studies. Although controlled studies are far better for evaluating a therapy, it is sometimes difficult to argue with the observation that "people used to die without a drug or treatment but now live with it."

CASE ANALYSIS

Researchers continue to investigate the process by which children learn to read. Debate continues over the most effective method to teach reading. The whole-word method, used in a majority of schools, emphasizes the reading of literature and understanding words by understanding the context. The phonics method emphasizes the decoding of words by focusing on the sounds of the alphabet. A researcher decides to compare two classes that will use the two different methods.

The researcher knows that School A uses the whole-word method and that School B uses the phonics method. The researcher randomly samples one first-grade class from School A and one first-grade class from School B. At the end of the school year, the researcher receives consent to administer a standardized reading test to the children in both classes. Scores show that children in the phonics class scored significantly higher on the

reading test than children in the whole-word class. The researcher concludes that the phonics method is more effective than the whole-word method.

Critical Thinking Questions

1. Do you believe that this conclusion is warranted?
2. Does this represent a true experimental design? Why or why not?
3. Which extraneous variables were effectively controlled by the methodology used?
4. Which extraneous variables were not effectively controlled by the methodology used?
5. Which control techniques would be effective in reducing the extraneous variables?
6. Which experimental design would be more effective, and how would it be conducted?

GENERAL SUMMARY

A true experiment is characterized by a high degree of experimental control, the hallmark of which is random

assignment. The research techniques described in this chapter provide the tools with which a researcher can confidently answer questions in the field of behavioral research. The challenge is to understand the tools that are available and to know when to use them. The good researcher knows that extraneous variables can creep in at every step of the research process. Researchers can control extraneous variables through the experimental setting, consent, instructions, sampling techniques, assignment techniques, observation techniques, measurement techniques, interactions with participants, and the use of research designs with control groups.

The experimental setting should be selected so that the researcher can control the stimuli and events that the participant will experience, without sacrificing external validity. Informed consent and experiment instructions should be carefully worded to avoid demand characteristics, evaluation apprehension, diffusion of treatment, and other unwanted effects. In addition to random sampling of participants, random assignment to groups can be a very effective deterrent to extraneous variables. In other situations, random error due to individual differences or systematic error due to a confound can be controlled by pairing the scores in the groups via natural pairs, matched pairs, or repeated measures designs. Precise observation and measurement techniques are critical, along with a professional demeanor on the part of the experimenter. Finally, use of a control condition that does not receive the treatment provides a critical comparison condition against which to judge the effect of the treatment in the experimental condition. A control condition is particularly important when placebo effects are a concern.

Before we turn to specific experimental designs, the next chapter will review some basic statistical issues.

DETAILED SUMMARY

1. A variety of research design techniques are available to control extraneous variables. Random assignment and the extensive use of other control techniques are hallmarks of the true experiment.

2. The true experiment has advantages and disadvantages. Advantages relate to the extensive use of control to reduce the influence of extraneous variables and thus alternative interpretations of the data. Disadvantages, in some cases, relate to the ability to generalize findings to the "real" world. In addition, some research questions cannot be addressed with a true experiment, either because the independent variable cannot be manipulated or because it would be unethical to do so.

3. Control techniques include control through sampling, assignment to conditions, setting, consent, instructions, observation, measurement, experimenter interactions, use of control groups, and research design.

4. Control through sampling refers to the use of random sampling to increase both internal validity (reduce systematic and random error) and external validity. Sampling refers to the way in which participants are selected for the study. With random sampling, each element in the population has an equal chance of being in the study. When random samples are not practically possible (you then have a sample in search of a population), the researcher should nevertheless strive for the characteristics of random sampling.

5. Control through assignment to conditions refers to the ways in which research participants who have been sampled for the study are assigned to particular groups or conditions. Control can be exercised by the use of random assignment to create an independent samples design or the use of correlated samples designs (natural pairs, matched pairs, repeated measures) in which control is achieved by pairing scores in the different groups/conditions.

6. Control through experimental setting refers to the researcher's ability to determine stimuli and events in the research setting. Greater control of the setting reduces sources of systematic and random error.

7. Control through consent refers to the use of relaxed but professional language during informed consent. We do not want to create anxiety, and we do not want to reveal details that might lead to unnecessary demand characteristics. In many situations, we can use a single-blind technique in which participants are not aware of the group or condition that they are in.

8. Control through instructions refers to the use of identical instructions for all participants (unless the instructions serve as the independent variable). It often includes a request to not discuss the study with other individuals who might participate in the future.

9. Control through observation and measurement refers to observation conducted without participant awareness and/or the use of a double-blind technique, whereby participants do not know what group they are in and observers do not know what group participants are in when observations are made. Clear operational definitions and periodic checks of recording equipment also contribute to control.

10. Control through experimenter interactions refers to the professionalism with which the experimenter presents him/herself.

11. Control through use of control groups and research design refers to research designs that include a comparison group that receives either a different treatment or no treatment (control group). Examples of such designs are the randomized pre- and posttest control-group design and the randomized posttest-only control-group design.

12. Specific types of control groups include the yoked control and placebo control. Yoked control refers to an experimental situation in which two participants experience exactly the same environmental events at the same moments in time with the exception of the one variable that is manipulated by the researcher (the IV). Placebo control refers to the fact that for some treatments (especially drug treatments), participants readily expect specific effects, and these expectations can mimic the effect of the treatment. A placebo control group provides a measure of these expectancy effects when the treatment is not actually administered.

KEY TERMS

active control *(p. 154)*

correlated samples *(p. 141)*

double-blind study *(p. 145)*

historical control *(p. 154)*

independent samples *(p. 140)*

matched pairs *(p. 141)*

natural pairs *(p. 141)*

placebo control *(p. 153)*

random assignment *(p. 141)*

repeated measures *(p. 141)*

single-blind study *(p. 144)*

yoked control *(p. 151)*

REVIEW QUESTIONS/EXERCISES

1. Briefly describe a hypothetical study of emotions in which random assignment of participants to treatment conditions is possible. Briefly describe a hypothetical study of emotions in which random assignment is not possible. Briefly describe a hypothetical study of emotions in which random assignment is unethical.

2. Consider a research topic in which you are interested, and conduct a database search for journal articles on that topic using your InfoTrac College Edition subscription (log on at http://www.infotrac-college.com). Locate a study that is a true experiment, and provide a summary of the experiment.

3. Read the Method section of the article you chose in question 2. Using the summary of control techniques illustrated in Figure 9.1, identify which of the techniques were used in the experiment, and provide a description of how each was used.

 ## WEB RESOURCES TO INCREASE LEARNING

The chapter outline, chapter summaries, key terms and definitions, additional chapter questions, chapter exercises, and links to relevant Web sites are available at the course Web site (**http://psychology.wadsworth.com/lammers_badia1e**). Explore the interactive workshops "Experimental Methods," "True Experiments," and "Controls."

CHAPTER **10**

EXPERIMENTAL DESIGN
STATISTICAL ANALYSIS
OF DATA

● Purpose of Statistical Analysis

In previous chapters, we have discussed the basic principles of good experimental design. Before examining specific experimental designs and the way that their data are analyzed, we thought that it would be a good idea to review some basic principles of statistics. We assume that most of you reading this book have taken a course in statistics. However, our experience is that statistical knowledge has a mysterious quality that inhibits long-term retention. Actually, there are several reasons why students tend to forget what they learned in a statistics course, but we won't dwell on those here. Suffice it to say, a chapter to refresh that information will be useful.

When we conduct a study and measure the dependent variable, we are left with sets of numbers. Those numbers inevitably are not the same. That is, there is variability in the numbers. As we have already discussed, that variability can be, and usually is, the result of multiple variables. These variables include extraneous variables such as individual differences, experimental error, and confounds, but may also include an effect of the independent variable. The challenge is to extract from the numbers a meaningful summary of the behavior observed and a meaningful conclusion regarding the influence of the experimental treatment (independent variable) on participant behavior. Statistics provide us with an objective approach to doing this.

● Descriptive Statistics

Central Tendency and Variability

In the course of doing research, we are called on to summarize our observations, to estimate their reliability, to make comparisons, and to draw inferences. **Measures of central tendency** such as the mean, median, and mode summarize the performance level of a group of scores, and **measures of variability** describe the spread of scores among participants. Both are important. One provides information on the level of performance, and the other reveals the consistency of that performance.

Let's illustrate the two key concepts of central tendency and variability by considering a scenario that is repeated many times, with variations, every weekend in the fall and early winter in the high school, college, and professional ranks of our nation. It is the crucial moment in the football game. Your team is losing by four points. Time is running out, it is fourth down with two yards to go, and you need a first down to keep from losing possession of the ball. The quarterback must make a decision: run for two or pass. He calls a timeout to confer with the offensive coach, who has kept a record of the outcome of each offensive play in the game. His report is summarized in Table 10.1.

To make the comparison more visual, the statistician had prepared a chart of these data (Figure 10.1).

What we have in Figure 10.1 are two frequency distributions of yards per play. A **frequency distribution** shows the number of times each score (in this case, the number of yards) is obtained. We can tell at a glance that these two distributions are markedly different. A pass play is a study in contrasts; it leads to extremely variable outcomes. Indeed, throwing a pass is somewhat like playing Russian roulette. Large gains, big losses, and incomplete passes (0 gain) are intermingled. A pass doubtless carries with it considerable excitement and apprehension. You never really know what to expect. On the other hand, a running play is a model of consistency. If it is not exciting, it is at least dependable. In no case did a run gain more than ten yards, but neither were there any losses. These two distri-

Table 10.1	Yards Gained (or Lost) on 20 Pass and 20 Running Plays, Ordered from Largest Gain (Left Column) to Smallest Gain or Largest Loss (Right Column)							
	PASS PLAYS				RUNNING PLAYS			
31	9	0	−1	10	5	3	2
29	8	0	−5	10	4	3	1
20	5	0	−10	8	4	3	1
15	1	0	−15	8	3	3	1
10	0	0	−17	6	3	2	0

Figure 10.1	Yards Gained or Lost by Passing and Running Plays

The mean gain per play, +4 yards, is identical for both running and passing plays.

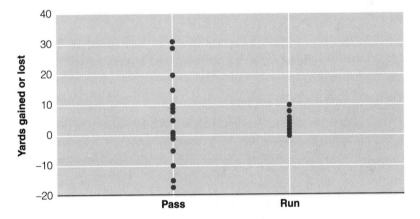

butions exhibit extremes of variability. In this example, a coach and quarterback would probably pay little attention to measures of central tendency. As we shall see, the fact that the mean gain per pass and per run is the same would be of little relevance. What is relevant is the fact that the variability of running plays is less. It is a more dependable play in a short yardage situation. Seventeen of 20 running plays netted two yards or more. In contrast, only 8 of 20 passing plays gained as much as two yards. Had the situation been different, of course, the decision about what play to call might also have been different. If it were the last play in the ball game and 15 yards were needed for a touchdown, the pass would be the play of choice. Four times out of 20 a pass gained 15 yards or more, whereas a run never came close. Thus, in the strategy of football, variability is a fundamental consideration. This is, of course, true of many life situations.

Some investors looking for a chance of a big gain will engage in speculative ventures where the risk is large but so, too, is the potential payoff. Others pursue a strategy of investments in blue chip stocks, where the proceeds do not fluctuate like a yo-yo. Many other real-life decisions are based on the consideration of extremes. A bridge is designed to handle a maximum rather than an average load; transportation systems and public utilities (such as gas, electric, water) must be prepared to meet peak rather than average demand in order to avoid shortages and outages.

Researchers are also concerned about variability. By and large, from a researcher's point of view, variability is undesirable. Like static on an AM radio, it frequently obscures the signal we are trying to detect. Often the signal of interest in psychological research is a measure of central tendency, such as the mean, median, or mode.

Measures of Central Tendency

The Mean Two of the most frequently used and most valuable measures of central tendency in psychological research are the mean and median. Both tell us something about the central values or typical measure in a distribution of scores. However, because they are defined differently, these measures often take on different values. The **mean,** commonly known as the arithmetic average, consists of the sum of all scores divided by the number of scores. Symbolically, this is shown as

$$\overline{X} = \frac{\Sigma X}{n}$$

in which $\overline{X}$ is the mean; the sign Σ directs us to sum the values of the variable X. (Note: When the mean is abbreviated in text, it is symbolized M). Returning to Table 10.1, we find that the sum of all yards gained (or lost) by pass plays is 80. Dividing this sum by n (20) yields $M = 4$. Since the sum of yards gained on the ground is also 80 and n is 20, the mean yards gained per carry is also 4. If we had information only about the mean, our choice between a pass or a run would be up for grabs. But note how much knowledge of variability adds to the decision-making process. When considering the pass play, where the variability is high, the mean is hardly a precise indicator of the typical gain (or loss). The signal (the mean) is lost in a welter of static (the variability). This is not the case for the running play. Here, where variability is low, we see that more of the individual measures are near the mean. With this distribution, then, the mean is a better indicator of the typical gain.

It should be noted that each score contributes to the determination of the mean. Extreme values draw the mean in their direction. Thus, if we had one running play that gained 88 yards, the sum of gains would be 160, n would equal 21, and the mean would be 8. In other words, the mean would be doubled by the addition of one very large gain.

The Median The median does not use the value of each score in its determination. To find the **median,** you arrange the values of the variable in order—either ascending or descending—and then count down $(n + 1)/2$ scores. This score is the median. If n is an even number, the median is halfway between the two middle scores. Returning to Table 10.1, we find the median gain on a pass play by counting down to the 10.5th case $[(20 + 1)/2 = 10.5]$. This is halfway between the 10th and 11th scores. Because both are 0, the median gain is 0. Similarly, the median gain on a running play is 3.

The median is a particularly useful measure of central tendency when there are extreme scores at one end of a distribution. Such distributions are said to be skewed in the direction of the extreme scores. The median, unlike the mean, is unaffected by these scores; thus, it is more likely than the mean to be representative of central tendency in a skewed distribution. Variables that have restrictions at one end of a distribution but not at the other are prime candidates for the median as a measure of central tendency. A few examples are time scores (0 is the theoretical lower limit and there is no limit at the upper end), income (no one earns less than 0 but some earn in the millions), and number of children in a family (many have 0 but only one is known to have achieved the record of 69 by the same mother).

The Mode   A rarely used measure of central tendency, the **mode** simply represents the most frequent score in a distribution. Thus, the mode for pass plays is 0, and the mode for running plays is 3. The mode does not consider the values of any scores other than the most frequent score. The mode is most useful when summarizing data measured on a nominal scale of measurement. It can also be valuable for describing a multimodal distribution, one in which the scores tend to occur most frequently around two or three points in the distribution.

Measures of Variability

We have already seen that a measure of central tendency by itself provides only a limited amount of information about a distribution. To complete the description, it is necessary to have some idea of how the scores are distributed about the central value. If they are widely dispersed, as with the pass plays, we say that variability is high. If they are distributed compactly about the central value, as with the running plays, we refer to the variability as low. But *high* and *low* are descriptive words without precise quantitative meaning. Just as we needed a quantitative measure of centrality, so also do we require a quantitative index of variability.

The Range   One simple measure of variability is the **range**, defined as the difference between the highest and lowest scores in a distribution. Thus, referring to Table 10.1, we see that the range for pass plays is 31 − (−17) = 48; for running plays, it is 10 − 0 = 10. As you can see, the range provides a quick estimate of the variability of the two distributions. However, the range is determined by only the two most extreme scores. At times this may convey misleading impressions of total variability, particularly if one or both of these extreme scores are rare or unusual occurrences. For this and other reasons, the range finds limited use as a measure of variability.

The Variance and the Standard Deviation   Two closely related measures of variability overcome these disadvantages of the range: **variance** and **standard deviation.** Unlike the range, they both make use of all the scores in their computation. Indeed, both are based on the squared deviations of the scores in the distribution from the mean of the distribution.

Table 10.2 illustrates the number of aggressive behaviors during a one-week observation period for two different groups of children. The table includes measures of central tendency and measures of variability. Note that the symbols and formulas for variance and standard deviation are those that use sample data to provide estimates of variability in the population.

Notice that although the measures of central tendency are identical for both groups of scores, the measures of variability are not and reflect the greater spread of scores in Group 2. This is apparent in all three measures of variability (range, variance, standard deviation). Also notice that the variance is based on the squared deviations of scores from the mean and that the standard deviation is simply the square root of the variance. For most sets of scores that are measured on an interval or ratio scale of measurement, the standard deviation is the preferred measure of variability. Conceptually, you should think of standard deviation as "on average, how far scores are from the mean."

Now, if the variable is distributed in a bell-shaped fashion known as the normal curve, the relationships can be stated with far more precision. Approximately 68% of the scores lie

Table 10.2	Measures of Central Tendency and Measures of Variability for Aggression Scores From Two Different Groups of Children					
	GROUP 1			**GROUP 2**		
	Score (X)	$X - \bar{X}$	$(X - \bar{X})^2$	Score (X)	$X - \bar{X}$	$(X - \bar{X})^2$
	14	2	4	18	6	36
	13	1	1	15	3	9
	12	0	0	12	0	0
	12	0	0	12	0	0
	11	−1	1	9	−3	9
	10	−2	4	6	−6	36
	$\Sigma = 72$	$\Sigma = 0$	$\Sigma = 10$	$\Sigma = 72$	$\Sigma = 0$	$\Sigma = 90$
Mean $(\bar{X})$	12			12		
Median	12			12		
Range	4			12		
Variance (s^2) $s^2 = \dfrac{\Sigma(X - \bar{X})^2}{n-1}$	2			18		
Standard deviation (s) $s = \sqrt{\dfrac{\Sigma(X - \bar{X})^2}{n-1}}$	1.41			1.97		

between the mean and ±1 standard deviation, approximately 95% of the scores lie between ±2 standard deviations, and approximately 98% of the scores lie between ±3 standard deviations. These features of normally distributed variables are summarized in Figure 10.2.

Note that these areas under the normal curve can be translated into probability statements. Probability and proportion are simply percentage divided by 100. The proportion of area found between any two points in Figure 10.2 represents the probability that a score, drawn at random from that population, will assume one of the values found between these two points. Thus, the probability of selecting a score that falls between 1 and 2 standard deviations above the mean is 0.1359. Similarly, the probability of selecting a score 2 or more standard deviations below the mean is 0.0228 (0.0215 + 0.0013).

Many of the variables with which psychologists concern themselves are normally distributed, such as standardized test scores. What is perhaps of greater significance for the researcher is the fact that distributions of sample statistics tend toward normality as sample size increases. This is true even if the population distribution is not normal. Thus, if you were to select a large number of samples of fixed sample size, say $n = 30$, from a nonnormal distribution, you would find that separate plots of their means, medians, standard deviations, and variances would be approximately normal.

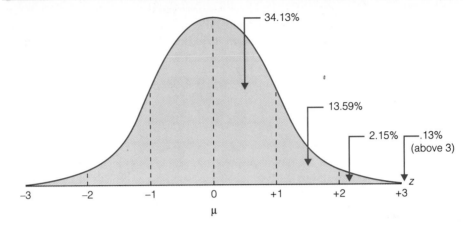

Figure 10.2 Areas Between the Mean and Selected Numbers of Standard Deviations Above and Below the Mean for a Normally Distributed Variable

The Importance of Variability

Why is variability such an important concept? In research, it represents the noisy background out of which we are trying to detect a coherent signal. Look again at Figure 10.1. Is it not clear that the mean is a more coherent representation of the typical results of a running play than is the mean of a pass play? When variability is large, it is simply more difficult to regard a measure of central tendency as a dependable guide to representative performance.

This also applies to detecting the effects of an experimental treatment. This task is very much like distinguishing two or more radio signals in the presence of static. In this analogy, the effects of the experimental variable (treatment) represent the radio signals, and the variability is the static (noise). If the radio signal is strong, relative to the static, it is easily detected; but if the radio signal is weak, relative to the static, the signal may be lost in a barrage of noise.

In short, two factors are commonly involved in assessing the effects of an experimental variable: a measure of centrality, such as the mean, median, or proportion; and a measure of variability, such as the standard deviation. Broadly speaking, the investigator exercises little control over the measure of centrality. If the effect of the treatment is large, the differences in measures of central tendency will generally be large. In contrast, control over variability is possible. Indeed, much of this text focuses, directly or indirectly, on procedures for reducing variability—for example, selecting a reliable dependent variable, providing uniform instructions and standardized experimental procedures, and controlling obtrusive and extraneous experimental stimuli. We wish to limit the extent of this unsystematic variability for much the same reasons that a radio operator wishes to limit static or noise—to permit better detection of a treatment effect in the one case and a radio signal in the other. The lower the unsystematic variability (random error), the more sensitive is our statistical test to treatment effects.

Tables and Graphs

Raw scores, measures of central tendency, and measures of variability are often presented in tables or graphs. Tables and graphs provide a user-friendly way of summarizing information and revealing patterns in the data. Let's take a hypothetical set of data and play with it.

One group of 30 children was observed on the playground after watching a TV program without violence, and another group of 30 children was observed on the playground after watching a TV program with violence. In both cases, observers counted the number of aggressive behaviors. The data were as follows:

Program with no violence: 5, 2, 0, 4, 0, 1, 2, 1, 3, 6, 5, 1, 4, 2, 3, 2, 2, 2, 5, 3, 4, 2, 2, 3, 4, 3, 7, 3, 6, 3, 3

Program with violence: 5, 3, 1, 4, 2, 0, 5, 3, 4, 2, 6, 1, 4, 1, 5, 3, 7, 2, 4, 2, 3, 5, 4, 6, 3, 4, 4, 5, 6, 5

Take a look at the raw scores. Do you see any difference in number of aggressive behaviors between the groups? If you are like us, you find it difficult to tell.

One of the first ways we might aid interpretation is to place the raw scores in a table called a frequency distribution and then translate that same information into a graph called a frequency histogram (see Figure 10.3).

Both the frequency distribution and the frequency histogram in Figure 10.3 make it easy to detect the range of scores, the most frequent score (mode), and the shape of the distribution. A quick glance at the graphs now suggests that the children tended to exhibit fewer aggressive behaviors after the TV program with no violence. We can further summarize the data by calculating the mean and standard deviation for each group and presenting these values in both a table and a figure (see Table 10.3 and Figure 10.4).

In Figure 10.4, the mean is depicted by a square, and the bars represent 1 standard deviation above and below the mean. Thus, although the means differ by 0.6 units, one can see from the standard deviation bars that there is quite a bit of overlap between the two sets of scores. Inferential statistics will be needed to determine whether the difference between the means is statistically significant.

In the preceding description of data, we selected a few ways that the data could be summarized in both tables and figures. However, these methods are certainly not exhaustive. We can display these data and other data in a variety of other ways, in both tabular and graphical form, and we encourage students to experiment with these techniques. Remember that the data are your window into participant behavior and thought. You can only obtain a clear view by careful examination of the scores.

Before we turn to inferential statistics, let's think about the added clarity that descriptive statistics can provide when observed behavior is described. To do this, we return to the report of a study that was first described in Chapter 6 and is considered again here in the box "Thinking Critically About Everyday Information."

Table 10.3	Descriptive Statistics for the No Violence and Violence Groups	
	No Violence	**Violence**
M	3.00	3.60
SD	1.74	1.73
n	30	30

Figure 10.3 **Number of Aggressive Behaviors Illustrated in Both Frequency Distributions and Frequency Histograms**

No Violence Group

Score (X)	Frequency (f)
7	1
6	2
5	3
4	4
3	7
2	8
1	3
0	2

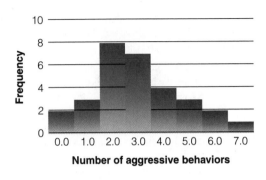

Violence Group

Score (X)	Frequency (f)
7	1
6	3
5	6
4	7
3	5
2	4
1	3
0	1

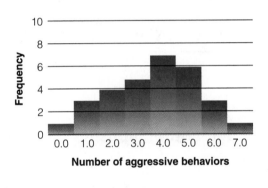

Figure 10.4 **Graphical Depiction of the Mean and Standard Deviation for the No Violence and Violence Groups**

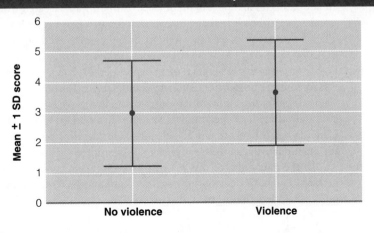

Thinking Critically About Everyday Information

School Backpacks and Posture Revisited

A news report by MSNBC describes a study in which children were observed carrying school backpacks. The article states:

> Thirteen children ages 8 and 9 walked about 1,310 feet without a backpack, and wearing packs weighing 9 and 13 pounds, while researchers filmed them with a high-speed camera.... The kids did not change their strides, the images showed. Instead, the youngsters bent forward more as they tried to counter the loads on their backs, and the heavier loads made them bend more, the study found. As they grew more tired, their heads went down, Orloff said.

In Chapter 6, we focused our critical thinking questions on the method of observation. Now, let's think about the description of the observations:

- The article states that when children carried the backpacks, they "did not change their strides" but

"bent forward more." Although this description is typical of a brief news report, what specific measure of central tendency could be reported for each dependent variable to clarify the description?

- What measure of variability would clarify the description?

- How would you create a graph that would nicely summarize the pattern of results reported in the article?

- Why is it that most reports of research in the everyday media do not report measures of central tendency and variability, with related tables or graphs?

SOURCE: Retrieved June 11, 2003. online at http://www.msnbc.com/news/922623.asp?0si=-

Inferential Statistics

From Descriptions to Inferences

We have examined several descriptive statistics that we use to make sense out of a mass of raw data. We have briefly reviewed the calculation and interpretation of statistics that are used to describe both the central tendency of a distribution of scores or quantities (mean, median, and mode) and the dispersion of scores around the central tendency (range, standard deviation, and variance). Our goal in descriptive statistics is to describe, with both accuracy and economy of statement, aspects of samples selected from the population.

It should be clear that our primary focus is not on the sample statistics themselves. Their value lies primarily in the light that they may shed on characteristics of the population. Thus, we are not interested, as such, in the fact that the mean of the control group was higher or lower than the mean of an experimental group, nor that a sample of 100 voters revealed a higher proportion favoring Candidate A. Rather, our focus shifts from near to far vision; it shifts from the sample to the population. We wish to know if we may justifiably conclude that the experimental variable has had an effect; or we wish to predict that Candidate A is likely to win the election. Our descriptive statistics provide the factual basis for the inductive leap from samples to populations.

In the remainder of this chapter, we will take a conceptual tour of statistical decision making. The purpose is not to dwell on computational techniques but rather to explore the rationale underlying inferential statistics.

The Role of Probability Theory

Recall the distinction between deductive and inductive reasoning. With deductive reasoning, the truth of the conclusion is implicit in the assumptions. Either we draw a valid conclusion from the premises, or we do not. There is no in-between ground. This is not the case with inductive or scientific proof. Conclusions do not follow logically from a set of premises. Rather, they represent extensions of or generalizations based on empirical observations. Hence, in contrast to logical proof, scientific or inductive conclusions are not considered valid or invalid in any ultimate sense. Rather than being either right or wrong, we regard scientific propositions as having a given probability of being valid. If observation after observation confirms a proposition, we assign a high probability (approaching 1.00) to the validity of the proposition. If we have deep and abiding reservations about its validity, we may assign a probability that approaches 0. Note, however, we never establish scientific truth, nor do we disprove its validity, with absolute certainty.

Most commonly, probabilities are expressed either as a proportion or as a percentage. As the probability of an event approaches 1.00, or 100%, we say that the event is likely to occur. As it approaches 0.00, or 0%, we deem the event unlikely to occur. One way of expressing probability is in terms of the number of events favoring a given outcome relative to the total number of events possible. Thus,

$$P_A = \frac{\text{number of events favoring A}}{\text{number of events favoring A} + \text{number of events not favoring A}}$$

To illustrate, if a population of 100,000 individuals contains 10 individuals with the disorder phenylketonuria (PKU), what is the probability that a person, selected at random, will have PKU?

$$P_{PKU} = \frac{10}{10 + 99,990} = 0.0001 \text{ or } 0.01\%$$

Thus, the probability is extremely low: 1 in 10,000.

This definition is perfectly satisfactory for dealing with discrete events (those that are counted). However, how do we define probability when the variables are continuous—for example, weight, IQ score, or reaction time? Here, probabilities can be expressed as a proportion of one area under a curve relative to the total area under a curve. Recall the normal distribution. The total area under the curve is 1.00. Between the mean and 1 standard deviation above the mean, the proportion of the total area is 0.3413. If we selected a sample score from a normally distributed population, what is the probability that it would be between the mean and 1 standard deviation above the mean? Because about 34% of the total area is included between these points, $p = 0.34$. Similarly, $p = 0.34$ that a single randomly selected score would be between the mean and 1 standard deviation below the mean. Table A.2 (Appendix A) shows areas under the standard normal curve and permits the expression of any value of a normally distributed variable in terms of probability.

Probability looms large on the scene of inferential statistics because it is the basis for accepting some hypotheses and rejecting others.

The Null and Alternative Hypotheses

Before beginning an experiment, the researcher sets up two mutually exclusive hypotheses. One is a statistical hypothesis that the experimenter expects to reject. It is referred to as the **null hypothesis** and is usually represented symbolically as H_0 The null hypothesis states some expectation regarding the value of one or more population parameters. Most commonly, it is a hypothesis of no difference (no effect). Let us look at a few examples:

- If we were testing the honesty of a coin, the null hypothesis (H_0) would read: The coin is unbiased. Stated more precisely, the probability of a head is equal to the probability of a tail: $P_h = P_t = 1/2 = 0.5$.

- If we were evaluating the effect of a drug on reaction time, the null hypothesis might read: The drug has no effect on reaction time.

The important point to remember about the null hypothesis is that it always states some expectation regarding a population parameter—such as the population mean, median, proportion, standard deviation, or variance. It is never stated in terms of expectations of a sample. For example, we would never state that the sample mean (or median or proportion) of one group is equal to the sample mean of another. It is a fact of sampling behavior that sample statistics are rarely identical, even if selected from the same population. Thus, ten tosses of a single coin will not always yield five heads and five tails. The discipline of statistics sets down the rules for making an inductive leap from sample statistics to population parameters.

The **alternative hypothesis (H_1)** denies the null hypothesis. If the null hypothesis states that there is no difference in the population means from which two samples were drawn, the alternative hypothesis asserts that there is a difference. The alternative hypothesis usually states the investigator's expectations. Indeed, there really would be little sense embarking upon costly and time-consuming research unless we had some reason for expecting that the experimental variable will have an effect. Let's look at a few examples of alternative hypotheses:

- In the study aimed at testing the honesty of a coin, the alternative hypothesis would read: H_1: $P_h \neq P_t \neq 1/2$; the probability of a head is not equal to the probability of a tail, which is not equal to one-half.

- In the effect of a drug on reaction time, the alternative hypothesis might read: The administration of a given dosage level of a drug affects reaction time.

The Sampling Distribution and Statistical Decision Making

Now that we have stated our null and alternative hypotheses, where do we go from here? Recall that these hypotheses are mutually exclusive. They are also *exhaustive.* By exhaustive we mean that no other possibility exists. These two possible outcomes in our statistical decision exhaust all possible outcomes. If the null hypothesis is true, then the alternative hypothesis must be false. Conversely, if the null hypothesis is false, then the alternative hypothesis must be true.

Considering these realities, our strategy would appear to be quite straightforward—simply determine whether the null hypothesis is true or false. Unfortunately, there is one further wrinkle. The null hypothesis can never be proved to be true. How would you go about proving that a drug has no effect, or that males and females are equally intelligent, or that a coin is honest? If you flipped it 1,000,000 times and obtained exactly 500,000 heads, wouldn't that be proof positive? No. It would merely indicate that, if a bias does exist, it must be exceptionally small. But we cannot rule out the possibility that a small bias does exist. Perhaps the next million, 5 million, or 10 billion tosses will reveal this bias. So we have a dilemma. If we have no way of proving one of two mutually exclusive and exhaustive hypotheses, how can we establish which of these alternatives has the higher probability of being true?

Fortunately, there is a way out of this dilemma. If we cannot prove the null hypothesis, we can set up conditions that permit us to reject it. For example, if we had tossed the coin 1,000,000 times and obtained 950,000 heads, would anyone seriously doubt the bias of the coin? Clearly, we would reject the null hypothesis that the coin is honest. The critical factor in this decision is our judgment that an outcome this rare is unlikely to have been the result of chance factors. It happened for a reason, and that reason is to be found in the characteristics of the coin or in the way it was tossed.

In this particular example, we did not engage in any formal statistical exercise in order to reject H_0. Our lifelong experience with coin-tossing experiments provided a frame of reference that permitted us to make the judgment. Because the obtained outcome is monumentally rare, we conclude that it did not occur by chance. However, in science, we often do not have frames of reference, based on experience, that permit us to dispense with formal statistical analyses. Nor are we often afforded the luxury of a sample size equal to 1 million. The frame of reference for statistical decision making is provided by the **sampling distribution** of a statistic. A sampling distribution is a theoretical probability distribution of the possible values of some sample statistic that would occur if we were to draw all possible samples of a fixed size from a given population. There is a sampling distribution for every statistic— mean, standard deviation, variance, proportion, median, and so on.

To illustrate, imagine we had a population of six scores: 1, 2, 3, 3, 4, 5. Suppose we randomly select a single score from this population, return it, and randomly select a second score. We call these two scores a random sample of $n = 2$, and we calculate a mean. Now imagine that we selected all possible samples of $n = 2$ from that population and calculated a mean for each. Table 10.4 shows all possible outcomes of this sampling experiment. Each cell shows the mean of the two scores that make up each sample. Thus, if the first selection is 1 and the second is 1, the mean of the sample is 1.0.

Now we can record the frequency with which each mean would be obtained. When we do so, we have constructed a frequency distribution of means of sample size $n = 2$. Table 10.5 shows this frequency distribution of the sample means.

Table 10.4	Sample Means Resulting From Selecting All Possible Samples of $n = 2$ From a Population of Six Scores					
SECOND SELECTION	FIRST SELECTION					
	1	2	3	3	4	5
1	1.0	1.5	2.0	2.0	2.5	3.0
2	1.5	2.0	2.5	2.5	3.0	3.5
3	2.0	2.5	3.0	3.0	3.5	4.0
3	2.0	2.5	3.0	3.0	3.5	4.0
4	2.5	3.0	3.5	3.5	4.0	4.5
5	3.0	3.5	4.0	4.0	4.5	5.0

Table 10.5	Frequency Distribution and Sampling Distribution of Means Based on Samples of $n = 2$ Drawn at Random From a Population of Six Numbers

Note that the mean of the distribution of sample means is the same as the population mean.

	SAMPLE MEAN	FREQUENCY	p
	1.0	1	.028
	1.5	2	.056
	2.0	5	.139
	2.5	6	.167
Mean ⟶	3.0	8	.222
	3.5	6	.167
	4.0	5	.139
	4.5	2	.056
	5.0	1	.028
		Total = 36	Total = 1.002*

*The sum of the probabilities is 1.00. The slight disparity is due to rounding error.

Now, if we divide the frequency with which a given mean was obtained by the total number of sample means (36), we obtain the probability of selecting that mean (last column in Table 10.5). Thus, eight different samples of $n = 2$ would yield a mean equal to 3.0. The probability of selecting that mean is 8/36 = 0.222. Note that, by chance, we would rarely select a mean of 1.0 ($p = 0.028$) or a mean of 5.0 ($p = 0.028$).

In this example, we used a very small population to illustrate a sampling distribution of a statistic. In real life, the populations are often extremely large. Let us imagine that we had a large population of scores and we selected a large number of samples of a given size (say, $n = 30$). We could construct a distribution of the sample means. We would find that the mean of this distribution equals the mean of the population, and the form of the distribution would tend to be normal—even if the population distribution is not normal. In fact, the larger the sample size, the more closely the distribution of sample means will approximate a normal curve (see Figure 10.5).

It is a fortunate fact of statistical life that distributions of sample statistics often take on the form of other distributions with known mathematical properties. This permits us to use this known distribution as a frame of reference against which to evaluate a given sample statistic. Thus, knowing that the distribution of sample means tends toward normality when the sample size exceeds 30 permits us to evaluate the relative frequency of a sample mean in terms of the normal distribution. We are then able to label certain events or outcomes as common, others as somewhat unusual, and still others as rare. For example, note that in Figure 10.5 a score of 130 is fairly common when $n = 1$, whereas a mean of 130 is unusual when $n = 15$, and rare when $n = 30$. If we find that the occurrence of an event or the outcome of an experiment is rare, we conclude that nonchance factors (such as the experimental variable) are responsible for or have caused this rare or unusual outcome.

Figure 10.5 Distribution of Scores of a Population (*n* = 1) and Sampling Distributions of Means When Samples Are Randomly Selected From That Population and the Sample Sizes Are *n* = 15 and *n* = 30, Respectively

Note that the parent distribution is markedly skewed. As we increase *n*, the distribution of sample means tends toward normality and the dispersion of sample means decreases. (The Greek letter mu, μ, represents a population mean.)

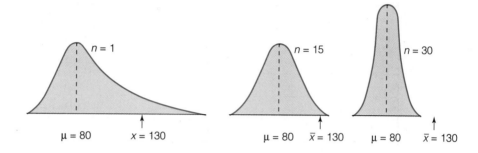

Table 10.6 shows the sampling distribution of a coin-tossing experiment when a single coin is tossed 12 times or when 12 coins are tossed once. It is the sampling distribution of a binomial or two-category variable when *n* = 12, and the probability of each elementary event (a head or a tail) is equal to 1/2.

This sampling distribution provides a frame of reference for answering questions about possible outcomes of experiments. Is 12 out of 12 heads a rare outcome? Yes, exceedingly rare. It occurs, by chance, about twice out of every 10,000 repetitions of the experiment. Note that 0 out of 12 is equally rare. What about 7 heads out of 12? This would be not at all unusual. This outcome will occur about 19 times out of every 100 repetitions of the coin-tossing experiment. Can we define *rare* more precisely? This will require an agreement among fellow scientists. If the event in question or an event more unusual would have occurred less than 5% of the time, most psychological researchers are willing to make the judgment that the outcome is rare and ascribe it to nonchance factors. In other words, they reject H_0 and assert H_1. This cutoff point for inferring the operation of nonchance factors is referred to as the 0.05 significance level. When we reject the null hypothesis at the 0.05 level, it is conventional to refer to the outcome of the experiment as statistically significant at the 0.05 level.

Other scientists, more conservative about rejecting H_0, prefer to use the 0.01 significance level, or the 1% significance level. When the observed event or one that is more deviant would occur by chance less than 1% of the time, we assert that the results are due to nonchance factors. It is conventional to refer to the results of the experiment as statistically significant at the 0.01 level.

The level of significance set by the investigator for rejecting H_0 is known as the **alpha (α) level**. When we employ the 0.01 significance level, α = 0.01. When we use the 0.05 significance level, α = 0.05.

Let us look at a few examples of this statistical decision-making process:

- Jeanette conducted a study in which she used α = 0.05. Upon completing her statistical analysis, she found that the probability of obtaining such an outcome simply by

Table 10.6	Sampling Distribution of a Binomial Variable in Which $P_h = P_t = 1/2$ and the Number of Trials Equals 12
OUTCOME EXPRESSED AS NUMBER OF HEADS	**PROBABILITY**
12	.0002
11	.0029
10	.0161
9	.0537
8	.1208
7	.1934
6	.2256
5	.1934
4	.1208
3	.0537
2	.0161
1	.0029
0	.0002
	$\Sigma P = .9998^*$

*The sum of the probabilities is 1.00. The slight disparity is due to rounding error.

chance was 0.02. Her decision? She rejects H_0 and asserts that the experimental variable had an effect on the dependent measure.

- Roger obtained a probability of 0.06, using $\alpha = 0.05$. Because his results failed to achieve the 0.05 cutoff point, he does not reject the null hypothesis. Note that he cannot claim to have proved the null hypothesis, nor should he claim "there is a trend toward significance." Once a significance level is set, its boundaries should be considered as quite rigid and fixed.

- A research team set alpha at 0.01 and found the probability of their obtained outcome to be $p = 0.03$. They fail to reject H_0 because the probability of this outcome is greater than α.

The statistical decision-making process is summarized in Table 10.7.

Many of the tables that researchers and statisticians use do not provide probability values for the sampling distributions to which they refer. Rather, they present **critical values** that define the **region of rejection** at various levels of α. The region of rejection is that portion of the area under a curve that includes those values of a test statistic that lead to rejection of the null hypothesis. However, Roger's results are so close to the cutoff point, he would be wise to consider repeating the study and increasing the n, if still possible.

To illustrate, the two curves in Figure 10.6 show the regions for rejecting H_0 when the standard normal curve is used.

Table 10.7	The Decision-Making Matrix in Inferential Statistics	
	ALPHA LEVEL (α)	
PROBABILITY OF OUTCOME	0.05	0.01
$p < 0.01$	Reject H_0	Reject H_0
$0.05 > p \geq 0.01$	Reject H_0	Fail to reject H_0
$p \geq 0.05$	Fail to reject H_0	Fail to reject H_0

Figure 10.6	Region of Rejection at α = 0.05 and α = 0.01 Under the Standard Normal Curve

If the obtained statistic is greater than 1.96 or less than −1.96 and α = 0.05, we reject H_0.
If α = 0.01 and the test statistic exceeds the absolute value of 2.58, we reject H_0.

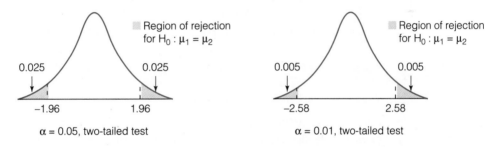

α = 0.05, two-tailed test α = 0.01, two-tailed test

Let's look at a few examples:

- If α = 0.05 and the test statistic equals 1.43, we fail to reject H_0 because the test statistic does not achieve the critical value.
- If α = 0.01 and the test statistic equals 2.83, we reject H_0 because the test statistic is in the region of rejection.
- If α = 0.05 and the test statistic equals 2.19, we reject H_0 because the test statistic is in the region of rejection for α = 0.05.

You may have noticed that in the above discussion we assumed a two-tailed test of significance. That is, the probability associated with the alpha level was split into the left and right tails of the sampling distribution to determine the critical values for the significance test. Most researchers use two-tailed tests, and most statistical software programs conduct two-tailed tests as the default. The two-tailed test is slightly more conservative, and it lets us reject the null hypothesis if the treatment increases *or* decreases scores on the dependent variable. However, if you are confident that your independent variable will only affect scores on the dependent variable in a particular direction, you may decide to use a one-tailed test of significance. In that case, you would place all of the probability associated with your alpha level into one tail of the sampling distribution. This results in a slightly more powerful analysis but risks the chance that the effect may go in the direction that is opposite of your prediction.

Type I Errors, Type II Errors, and Statistical Power

As we saw earlier in the chapter, we can make two types of statistical decisions: reject H_0 when the probability of the event of interest achieves an acceptable a level (usually $p < 0.05$ or $p < 0.01$), or fail to reject H_0 when the probability of the event of interest is greater than α. Each of these decisions carries an associated risk of error.

If we reject H_0 (conclude that H_0 is false) when in fact H_0 is true, we have made the error of falsely rejecting the null hypothesis. This type of error is called a **Type I error**. If we fail to reject H_0 (we do not assert the alternative hypothesis) when in fact H_0 is false, we have made the error of falsely accepting H_0. This type of error is referred to as a **Type II error**.

Let's look at a few examples:

- $H_0: \mu_1 = \mu_2,\ \alpha = 0.05$. Obtained $p = 0.03$.
  Statistical decision: Reject H_0. Actual status of H_0: True.
  Error: Type I (rejecting a true H_0).

- $H_0: \mu_1 = \mu_2,\ \alpha = 0.05$. Obtained $p = 0.04$.
  Statistical decision: Reject H_0. Actual status of H_0: False.
  Error: None (conclusion is correct).

- $H_0: \mu_1 = \mu_2,\ \alpha = 0.01$. Obtained $p = 0.10$.
  Statistical decision: Fail to reject H_0. Actual status of H_0: False.
  Error: Type II (failing to reject a false H_0).

- $H_0: \mu_1 = \mu_2,\ \alpha = 0.01$. Obtained $p = 0.06$.
  Statistical decision: Fail to reject H_0. Actual status of H_0: True.
  Error: None (conclusion is correct).

You should know that a Type I error can be made only when H_0 is true because this type of error is defined as the mistaken rejection of a true hypothesis. The probability of a Type I error is given by α. Thus, if $\alpha = 0.05$, about 5 times out of 100 we will falsely reject a true null hypothesis. In contrast, a Type II error can be made only when H_0 is false because this type of error is defined as the mistaken retention of a false hypothesis.

Table 10.8 summarizes the probabilities associated with retention or rejection of H_0 depending on the true status of the null hypothesis.

The probability of a Type II error must be obtained by calculation. It is beyond the scope of this book to delve into the calculation of β probabilities. Interested students may consult a more advanced statistics book. The concept of this error is important because,

Table 10.8 The Type of Error Made as a Function of the True Status of H_0 and the Statistical Decision Made

To illustrate, if H_0 is true (column 1) and we have rejected H_0 (row 2), we have made a Type I error. If H_0 is false (column 2) and we have rejected H_0, we have made a correct decision.

		TRUE STATUS OF H_0	
		H_0 **true**	H_0 **false**
STATISTICAL DECISION	**Retain H_0**	Correct $(1 - \alpha)$	Type II error (β)
	Reject H_0	Type I error (α)	Correct $(1 - \beta)$

among other things, it relates to the economics of research. It would make little sense to expend large amounts of funds, tie up laboratory space and equipment, and devote hours of human effort to the conceptualization, conduct, and statistical analysis of research if, for example, the β probability were as high as 90 percent. This would mean that the probability of making a correct decision—rejecting the false null hypothesis—would be only 10 percent. It would hardly seem worth the effort. This probability—the probability of correctly rejecting the null hypothesis when it is false—is known as the **power** of the test. Power is defined as $1 - \beta$. In other words, the power of a statistical test is the ability of the test to detect an effect of the IV when it is there.

There is a further risk when conducting research in which the power is low. A failure to find a significant difference may cause a researcher to prematurely abandon a promising line of experimentation. As a consequence, potentially important discoveries may never be made because the researcher relegated a seminal idea to the junk heap.

Clearly, one of the goals of the careful researcher must be to reduce the probability of β error and, thereby, increase the power of the test. A number of factors influence statistical power. Among them are sample size, alpha level, and precision in estimating experimental error. Fortunately, all are under the control of the experimenter.

Other things being equal, as you increase the sample size, you increase the power of your statistical test. In research in which the cost per participant is low, increasing the sample size may be an attractive way to boost power. However, the relationship between sample size and power is one of diminishing returns. Beyond a certain point, further increases in sample size lead to negligible increases in power.

As the α level is decreased, we decrease the probability of a Type I error and increase the probability of a Type II error. Conversely, as the α level is increased, we increase the probability of a Type I error and decrease the probability of a Type II error. Because the power of the test is inversely related to the probability of a Type II error (power increases as the probability of a Type II error decreases), it follows that the power can be increased by setting a higher alpha level for rejecting H_0.

Balanced against this is the fact that increasing the α level also increases the probability of falsely rejecting a true null hypothesis. The researcher must decide which of these risks is more acceptable. If the consequences of making a Type I error are serious (claiming that a chemical compound cures a serious disease when it does not), it is desirable to set a low α level. However, the commission of a Type II error can also have serious consequences, as when failure to reject the null hypothesis is treated as if the null hypothesis has been proved. Thus, a chemical compound "proved safe after exhaustive testing" could lead to the introduction of a lethal compound into the marketplace.

The third factor, control over the precision in estimating experimental error, is the one that should receive the most attention from a careful researcher. Any steps that lead to increased precision of our measurement of experimental error will also increase the power of the test. We can increase our precision in measuring experimental error in numerous ways, including improving the reliability of our criterion measure, standardizing the experimental technique, and using correlated measures. In a correlated samples design, for example, the power of the test will increase as the correlation between paired measures increases. We had more to say about this important topic in earlier chapters, where we noted that a feature of various research designs was the degree of precision in estimating both the effects of experimental treatments and the error variance.

In our consideration of Type I and Type II errors, it is important to remember that only one type of error is possible in any given analysis and that researchers never know whether one of these errors has occurred (if they knew, then they would obviously change their con-clusion to avoid the error!). Thus, it is critical for the researcher to consider all of the factors discussed in the previous paragraphs to increase confidence that an erroneous conclusion will not be made.

Effect Size

Generally speaking, we want a high degree of power in our experiment. That is, we want to be able to detect a difference if one in fact exists. As noted above, we can increase the power of our experiment by increasing the sample size. How far should we take this? Is it the case that the larger the sample the better? Not exactly. At some point, we can use such large sam-ples and have such high power that we begin to detect statistically significant differences that are, in fact, practically meaningless (the differences between the treatment group and control group are small and trivial). Significance tests (such as the *t* test or ANOVA) provide a way to decide whether an effect exists, but do not provide a clear indication of how large an effect is. Measures of **effect size** provide an indication of the size of an effect (strength of the IV) and, therefore, provide important additional information. Measuring effect size is a helpful technique for separating statistical significance and practical significance.

Several different measures of effect size are available. The APA *Publication Manual* (p. 25) provides a list and encourages authors to include an appropriate measure of effect size in the results section of a research report. You can use Table 10.9 as a guide to select the most appropriate measure of effect size for some of the most basic statistical analyses.

Your obvious next question is, What do these numbers tell you? Without getting into deep statistical explanations (you can find these in more advanced statistics books), let's summarize what are considered small, medium, and large effect sizes. For the point-biserial correlation, values less than .30 are considered small, values of .30–.50 are considered mod-erate, and values greater than .50 are considered large (Thompson & Buchanan, 1979). For

Table 10.9	Guide to the Selection and Calculation of Effect Size	
INFERENTIAL STATISTIC	**MEASURE OF EFFECT SIZE**	**STATISTICAL FORMULA**
t test	r_{pb} (point-biserial correlation)	$r_{pb} = \sqrt{\dfrac{t^2}{t^2 + df}}$
	d (Cohen's *d*)	$d = \dfrac{t(n_1 + n_2)}{\sqrt{df}\sqrt{n_1 n_2}}$
Analysis of variance (ANOVA)	η^2 (eta-squared)	$\eta^2 = \dfrac{SS_{between}}{SS_{total}}$
	ω^2 (omega-squared)	$\omega^2 = \dfrac{SS_{between} - (a-1)MS_{error}}{SS_{total} + MS_{error}}$
Pearson *r* correlation coefficient	r^2 (*r*-squared)	r^2
Chi-square test for independence	ϕ^2 (phi coefficient squared)	$\phi^2 = \dfrac{\chi^2}{N}$

Cohen's d, values of .20–.50 are considered small, values of .50–.80 are considered moderate, and values greater than .80 are considered large (Cohen, 1977). For η^2 and ω^2, the value indicates the proportion of variance (0.0–1.0) in the dependent variable that can be explained by the levels of the independent variable. For r^2 and ϕ^2, the value indicates the proportion of variance in the criterion variable that can be explained by the predictor variable. The larger the proportion of variance that can be explained, the larger is the effect size.

Meta-analysis

Whereas measures of effect size provide important information for a particular study, **meta-analysis** is a statistical technique that provides an indication of the size of an effect across the results of many studies. As different researchers continue to explore a particular research question, published studies begin to accumulate. After some period of time, it is common for someone to publish a review article to summarize the different studies that have been done and their findings. These review articles often reveal mixed findings; that is, some studies report effects, and some do not.

Meta-analysis provides a statistical method for combining the effects across studies to reach a decision regarding whether a particular independent variable affects a particular dependent variable. Essentially, a measure of effect size is calculated for each study and then weighted according to the sample size and quality of the study. These measures are then averaged across studies to produce an overall effect size. This overall value provides a measure of effect size in standard deviation units. Thus, a meta-analysis that produced an effect size of .33 would indicate that the size of the effect is one-third of the average standard deviation across studies.

Let's examine an actual meta-analysis. Do you believe that prevention programs targeted to children in school can reduce the incidence of child sexual abuse? A variety of such programs have been developed, implemented, and evaluated. Two researchers conducted a meta-analysis of 27 such studies (Davis & Gidycz, 2000). They reported an overall effect size of 1.07, which indicated that children who participated in prevention programs performed more than 1 standard deviation higher on outcome measures. Based on their analysis, they also concluded that long-term programs that required active involvement from the children were more effective. Such analyses effectively summarize a body of literature and direct further research.

Parametric Versus Nonparametric Analyses

Many data are collected in the behavioral sciences that either do not lend themselves to analysis in terms of the normal probability curve or fail to meet the basic assumptions for its use. For example, researchers explore many populations that consist of two categories—for example, yes/no, male/female, heads/tails, right/wrong. Such populations are referred to as dichotomous, or two-category, populations. Other populations consist of more than two categories—for example, political affiliation or year in college. (We dealt with these in Chapter 5 under the heading Nominal Scale.) Other data are best expressed in terms of ranks—that is, on ordinal scales. When comparing the attributes of objects, events, or people, we are often unable to specify precise quantitative differences. However, we are frequently able to state ordered relationships—for example, Event A ranks the highest with respect to the attribute in question, Event B the second highest, and so on. In addition to equivalence and nonequivalence, then, the mathematical relationships germane to such data are "greater than" (>) and "less than" (<). The relationship $a > b$ may mean that a is taller than *b*, of higher rank than *b*, more prestigious than *b*, prettier than *b*, and so on. Similarly, the relationship *a* < *b* may mean that *a* is less than *b*, of lower rank than *b*, less prestigious than *b*, and so on.

Finally, many data collected by psychologists are truly quantitative. They may be meaningfully added, subtracted, multiplied, and divided. These data are measured on a scale with equal intervals between adjacent values—that is, an interval or ratio scale. For example, in a timed task, a difference of 1 second is the same throughout the time scale. Most commonly, **parametric statistics** are used with such variables. Parametric tests of significance include the *t* test and analysis of variance (ANOVA).

Parametric tests always involve two assumptions. One is that the populations for the dependent variable are normally distributed. That is, the distribution of scores conforms to a bell-shaped distribution rather some other shape of distribution (such as positively or negatively skewed, or multimodal). The risk of a nonnormal distribution is particularly great with small *n*'s. With large *n*'s, the sampling distributions of most statistics approach the normal curve even when the parent distributions deviate considerably from normality. The second assumption is termed **homogeneity of variance**. Homogeneity of variance is the assumption that the populations for the dependent variable have equal variances. That is, the degree to which the scores are spread out around the mean is the same in the populations represented by the groups in the study. It is worth noting that parametric tests are robust. As long as the assumptions are not seriously violated, the conclusions derived from parametric tests will be accurate.

For data measured on a nominal scale, an ordinal scale, an interval scale with a nonnormal distribution, or a ratio scale with a nonnormal distribution, the investigator should use **nonparametric statistics** for the analysis. For data on a nominal scale, nonparametric analyses include the chi-square test for goodness of fit, the chi-square test for independence, the binomial test, and the median test. For data on an ordinal scale or for data on an interval/ratio scale that do not satisfy the assumption of normality, nonparametric analyses include the Wilcoxon test and the Mann–Whitney test. (It is beyond the scope of this text to review the many nonparametric tests that are available. If you wish to read further, you may consult a statistics textbook.)

Selecting the Appropriate Analysis: Using a Decision Tree

As you can see, deciding on the appropriate descriptive and inferential statistics for a given study is not easy and involves consideration of several factors. To aid in these decisions, we have included several decision trees. Figure 10.7 illustrates how to choose a descriptive statistic. Figure 10.8 illustrates how to choose a parametric statistic to evaluate group differences. Figure 10.9 illustrates how to choose a nonparametric statistic to evaluate group differences. Finally, Figure 10.10 illustrates how to choose a statistic to measure the relationship between two variables.

● Using Statistical Software

Computers have greatly increased the efficiency with which research data can be analyzed. Researchers rarely calculate statistics by hand. Typically, data are entered into some form of spreadsheet. Statistics can then be calculated by database software (such as Excel, Access,

Figure 10.7 **Decision Tree to Select a Descriptive Statistic**

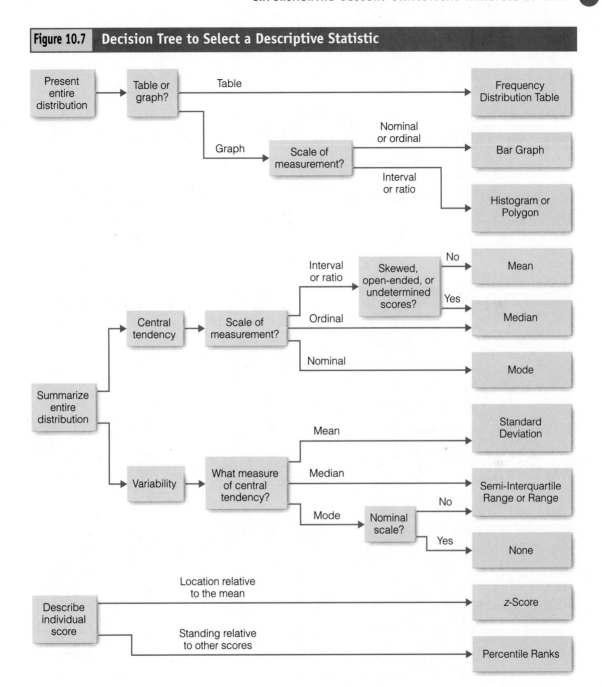

Figure 10.8 Decision Tree to Select a Parametric Statistic to Evaluate Group Differences

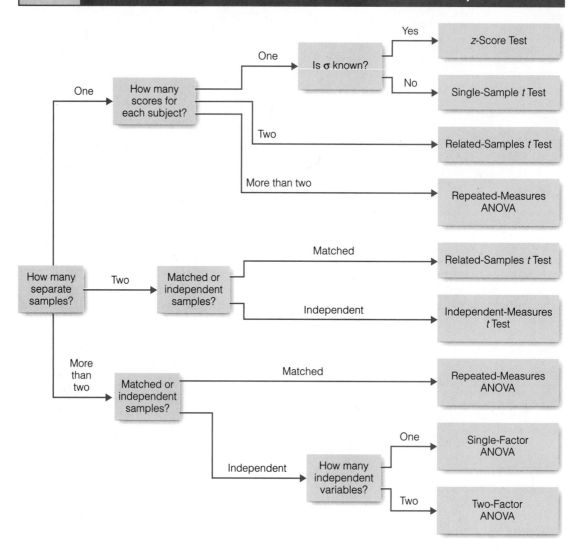

Lotus123, or Quattro pro) or by statistical software (such as SPSS, SAS, SYSTAT, or STATVIEW). The particular software that you use as a student researcher will depend on which software is available at your university and which software is familiar to your instructor. Each software program has advantages and disadvantages. Although we do not want to recommend a particular program, we do suggest that you learn at least one of them.

The statistical output that we present in the next several chapters is presented in generic form rather than the format of a particular software package. Whichever package you use, you should be able to locate the same information in the output.

Figure 10.9 **Decision Tree to Select a Nonparametric Statistic to Evaluate Group Differences**

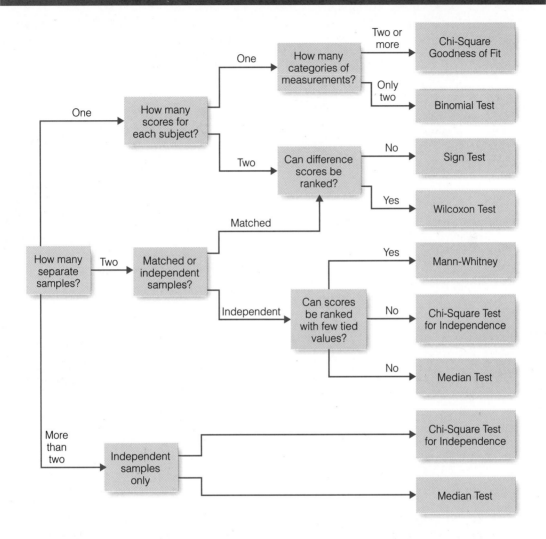

A caution is in order. The ease with which inferential statistics can be calculated by the computer creates a temptation to simply enter the data and click on the button to perform the inferential analysis so that a conclusion statement can be written. Be sure to perform descriptive statistics first. Get a strong feel for your data by calculating measures of central tendency and measures of variability. Let your data talk to you through various graphs that not only depict summary statistics, but also depict the distribution of raw scores. These graphs can show outliers and patterns in the data that would be overlooked by the inferential statistic and may, in fact, create inferential analyses that are misleading.

Figure 10.10 **Decision Tree to Select a Statistic to Measure the Relationship Between Two Variables**

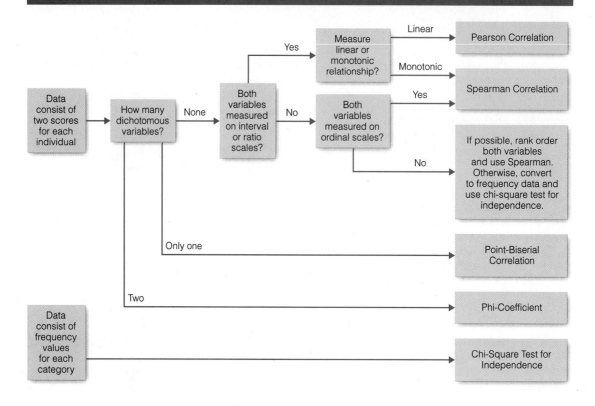

CASE ANALYSIS

One recent area of research in the behavioral sciences involves the positive impact that natural environments have on mental, social, and physical health. This research on "restorative environments" has implications for the design of homes, office space, and hospital recovery rooms. You decide to study this phenomenon by comparing two recovery rooms at your local hospital. The rooms are identical except that the view from one looks out over a park with trees and grass, and the view from the other simply shows a brick wall of the building. Patients recovering from routine surgeries are randomly assigned to one of the recovery rooms, and you record the number of days of recovery prior to discharge from the hospital. Because you understand the concept of confounding variables, you

make sure that the patients and nurses are unaware of the experiment. The data are shown in Table 10.10.

Critical Thinking Questions

1. Which measure of central tendency would you use? Why?

2. Which measure of variability would you use? Why?

3. Which type of graph would you use to illustrate the average days to recovery as a function of the type of view? Why?

4. Which type of inferential analysis would you use to determine whether there was any effect of the type of view on recovery rate? Why?

Table 10.10

DAYS TO DISCHARGE (DV)	EXPERIMENTAL CONDITION (IV)							
	View of Nature				View of Wall			
	1	3	6	3	4	3	1	8
	9	3	2	1	7	4	5	5
	2	1	3	4	10	8	9	7
	4	2	5	7	2	4	8	3
	3	3	2	4	5	7	6	3
	1	5	4	2	4	8	6	5

GENERAL SUMMARY

Statistics provide a way to summarize and interpret behavioral observations. Descriptive statistics, such as measures of central tendency, measures of variability, and graphical representations of data, summarize observations. Central tendency can be measured with the mean, median, or mode. The mean, the most common measure, has the advantage of considering the specific value of every score in the distribution. The median is often appropriate when the distribution of scores is skewed or contains a few extreme scores. The mode can be used when the data are measured on a nominal scale of measurement. Variability is most often measured using standard deviation, which provides an indication of how far, on average, scores are from the mean.

Inferential statistics, such as the *t* test and analysis of variance, provide a way to interpret the data and arrive at conclusions. The interpretation is based on a calculation of probabilities. Thus, inferential statistics never prove anything. Rather, they allow the researcher to draw a conclusion with some degree of confidence. Because probabilities are involved, there always exists the possibility of a Type I error or a Type II error. A Type I error occurs when the researcher concludes that an effect exists when, in fact, it does not. A Type II error occurs when the researcher concludes that no effect exists when, in fact, it does. Increasing the power of your study can reduce the chance of a Type II error.

Significance tests are often supplemented with a measure of effect size. Such measures provide an indication of how large an effect is and, thus, whether a significant effect is, in fact, a meaningful effect. Similarly, meta-analyses provide a way to summarize the size of effects across multiple studies so that an entire body of literature can be interpreted.

Inferential statistics come in the form of parametric statistics and nonparametric statistics. Parametric statistics are more powerful but require interval or ratio data and also require that certain assumptions about the nature of the data be met. A variety of factors must be considered to determine the most appropriate statistical analysis. Decision trees can be used to make such decisions, and computer programs can be used to perform the statistical analyses.

In the next chapter, we will begin to explore particular types of experimental design.

DETAILED SUMMARY

1. Statistics provide an objective approach to understanding and interpreting the behaviors that we observe and measure.

2. Descriptive statistics are used to describe and summarize data. They include measures of central tendency

(mean, median, mode) and measures of variability (range, variance, standard deviation). Descriptive statistics are often presented in the form of graphs.

3. Measures of central tendency provide an indication of the "center" of the distribution of scores, whereas

measures of variability provide an indication of the spread of scores.

4. The mean is the arithmetic average of a set of scores. It considers the precise value of each score in the distribution. It is the preferred measure of central tendency for interval or ratio data unless the distribution of scores is skewed by outlier (extreme) scores.

5. The median is the middle point in the distribution. That is, half of the scores are above the median, and half are below the median.

6. The mode is the most frequent score in the distribution—that is, the score that occurs most often.

7. The range is the number of units between the highest and lowest scores in the distribution. Because the range only considers the values of the two most extreme scores, it is less stable than other measures of variability and may not adequately reflect the overall spread of scores.

8. The variance is the average squared deviation of scores from the mean. The square root of variance is the standard deviation. Thus, standard deviation reflects, on average, how far scores are from the mean. It is the preferred measure of variability.

9. Many variables result in a distribution of scores that is normal in shape. This observation, along with the calculated mean and standard deviation, provide a wealth of additional information regarding the proportion of scores in particular parts of the distribution or the probability (or percentage chance) of obtaining a particular score in the distribution.

10. Variability is an essential concept in behavioral research because most of the principles of good research design involve methods to reduce variability due to extraneous variables so that variability due to systematic sources (our independent variables) is clear.

11. Researchers should make extensive use of tables and graphs to summarize data. Such techniques provide the researcher with a better "feel" for the data.

12. We usually conduct research on samples of participants and then want to draw conclusions about populations. Inferential statistics are tools used to make such inferences.

13. The conclusions made using inferential statistics are based on probabilities—specifically, the probabilities that certain events would occur simply by chance. Thus, our research hypotheses are never *proven* correct or incorrect. They are either retained or rejected based on probabilities.

14. The null hypothesis typically states that there is no difference in population parameters (usually population means), whereas the alternative hypothesis typically states that there is a difference in population parameters. The null hypothesis is the one that is statistically tested and either retained or rejected, whereas the alternative hypothesis usually reflects the researcher's expectation.

15. The frame of reference for statistical decision making is provided by the sampling distribution of a statistic. A sampling distribution is a theoretical probability distribution of the possible values of some sample statistic that would occur if we were to draw all possible samples of a fixed size from a given population.

16. If the probability of obtaining a sample statistic by chance is very rare, very unlikely, or less than our alpha level (often 0.05), then we conclude that the sample did not come from the population and that our independent variable had a significant effect (that is, we reject the null hypothesis).

17. Power is the probability of finding a certain size effect assuming that it, in fact, exists. Power can be increased by increasing sample size and by using control techniques to reduce extraneous variability.

18. Because all conclusions are based on probabilities, our conclusions can, in fact, be wrong. If we conclude that there is an effect and there really is not, then we have made a Type I error. If we conclude that there is no effect and there really is one, then we have made a Type II error. Good research designs and experimental control will reduce the chance of making these errors.

19. The decision to reject a null hypothesis does not reflect the *size* of an effect. Other statistics measure effect size, providing another valuable tool in data analysis.

20. A particular inferential technique called meta-analysis provides a statistical method for combining the effects across studies to reach a decision regarding whether a particular independent variable affects a particular dependent variable.

21. Parametric statistics are used when data are measured on an interval or ratio scale and meet a few additional assumptions regarding sample size and variability. Nonparametric statistics are used when data are measured on a nominal or ordinal scale or do not meet the assumptions of parametric statistics.

22. During data analysis, the researcher must decide on the most appropriate descriptive and inferential sta-

tistics. These decisions are not always easy, and flow-charts can be a useful aid.

23. Statistical software makes data analysis much more efficient and less prone to errors in calculation.

However, it is the responsibility of the researcher to understand what the software is doing to the data and to not blindly click the mouse on a series of buttons.

KEY TERMS

alpha (α) level *(p. 171)*
alternative hypothesis (H_1) *(p. 168)*
critical values *(p. 172)*
effect size *(p. 176)*
frequency distribution *(p. 158)*
homogeneity of variance *(p. 178)*
mean *(p. 160)*
measure of central tendency *(p. 158)*
measure of variability *(p. 158)*
median *(p. 160)*
meta-analysis *(p. 177)*
mode *(p. 161)*

nonparametric statistics *(p. 178)*
null hypothesis (H_0) *(p. 167)*
parametric statistics *(p. 178)*
power *(p. 175)*
range *(p. 161)*
region of rejection *(p. 172)*
sampling distribution *(p. 169)*
standard deviation *(p. 161)*
Type I error *(p. 174)*
Type II error *(p. 174)*
variance *(p. 161)*

REVIEW QUESTIONS/EXERCISES

Use the hypothetical study described in the Case Analysis above.

1. Either by hand or using a computer program, calculate the mean, median, and mode for each group. Comparing these values, what do you notice?

2. Either by hand or using a computer program, calculate the range and standard deviation for each group. Comparing these values, what do you notice?

3. Construct a graph similar to the one shown in Figure 10.4. Again, what do you notice?

4. In words, write both the null hypothesis and the alternative hypothesis.

5. Either by hand or using a computer program, calculate an appropriate inferential statistic that will test the null hypothesis. What is the probability of such a statistic assuming the null hypothesis is true? Do you reject or retain the null hypothesis?

6. Which type of statistical error could you be making with the statistical decision in question 5?

7. Either by hand or using a computer program, calculate an appropriate measure of effect size. What does this value indicate?

8. Based on all of the above information, write a conclusion statement for the study.

 ## WEB RESOURCES TO INCREASE LEARNING

Rice University maintains the Rice Virtual Lab in Statistics. This extensive Web site includes an online statistics textbook, simulations and demonstrations of statistical concepts, case studies, and several basic statistical analysis tools. We encourage you to visit this Web site and explore statistical concepts that you do not yet fully understand. The Web address is http://www.ruf.rice.edu/~lane/rvls.html.

The chapter outline, chapter summaries, key terms and definitions, additional chapter questions, chapter exercises, and links to relevant Web sites are available at the course Web site (**http://psychology.wadsworth.com/lammers_badia1e**). Explore the interactive workshops "Central Tendency and Variability," "Central Limit Theorem," "Hypothesis Testing," "Chi-Square," and "Choosing the Correct Statistical Test."

CHAPTER 11

EXPERIMENTAL DESIGN
ONE-WAY INDEPENDENT SAMPLES DESIGN

Advantages and Limitations

Now that we have introduced the basic concepts of behavioral research, the next five chapters discuss specific research designs. Chapters 11–14 focus on true experimental designs that involve experimenter manipulation of the independent variable and experimenter control over the assignment of participants to treatment conditions. Chapter 15 focuses on alternative research designs in which the experimenter does not manipulate the independent variable and/or does not have control over the assignment of participants to treatment conditions.

Let's return to a topic and experimental design that we discussed earlier. Suppose we are interested in the possible effect of TV violence on aggressive behavior in children. One fairly simple approach is to randomly sample several day-care centers for participants. On a particular day, half of the children in each day-care center are randomly assigned to watch *Mister Rogers* for 30 minutes, and the other half watch *Beast Wars* for 30 minutes. The children are given the same instructions by one of the day-care personnel and watch the TV programs in identical environments. Following the TV program, the children play for 30 minutes, and the number of aggressive behaviors is observed and recorded by three experimenters who are "blind" to which TV program each child saw. (You should be able to identify several experimental control techniques in this description.)

The subject of this chapter is *one-way independent samples designs*. The term *one-way* means that there is one independent variable (IV). In our example, the IV is level of TV violence. *Independent samples* means that random assignment was used to create groups whose scores are independent of each other.

In our example, the independent variable has two levels. One level is a TV program with violence, and the other level is a TV program without violence. Thus, we have one dependent variable and one independent variable with two levels (see Table 11.1).

Our design has several advantages. As noted in Chapter 9, our use of random sampling, at least in the geographical area that we are conducting the experiment, helps avoid bias that might be created by choosing one particular day-care center. It also permits us to generalize from our sample to the population of day-care centers from which our sample was drawn. Our use of random assignment is designed to avoid confounding variables associated with selection of participants. Can you imagine the characteristics of the two groups if you asked for volunteers to watch *Mister Rogers* and volunteers to watch *Beast Wars*? The two groups would almost certainly be different before you even introduced the independent variable. Also, it is clear that we have a control group (TV program without violence) with which to compare the children who receive the TV violence.

As we have mentioned, no design is perfect, and this design has limitations. We know that our two experimental conditions have different children in them. These different children have different backgrounds and different personalities that will certainly influence their

Table 11.1	Characteristics of Research Designs				
TYPE OF RESEARCH DESIGN	NUMBER OF INDEPENDENT VARIABLES	NUMBER OF LEVELS OF THE IV	NUMBER OF DEPENDENT VARIABLES	ASSIGNMENT TO CONDITIONS	MOST PROBABLE INFERENTIAL STATISTIC
One-way independent samples	1	2 or more	1	Random	*t* test or one-way ANOVA

aggressiveness regardless of the TV program watched. Although random assignment is a technique designed to equate the groups at the start, there is no guarantee that they are in fact equated. Thus, the fact that there are different participants in the different groups constitutes an important source of random error. As we know, random error makes it more difficult to identify variability in the scores that is due to the independent variable. We will explore designs (correlated samples designs) that attempt to deal with this problem in the next chapter.

Comparing Two Groups

In our example, we have two groups. This is the same as saying there are two conditions or two levels of the independent variable. A two-group study is the simplest design that incorporates a number of experimental control techniques. Let's look at some data that might be recorded from this study (see Table 11.2).

From the table we can see that 48 children were randomly sampled and $n=24$ children were randomly assigned to each of the two experimental groups. The numbers in each cell represent our dependent variable—the number of aggressive behaviors that were observed. Clearly, the mean number of aggressive behaviors for children who watched the TV program with violence is somewhat higher than that for children who watched the TV program without violence.

In addition to this variability between the groups, there is also variability within the groups (as indicated by the standard deviation) such that scores were, on average, about 3 units from their respective means. The variability within the groups (also called error variability) is due to random error; the variability between the groups is due to any systematic error due to confounds plus any systematic variability due to the type of TV program. Thus:

Variability Within Groups (error variability) = Random Error (extraneous variables)
Variability Between Groups = Systematic Error (confounds) + Systematic Variability (effect of IV)

Table 11.2	Number of Aggressive Behaviors Recorded				
TV PROGRAM WITH VIOLENCE (EXPERIMENTAL)			**TV PROGRAM WITHOUT VIOLENCE (CONTROL)**		
8	8	6	10	5	2
9	8	5	2	7	4
0	6	5	2	2	6
10	12	9	2	0	4
4	8	9	0	2	7
7	4	15	1	6	7
3	4	12	3	8	9
2	5	3	3	11	5
$n=24$; $M=6.75$; $SD=3.52$			$n=24$; $M=4.50$; $SD=3.12$		

Recall from Chapter 8 that random error includes extraneous variables such as individual differences in the participants, characteristics of the experimenter, and characteristics of the experimental procedure. Systematic error includes many of the same factors but in circumstances in which the error creates unintended differences *between* the groups.

The goal is for our experimental design and procedures to reduce random error due to extraneous variables, to eliminate systematic error due to confounds, and to maximize the systematic variability due to manipulation of the independent variable. Although this is our goal, we in fact expect some degree of error in the scores. Thus, we expect some difference between the two group means even if there is absolutely no effect of the independent variable. So, the basic question is whether the difference between the two group means is due to error alone or due to error plus an effect of the independent variable (TV violence).

● Comparing *t* Test to ANOVA

Let's return to the data in Table 11.1. Notice that we have already used descriptive statistics (mean and standard deviation) to summarize the data. We now need to use inferential statistics to determine whether our independent variable had a significant effect on our dependent variable. That is, did the level of TV violence have an effect on aggressive behavior? We actually have two options. An independent samples design with two groups can be analyzed with either an **independent samples *t* test** or a **one-way independent samples ANOVA**. Recall from Chapter 10 that parametric tests require assumptions of normality and homogeneity of variance. If there is reason to suspect that these assumptions are seriously violated in an independent samples design, then a nonparametric test such as the Mann–Whitney test is more appropriate. For the examples in this chapter, we will assume normality of the data and homogeneity of variance.

Whereas *t* tests are restricted to the comparison of two groups, ANOVAs can be used with two groups or more. In either case, the inferential statistic is based on a ratio of variability between groups to variability due to error.

$$\text{Inferential Statistic} = \frac{\text{Variability Between Groups}}{\text{Error Variability}}$$

Let's look at each one.

Independent Samples *t* Test

The independent samples *t* test uses the difference between the two group means as a measure of variability between groups and uses the standard error of the difference between means as a measure of error variability.

$$t = \frac{\text{Difference Between the Two Group Means}}{\text{Standard Error of the Difference Between Means (Error)}}$$

The difference between the two group means is a straightforward calculation. The standard error of the difference between means tells you, on average, how different the two group means should be if the difference is due solely to error variability. If you examine the formulas in a statistics book, you will see that the standard error is based on the variance of the scores within each of the groups.

Table 11.3	Output From an Independent Samples *t* Test		
t	*df*	*p*	
2.34	46	0.023	

If the null hypothesis (H_0) is true—that is, there is no effect of the independent variable—then you would expect the difference between the two group means to be small and the *t*-statistic to be near 0. If, on the other hand, the null hypothesis is false, then you would expect the difference between the two group means to be large (in either a positive or a negative direction) relative to the standard error. This would produce a *t*-statistic that has a value away from 0 (in either a positive or a negative direction). The larger the absolute value of the *t*-statistic, the lower is the probability that the difference between the group means is due solely to error variability. If the probability is low enough (lower than the alpha level), then we reject the null hypothesis (H_0) and accept the alternative hypothesis (H_1). We conclude that the independent variable had an effect.

Because this is not a statistics book, we are not going to present the detailed calculations of the *t*-statistic here. You can consult a statistics textbook for the relevant formulas. Most people now do the statistical analyses using a computer with statistical software. For the data presented in this example, the output from one of these programs would include the information in Table 11.3.

This table shows that the *t*-statistic is 2.34, the degrees of freedom are 46, and the probability value is 0.023. The probability value tells you the probability (likelihood) of obtaining that *t*-statistic assuming the null hypothesis is true. Typically, researchers set their alpha level at .05 for deciding to reject the null hypothesis. Because the probability is low enough ($0.023 < .05$), we decide to reject the null hypothesis and conclude that there was a significant effect of the independent variable on the dependent variable. Specifically, children who watched a TV program with violence showed significantly more aggressive behaviors than children who watched a TV program without violence, $t(46) = 2.34, p = 0.023$.

Independent Samples ANOVA

As noted earlier, these same data could be analyzed with an independent samples analysis of variance (ANOVA). By the way, the results based on a *t* test will always match those based on an ANOVA. The logic of the ANOVA is very similar to that of the *t* test. Again, a ratio of variability between the groups to error variability is calculated. The resulting statistic is referred to as the *F*-ratio.

$$F\text{-ratio} = \frac{\text{Variability Between Groups (Mean Square Between)}}{\text{Error Variability (Mean Square Error)}}$$

$$F\text{-ratio} = \frac{\text{Treatment Effect} + \text{Systematic Error}}{\text{Random Error}}$$

Here, the numerator of the formula is not simply the difference between the group means. It is a measure of variability based on how different the group means are. Therefore, whereas the *t*-statistic can have negative values and has an expected value of 0, the *F*-ratio must be positive (because variability is always positive) and has an expected value of 1. Remember that expected values are based on the null hypothesis being true.

Table 11.4	Output From an Independent Samples ANOVA				
SOURCE OF VARIABILITY	DEGREES OF FREEDOM (df)	SUM OF SQUARES	MEAN SQUARES	F RATIO	F PROBABILITY
Between groups	1	60.75	60.75	5.50	0.023
Within groups (error)	46	508.50	11.05		
Total	47	569.25			

Output from a computer program would include the information in Table 11.4.

As in the analysis using the t test, the probability of the F-ratio (0.023) is less than the alpha level (.05), so the decision would be to reject the null hypothesis and conclude that the independent variable had a significant effect on the dependent variable. Specifically, children who watched a TV program with violence showed significantly more aggressive behaviors than children who watched a TV program without violence, $F(1,46) = 5.50$, $p = 0.023$.

We hope that you get the sense that the independent samples design with two groups is a relatively simple, yet powerful, design that requires a relatively simple analysis. We arrived at a conclusion without too much effort. But let's take a closer look at our conclusion.

● Comparing More Than Two Groups

Based on the above experiment, we concluded that children who watched a TV program with violence showed significantly more aggressive behaviors than children who watched a TV program without violence. We bet that you are thinking the TV violence increased aggressive behaviors. We bet that most people would think that and naturally conclude that violence on TV is "bad." But is there another possible interpretation of the results? Is it possible that the children who watched *Beast Wars* showed normal levels of aggression and the children who watched *Mister Rogers* showed unusually low levels of aggression? In other words, it could be that *Beast Wars* had no effect and *Mister Rogers* actually caused a decrease in aggression. In fact, there is yet a third possibility: that *Beast Wars* increased aggression and *Mister Rogers* decreased aggression. This is a very important distinction and one that cannot be answered with the design that we have used.

To help us distinguish among these possibilities, we could add a third group of children to our experimental design. The experimental procedures would be the same as previously described with the exception that there is an additional group of children who watch no TV program in the 30 minutes prior to the observation period. This third group will serve as something of a baseline with which we can compare the other two groups. Let's add this third group to our hypothetical data set (see Table 11.5; note that each number represents the score of a single participant).

An inspection of the group means suggests that it may be the *Mister Rogers* program that reduced aggression in that group. We need to conduct analyses to tell us whether there are any significant differences, and if so, where they are. A t test is not an option because it is restricted to the comparison of two groups. Therefore, an independent samples ANOVA is the appropriate analysis. Output from a computer program would include the information in Table 11.6.

Table 11.5	Number of Aggressive Behaviors Recorded							
VIOLENCE			**NO VIOLENCE**			**NO TV**		
8	8	6	10	5	2	7	5	9
9	8	5	2	7	4	7	8	9
0	6	5	2	2	6	10	2	11
10	12	9	2	0	4	4	11	7
4	8	9	0	2	7	3	12	10
7	4	15	1	6	7	12	3	4
3	4	12	3	8	9	6	3	5
2	5	3	3	11	5	6	5	4
$n = 24$; $M = 6.75$; $SD = 3.52$			$n = 24$; $M = 4.50$; $SD = 3.12$			$n = 24$; $M = 6.79$; $SD = 3.11$		

Table 11.6	Output From an Independent Samples ANOVA				
SOURCE OF VARIABILITY	**DEGREES OF FREEDOM (df)**	**SUM OF SQUARES**	**MEAN SQUARES**	**F RATIO**	**F PROBABILITY**
Between groups	2	82.53	41.26	3.90	0.025
Within groups (error)	69	730.46	10.59		
Total	71	812.99			

This output tells us that there is a significant difference among the three group means, $F(2,69) = 3.90$, $p = 0.025$. Because there are more than two groups, we cannot be sure where the differences are. To determine this, we need to conduct a **post hoc specific comparison test** (such as Tukey HSD, Bonferroni, or Sheffé). Output from a Tukey HSD showed that the means for Group 1 (TV Violence) and Group 3 (No TV) are significantly higher than the mean for Group 2 (No Violence). Therefore, we can now conclude that watching *Mister Rogers* for 30 minutes significantly reduced aggressive behavior when compared to watching either *Beast Wars* or no TV.

It is important to note that post hoc specific comparison tests are only applied when there are more than two groups and the F-statistic in the ANOVA is significant. Sometimes, the researcher plans comparisons between specific groups before the experiment is conducted. In these situations, the experimenter can apply an **a priori specific comparison test** (planned comparisons) even if the F-statistic in the ANOVA is not significant (see an advanced statistics book for a complete discussion of specific comparison tests).

Although the independent samples design seems simple and easy to identify, it possesses important characteristics that require a critical evaluation. Practice your skills by considering research that studied video games (see "Thinking Critically About Everyday Information").

Thinking Critically About Everyday Information

Can Video Games Sharpen Your Mind?

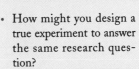

The Associated Press reported on a set of studies that examined the relationship between playing video games and skills in processing visual information. Portions of the report are shown below:

Study: Video Games Hone the Mind

(AP) All those hours spent playing video games may not be wasted time after all: A new study suggests action-packed video games like "Grand Theft Auto III" and "Counter-Strike" may sharpen your mind.

Researchers at the University of Rochester found that young adults who regularly played video games full of high-speed car chases and blazing gun battles showed better visual skills than those who did not. For example, they kept better track of objects appearing simultaneously and processed fast-changing visual information more efficiently.

In the Rochester study, 16 men ages 18 to 23 took a series of tests that measured their ability to locate the position of a blinking object, count the number of simultaneous objects on a screen and pick out the color of an alphabet letter. Those who played video games for the previous six months (self-report on a questionnaire) performed better in all those tests than those who did not.

Before we read about the next study that was reported, think about the following:

- How many groups were compared?

- Did the researchers use an independent samples design?

- Although the report suggests a causal link between video gaming and visual perception skills, what is an alternative interpretation for the results?

- How might you design a true experiment to answer the same research question?

Now that you've thought about these questions, let's continue with the report:

To rule out the possibility that visually adept people are simply drawn toward video games, the researchers conducted a second experiment. They found that people who do not normally play video games but were trained to play them developed enhanced visual perception.

In a separate test, a group of 17 who never played video games were trained to play the military game "Medal of Honor" and the puzzle game "Tetris." After playing for 10 days, those who learned "Medal of Honor" scored better on the performance tests than those who didn't.

Let's return to some critical thinking questions:

- The researchers understood that there was an alternative interpretation for the first study. Based on the description in the last paragraph, did the researcher do a good job of resolving the issue? Do you believe that the second study represents a true experiment?

- Although the second study represents a research design similar to what will be discussed in the next chapter (thus, you may not be familiar with the issues involved), do you believe that the second study convincingly demonstrates an effect of video gaming on visual perception? Can you think of an alternative explanation?

SOURCE: "Study: Video Games Hone the Mind," May 28, 2003. The Associated Press. Reprinted with permission of the Associated Press.

Quasi-experiments

The studies discussed so far in this chapter represent true experiments that included manipulation of the independent variable and random assignment of participants to conditions. Many studies closely mimic a true experiment but lack one or more essential characteristics. In some cases, the investigator may manipulate the independent variable but be unable to

Table 11.7	Number of Aggressive Behaviors Recorded				
TV PROGRAM WITH VIOLENCE (EXPERIMENTAL)			TV PROGRAM WITHOUT VIOLENCE (CONTROL)		
8	8	6	10	5	2
9	8	5	2	7	4
0	6	5	2	2	6
10	12	9	2	0	4
4	8	9	0	2	7
7	4	15	1	6	7
3	4	12	3	8	9
2	5	3	3	11	5
$n = 24$; $M = 6.75$; $SD = 3.52$			$n = 24$; $M = 4.50$; $SD = 3.12$		

randomly assign participants to conditions. Such designs are termed **quasi-experiments** and are very similar to true experiments except for the important feature of random assignment. It is important to distinguish between a true experiment and a quasi-experiment because the conclusions that may be drawn from the research depend upon this distinction. The degree of risk in inferring causal relationships is much greater with quasi-experiments.

Let's look at an example of a quasi-experiment that resembles a true experiment. To investigate the effect of TV violence, a researcher selects two day-care centers to participate in the study. In one day-care center, the experimenter presents *Mister Rogers;* in the other day-care center, the experimenter presents *Beast Wars.* In both day-care centers, the researcher observes the number of aggressive behaviors during a play period following the TV programs. Assume that the data collected are identical to those for the first study in this chapter (see Table 11.7).

The results from the *t* test or ANOVA would again show the difference between the two group means to be significant. Can we conclude that the manipulation of the independent variable (level of TV violence) caused a change in the dependent variable (aggressive behavior)? The answer is no. The difference in aggressiveness may be due to differences that already existed between the children in the two day-care centers. It is likely that these two day-care centers differ in many ways other than the type of TV program that was presented. They may differ in quality of the staff, types of activities, typical TV programming, income level of the children's parents, educational level of the children's parents, and many other factors. The differences that were observed in the children's aggressiveness could be due to one or more of these other factors rather than to the type of TV program presented by the researcher. Unfortunately, we cannot choose among these alternative interpretations. On the other hand, if this study had used random assignment of participants, alternative interpretations would have been eliminated and strong, confident conclusions could have been drawn.

Other examples of quasi-experiments are **cross-sectional research** designs. Developmental psychologists are often interested in how the behaviors of individuals may change across portions of the life span or across the entire life span. We could ask the question "Do people's responses to violence on TV change as they develop from young children to school-age children to teenagers?" An approach using a cross-sectional design might involve testing children of different specific age groups and then making comparisons across the age groups. Once again, notice that the researcher can manipulate the independent variable (level of TV violence) but does not use random assignment to form the age groups. The different age groups are preexisting groups.

When quasi-experiments are conducted using an experimental group and a comparison group, there is always concern about the equality of the two (or more) groups because random assignment is absent. Any differences between the two groups could be due to the treatment that only the experimental group received or to differences between participants in the two groups (perhaps brighter, healthier, or more motivated in one group than the other). Researchers conducting quasi-experiments may try to minimize participant differences by selecting participants as similar as possible for the two groups, but this is very difficult. There is no way to be sure that the composition of participants in the two groups will be equal, but a random assignment procedure comes closest to achieving this goal.

As we have just discussed, quasi-experiments involve manipulation of an independent variable but lack random assignment. Other studies may lack both manipulation of the independent variable and random assignment. Common examples include many typical undergraduate studies that involve comparisons of gender, race, socioeconomic status, fraternity/sorority status, and other preexisting characteristics. Because these are not true experiments, strong cause–effect conclusions cannot be made. These types of studies will be discussed further in Chapter 15.

CASE ANALYSIS

One important area of behavioral research involves attempts to reduce the occurrence of risky sexual behaviors in teenagers. A recent study showed that a high school program taught by teachers was more effective in the long term than a similar program taught by peers (Fisher, Fisher, & Bryan, 2002). You decide to determine whether the same principle applies to drug education. Using three high schools, you implement a teacher-based program in one school, a peer-based program in a second school, and no program in a third school. For the dependent variable, you ask students to anonymously report the number of times they have used drugs in the previous month. You measure level of drug use at the beginning of the school year and at the end of the school year and calculate a "change" score by subtracting one from the other. Thus, a score of 0 would indicate no change, a positive score would indicate an increase in drug use, and a negative score would indicate a decrease in drug use. From the samples tested in each high school, you obtain the statistics shown in Tables 11.8–11.10.

Critical Thinking Questions

1. Based on the ANOVA, is there a significant effect of type of program on drug use?

2. Based on the post hoc analysis, which groups differ from each other?

Table 11.8	Descriptive Statistics		
PROGRAM	*n*	MEAN	STANDARD DEVIATION
Teacher-based	60	−2.68	2.68
Peer-based	58	−1.83	2.90
None	65	2.37	2.58

Table 11.9 — Output From an Independent Samples ANOVA

SOURCE OF VARIABILITY	DEGREES OF FREEDOM (df)	SUM OF SQUARES	MEAN SQUARES	F RATIO	F PROBABILITY
Between groups	2	920.82	460.41	62.39	<.001
Within groups (error)	180	1328.40	7.38		
Total	182	2249.23			

Table 11.10 — Results From the Post Hoc Tukey Test

COMPARISON	MEAN DIFFERENCE	SIGNIFICANCE (PROBABILITY)
Teacher-based/Peer-based	−0.856	0.201
Teacher-based/Control	−5.053	< 0.01*
Peer-based/Control	−4.197	< 0.01*

3. Write a conclusion for the study that includes the direction of the effects.

4. Was this study a true experiment?

5. Can you conclude that the programs caused a change in drug use? Why or why not?

6. Identify at least two variables that were not measured but that may be confounding variables.

7. How could the study be improved so that the conclusion would be stronger?

GENERAL SUMMARY

An independent samples design is a true experiment characterized by random assignment of participants to conditions and manipulation of the independent variable. In conjunction with the use of control groups, this design permits cause–effect conclusions and results in fewer alternative interpretations of the data. Such conclusions are derived from the use of descriptive statistics and inferential statistics (t test, ANOVA).

Quasi-experiments are similar to true experiments with the exception that there is no random assignment of participants to conditions. Thus, there is no experimental procedure that adequately equates the groups prior to introduction of the independent variable. Therefore, quasi-experiments do not lend themselves to cause–effect conclusions. Differences between the groups could be due to a host of factors other than the independent variable.

The next chapter will explore true experiments that consist of correlated samples.

DETAILED SUMMARY

1. When a research design is a "one-way" design, it involves only one independent variable. When a research design is an "independent samples" design, random assignment is used to place participants into comparison groups.

2. Random assignment is the best method to create initial equality of comparison groups before the independent variable is introduced. Thus, random assignment is designed to eliminate potential confounds. However, the technique does not guarantee equality of groups, and random error due to individual differences is still expected.

3. In a two-group study, the variability of the scores is composed of variability within groups and variability

between groups. Variability within groups is the result of extraneous variables. Variability between groups is the result of confounding variables plus the effect of the independent variable.

4. The objective of the researcher is to reduce extraneous variables and confounds so that any effect of the independent variable is revealed.

5. An independent samples design with two groups can be analyzed with either an independent samples t test or a one-way independent samples analysis of variance (ANOVA). The t tests are restricted to the comparison of two groups while ANOVAs are appropriate when there are two or more groups.

6. The t-statistic in a t test is a standardized score that reflects the size of the difference between the two group means. The t-statistic can be used to determine the probability that the difference was simply due to chance. If that probability is low enough (less than the alpha level, usually .05), then the researcher can reject the null hypothesis and accept the alternative hypothesis—that is, conclude that there was a significant effect.

7. The F-ratio in an analysis of variance (ANOVA) is a standardized score that reflects the degree to which the variability between groups is greater than the variability within groups. Like the t-statistic, the F-ratio is used to determine the probability that the difference between group means is significant.

8. An independent samples design with more than two groups should be analyzed with ANOVA. To determine where differences may exist between specific groups, a priori planned comparisons or post hoc comparisons can be performed.

9. Quasi-experiments are similar to true experiments in that the researcher manipulates the independent variable but different in that the researcher does not randomly assign participants to the comparison groups. Absence of random assignment creates a greater concern that differences between the comparison groups are the result of confounding variables rather than manipulation of the independent variable. Thus, cause–effect conclusions are typically unwarranted and should only be made with great caution.

KEY TERMS

a priori specific comparison test *(p. 192)*
cross-sectional research *(p. 194)*
independent samples *t* test *(p. 189)*

one-way independent samples ANOVA *(p. 189)*
post hoc specific comparison test *(p. 192)*
quasi-experiment *(p. 194)*

REVIEW QUESTIONS/EXERCISES

1. Summarize the essential characteristics of a one-way independent samples research design.

2. Briefly describe a true experiment regarding the effectiveness of a particular drug for which an independent samples *t* test would be the appropriate inferential statistic.

3. Briefly describe a true experiment regarding the effectiveness of a particular drug for which an independent samples ANOVA would be the appropriate inferential statistic.

4. Briefly describe a quasi-experiment regarding the effectiveness of a particular drug for which an independent samples ANOVA would be the appropriate inferential statistic.

5. In your own words, describe the purpose of post hoc specific comparison tests, including a description of when it is appropriate to use them.

LABORATORY EXERCISES

Chapter 4 in *Research Methods Laboratory Manual for Psychology* (Langston, 2005) explores the interesting phenomenon called the Stroop Effect. Several ideas for experiments are provided, and we suggest that you

consider at least one of these using an independent samples design.

If you are like us, you know of several people who use their hands a lot when they talk. What function might this gesturing serve? Chapter 5 in *Research*

Methods Laboratory Manual for Psychology explores this issue. Several ideas for experiments are provided, and we suggest that you consider at least one of these using an independent samples design.

In our experience, when students develop ideas for experiments, one independent variable frequently mentioned is color and how color affects this or that. Chapter 6 in *Research Methods Laboratory Manual for Psychology* provides several ideas for experiments involving color as the independent variable. Consider at least one of these experiments using an independent samples design.

Have you heard that people (particularly the elderly) who own pets are healthier? This has been a "hot topic" during the last decade, and Chapter 3 in *Research Methods Laboratory Manual for Psychology* suggests several projects related to this issue. Consider conducting one of the projects that conforms to a quasi-experimental design (measure pet ownership as a dichotomous variable).

 ## WEB RESOURCES TO INCREASE LEARNING

The chapter outline, chapter summaries, key terms and definitions, additional chapter questions, chapter exercises, and links to relevant Web sites are available at the course Web site (**http://psychology.wadsworth.com/** **lammers_badia1e**). Explore the interactive workshops "Independent vs. Repeated *t* Tests" and "One-Way ANOVA."

CHAPTER 12

EXPERIMENTAL DESIGN
ONE-WAY CORRELATED SAMPLES DESIGN

● Advantages and Limitations

In the previous chapter, we included the powerful technique of random assignment in our research design to reduce systematic error (confounding variables). The assignment of participants to groups in a random fashion is one of the best ways to equate the groups on both known and unknown factors prior to administration of the independent variable. However, as we noted, there is no guarantee that they will be equated. To enhance experimental control, you may want to guarantee that one or more variables are equated among your treatment levels, and you may not want to rely on random assignment to establish that equality. Remember that any variable that varies systematically among your treatment levels and is not an independent variable is a confounder that can mask the effect of the independent variable. For example, in the previous chapter we discussed random assignment of children to two groups in a TV violence study. Random assignment, by chance, could result in having more boys in one group and more girls in the other group. If gender of the child is related to the dependent variable (aggressiveness), then we have created a confounding variable that will result in systematic error. As we will see, one advantage of the correlated samples designs discussed in this chapter is the reduction of systematic error between the treatment conditions.

However, the primary advantage of the correlated samples designs is the reduction of random error due to individual differences. Recall that random error creates "noise" that makes it more difficult to detect systematic effects of the independent variable. Reducing the noise enables us to detect smaller differences (systematic variance) between treatments. In terms of statistical formulas, we will see that the denominator of the formulas for our test statistic (t or F) consists of random error and the numerator consists primarily of the treatment (systematic variance). The larger the random error, the smaller the value is for the test statistic, and the less likely we are to find a treatment effect that is statistically significant.

The three techniques introduced in this chapter are all correlated samples designs. Correlated samples designs do not use random assignment of participants to conditions. Instead, they either test the same research participants under each treatment condition or match different participants on a related factor. Similar to random assignment designs, correlated samples designs can be used with two treatment conditions or more. The three types of correlated samples designs are natural pairs, matched pairs, and repeated measures. We should note that the appropriate statistical test is related to the research design that is used. For example, the t test for correlated samples design is calculated differently than that for independent samples design. (See Table 12.1.)

Table 12.1	Characteristics of Research Designs				
TYPE OF RESEARCH DESIGN	NUMBER OF IVS	NUMBER OF LEVELS OF THE IV	NUMBER OF DVS	ASSIGNMENT TO CONDITIONS	MOST PROBABLE INFERENTIAL STATISTIC
One-way independent samples	1	2 or more	1	Random	t test or one-way ANOVA
One-way correlated samples	1	2 or more	1	Natural pairs Matched pairs Repeated measures	t test or one-way ANOVA

Natural Pairs

In a natural pairs design, the scores in the groups are paired for some natural reason; an effort is made to match the participants on some natural basis. A good example of this matching would be twin studies. Returning to our TV violence study, research suggests that there is a genetic component to some aspects of personality, including aggressiveness. That is, babies come into this world with temperaments that help shape their developing personalities. Therefore, when we observe levels of aggressive behavior in children in a day-care center, we suspect that part of the explanation for their behavior is their genetic profile. Thus, variability of scores within and between groups is partly due to different participants' having different genetic profiles. This factor contributes to random error and makes it more difficult to detect variability due to the independent variable.

One solution is to eliminate genetic differences between groups by using identical twins. If we place one of the twins in one treatment condition and the other twin in the other treatment condition, we have created a situation in which there is no genetic difference between the groups. Differences between the group means could no longer be partly explained by differences in genetic profiles. Thus, in this natural pairs design, the scores in the two groups would be paired up because they are identical twins.

The primary advantage of the natural pairs design is that it uses a natural characteristic of the participants to reduce sources of error. The primary limitation of this design is often the availability of participants. The researcher must locate suitable pairs of participants (such as identical twins) and must obtain consent from both participants.

Matched Pairs

In a natural pairs design, scores were paired for some natural reason. In a matched pairs design, scores are paired because the experimenter decides to match them on some variable. The rationale for the matched pairs design is the same as that for the natural pairs design—to reduce error variability by controlling extraneous variables.

Once again, let's return to our TV violence study. It is important for the researcher to consider possible matching variables prior to the study. As the researcher, you may decide that the gender and age of the child are critical variables that relate not only to the child's aggressive behavior, but also to how the TV program may affect them. You suspect that 5-year-old boys may be more aggressive, in general, than 3-year-old girls and may be more affected by the violence in a TV program. In the next chapter, we will see how these variables can be included as additional independent variables in the research design. But for now our goal will be to control them.

Instead of relying on simple random assignment to balance these variables (gender and age) across your groups, you begin by pairing participants in your sample. A 3-year-old girl is paired with another 3-year-old girl, a 5-year-old boy is paired with a 5-year-old boy, and so on. After all the pairs are created, you use random assignment to determine which of the participants in each pair will be in the experimental group and which one will be in the control group. Now the two groups are matched in terms of both age and gender. Differences between the group means can no longer be explained by differences in age or gender of the participants.

The primary advantage of the matched pairs design is to use experimental control to reduce one or more sources of error variability. One limitation of this design can be the availability of participants. At times, there may not be a suitable match for a participant. For this reason, the researcher should not try to match the groups on too many variables. The design can quickly become too difficult to manage. Usually one or two matching variables are sufficient. But remember, the matching variable(s) must be related to scores on the dependent variable. Otherwise, error variability will not be reduced.

Repeated Measures

With both the natural pairs and the matched pairs designs, our objective is to better equate the groups and to reduce random error due to individual differences. However, notice that we still have different participants in the different groups. Different participants will not only have different genetic backgrounds (unless they are identical twins), they will have very different sets of life experiences (including identical twins). These different life experiences shape a person and influence how he or she will behave in any given situation. Whenever you have different participants in the different experimental conditions, there will be some error variability due to individual differences. A solution is to use a repeated measures design, in which the same group of participants experiences all the conditions; that is, each research participant is tested under each treatment condition.

For our TV violence study, we would sample a group of children from day-care centers and then have them participate in both experimental conditions. On one day, the children would be observed after they had watched a TV program with violence. On another day, the same children would be observed after they had watched a TV program without violence. To avoid confounding due to order effects, we would have to counterbalance the order of TV programs so that half the participants watch the violent program first and half watch the program without the violence first.

Advantages of Repeated Measures Designs   The beauty of this design is that it provides a means of controlling all of the extraneous variables associated with individual differences, including genetic background, socioeconomic status, age, gender, family structure, and type of parents. We have indicated that the greatest advantage of using a repeated measures design is the marked control over individual participant variation. Because each participant receives each treatment, participants with identical characteristics necessarily receive each of the different treatment conditions. Thus, any differences in performance should result only from the treatment conditions. In fact, however, this does not happen. Even though the same participant is used across treatments, the participant may change in some systematic fashion. The participant may be less observant or attentive from one treatment to the other, motivational levels may increase or decrease, fatigue or boredom may occur, or perceptions may change. Further, inevitable variations in the experimental setting, such as noise level or distractions, may affect performance. Therefore, because the participant and the environment may differ from treatment to treatment, there will still be some error variability, but far less than if an independent samples design had been used.

Another advantage of the repeated measures design relates to the population of available participants. If the availability of participants is low, then an independent samples design may not be possible. This predicament arises on occasion, especially when the population of interest is very small—for example, left-handed individuals with split-brain operations, identical twins separated at birth, or patients in therapy. The independent groups designs require k times as many participants as repeated measures designs (where k is the number of different treatments).

With fewer participants come greater efficiency and economy. In many cases, pretraining on a task may be needed one time only, after which a number of different treatments can be given. To illustrate, with four treatments and a task that requires a 10-minute pre-training period, a repeated measures design would save 30 minutes of training time per participant over an independent groups design. Thus, having only one training period may result in considerable savings in time, effort, and expenses. A similar savings can occur with instructions. In experiments involving different treatment conditions, the same instructions or similar instructions are commonly used. These instructions can be long and tedious. A repeated measures design can reduce the time devoted to instructions, particularly when instructions are the same across treatments.

A final important advantage is that a repeated measures design may be the most appropriate for the study of certain phenomena. It is the design of choice for studying learning and transfer of information, or for assessing the effects of practice or repetition on performance. The independent variable is commonly the number of practice sessions given to individual participants. In this case, we are interested in the effects that earlier treatments have on later performance. In Chapter 8, we introduced the notion of carryover effects as a potential source of extraneous variability (confounder). However, they may be the phenomenon of interest to the researcher. Moreover, the concept of external validity enters into the choice of experimental design. The generalizability or representativeness of the research is related to the context in which it takes place, especially when the results of the research are to be used in applied settings. The setting in which the research takes place should be similar to the setting to which the experimenter wishes to generalize his or her results. It may be the case that the researcher is interested in situations where each individual receives a number of conditions or receives extensive practice. If so, then a repeated measures design would have greater external validity. On the other hand, if the researcher is interested in performance under conditions that minimize practice, an independent groups design is necessary.

A final example of a research project that lends itself to a repeated measures design is a **longitudinal research** study. As noted in the previous chapter, developmental psychologists are often interested in how the behaviors of individuals may change across portions of the life span or across the entire life span. We could ask the question "Do people's responses to violence on TV change as they develop from young children to school-age children to teenagers?" Instead of comparing preexisting age groups (cross-sectional research), such a study might involve repeated annual testing of the same children over a dozen years.

Methodological Issues With Repeated Measures Designs   A major methodological problem found with repeated measures designs is that they give rise to unwanted carryover effects. Any treatment other than the independent variable that changes the organism in such a way that it has a persistent effect on other treatments, we call carryover. We will distinguish three categories of carryover effects: (1) **transient effects**—short-term effects that dissipate with time; (2) permanent effects, most often due to learning; and (3) sensitization effects, resulting from experiencing all treatments. These carryover effects pose a problem for us when they are unwanted and their occurrence is confounded with the effects of treatment.

Short-term transient effects are often due to fatigue, boredom, or drugs. For example, let us assume that we are interested in evaluating the effects of Drugs A and B against a placebo condition using a psychomotor task involving coordination. We decide to use a repeated measures design in which each participant will receive each drug, including the placebo, in some random order. A tracking task is used in which the duration of contact with a moving target is recorded. Each participant is tested once each day, but under a different condition. Imagine that on Day 1, one drug was evaluated, and on Day 2, the second drug was tested. What would happen if the effects of the first drug had not worn off?

Performance on Day 2 would be a function of the second drug plus the persistent effects of the first drug. In short, the effects of one drug treatment would still be present when testing the effects of the other drug. Obviously, this is a case of blatant confounding, since we are not interested in the combined effects of the two drugs. This transient carryover effect can be easily corrected. Assuming that the changes in performance due to the drugs are not permanent, we could reduce this carryover by widely separating the treatments in time so that the previous drugs are out of the physiological system.

Another type of transient effect is that due to fatigue or boredom. Fatigue or boredom is especially likely to occur in nonchallenging studies requiring repetitive responding or in studies that take place over a long period of time. Therefore, when one treatment condition follows another, factors such as fatigue or boredom may contribute more to one condition than to the other. These factors would be mixed with our independent variable, thus making it impossible to evaluate. In short, we have confounding.

An example of the fatigue or boredom effect may help. Let us say that we are interested in evaluating the speed of responding to an auditory signal versus a visual signal. For one treatment condition, we use a five-second auditory signal and for the other, a five-second visual signal. Our dependent variable is speed of responding (pressing a key on a computer keyboard) to the two different signals. Participants first receive 100 trials of practice without any signal to assure that rapid responding will occur at the start of the experiment. All participants then receive the auditory signal first for 500 trials, followed immediately by the visual signal for another 500 trials. If we were to use the described procedure, we could not adequately evaluate the effects of signal modality. The possibility exists that the participants may experience fatigue, boredom, or both during the second 500 trials with the visual signal. If so, then there could be a systematic decrease in reaction time due to fatigue and/or boredom, thus resulting in our underestimating reaction time to a visual signal.

One way to avoid the problem of fatigue or boredom contributing more to one condition than the other is to use a **counterbalancing** procedure. Counterbalancing does not eliminate transient effects, but it allows us to distribute them evenly across the treatment conditions. It can be used easily with two treatments, less so with three, and only with difficulty with four or more treatments. Counterbalancing could be achieved in our reaction time experiment in several ways. The easiest way would be to have an equal number of participants receive the treatments in an A-B order as in a B-A order. A and B would represent either the visual or the auditory signal. It is important to note that the use of such a procedure assumes that the transient effects of fatigue or boredom when going from Treatment A to Treatment B are the same as the transient effects when going from Treatment B to Treatment A. If, in our example, the second treatment were more fatiguing or boring than the first, then our assumption would be in error. In this case, counterbalancing would not distribute the transient effects evenly for the two conditions. The problem of equal treatment effects could be avoided and a repeated measures design still used by conducting the experiment over a two-day period. In this case, A and B would correspond to Days 1 and 2.

We previously noted that counterbalancing gets more difficult as the number of treatments increases. With two treatments, only two orders are possible: A-B and B-A. With three treatments, we have six possible orders: A-B-C, B-C-A, C-A-B, A-C-B, B-A-C, and C-B-A. However, with four treatments, we would have 24 orders, and with five treatments, we would be overwhelmed with 120 orders. When the number of treatments is greater than three, a random assignment procedure is far easier to use.

When repeated measures are taken on the same individual, we often see special kinds of permanent carryover effects. These are referred to as practice effects or learning effects. In many instances, practice effects are the independent variable of primary interest, but in other instances we try to avoid them. Practice effects can confound our research in ways that make our results uninterpretable. As we have noted, when our interest is in an independent variable other than practice, we must control practice effects so that they do not intrude on our results. In the preceding example where Drugs A and B were evaluated, we noted that the transient carryover effects of one drug on the other could be eliminated by widely spacing the time between tests. Knowing how long the drug remained active in the body would virtually assure us that we could eliminate transient effects. However, if for some unfortunate reason we did not randomize or counterbalance the presentation of drugs to each participant, a new problem would emerge. For example, if the effects of Drug A on the pursuit motor task were always tested first and the effects of Drug B were always tested second, then a marked practice effect (change in skill) could confound our results. Because trying to maintain contact with a moving target (pursuit motor task) is difficult, participants would initially do poorly on the task but would subsequently improve. Therefore, always practicing the task under Drug A first may lead to better performance under Drug B. However, the improvement may have little to do with the drug. The individual may simply now be more skilled because of practice. If our results came out the reverse, we could propose a reasonable alternative explanation—namely, that participants became more fatigued by the time of the second treatment. However, this argument could be weakened by lengthening the time interval between treatments.

Two things could be done to avoid practice effects. One would be to give sufficient practice on the pursuit motor task before giving any treatment condition. After improvement had stabilized or the limit of learning was attained, we could then introduce the treatments. This procedure would virtually assure that no increases in performance under the second treatment could occur as a result of practice. If our treatments were widely separated in time, we could also rule out fatigue factors. But the solution to the problem may create a new one if our interest is directed toward evaluating improvement in performance. If, because of our extended practice, participants are performing at their upper limits, further improvement in performance as a result of our treatment may not be possible. This ceiling effect would obscure any enhancing effect on the pursuit motor task that the drugs might have. We would only be able to determine if they detracted from performance.

We could also deal with order effects by randomly assigning the order of treatments to each participant or counterbalancing them as described in the preceding section. When random assignment or counterbalancing is used, we assume that the effects of practice due to the order of presenting the treatments are the same for each treatment. If the carryover effects of practice are different, we then have confounded practice (order of presenting treatments) with the treatment effects. Whether this type of confounding has occurred can be determined by plotting performance across the different testing orders. Figure 12.1 illustrates the absence and presence of confounding due to order of presentation.

If the results look like those at the top of the figure, then there is not a problem, because the practice effect is the same for each treatment whether it is given first, second, or third in the sequence. On the other hand, if the data look like those at the bottom of the figure, then we have confounded practice (that is, order) with the treatment effects. The bottom of the figure shows an interaction between the treatment conditions and the order of testing. What this means is that the practice effect is different for different treatments and the effect on performance that we observed is not a pure treatment effect. Clearly, the order of presenting the conditions has some effect. Our performance measure reflects the effect of the treatments plus the practice due to the preceding treatment. Results such as this suggest that an independent samples design would be more appropriate.

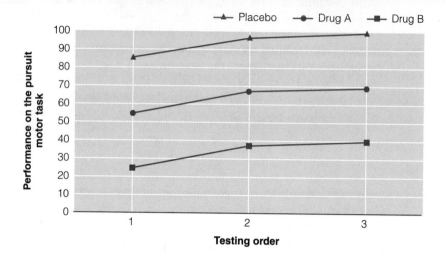

Figure 12.1 Graphic Illustration of the Absence or the Presence of Confounding Due to Order of Presentation of Treatment Conditions

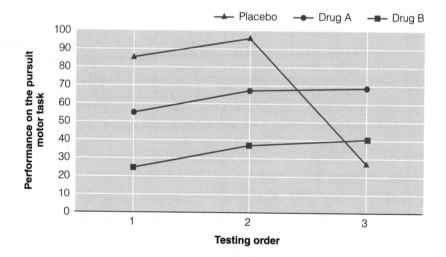

A final category of carryover effects is referred to as sensitization. Experiencing the full range of treatments in an experiment may enhance participants' ability to distinguish differences in treatments and the extent of these differences. This may, in turn, allow the participants to contrast the various treatment conditions. Thus, their responses to a particular treatment may depend upon how they perceive that condition relative to the preceding one. Because participants are exposed to the entire range of stimuli when a repeated measures design is used, the context in which participants respond is very different from that of participants receiving only one treatment. Moreover, the demand characteristics are likely to differ from one design to another. After participants have received several treatments, they are more likely to form expectancies or hypotheses about the purpose of the experiment. If so, then these hypotheses may affect their performance over and above that of the treatments.

For example, sensitization effects may occur in a repeated measures design in which participants are asked to judge personality traits of persons pictured in photographs and the independent variable is the body size of the person in the photograph (overweight vs. not overweight). Although the order of the photographs could be randomized, it is likely that many participants would notice that the weight of the person is being manipulated and that the researchers are specifically studying how weight might affect personality judgments. This awareness of the relevant conditions might then affect their personality judgments on all remaining photographs (in a manner that might conceal a bias due to weight). Note that such a response by participants would not occur in an independent samples design.

Comparing Repeated Measures Designs With Independent Samples Designs   Because the context provided by exposure to all treatments is very different from the context provided by exposure to a single treatment, the participant's response to any given treatment may be, in part, a function of the research design. The most effective way to determine if different designs lead to different findings or behavioral laws is to compare experiments using repeated measures designs with those using independent samples designs. Determining the equivalence or nonequivalence of the two types of designs is important whenever different relationships are discovered and different designs are used to reveal them. This determination should also be made in other circumstances that go beyond methodological considerations. For example, it may be important for the construction of theories or for the application of findings to some practical problems.

Before we turn to the statistical analysis of correlated samples designs, there is one final statistical issue related to the comparison of independent samples designs and correlated samples designs. As we have noted in this chapter, the primary advantage of correlated samples designs is the reduction of random error due to individual differences. This results in a larger value for either the t or F statistic and, therefore, a greater likelihood of detecting a significant treatment effect. However, the probability assigned to a particular t or F statistic also depends on the degrees of freedom associated with the analysis. The lower the degrees of freedom, the less likely we are to find a significant effect. For the independent samples design with two groups, the degrees of freedom are $(n_1 - 1) + (n_2 - 1)$ where n is equal to the sample size for each group. For the correlated samples design with two groups, the degrees of freedom are $(n - 1)$ where n is equal to the number of pairs of scores. For an experiment with 20 scores in each of two conditions, an independent samples design would have 38 degrees of freedom, whereas a correlated samples design would have 19 degrees of freedom. Thus, it is important for the reduction in random error associated with correlated samples to outweigh the reduction in degrees of freedom. This is generally the case for natural pairs and repeated measures designs because of the multitude of extraneous variables that are controlled. It is a more relevant consideration for matched pairs designs. If the matching variable does not substantially reduce the random error, the design is at a disadvantage.

Let's now take a look at the box "Thinking Critically About Everyday Information" and consider a repeated measures design that has some methodological problems.

Thinking Critically About Everyday Information

Effect of Frustration on Constructive Play in Children

Consider the following research report:

A researcher was interested in the effect of frustration on constructive play in children between the ages of 5 and 8 years. The hypothesis was that frustration would have an adverse effect on such play. Frustration was induced in the traditional way by thwarting or blocking performance of certain activities that children found pleasurable. A random sample of children in the proper age range was selected for study. The researcher then began the experiment with a 30-minute period during which the children played in the schoolyard in groups of ten. Groups of ten were used so that the experimenter could easily record both frequency and duration of constructive play. Then the children were brought into another condition, where frustration was induced. The children were then placed back into the original play situation, and frequency and duration of constructive play were again observed and recorded by the experimenter. Results of the study were unambiguous: Constructive play declined considerably following the frustration condition. Statistical tests revealed this outcome to be significant. The experimenter concluded that frustration was detrimental to constructive play, thus confirming the hypothesis.

Think about the following questions:

- What methodological issue is most problematic?

- What are some alternative explanations for the pattern of results?

- How would you improve the research design?

● Comparing Two Groups

We have already mentioned how we might approach our TV violence study with a natural pairs, matched pairs, or repeated measures design. Because all three designs involve correlated samples, they can be analyzed the same way. Let's return to our repeated measures design in which the same group of children watched both types of TV programs. Data that might be recorded from this study are shown in Table 12.2.

Table 12.2	Number of Aggressive Behaviors Recorded								
TV PROGRAM WITH VIOLENCE (EXPERIMENTAL)					**TV PROGRAM WITHOUT VIOLENCE (CONTROL)**				
8	9	0	10	4	10	2	2	2	0
7	3	2	8	8	1	3	3	5	7
6	12	8	4	4	2	0	2	6	8
5	6	5	5	9	11	2	4	6	4
9	15	12	3		7	7	9	5	
$n = 24$; $M = 6.75$; $SD = 3.52$					$n = 24$; $M = 4.50$; $SD = 3.12$				

Clearly, the mean number of aggressive behaviors when the children watched the TV program with violence (*Beast Wars*) is somewhat higher than when the children watched the TV program without violence (*Mister Rogers*). In addition to this variability between the groups, there is also variability within the groups such that scores were, on average, about 3 units from their respective means. The variability within the groups is due to random error, and the variability between the groups is due to any systematic error due to confounds plus any systematic variability due to the type of TV program. Again, the advantage of the repeated measures design is that individual differences do not contribute to the error between the groups of scores.

Variability Within Groups = Random Error (Extraneous Variables)
Variability Between Groups = Systematic Error (Confounds) + Systematic Variability
(Effect of IV)

As with the independent samples design, the basic question is whether the difference between the two group means is due to error alone or due to error plus an effect of the independent variable (TV violence).

● Comparing *t* Test to ANOVA

As with the independent samples design, the correlated design with two groups can be analyzed with either a **correlated samples *t* test** or a **one-way correlated samples ANOVA**. The correlated samples *t* test is sometimes referred to as a related samples *t* test or a paired samples *t* test. Likewise, the correlated samples ANOVA is often referred to as a repeated measures ANOVA. Recall from Chapter 10 that parametric tests require assumptions of normality and homogeneity of variance. If there is reason to suspect that either of these assumptions is seriously violated in a correlated samples design, then a nonparametric test such as the Wilcoxon test is more appropriate. For the examples in this chapter, we will assume normality and homogeneity of variance.

Recall that *t* tests are restricted to the comparison of two groups, whereas ANOVAs can be used with two or more groups. In either case, the inferential statistic is based on a ratio of variability between groups to variability due to error.

$$\text{Inferential Statistic} = \frac{\text{Variability Between Groups}}{\text{Error Variability}}$$

Let's examine each one.

Correlated Samples *t* Test

The correlated samples *t* test uses the difference between the two group means as a measure of variability between groups and uses the standard error of the difference between means as a measure of error variability. The difference between the two group means is a straightforward calculation. The standard error of the difference between means tells you, on average, how different the two group means should be if the difference is due solely to error variability. If you examine the formulas in a statistics book, you will see that the standard error is based on the variability of the difference scores, where the difference scores are calculated for each pair of scores.

$$t = \frac{\text{Difference Between the Two Group Means}}{\text{Standard Error of the Difference Between Means (Error)}}$$

If the null hypothesis (H_0) is true—that is, there is no effect of the independent variable—then you would expect the difference between the two group means to be small and the t-statistic to be near 0. If, on the other hand, the null hypothesis is false, then you would expect the difference between the two group means to be large (in either a positive or a negative direction) relative to the standard error. The resulting t-statistic would have a value away from 0 (in either a positive or a negative direction). The larger the absolute value of the t-statistic, the lower is the probability that the difference between the group means is due solely to error variability. If the probability is low enough (what we refer to as the alpha level), then we reject the null hypothesis and accept the alternative hypothesis (H_1). We conclude that the independent variable had an effect.

For the data presented in this example, the output from a statistical analysis program would include the information in Table 12.3.

Table 12.3	Output From a Correlated Samples t Test		
	t	df	p
	−2.52	23	0.019

This table shows that the t-statistic was −2.52, the degrees of freedom were 23, and the probability value was 0.019. Using an alpha level of .05, we decide to reject the null hypothesis and conclude that there was a significant effect of the independent variable on the dependent variable. Specifically, children who watched a TV program with violence showed significantly more aggressive behaviors than children who watched a TV program without violence, $t(23) = -2.52$, $p = 0.019$.

Correlated Samples ANOVA

As noted earlier, these same data could be analyzed with a correlated samples analysis of variance. As noted in the previous chapter, the logic of the ANOVA is very similar to that of the t test. Again we calculate a ratio of variability between the groups to error variability, referred to as the F-ratio. However, the numerator of the formula is not simply the difference between the group means. It is a measure of variability based on how different the group means are. Therefore, whereas the t-statistic can have negative values and has an expected value of 0, the F-ratio must be positive (because variability is always positive) and has an expected value of 1. Remember that expected values are based on the null hypothesis being true.

$$F\text{-ratio} = \frac{\text{Variability Between Groups (Mean Square Between)}}{\text{Error Variability (Mean Square Error)}}$$

Output from a computer program would include the information shown in Table 12.4.

Table 12.4	Output From a Correlated Samples ANOVA				
SOURCE OF VARIABILITY	DEGREES OF FREEDOM (df)	SUM OF SQUARES	MEAN SQUARES	F RATIO	F PROBABILITY
Between groups	1	60.75	60.75	6.37	0.019
Within groups (error)	23	219.25	9.53		
Total	24	280.00			

As in the analysis using the t test, the probability of the F-ratio (0.019) is less than the alpha level (.05), so the decision would be to reject the null hypothesis and conclude that the independent variable had a significant effect on the dependent variable. Specifically, children who watched a TV program with violence showed significantly more aggressive behaviors than when the same children watched a TV program without violence, $F(1,23) = 6.37$, $p = 0.019$.

Comparing More Than Two Groups

Based on the above experiment, we concluded that children who watched a TV program with violence (*Beast Wars*) showed significantly more aggressive behaviors than when they watched a TV program without violence (*Mister Rogers*). As with the independent samples design in the previous chapter, a control condition with no TV program would help us to determine which type of program is actually affecting aggressive behavior. The experimental procedures will be the same as previously described with the exception that there will be an additional condition in which the children watch no TV program in the 30 minutes prior to the observation period. This third condition will serve as something of a baseline with which we can compare the other two conditions. Let's add this third group to our hypothetical data (see Table 12.5).

An inspection of the group means suggests that it may be the *Mister Rogers* program that reduced aggression in that group. You might also observe that the standard deviations are similar across the groups, thus supporting the homogeneity of variance assumption. We

Table 12.5	Number of Aggressive Behaviors Recorded													
TV PROGRAM WITH VIOLENCE					TV PROGRRAM WITH NO VIOLENCE					NO TV PROGRAM				
8	9	0	10	4	10	2	2	2	0	7	7	10	4	3
7	3	2	8	8	1	3	3	5	7	12	6	6	5	8
6	12	8	4	4	2	0	2	6	8	2	11	12	3	3
5	6	5	5	9	11	2	4	6	4	5	9	9	11	7
9	15	12	3		7	7	9	5		10	4	5	4	
$M = 6.75$; $SD = 3.52$					$M = 4.50$; $SD = 3.12$					$M = 6.79$; $SD = 3.11$				

Table 12.6	Output From a Correlated Samples ANOVA				
SOURCE OF VARIABILITY	DEGREES OF FREEDOM (df)	SUM OF SQUARES	MEAN SQUARES	F RATIO	F PROBABILITY
Between groups	2	82.53	41.26	3.87	0.028
Within groups (error)	46	490.14	10.66		
Total	48	572.67			

need to conduct analyses to tell us whether there are any significant differences, and if so, where they are. A t test is not an option because it is restricted to the comparison of two groups, and the use of multiple t tests is not an acceptable procedure because it inflates the Type I error rate. Therefore, a correlated samples ANOVA is the appropriate analysis. Output from a computer program would include the information in Table 12.6.

This output tells us that there is a significant difference among the three group means, $F(2,46) = 3.87$, $p = 0.028$. Because there are more than two groups, we cannot be sure where the differences are. To determine this, we conduct a post hoc specific comparison test (such as Tukey HSD or Sheffé). Output from a Tukey HSD shows that the means for Group 1 (TV Violence) and Group 3 (No TV) are significantly higher than the mean for Group 2 (No Violence). Therefore, we can now conclude that watching *Mister Rogers* for 30 minutes significantly reduced aggressive behavior when compared to watching *Beast Wars* or no TV. Notice the additional information that was provided by the multiple-group design.

CASE ANALYSIS

Let's consider a study in which the research participants experience both levels of an independent variable. An industrial/organizational psychologist is consulting with a large company that operates its factory 24 hours a day. The employees work on three rotating shifts: day shift (7 A.M.–3 P.M.), evening shift (3 P.M.–11 P.M.), and night shift (11 P.M.– 7 A.M.). Every month, employees rotate to a new shift. The research question is whether employee productivity is better with a clockwise rotation (day to evening to night to day) or with a counterclockwise rotation (day to night to evening to day). For the first six months, employees rotate clockwise, and for the second months, employees rotate clockwise, and for the second

six months, employees rotate counterclockwise. The total number of production mistakes for each six-month period is recorded for 100 employees. Table 12.7 shows the descriptive statistics, and Table 12.8 shows the inferential statistics.

Critical Thinking Questions

1. Based on the t test, is there a significant effect of the direction of rotation on employee mistakes?

2. Write a conclusion for the study that includes the direction of the effect.

Table 12.7	Descriptive Statistics		
SHIFT WORK ROTATION	n	M	SD
Clockwise	100	19.96	5.63
Counterclockwise	100	24.45	5.99

Table 12.8	Output From a Correlated Samples *t* Test		
	t	*df*	*p*
	−5.20	99	<.01

3. Was this study a true experiment?

4. Can you conclude that the direction of rotation caused a change in worker productivity? Why or why not?

5. How could the study be improved so that the conclusion would be stronger?

GENERAL SUMMARY

A correlated samples design is a true experiment characterized by assignment of participants to conditions in pairs or sets. The pairs or sets may be natural, matched, or repeated measures on the same participants. The design also includes manipulation of the independent variable. In conjunction with the use of control groups, this design permits cause–effect conclusions. Such conclusions are derived from the use of descriptive statistics and inferential statistics (*t* test, ANOVA).

The repeated measures design is quite common. Although this design has advantages, it also raises statistical and methodological issues. Advantages include a need for fewer participants and the ability to eliminate individual differences as a source of error between groups.

Statistical issues involve assumptions of homogeneity of variance and covariance, wherein one assumes equal variability of scores in each of the treatment conditions and that participants maintain their relative standing in the different treatment conditions. Methodological issues include the effects of repeated testing—transient effects, permanent carryover effects, and sensitization. Counterbalancing techniques can be used to address the methodological issues.

Now that we have a fundamental understanding of experimental designs with one independent variable, the next chapter will explore designs with multiple independent variables.

DETAILED SUMMARY

1. Correlated samples designs do not use random assignment of participants to conditions. Rather, scores in the groups are paired up (assuming two groups) because they are natural pairs of participants, matched pairs of participants, or repeated measures from the same participants.

2. Correlated samples designs involve strategies to equate the comparison groups on variables other than the independent variable so that any differences between the comparison groups can be attributed to the manipulation of the independent variable.

3. Natural pairs designs involve the use of a natural variable (such as twins, siblings, or married couples) to equate the comparison groups. Good examples are identical twin studies in which one twin is randomly assigned to one of the treatment conditions and the other twin to the other treatment condition. These

natural pairs equate the groups in terms of the genetic profiles of the participants.

4. The primary advantage of the natural pairs design is to use a natural characteristic of the participants to reduce one or more sources of error between the groups. The primary limitation of this design is often the availability of participants.

5. Matched pairs designs involve the use of an experimenter-chosen variable to equate the comparison groups. After pairs are established, one participant from each pair is randomly assigned to one treatment condition and the other participant to the other treatment condition.

6. The primary advantage of the matched pairs design is to use experimental control to reduce one or more sources of error between the groups. One limitation of this design can be the availability of participants.

At times, there may not be a suitable match for a participant.

7. Repeated measures designs involve the repeated testing of the same participants such that each participant experiences all treatment conditions. This procedure eliminates error variability due to individual differences between the groups. Other advantages include efficiency, economy, and the ability to study phenomena that lend themselves to repeated testing (such as learning and practice).

8. Methodological concerns with repeated measures designs focus on three categories of carryover effects:

(1) transient effects—short-term effects that dissipate with time; (2) permanent effects, most often due to learning; and (3) sensitization effects, resulting from experiencing all treatments. These carryover effects pose a problem when their occurrence is confounded with the effects of treatment.

9. All three types of correlated samples designs are analyzed in the same way. A two-group study can be analyzed with either a correlated samples *t* test or a correlated samples ANOVA. A multiple-group study must be analyzed with a correlated samples ANOVA.

KEY TERMS

correlated samples *t*-test *(p. 209)*
counterbalancing *(p. 204)*
longitudinal research *(p. 203)*

one-way correlated samples ANOVA *(p. 209)*
transient effects *(p. 203)*

REVIEW QUESTIONS/EXERCISES

1. Summarize the essential characteristics of a one-way correlated samples research design.

2. Briefly describe a matched pairs experiment for which a correlated samples *t* test would be the appropriate inferential statistic. The experiment should test which is more effective in treating depression: a behavior modification program or a cognitive therapy program.

3. Briefly describe a repeated measures experiment for which a repeated measures ANOVA would be the appropriate inferential statistic. The experiment should

test the effect of 4-hour food deprivation, 8-hour food deprivation, and 12-hour food deprivation on how fast a rat will run through a maze to obtain food.

4. In your own words, describe the methodological and statistical advantages of the repeated measures design. Also describe the statistical disadvantage and the potential methodological disadvantages.

5. Describe a repeated measures experiment related to human memory for which counterbalancing would be an essential methodological tool.

LABORATORY EXERCISES

 As noted in the previous chapter, Chapter 4 in *Research Methods Laboratory Manual for Psychology* (Langston, 2005) provides several ideas for experiments involving the phenomenon called the Stroop Effect. Consider at least one of these experiments using a correlated samples design.

As noted in the previous chapter, Chapter 5 in *Research Methods Laboratory Manual for Psychology* pro-

vides several ideas for experiments involving the issue of gesturing while one speaks. Consider at least one of these experiments using a correlated samples design.

As noted in the previous chapter, Chapter 6 in *Research Methods Laboratory Manual for Psychology* provides several ideas for experiments involving color as the independent variable. Consider at least one of these experiments using a correlated samples design.

WEB RESOURCES TO INCREASE LEARNING

The chapter outline, chapter summaries, key terms and definitions, additional chapter questions, chapter exercises, and links to relevant Web sites are available at the course Web site (**http://psychology.wadsworth.com/** **lammers_badia1e**). Explore the interactive workshops "Between vs. Within Designs" and "Independent vs. Repeated t Tests."

CHAPTER 13

EXPERIMENTAL DESIGN
MULTIPLE INDEPENDENT VARIABLES

Characteristics of Factorial Designs

Why do children engage in aggressive behaviors? From our discussions so far, it is clear that aggression is the result of several factors. Indeed, nearly all behaviors have their cause in a multitude of factors, both genetic and environmental factors. Thus, when we attempt to understand some area of human or animal behavior, it is often advantageous to be able to study more than one independent variable at a time. In the previous two chapters, we discussed experimental designs that involved only one independent variable and one dependent variable. In this chapter, we examine factorial designs that include more than one independent variable.

In this book, we have continued to discuss the independent variable of TV violence and its potential impact on the aggressive behavior of children. One issue that we have not discussed, but others have, is whether the violence depicted on television programs is perceived as real. Does a child realize that violence seen in cartoons is not real? Might exposure to such violence affect the child's behavior in a way different from exposure to violence by real characters? This is an interesting question. In previous chapters, we did not control the type of character in our television show. Therefore, type of character could have been an extraneous variable with unknown effects. One solution to the problem would be to treat the type of TV character as an independent variable. In this chapter, we treat the realism of the TV program (real characters versus cartoon characters) as a second independent variable and examine its possible effect on aggressive behavior.

As you will see, the primary advantage of this design is the ability to study more than one independent variable at a time and to see how these variables interact with one another. For our study, we will examine (1) the effect of TV violence on aggressive behavior (violent versus nonviolent TV programs), (2) the effect of program realism on aggressive behavior (cartoon versus real characters), and (3) the possible interaction effect of TV violence and program realism on aggressive behavior. Notice that the first two effects could be tested by conducting two separate one-way designs. One study could test the effect of TV violence, and the other could test the effect of program realism. However, two separate studies would not permit us to examine the possible interaction of these two variables. That is, could the effect of TV violence depend on whether the program characters are real? We will return to this experiment a little later in the chapter.

In a two-way factorial design, there are two experimental or treatment variables (independent variables). One or both of these variables may be either qualitative (distinct categories) or quantitative (different amounts). Although a two-way design has only two experimental variables, each variable may have any number of subclasses or levels of treatment. A given study might involve two levels of one variable and four levels of a second variable, or three levels of each variable, or any other combination. The traditional way of designating a two-way design is by citing the number of levels (or subclasses) of each variable. For example, a study with two levels of one variable and four levels of a second variable is referred to as having a 2 × 4 design. This 2 × 4 study would have 8 cells (groups). A study with three levels of each variable is referred to as having a 3 × 3 design. This design would have 9 groups. A study with three levels of one variable and four levels of a second variable is referred to as having a 3 × 4 design (12 groups).

The only inherent limitation of designs with multiple independent variables is that they are a bit more complex than the one-way designs. Data analysis and interpretation are a little more challenging, and the design often requires more participants than designs with one independent variable. This is particularly true as the design is expanded to include three or

Table 13.1	Characteristics of Research Designs				
TYPE OF RESEARCH DESIGN	NUMBER OF IVS	NUMBER OF LEVELS OF THE IV	NUMBER OF DVS	ASSIGNMENT TO CONDITIONS	MOST PROBABLE INFERENTIAL STATISTIC
One-way independent samples	1	2 or more	1	Random	*t* test or one-way ANOVA
One-way correlated samples	1	2 or more	1	Natural pairs Matched pairs Repeated measures	*t* test or one-way ANOVA
Two-way design	2 or more	2 or more	1	Random Repeated measures Mixed	Two-way ANOVA

more independent variables or three or more levels for the independent variables. Fortunately for you, we will restrict our focus to two-way designs—that is, only two independent variables.

Table 13.1 summarizes the experimental designs discussed so far.

Possible Outcomes of a 2 × 2 Factorial Experiment

The total number of treatment combinations in any factorial design is equal to the product of the treatment levels of all factors or variables. Thus, a 2 × 2 factorial design has four treatment combinations; a 2 × 3 factorial design has six treatment combinations. In more complex factorial designs, the same principle applies. A 2 × 3 × 4 factorial design would have 24 treatment combinations.

As noted, factorial designs introduce the concept of **interaction**. This concept is very important for the proper analysis and understanding of complex designs. Indeed, often the main focus of interest in a study is the interaction of variables: Is the effect of one variable dependent on either the presence or the amount of a second variable? For example, a psychoactive drug alone may have little effect on the treatment of mentally ill patients. Psychotherapy alone may be equally ineffective. However, the combination of the two may produce the desired behavioral change. Without the two-variable design, this interaction might never be discovered.

Figure 13.1 illustrates a possible interaction of two variables: psychotherapy versus no psychotherapy, and drug versus no drug. Note that psychotherapy alone or the drug alone did not appear to bring about much improvement in the patients' behavior. However, when the two were combined, an improvement is noted (right side of top line).

Let's look at another example. Imagine you have conducted a study involving two levels of anxiety (A1 = low, A2 = high) and two levels of perceived difficulty of task (B1 = easy, B2 = difficult). The dependent measure is the time the individual continues to work at an unsolvable task. Figure 13.2 illustrates six different, although not exhaustive, possible outcomes of the experiment. In (a), there is no effect of either independent variable, and there is no interaction effect of the variables. In short, none of the experimental treatments had an

| Figure 13.1 | Interaction of Psychotherapy Treatment and Drug Treatment on Therapeutic Effectiveness |

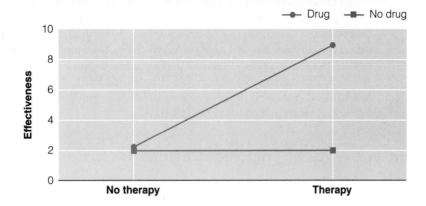

| Figure 13.2 | Several Possible Outcomes of an Experiment Involving a 2 × 2 Factorial Design |

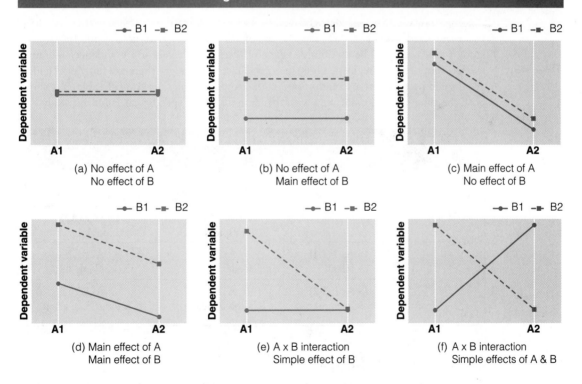

effect on the dependent variable of time on task. Note that in (b), (c), and (d), the observed effect of one variable is found over both levels of a second variable. When this happens, we refer to the outcome as a **main effect.** A main effect of a given variable describes an effect of that variable over all levels of a second variable.

Thus, in (b), high levels of perceived difficulty (B2) is found to produce longer periods of task-related activities at both levels of induced anxiety. Similarly, in (c), time on task is greater with low levels of anxiety than with high levels of anxiety, whether the task is perceived as easy (B1) or difficult (B2). In (d), we see both of these main effects. In contrast, (e) and (f) show interactions between the two independent variables. In (e), the time spent at a task perceived as difficult (B2) increases only when induced anxiety is low (A1). Because the difference between low and high perceived difficulty is not found at both levels of induced anxiety, the effect is a **simple effect.** In (f), the interaction is complete. Here, a high level of perceived difficulty produces a greater effect than a low level only when induced anxiety is low (A1), whereas a low level of perceived difficulty produces longer periods of task orientation only when induced anxiety is high (A2).

● Different Types of Factorial Designs

The previous two chapters discussed several different ways in which participants can be assigned to experimental conditions. These methods included randomization, natural pairs, matched pairs, and repeated measures. These options continue to be available to us in the two-way design.

Completely Randomized Factorial Design (Independent Samples)

A **completely randomized factorial design** uses randomization to assign participants to all treatment conditions. Let's consider the use of a 2×2 factorial design for our TV violence study. Participants will be randomly assigned to one of the levels of TV violence and one of the levels of program realism. Thus, in a 2×2 factorial design, there are four independent groups and participants are randomly assigned to one of the four groups. Table 13.2 shows both the general terms associated with this design and the specific labels for our study.

Table 13.2	General Diagram and Specific Example of a 2 × 2 Factorial Design		
		FACTOR A **(TV VIOLENCE)**	
		Level 1 (A1) **(Violent)**	**Level 2 (A2)** **(Nonviolent)**
FACTOR B **(REALISM)**	**Level 1 (B1)** **(Real)**	A1B1 (Real/Violent)	A2B1 (Real/Nonviolent)
	Level 2 (B2) **(Cartoon)**	A1B2 (Cartoon/Violent)	A2B2 (Cartoon/Nonviolent)

Repeated Measures Factorial Design

A **repeated measures factorial design** uses multiple observations on the same participants, possibly in combination with natural pairs or matched pairs, to assign participants to treatment conditions. The most typical design involves all participants participating in all conditions. Let's look at how a two-way repeated measures design might be used in the TV violence study.

Table 13.3	Example of a Repeated Measures Factorial Design			
	EXPERIMENTAL CONDITION			
	Real/ Violent	Real/ Nonviolent	Cartoon/ Violent	Cartoon/ Nonviolent
Participant 1				
Participant 2				
Participant 3				
.				
.				
.				
Participant 12				

As in the factorial design described earlier, we will have two independent variables, each with two levels. But rather than randomly assigning participants to each of the four conditions, we will now have all participants participate in all four conditions. Table 13.3 illustrates this design.

As discussed previously, advantages of the repeated measures design include the reduction of error due to individual differences and the efficiency of using fewer participants. Disadvantages include concern for homogeneity of variance, homogeneity of covariance, and carryover effects. Regarding carryover effects, it may be that the effect of watching a violent program may carry over into an observation period following a nonviolent program. Although the statistical concerns are difficult to control, carryover effects can be addressed by counterbalancing the conditions.

For our example with four different conditions, complete counterbalancing would require 24 different orders for the conditions. In many situations, the experimenter is unable to accommodate such complete counterbalancing. One possible solution is to select a random order for each participant. Another technique uses a simpler version in which each condition occurs in a different position in the order. For example, if we label the real/violent condition as condition 1, the real/nonviolent as condition 2, and so on, then we would arrange the ordering as shown in Table 13.4. Thus, each condition occurs in the first position three times, each condition occurs in the second position three times, and so on. One potential danger of this simpler counterbalancing occurs if the effect of one condition depends on the particular condition that preceded it in the order.

Mixed Factorial Design

A mixed factorial design uses a combination of randomization and repeated measures (although natural pairs and matched pairs are possible) to assign participants to treatment conditions. Participants are randomly assigned to the different levels of one independent variable and participate in all levels of another independent variable. For our TV violence study, we might decide to randomly assign participants to watch either TV programs with violence or ones without violence, but all participants will watch one show involving real characters

Table 13.4	Counterbalancing in a Repeated Measures Factorial Design			
	EXPERIMENTAL CONDITION			
Participant 1	1	2	3	4
Participant 2	1	2	3	4
Participant 3	1	2	3	4
Participant 4	2	3	4	1
Participant 5	2	3	4	1
Participant 6	2	3	4	1
Participant 7	3	4	1	2
Participant 8	3	4	1	2
Participant 9	3	4	1	2
Participant 10	4	1	2	3
Participant 11	4	1	2	3
Participant 12	4	1	2	3

and one show involving cartoon characters. We might visualize this design as shown in Table 13.5.

Let's turn to a recent report on the effects of diet on blood pressure and consider how this study might be converted into a factorial design (see "Thinking Critically About Everyday Information").

Thinking Critically About Everyday Information

Effect of Diet on Blood Pressure

A report by ABC News refers to research (Appel et al., 2003) that studied the effect of lifestyle changes on lowering blood pressure. In the study, participants with above-normal blood pressure were randomly assigned to one of three treatment conditions. One group received one advice session regarding dietary changes, the second group received 28 counseling sessions that focused on lowering fat intake, and the third group received the 28 counseling sessions plus a specific diet plan. After six months, results showed substantial improvements in both the second and third groups.

• What type of research design was used?

• Was the study a true experiment? Why or why not?

• As you know, lifestyle change can involve more than changes in diet. What second independent variable could be added to create a factorial design? What levels of this second IV would you test?

• What type of factorial design do you now have (completely randomized, repeated measures, or mixed design)?

• What would be your prediction for your new factorial design?

SOURCE: Retrieved June 11, 2003, online at http://abcnews.go.com/sections/living/Healthology/ho_bpsqueeze.html

Table 13.5 Example of a Mixed Factorial Design			REALISM	
			Real	Cartoon
TV VIOLENCE	Violent	Participant 1		
		Participant 2		
		Participant 3		
		Participant 4		
		Participant 5		
		Participant 6		
		Participant 7		
		Participant 8		
	Nonviolent	Participant 9		
		Participant 10		
		Participant 11		
		Participant 12		
		Participant 13		
		Participant 14		
		Participant 15		
		Participant 16		

● Interpreting Main Effects and Interactions

Let's return to our two-way randomized factorial design to discuss the interpretation of main effects and interactions. Although we won't do the same for two-way repeated measures or mixed designs, the logic of the interpretation is the same.

Assume that we began with a sample of 80 participants, randomly assigned 20 to each of the four groups, and calculated the mean number of aggressive behaviors for each group. Table 13.6 shows the design and descriptive statistics. To aid interpretation, Figure 13.3 provides both a bar graph and a line graph of the means. Based on the graphs, can you guess which effects might be significant?

Inferential analysis consisted of a 2×2 independent samples ANOVA. The ANOVA Summary Table is shown in Table 13.7.

Notice that there are three F-values in the analysis—one for each effect to be analyzed. The analysis (assuming alpha = .05) reveals a significant main effect for the level of violence, a significant effect for the type of characters, and a significant interaction, $F(1,76) = 46.94$, $p < .001$, $F(1,76) = 4.35$, $p = .04$, and $F(1,76) = 4.86$, $p = .031$, respectively. Let's work to understand each of these effects individually. Using the graphs in Figure 13.3, the main effect for the level of violence shows that a program with violence resulted in significantly more

Table 13.6	Example of a 2 × 2 Factorial Design		
		TV VIOLENCE	
		Violent	**Nonviolent**
CHARACTERS	**Real**	M = 7.75 SD = 2.63	M = 3.95 SD = 1.32
	Cartoon	M = 5.95 SD = 1.88	M = 4.00 SD = 1.38

Figure 13.3	Graphical Depictions of the Means for the TV Violence Study

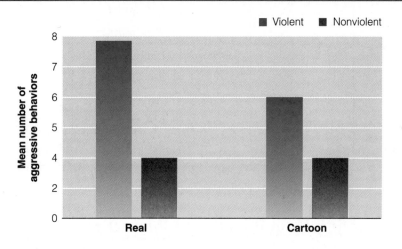

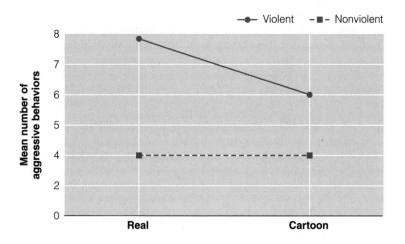

Table 13.7	ANOVA Summary Table				
SOURCE OF VARIABILITY	DEGREES OF FREEDOM (df)	SUM OF SQUARES	MEAN SQUARES	F RATIO	F PROBABILITY
Level of Violence	1	165.31	165.31	46.94	<.001
Type of Characters	1	15.31	15.31	4.35	.040
Violence × Characters	1	17.11	17.11	4.86	.031
Error	76	3.52	3.52		
Total	79	201.25			

aggressive behaviors than a program without violence. Notice that this interpretation ignores the levels of the other variable (type of characters). The main effect for the type of characters shows that real characters resulted in significantly more aggressive behaviors than cartoon characters. Notice that this interpretation ignores the levels of the other variable (level of violence). The interaction effect shows that the increase in aggressive behavior as a result of TV violence was enhanced when the TV characters were real. Notice that this interpretation considers both levels of both variables.

Are we done with the interpretation of results? Not yet. Whenever a significant interaction is found, you must determine whether the conclusions for the main effects still make sense. In other words, a statistically significant main effect can be explained by a significant interaction. So, let's return to each of our main effects. We concluded that TV violence resulted in more aggression. Does examination of our graphs show this to be always true? The answer is yes. TV violence resulted in more aggression when the TV program contained either type of character. We also concluded that real characters resulted in more aggression. Does examination of our graphs show this to be always true? The answer is no. Real characters only resulted in more aggression when the TV program contained violence. Thus, this main effect is actually a simple effect and a result of the significant interaction. Our overall conclusion would be that watching a TV program with violence resulted in more aggressive behaviors and that this effect was enhanced by the use of real characters in the TV program.

It is important to notice in this example, as well as the other examples in this chapter, that the researcher was able to randomly assign participants to the various conditions and was able to manipulate the factors of interest (independent variables). As we have noted before, these are important characteristics of a true experiment and permit cause–effect conclusions. As we stated in Chapter 11, students are often interested in factors such a gender, race, personality traits, political affiliation, fraternity/sorority status, and other attributes where random assignment is not possible—designs in which one or more factors consist of preexisting groups. Again, you should exercise caution when drawing conclusions regarding the effects that result when you are unable to randomly assign participants to conditions.

More Complex Factorial Designs

Before we end this chapter, we would like to say a few words about factorial designs that go beyond the relatively simple 2 × 2 design. The logic of main effects and interactions can be extended to 2 × 3 designs, 2 × 4 designs, 3 × 5 designs, and so on, and these designs can be of the three different varieties presented in this chapter—namely, independent samples, correlated samples, or mixed designs. With these more complex two-way designs, significant effects must often be followed by more specific comparison tests to determine exactly where significant differences exist. As illustrated earlier in this chapter, graphic depiction of the cell means is critical to a complete understanding of the data.

In addition to two-way designs, the logic of factorial designs can be extended to three-way designs (for example, $2 \times 2 \times 2$ or $2 \times 4 \times 3$). Although the logic could be extended to four-way designs, five-way designs, and beyond, very few researchers employ such complicated experimental designs. In a three-way design, the ANOVA would analyze the main effect of factor A, the main effect of factor B, the main effect of factor C, the $A \times B$ interaction, the $A \times C$ interaction, the $B \times C$ interaction, and the $A \times B \times C$ interaction. If the complexity of such an analysis seems daunting, we certainly understand.

CASE ANALYSIS

One fascinating area of psychological research involves understanding the brain mechanisms responsible for learning and memory. Both human and animal research suggests that a structure in the brain called the hippocampus is important for the formation of certain types of memory, including spatial memory (memory for where things are located in your environment). In one research paradigm, rats are placed in a pool of milky water. At a particular location in this pool, a platform is hidden just beneath the surface of the milky water. When the rat locates this platform, it will climb onto it so that it can get most of its body out of the water (as you might guess, rats don't like water). After several trials in the pool, a normal rat will locate the platform quickly by using the spatial cues present in the room (such as unique items hanging on the wall).

As a researcher, you are interested in the effect of hippocampal damage on spatial learning and also whether the hippocampus is necessary for the retrieval of spatial memories that have already been learned. To study these questions, you randomly assign rats to one of four groups. Group 1 are rats with no damage to the hippocampus and no prior experience in the pool. Group 2 are rats with no damage to the hippocampus and prior experience in the pool. Group 3 are rats with damage to the hippocampus and no prior experience in the pool. Group 4 are rats with damage to the hippocampus and prior experience in the pool (experience was prior to

damage). For each rat, you measure the time it takes for the rat to locate the platform. The group means are as follows:

Group 1	30 seconds
Group 2	5 seconds
Group 3	29 seconds
Group 4	32 seconds

Critical Thinking Questions

1. What are the independent variables and the dependent variable for this experiment?

2. What type of research design is this?

3. Create a 2×2 table that depicts the conditions and means.

4. Create a line graph that depicts the conditions and means.

5. Based on the table and graph, does there appear to be a significant main effect of "damage"? A significant main effect of "experience"? A significant interaction? (Note: Your answers are guesses. You would need to know the variability in the groups and the results of the ANOVA to make definitive judgments.)

6. Based on your answers in question 5 and your evaluation of simple effects, write a conclusion for the experiment.

GENERAL SUMMARY

Factorial designs permit the researcher to determine the effect of more than one independent variable on a dependent variable and to determine the possible interaction of multiple independent variables. That is, the effect of one independent variable may differ across different levels of another independent variable. With an independent samples design, participants are randomly assigned to levels of each independent variable. With a correlated samples design, participants are usually measured repeatedly; that is, they participate in each level of each independent variable. With a mixed design, participants are randomly assigned to the levels of one independent variable and are repeatedly measured on the levels of the other independent variable.

A 2 × 2 factorial design requires interpretation of three effects: a main effect for the first IV, a main effect for the second IV, and the interaction of the two IVs. A main effect signifies that there is an effect of that IV on the DV regardless of the levels of the other IV. An inter-action signifies that the effect of one IV depends on the levels of the other IV. In some cases, a significant main effect may be due solely to the interaction. We refer to this as a simple effect, and interpretation of this effect must be done with caution.

In the next chapter, we will explore how to design an experiment that involves only a single participant and how we can systematically manipulate an independent variable over time to determine its effect on a dependent variable.

DETAILED SUMMARY

1. Factorial designs permit the systematic investigation of two or more independent variables in a single study.

2. According to conventional terminology, a 2 × 3 factorial design would have two levels of one IV and three levels of the other IV.

3. Disadvantages of factorial designs can include the complexity of design and interpretation and, at times, the increased number of participants necessary to conduct the study.

4. A factorial design will reveal whether there is an effect of each independent variable on the dependent variable (main effects) plus whether there is an interaction effect. A main effect indicates that one IV has an effect on the DV regardless of the levels of a second IV. An interaction indicates that the effect of one IV depends on the levels of a second IV.

5. Different types of factorial designs can be distinguished based on how participants are assigned to treatment conditions. The three most common types are the completely randomized design, the repeated measures design, and the mixed design.

6. A completely randomized factorial design involves the random assignment of participants to all treatment conditions (all levels of all IVs). A repeated measures design involves testing each participant in each and every treatment condition. A mixed design involves a combination of random assignment to the levels of one IV and repeated testing across the levels of another IV.

7. A factorial design is analyzed with a factorial ANOVA that will calculate an F-value for each main effect and for the interaction. The statistical significance of these effects, along with a close inspection of a graph of the means, provides an accurate conclusion for the study.

8. The logic of the 2 × 2 factorial design can be extended to designs in which there are more than two levels of an independent variable (such as 2 × 3 or 3 × 4) and/or more than two independent variables (for example, 2 × 2 × 2 or 2 × 3 × 4).

KEY TERMS

completely randomized factorial design *(p. 220)*
interaction *(p. 218)*
main effect *(p. 219)*

mixed factorial design *(p. 221)*
repeated measures factorial design *(p. 220)*
simple effect *(p. 220)*

REVIEW QUESTIONS/EXERCISES

1. Briefly describe a memory recall study that would be a 2 × 2 independent samples design in which the independent variables are mode of sensory experience (see the object versus touch the object) and type of object (natural versus man-made).

2. Briefly describe a memory recall study that would be a 2 × 2 correlated samples (repeated measures) design in which the independent variables are the same as in question 1.

3. Briefly describe a memory recall study that would be a 2×2 mixed design in which the independent variables are the same as in question 1.

For questions 4–8, consider the following experiment:

An experimenter wanted to test the hypothesis that males are more creative than females. She also hypothesized that the male superiority in creativity would be heightened under conditions involving ego. She manipulated ego involvement by telling half of the males and females that the task was a measure of intelligence and that their scores would be posted on a bulletin board (high ego involvement). She told the other half of the males and females that she wanted to test the reliability of a task she was developing and that they shouldn't put their names on the answer sheets (low ego involvement). Her test of creativity was an "unusual uses" test in which a person is given the name of an object (army compass, monkey wrench) and has to write as many different unusual uses for that object as possible in five minutes. Twenty-five males and 25 females were randomly as-

signed to each of the two ego-involvement conditions. The males were members of a senior ROTC class, and the females came from sorority pledge classes. All participants were given five minutes to write down as many unusual uses as they could for each object. Results showed that mean number of unusual uses written by males was 6.1 under low ego involvement and 9.2 under high ego involvement. Mean number of unusual uses written by females was 2.3 under low ego involvement and 2.3 under high ego involvement.

4. How many independent variables were used? How many dependent variables?

5. How would you describe the experimental design that was used?

6. Does the pattern of means suggest a main effect of Sex? A main effect of Ego Involvement? A Sex × Ego Involvement interaction?

7. What is the primary threat to internal validity?

8. What is the primary threat to external validity?

LABORATORY EXERCISES

Does your mood influence the way that you process information in the world? This question is the topic of Chapter 7 in *Research Methods Laboratory Manual for Psychology* (Langston, 2005). A description of factorial designs and several ideas for such experiments are provided, and we suggest that you consider at least one of these.

Chapter 8 in Langston's manual asks whether measures of reading time can be used to support the use of the

word "they" as a gender-neutral pronoun in writing. Consider one of these factorial designs for your own research project.

How can you improve your chances that a person will comply with a request? Chapter 9 in Langston's manual explores this issue using a factorial design for a field experiment. Consider one of the suggested projects.

 ## WEB RESOURCES TO INCREASE LEARNING

The chapter outline, chapter summaries, key terms and definitions, additional chapter questions, chapter exercises, and links to relevant Web sites are available at the course Web site (**http://psychology.wadsworth.com/lammers_badia1e**). Explore the interactive workshop "Two-Way ANOVA."

CHAPTER 14

EXPERIMENTAL DESIGN
SINGLE-SUBJECT DESIGNS
AND TIME-SERIES DESIGNS

● Introduction to Single-Subject Designs

A 3-year-old boy diagnosed with autism showed characteristic language deficits. His level of spontaneous speech was equivalent to what is expected of a boy less than 2 years old. Monica Bellon, Billy Ogletree, and William Harn (2000) conducted a study to increase the level of spontaneous speech in this young boy. They began by recording the boy's normal level of spontaneous speech during four 45-minute sessions in which an adult read storybooks to the child and periodically asked questions. During the next phase (treatment phase), which consisted of eight 45-minute sessions, the adult again read storybooks but also used a technique called scaffolding. The scaffolding procedure includes pauses to allow the child to provide information, choices posed to the child, elaborations of the story by the adult, and questions asked of the child. The final phase consisted of two 45-minute sessions that were identical to the baseline phase. Results showed that spontaneous speech was relatively low and stable during the baseline phase, increased during the treatment phase, and remained elevated during the final phase. The authors concluded that repeated storybook reading with adult scaffolding effectively increased spontaneous speech in an autistic boy.

This example illustrates the single-subject approach. It is a method designed to study the behavior of individual organisms. As the method continues to evolve and improve, it also has become more popular for both scientific and therapeutic purposes. Its track record in both areas is impressive. The single-subject approach should not be confused with the case study or case history approach, in which a single individual is also studied exhaustively. The case study approach is often an uncontrolled inquiry into history (retrospective). It may yield interesting information, but the lack of control severely limits any conclusions that can be drawn. The case study approach has two serious problems: (1) lack of experimental control, and (2) obtaining precise measures of behavior. Neither of these problems applies to the single-subject approach.

The method is relatively popular today, but it hasn't always been. Research in psychology started out using small numbers of participants, and investigators relied heavily on their ability to control conditions so that the conditions were reasonably constant among participants. Rigorous methodology was only beginning to evolve. After the data were gathered, conclusions about effects of the independent variable were based on subjective visual inspection of the data. Groups were not formed randomly, and objective statistical analyses for decision making were not yet available. Investigators realized the shortcomings of their method and made attempts to minimize subjectivity in their analyses.

The introductions of random assignment and statistical analyses were tremendous advances for research. Random assignment enhanced the likelihood that groups were initially equal on all variables. Statistical procedures permitted researchers to decide objectively whether the observed effect was more likely a chance occurrence or an outcome of the treatment condition. Investigators readily accepted these powerful research tools, and large-sample statistical studies rapidly became popular. As interest in large-sample methods increased, it became difficult to publish nonstatistical research or even studies based on a small number of participants. Some researchers strongly preferred the single-subject approach refined by B. F. Skinner and elaborated by others. They continued using and refining it. Controversies and arguments frequently erupted between researchers using the single-subject approach and those using a statistical one. It is ironic that, even though psychology was defined as the study of individual behavior, investigators studying individual behavior could not easily get their research published in the established journals. This was the case even though strong behavioral control by the treatment condition was shown repeatedly in individual participants. It was this difficulty in getting their research published that led to the formation of the Society for the Experimental Analysis of Behavior and the subsequent establishment of the *Journal of the Experimental Analysis of Behavior.* This journal publishes basic research involving the study of individual participants. Subsequently, a second journal devoted to the study of individual participants, the *Journal of Applied Behavior Analysis,* was established with a focus on applied research.

With the passage of time, both the large-sample and single-subject procedures have become better developed and their strengths and weaknesses more apparent. These methods continue to evolve, as do other research methods. As a result, a greater variety of useful tools are becoming available to those interested in either basic or applied research.

Using the single-subject approach does not mean that you must investigate only a single participant, although you can. More often than not, several participants—usually three to five—are studied very intensively. However, interest is always in the careful analysis of the individual participant separately and not in the average performance of the group. With the single-subject approach, there is very little interest in averaging across participants. Great emphasis is placed on careful and rigorous experimental control. Unwanted environmental variables are either excluded from the study or are held constant so that their effects are the same across participants and conditions. As we shall see, important features of this procedure for determining the reliability of the findings are actual **replications** rather than inferential statistics. We will describe two types of replication: intraparticipant replication (replications within an individual participant) and interparticipant replication (replications between individual participants). As with other research methods, the single-subject approach has both advantages and limitations.

● Advantages and Limitations

Advantages of the Single-Subject Approach

Those who use the single-subject approach find it both a powerful and a satisfying research method. One reason is that the method provides feedback quickly to the investigator about the effects of the treatment conditions. The experimenter knows relatively soon whether the treatment is working or not working. Day-to-day changes can be observed firsthand, quickly and in individual participants. If changes are necessary on a day-to-day basis, they can be made. Seldom do scientists have available procedures that do this. In contrast to the single-subject approach, a large-sample statistical approach may take weeks or months of testing participants, calculating means, and then performing statistical analyses; unfortunately, often nothing can be known about the effects of the treatment conditions until the final statistical analysis is complete. Even then, as we have seen, the derived knowledge is limited to statements regarding group performance, not the performance of specific individual participants.

The single-subject method also allows us to draw strong conclusions regarding the factors controlling the dependent variable, even though the method does not use random assignment. The method allows strong conclusions because investigators employing it use procedures that provide rigorous control over environmental/experimental conditions, with great emphasis on obtaining stable behavior with each participant. To be an acceptable scientific work, the research must demonstrate for each participant that behavior is controlled by the treatment condition and must also show both intra- and interparticipant replication. That is, control must be shown both within a single participant and between the participants.

Limitations of the Single-Subject Approach

One obvious limitation of the single-subject approach is that the method is unsuitable for answering actuarial types of questions, such as "How many of the 100 people exposed to a particular treatment will respond favorably, and how many will respond unfavorably?" A related limitation involves studies comparing two or more different treatments on the same behavioral measure. For example, which of the various treatments is the most effective? Least effective? Most debilitating? The method cannot be used if you are interested in treating an entire group of participants, such as a classroom, in an identical way on a daily basis—that is, when any changes in procedures are made for everyone in the group at the same time and for the same period. A different method is also required if "after the fact" studies (ex post facto, correlational, passive observational) are of interest. Moreover, the single-subject approach makes heavy time demands. It may, on occasion, take several months to completely test a single participant under the various conditions of interest. Often researchers are unwilling or unable to devote the required time.

In addition to these limitations, single-subject designs also have some recurring problems. Establishing a criterion and acquiring stable baselines for the response of interest are sometimes very difficult. Further, determining whether variability in behavior is intrinsic or extrinsic can be troublesome. Nonreversible (irreversible) behavior poses its own set of problems, and it precludes the use of a design in which the researcher removes the treatment to observe a return to baseline levels of responding. Failure to obtain intra- and interparticipant replication for whatever reason creates problems for the single-subject approach. Sometimes decisions regarding the necessary number of both intra- and interparticipant replications are largely subjective. Nevertheless, despite the limitations and problems described here, the single-subject method does provide researchers with another powerful way to assess behavior.

● Why Some Researchers Use the Single-Subject Method

Investigators who use the single-subject method do so for different reasons. One of the main reasons is that their interest is in the behavior of individual participants. The large-sample approach places emphasis on group averages rather than individual participants. Unfortunately, the behavior reflected by the group average may not represent the individual participant. The following example illustrates how distant the overall results for the group may be from the performance of any given individual participant. Say that we are interested in learning as a function of practice. The particular form or shape of the curve is what we are trying to determine. We choose 20 participants to participate in our study, choose a learning task that we want to evaluate, and then give practice trials to the participants until the task is learned. After all the data are gathered, we plot a learning curve to determine its form or shape (see Figure 14.1), which in turn will reveal to us how quickly and smoothly participants learned the task. The learning curve in Figure 14.1 is based on the performance of all 20 participants. Each data point on the graph represents an average (five trials) of an average (20 participants).

A description of how these averages were computed may be helpful. First the performance of each participant on each block of five trials was averaged. Then the average for each average block of five trials was obtained for all 20 participants. This average of averages produces a smooth, negatively accelerated learning curve. But does this group curve reflect the performance of a single individual? It is quite unlikely that any one individual in a group of

| **Figure 14.1** | **Mean Performance of 20 Participants on Each of Six Blocks of Five Practice Trials** |

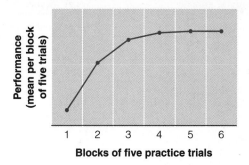

20 participants would perform like the group curve. In other words, plots of each individual participant may differ from the group curve. Usually, a statistical approach that relies on the analysis of group means masks the performance of each participant, whatever the problem being studied. A related point follows.

A group performance curve may not only mask the performance of an individual but may also be misleading. Although the group average may indicate an increase in performance as a result of the treatment condition, not all participants may have increased; some individuals within the group may, in fact, perform at a lower than normal level. The point is that individual reactions to the experimental conditions are not taken into account. Failure to address individual reactions may be especially unfortunate in more applied research, particularly if assessing different therapeutic techniques. If the therapy is harmful (or helpful) to certain individuals, this fact may be lost in the group mean. Others have made a similar argument regarding statistical analysis. The analysis may reveal statistically significant differences between groups, but the differences may be due to only a few participants. Conversely, the analysis may not be statistically significant overall, but some participants may change markedly as a result of the treatment conditions.

The dependence on statistical evaluation of the data with large-sample methods is also a source of unhappiness for some researchers. Have the assumptions underlying the statistical test been satisfied? Is the sample size sufficiently large to give the needed power? Is the sample size too large, so that trivial differences between groups will be significant? What about Type I and Type II errors? Some researchers are concerned that investigators are placing greater emphasis on statistical issues per se and less emphasis on rigorous methodology. Statistical analysis cannot salvage a poor experiment. Complete confounding of variables cannot be corrected by statistical analysis.

Other researchers favor the single-subject method because, for some interests, large numbers of participants may not be available. Consequently, a large-sample procedure cannot be used. In applied research dealing with specific behavioral problems, the researcher/therapist might have to wait months or years before obtaining a sufficiently large sample. Applied psychologists are often interested only in a small number of individuals. They need a method sufficiently flexible to allow treatment of individual cases, one that can be altered quickly to adjust to the responsiveness of the individual. Large-sample statistical procedures do not have this flexibility.

Table 14.1	Comparison of Single-Subject and Large-Sample Approaches	
ISSUE	SINGLE SUBJECT	LARGE SAMPLE
Random assignment	Not applicable	Yes
Control groups	Not applicable	Yes
Manipulation	Yes	Yes
Determining reliability	Replications	Statistically
Determining generality	Replications	Sampling
Number of participants	Usually 1–5	Usually >10 per group
Flexibility of procedure	High	Low
Measurement of behavior	Continuous monitoring	Varies
Focus of interest	Individual	Group
Time to complete experiment	Relatively long term	Relatively short term
Knowledge of results	Moment to moment	After study is complete
Type I and Type II errors	Not applicable	Yes
Statistical assumptions	Not applicable	Yes
Statistical power	Not applicable	Yes
Laboratory experiments	Yes	Yes
Field experiments	Yes	Yes
Actuarial experiments	No	Yes
Comparison experiments	No	Yes

Table 14.1 compares characteristics of the single-subject approach and the large-sample statistical approach.

● Procedures for the Single-Subject Method

As noted, the single-subject method means that the effects of the treatment must be shown in individual participants. To accomplish this, the experimenter must have considerable control over the experimental situation at all stages of the research and must use the proper methodology. As with other research methods, the dependent variable must be clearly defined. Where possible, it should be defined in terms of operations that objectively identify the occurrence or nonoccurrence of the response. In single-subject research, the dependent variable is often "rate of responding," and great emphasis is placed on steady-state (stable) performance rather than behavior in transition (in the process of changing).

Establishing a Baseline

When assessing steady-state behavior in a given condition, we assess the behavior relative to some comparison point. With the single-subject approach, the comparison point is the **baseline** condition. To establish a baseline, we first make repeated observations of the natural frequency of the behavior of interest (the dependent variable). In effect, we observe the frequency with which the behavior occurs before the treatment (the independent variable) is introduced. This baseline serves as a sort of benchmark against which to measure whether the subsequent introduction of the treatment condition has an effect. The behavioral effect may be either an increase over baseline responding **(facilitation)** or a decrease below baseline responding **(suppression)**.

Because the baseline serves as a point from which the treatment effects are judged, it is important that a stable baseline be established. There is no set number of days or experimental sessions that define baseline stability. Instead, we establish a criterion of stability, such as "four experimental sessions in which the frequency of the target behavior does not vary by more than 5%." In other instances, a less demanding criterion of 10% may be used. Some participants may take only four days to meet the criterion, whereas others may take a week or more before the session-to-session variability is less than 5% or 10%. The choice between 5% and 10% is somewhat arbitrary, but these values are often used. If baseline behavior is so variable that a 5% or 10% criterion of stability cannot be met, then the investigator should strive to acquire greater control over all variables related to the experimental situation. This can be a very difficult task. What is needed is a careful assessment of all aspects of the experiment for possible sources of unwanted variability. This would include assessing the instructions, procedure, apparatus, independent variable, dependent variable, and any other possibilities. It is wiser to assume that the reason for the variability is extrinsic (environmentally induced) and then seek ways to reduce it, rather than to assume that the variability is intrinsic (inherent) and cannot be reduced. If all efforts to reduce variability fail, then the percentage criterion under baseline conditions (5% or 10%) may have to change upward. Some criterion is necessary to avoid arbitrary decision making.

Optimal Baseline   An **optimal baseline** requirement for any given response is that it be stable—that is, there is little change in frequency from session to session under natural (baseline) conditions. In addition, if the treatment is expected to lead to increases in frequency of responding, then baseline responding should not be so high that further increases would be difficult to obtain (ceiling effect). On the other side of the coin, what if the treatment is expected to lead to decreases in frequency of responding? Now the opposite is true. Baseline responding should not be so low that further decreases would be difficult to achieve (floor effects). In some situations, the experimenter may be interested in demonstrating both increases and decreases in responding but at different phases of the experiment. If this is the case, then a baseline level that permits both increases and decreases in responding would be necessary. Such a baseline level is shown in Figure 14.2.

After the treatment condition is introduced, departures from the baseline, either upward or downward, can be easily observed. If the frequency of responding neither increased nor decreased nor changed in terms of session-to-session variability, then our independent variable (treatment condition) obviously had no measurable effect.

Recall that in Chapter 4 we discussed the use of different degrees of an independent variable for purposes of identifying a function or trend. We saw that a minimum of three different points or values was needed. A similar requirement applies to establishing a baseline across sessions. We can never use fewer than three sessions to establish a stable baseline, because it is not possible to identify a stable pattern with fewer than three sessions. Reasons for this will become more apparent as we describe different possible baseline conditions.

Baselines to Avoid   Several types of baselines should be avoided simply because they evidence trends that make it difficult to interpret the effects of the treatment condition. For

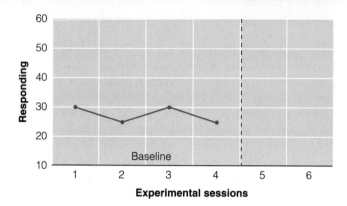

Figure 14.2 Baseline When Treatment Is Expected to Lead to Both Increases and Decreases in Responding at Different Phases of the Experiment

example, if you were evaluating the effects of praise on the amount of time spent studying, the baseline depicted in Figure 14.3 would not be appropriate. It would be difficult to assess whether obtaining an increase in study time on the fifth session when praise was introduced was a result of the treatment (praise) or a result of continued increases in study time under the baseline condition.

Imposing a treatment on a steadily increasing baseline should be avoided where possible. Similarly, the effects of an independent variable may be difficult to interpret with a decreasing baseline when the effects of the treatment are also expected to lead to a decrease in performance. For example, if we were interested in assessing the effects of punishment on disruptive classroom behavior, we would not want to use a baseline as shown in Figure 14.4. Further decreases at Session 5 and beyond may be a result of the natural downward trend, the punishment, or both factors. In fact, with a baseline either increasing throughout or decreasing throughout, any change or no change in the pattern would be difficult to assess.

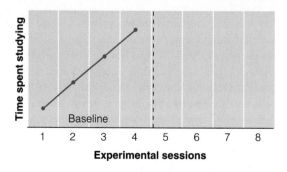

Figure 14.3 An Inappropriate Baseline to Use in a Single-Subject Design When Evaluating a Condition That Is Expected to Lead to Increases in the Dependent Variable

Figure 14.4	An Inappropriate Baseline to Use When Evaluating a Condition That Is Expected to Lead to Decreases in the Dependent Variable

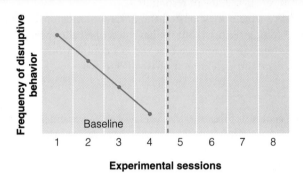

The soundest procedure would be for the researcher to continue baseline measurement until it leveled off and reached a rigorous criterion of stability. If the measure fails to reach the stability criterion, then we should attempt to achieve greater control over the conditions or find a different measure. Additional options are available to experienced researchers (Sidman, 1960).

Finally, if marked variability in responding occurs from one experimental session to the next, it is difficult to interpret any effect that the treatment might have. Figure 14.5 depicts such a pattern. In basic laboratory research, a baseline pattern of this type is of little use. The investigator should make an effort to reduce the variability by eliminating sources of extrinsic (environmental) variability. If these efforts are unsuccessful, a different response measure should be considered. At times, simply extending the period across more sessions results in a more stable baseline. However, most investigators would suggest that a careful, systematic assessment of the experimental situation be undertaken to identify sources of variability and then remove or alter them. Again, this means assessing the procedure, apparatus, task, instructions, experimenter, and other factors.

Figure 14.5	An Inappropriate Baseline to Use When Evaluating Conditions That Are Expected to Lead to Either Increases or Decreases in the Dependent Variable

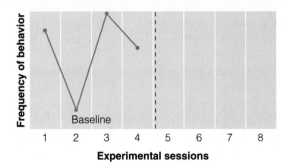

In applied areas, such as evaluation of therapeutic techniques, efforts to obtain a stable baseline may be less successful, and the investigator, after an exhaustive search for solutions, may have to impose a treatment condition over an unstable baseline. If the effects of the treatment are strong, then they may be seen in terms of both greater stability and a higher (or lower) frequency of responding.

We have not exhausted the different kinds of difficult baselines that are encountered when doing research, but we have described the more bothersome ones. The issue of what constitutes an acceptable baseline is a complex one that we have tried to simplify. We will now discuss the treatment phase of research.

Analysis of Treatment Effects

The analysis of treatment effects will be more understandable to you if we give an overview of the design strategy. It is customary to refer to the baseline phase of an experiment as the "A" condition and the treatment phase as the "B" condition. If there are different kinds of treatment conditions, then the others are referred to as "C," "D," and so on.

AB and ABA Designs   The weakest design in terms of drawing conclusions and ruling out alternative interpretations is the AB design (a single presentation of the baseline and treatment condition). This design does not permit the systematic assessment of the treatment condition. For example, what would be the natural course of the behavior across the same time period if the treatment had not been presented? It is similar to conducting an experiment without using a nontreatment control group. Without a control group, we cannot be sure that the behavior was altered by the treatment condition rather than by some extraneous variable. Similarly, with the AB design, it is possible that changes in behavior during the treatment phase resulted from some unknown environmental event not related to the treatment. The AB design does not permit ruling out this alternative hypothesis. It is sometimes tempting to accept the results of an AB design and conclude that the treatment had an effect when low levels of baseline behavior (A) are followed by sudden dramatic increases with the introduction of the treatment (B). To do so would be inappropriate, however, because control procedures were not present. Nevertheless, results of this kind would certainly be very encouraging; they should be pursued further, but with a more powerful design such as the ABA procedure. The AB design should be used only under circumstances that do not permit a more adequate method. These circumstances are more common in applied settings.

The ABA design is a far more powerful design than the AB design simply because the treatment condition is *introduced* for a period of time and then *withdrawn*. This design gives us two opportunities to assess whether the treatment condition is effective—introducing it and withdrawing it. If behavior shows a systematic change, then our confidence is increased that the treatment, rather than some unknown environmental event, is the reason for the behavioral change. It is quite unlikely that natural conditions would increase and then decrease behavior as it did when the treatment was presented and then withdrawn. Showing the same or similar relationships in other participants would further strengthen our confidence that the treatment was responsible.

The ABA design is generally criticized on two counts. One is that replication of the effect within a participant is not shown. The importance of this type of replication will be described in more detail below. The second problem relates to the applied setting where behavior modification is considered desirable. If the treatment (therapy) is effective in modifying behavior, then it is desirable to end the investigation on a treatment phase rather than a baseline phase.

ABAB Design   The most powerful design strategy (best method for assessing treatment effects) that we will discuss is the ABAB design. The ABAB design is a shorthand way for stating that we first determine a baseline (A), then we introduce the treatment for the first time (B). After the criterion of ability is achieved, we then withdraw the treatment and reintroduce the baseline condition (A). Finally, after baseline stability is reestablished, we present the treatment condition (B) a second time. This ABAB design, when used, is a very powerful design that allows the researcher to make strong conclusions regarding the treatment effects. With this design, the researcher demonstrates the degree of control over behavior in two ways—first by *introducing* the treatment condition, then by *removing* it. Again, we will repeat the procedure. After the baseline is established (A), the treatment condition (B) is introduced, and the extent to which the treatment influences behavior (the extent to which behavior departs from baseline) is assessed. Then, following stable performance, the treatment condition is removed; baseline condition (A) is again presented. Performance should then return to the original baseline. The final phase requires that we again present the treatment condition (B) and end the experiment with it. We will now give an example of an ABAB design strategy.

Over the years, researchers have been interested in whether participants prefer predictable over unpredictable painful events. Many studies used the single-subject method with a sample of three or four participants. It is interesting to note that the studies used very similar procedures even though different species were involved, including fish, birds, rats, and humans. The initial studies in this area used rats as participants, a brief electric shock as the mildly painful stimulus, and a tone to signal if shock was to occur. Researchers first exposed the animals to predictable shock (a five-second tone signaled when a half-second shock would occur) and to unpredictable shock (unsignaled shock) to acquaint them with the conditions and to make sure that they had equal experience with both. (The number of shocks was the same whether predictable or unpredictable. The only difference was that a signal preceded one condition but not the other.)

During this initial exposure to the two conditions, participants could not alter (change) the condition from one to the other. However, their responses on a response lever were recorded, even though responses on this lever had no effect. This period served as a baseline period (A) to measure how frequently they pressed the lever when there were no consequences. Responses on the lever occurred but were low in frequency during the baseline phase. After four days of being exposed to both signaled and unsignaled shock and with baseline responding stable, animals were given a choice between the signaled and unsignaled conditions. During this choice phase (treatment phase), the response lever was functional; responses now changed the conditions from one to the other. Animals at this time were placed in the unsignaled condition, but if the lever was pressed, the condition changed. A response on the lever changed the condition to the signaled one for a period of one minute. At the end of this one-minute period, the condition automatically changed back to the unsignaled condition and remained there unless another lever response was made. If the predictable (signaled) condition was reinforcing (preferred), response rate should increase over baseline; if it was punishing (not preferred), response rate should decrease. After choice behavior stabilized and preference was determined, the baseline condition was reinstated. This was followed by another treatment condition (preference testing). The results of the experiment were similar to those shown in Figure 14.6.

During the baseline conditions (A), participants lever-pressed at a rate sufficient to remain in the predictable shock schedule (had the levers been effective) only about 20% of the time. When the treatment condition (B) was introduced, participants changed from the

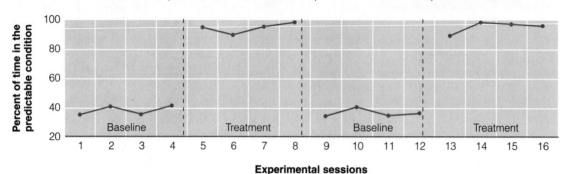

Figure 14.6 Single-Subject ABAB Design in Which the Participant Could Choose Between Predictable (Signaled) or Unpredictable (Unsignaled) Shock

The results would be similar whether percent of time or number of lever presses were used as the dependent variable.

unpredictable schedule at a rate sufficient to spend 90% of the time in the predictable condition. When the treatment condition was withdrawn and the baseline condition reinstated (Session 9), responding again returned to a low level. This showed that withdrawing the treatment *reversed* performance from high to low responding. Finally, when the treatment condition was introduced for the second time (Session 13), responding on the levers increased to a high level. Data such as this demonstrate convincingly, without the need for a statistical analysis, that the treatment condition is systematically controlling behavior.

Let's apply the ABAB design to our question regarding the effect of TV violence on aggressive behavior in children. It should not be too difficult for you to imagine how such a single-subject design could be implemented. First, a child is selected for the study. Typically, the participant is someone who is readily available to the researcher and has the characteristics of interest (such as a particular age). Then a baseline level of aggressive behavior is established during a week in which the child does not watch TV programs that contain violence. All of the issues regarding observation and measurement that have been discussed in previous chapters must be considered to develop a quality protocol for recording the dependent variable (level of aggressive behavior). After the one-week baseline, the treatment is imposed in the second week. During this second week, the participant is exposed to TV programs with violence, and aggressive behavior continues to be recorded in the same manner as during the previous week. The third and fourth weeks are replications of the first and second weeks. That is, the third week involves TV programs without violence, and the fourth week involves TV programs with violence. Remember that measurement of the participant's aggression (dependent variable) remains consistent throughout the experiment.

Some products advertise their effectiveness by pointing to "single-subject research" that consists of testimonials from individuals. Let's examine some information regarding claims that slippers can help you lose weight (see "Thinking Critically About Everyday Information").

Intraparticipant Replication

The preceding study regarding TV violence exposed each participant twice to the baseline and treatment conditions. When the conditions are repeated with the *same* participant, we are using **intraparticipant replication**. This is an important part of the single-subject

Thinking Critically About Everyday Information

Diet Slippers That Help You Lose Weight

A Japanese company sells HATSUKOI diet slippers that are designed to help a person lose weight. In support of their product, the company provides testimonials from individuals who have tried the slippers. Some of the testimonials include the following:

Testimonial No. 1

I always wear diet slippers. It's been more than two years since I tried these slippers for the first time. I have lost weight. Also minor health problems that I had are gone. I feel great every day. I want to share the benefits with lots of people. Therefore, I encourage them to try Diet Slippers. They are very happy with the results.

Testimonial No. 2

Hello, I'm a great fan of diet slippers. It's been almost one and a half years since I started wearing these. I lost about 5 lb. Before I wore the Diet Slippers, I could not afford to take three meals a day because the fear of gaining weight. Now I don't have to worry about it. It took a little while for me to get used to the Diet Slippers. First I felt a little tired after the first use. But now, I feel totally comfortable in them and can't go without

them even one day. I thank you for your wonderful creation.

Testimonial No. 3

Thanks to Diet Slippers, I have lost 9 lb.

Testimonial No. 4

My mother-in-law is quite impressed with Diet Slippers, because without causing any negative effect to her health, she was able to lose 5 lb. I thank you on behalf of my mother-in-law.

Consider the following questions:

- How are these testimonials similar to single-subject designs?

- Do the testimonials provide evidence of stable baselines?

- Do the testimonials provide evidence of intra-participant replication of the effect?

- What might be an alternative explanation for the reported weight loss?

SOURCE: Retrieved June 10, 2003, online at http://www.myshaldan.com/testimo.htm. Reprinted with permission.

method. As we have noted, the primary interest among psychologists is focused on the behavior of individual organisms. Intraparticipant replication focuses on the individual participant and identifies the factors affecting the participant. Systematic behavioral changes can be observed in individual participants by introducing and withdrawing the treatment condition. Intraparticipant replication, then, demonstrates that our method is reliable, that the treatment effect is real, and that we have control over behavior.

The decision on the number of intraparticipant replications that are necessary is sometimes difficult and may vary from experiment to experiment. Often a single replication is enough—that is, ABAB. The number of intraparticipant replications decided upon may vary according to the size of the treatment effects, the stability of the behavior, whether interparticipant replication is obtained, whether interspecies replications exist, whether similar related findings exist, and how well the present findings fit in with established findings.

A word should be said about the size of the effect. Small but consistent treatment effects combined with stable individual baselines can be important. Such effects, even though small, indicate experimental control over behavior. Perhaps with more effort and exploration, the conditions leading to a larger effect will be discovered.

Interparticipant Replication

We have seen that it is possible to demonstrate repeatedly consistent behavioral changes as a function of the treatment in an individual participant. It is also possible to demonstrate the same effect consistently in other participants. This **interparticipant replication** establishes the generality of the findings, showing that the effect occurs in more than one research participant. There are no hard-and-fast rules on the number of participants for which interparticipant replication must be shown. Much of the published research involves three to five participants per experiment. However, it is not unusual to find either fewer or more participants in different experiments. In addition to demonstrating that your findings can be generalized to other participants, interparticipant replication also demonstrates that the researcher has identified the controlling factors sufficiently to permit replication to other participants. On occasion, however, interparticipant replication is unsuccessful. When this occurs, additional detective work is usually necessary. It may be that greater control over the experimental situation is necessary. It is also possible that, because of individual differences, some participants react less to a given treatment. If the treatment were increased slightly (in intensity, duration, or frequency), interparticipant replication might be successful. This ability to treat individual participants in a flexible manner is one of the great strengths of the single-subject approach.

Reversible and Irreversible Behavior

When intraparticipant replication is achieved, we have demonstrated that baseline responding under the nontreatment condition can be recovered again once the treatment condition is withdrawn. We refer to the behavior as being **reversible behavior**. Without this feature, intraparticipant replication is not possible. In contrast, **irreversible behavior** refers to those occasions when the original baseline cannot be recovered after the treatment has been withdrawn. The baseline level of responding remains at the same level as it was under the treatment condition. Many critics of the single-subject approach argue that this is one of its weaknesses and that the method cannot be used when baseline responding is not recoverable. However, supporters argue that irreversible behavior may not be due to uncontrollable intrinsic factors (factors within the participant) but, instead, may be due to extrinsic controlling factors (experimental/environmental factors). They argue that a careful assessment of the situation and thoughtful changes based upon this assessment, more often than not, will produce reversible behavior. Often it is achieved only after a number of attempts. However, they do not argue that all behavior is reversible.

There may be situations in which the behavior is not reversible. For example, drug research may encounter carryover effects in which the effects of the drug last longer than anticipated and continue to affect behavior after the treatment (drug) is thought to be removed. The solution to this problem is to allow enough time for the drug to dissipate. A more difficult problem may arise when a single-subject design involves experimentally induced brain lesions in animal research. If the tissue damage is permanent, the treatment cannot be withdrawn, thus precluding the ABAB design. To overcome this difficulty, researchers have used pharmacological agents that only temporarily affect brain functions instead of producing permanent impairment. In other instances, behavior appears irreversible because of learning factors. The example of spontaneous speech in an autistic boy at the beginning of this chapter is one example. Consider another example. If a number of problems have the same solution and the solution is learned through a reinforcement procedure, you can withdraw the reinforcement but the solution to the problem will remain. Conceivably, then, researchers on occasion will encounter behavior that does not reverse (return to baseline levels) when the treatment condition is withdrawn. In such cases, the powerful ABAB design strategy cannot be used. For this reason and others, there is an alternative procedure, referred to as the **multiple baseline procedure.** This procedure is also useful in therapeutic situations where withdrawing a therapeutic treatment for purposes of identifying the controlling factor may be undesirable or unethical.

Multiple Baseline Procedures

As we noted, the ABAB design is not appropriate when we are unable to recover our baseline level of performance or when the withdrawal of treatment poses an ethical dilemma. Under these circumstances, a different design strategy such as the multiple baseline procedure is necessary. In effect, the multiple baseline procedure allows the researcher to perform intraparticipant replication with *different responses* rather than the same response.

The multiple baseline procedure requires that baselines be established for several different responses and that these responses be independent of one another. To say that the responses are independent implies that increases or decreases in the frequency of one response do not affect (lead to increases or decreases in) the frequency of other responses (see Figure 14.7). Usually, the multiple baseline procedure requires baselines for three or more different responses. Baseline responding is established in the same manner as described previously except that baselines for several responses are plotted at the same time. Then the different responses are treated one at a time.

To illustrate, after stable baseline levels are established, the treatment condition is applied to only one of the responses (the target response). The other responses are not treated and remain under the baseline condition. Changes in the target response are recorded to assess the treatment effects, but the other responses (those not receiving any treatment) continue to be monitored in the baseline condition. After the target response stabilizes to the treatment condition, the experimenter then applies the treatment to the second response until it stabilizes; then the third response is treated. Since a withdrawal phase is not used with this procedure, the treatment of each response following the establishment of the baseline is essentially an AB design. As with any of the single-subject designs, the effectiveness of the treatment condition is assessed by a change in behavior relative to the baseline level. In the case of the multiple baseline procedure, the treatment effects are assessed by comparing the response receiving the treatment with its no-treatment baseline and also with the baseline of the untreated responses. The latter would be meaningless if the responses were not independent. Although the multiple baseline procedure is not as effective as ABA or the ABAB design, it does demonstrate replication of the treatment condition *across responses.*

Let's consider an actual study that is not recent but is nonetheless interesting (cited by Leitenberg, 1973). Two investigators used punishment to deal with a case of transvestism. A male patient reported becoming sexually excited by dressing as a woman and was apparently unhappy about his feelings. Although, at the age of 21, the patient had never had girlfriends, he wanted to have a normal heterosexual relationship. Aversion therapy was used twice daily. It consisted of shocks to his arm or leg while he was either dressing as a woman (crossdressing) or thinking (fantasizing) about dressing as one. In the latter instance, the participant signaled the investigator when fantasies occurred. Shocks were withheld if the participant discarded the female garments. One response measure was sexual arousal, as determined by the circumference of the penis, to female pajamas, panties, slips, skirts, or a slide of a nude woman. Latency of the response was also recorded. After baseline responses

Figure 14.7 Illustration of Multiple Baseline Procedures When Responses Are (a) Independent and (b) Not Independent

Note that when experimental treatments are introduced in (a), the baselines of the remaining responses are unaffected. In (b), the introduction of each treatment produces a change in the baseline levels of the remaining responses (hypothetical data).

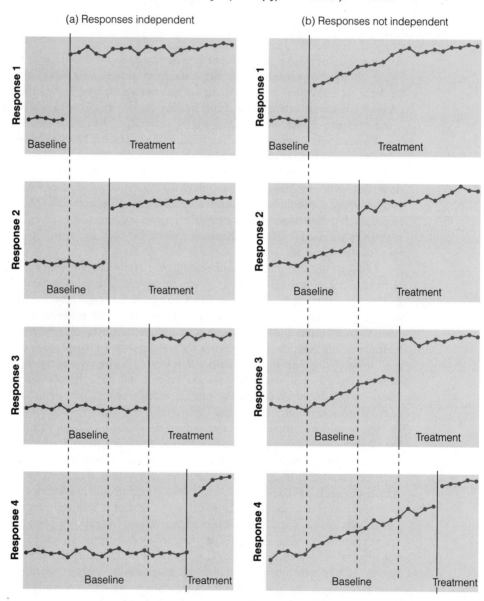

to these garments were determined, the treatment of shock was introduced. The investigators found that after the response of putting on panties was shocked a number of times, penile erection to this stimulus was suppressed. However, erections to the other garments continued to occur. Then responses of dressing up in the other garments were shocked until erections ceased to each. It was shown by the investigators that while erection no longer occurred to the female clothing, it continued to occur to the nude slide.

The multiple baseline procedure is also illustrated in an interesting study in which investigators used punishment to successfully modify undesirable mealtime behaviors among 16 severely retarded males (Barton, Guess, Garcia, & Baer, 1970). The undesirable behaviors included stealing food from others, eating with fingers rather than utensils, pigging (eating spilled food from the floor or lapping food directly from the tray), and making a mess, such as spilling or dropping food. The study ran nearly four months. Punishment consisted of removal (timeout) from the dining area whenever the undesired behavior occurred. In some instances, removal was for the entire meal; in other instances, for a shorter period. The investigators started by recording baseline frequencies for each behavior (stealing, pigging, and so on). The first response—for example, stealing—had only a six-day baseline before the punishment (treatment timeout) was introduced. While punishment was being given for stealing behavior, baseline recording continued for the other responses. When stealing stabilized, then punishment was introduced for the second response while baseline recording continued for the remaining two responses. This procedure continued until all responses were under the punishment procedure. For the most part, but not entirely, independence among the responses was observed; that is, punishing one response affected primarily only that response and not the others. The efforts of the researchers were successful: The undesirable mealtime behaviors greatly improved, as did the morale of the workers. An idealized depiction of the study appears in Figure 14.8, which also clearly outlines the procedure.

We want to repeat, before leaving this topic, that the multiple baseline procedure is used either because the baseline level of responding cannot be recovered when the treatment condition is withdrawn or because withdrawal of the treatment may have an adverse effect on the participant, especially in a therapeutic setting. The multiple baseline procedure is not as powerful as the ABAB design, in which both intra- and interparticipant replication can be shown by both the introduction and withdrawal of the treatment. However, as we have shown, replication across responses within the same participant can be shown with this procedure.

Time-Series Designs

In many ways, the single-subject approach is similar to a time-series analysis, in that the stability and changes in behavior are studied across time or experimental sessions. A **time-series design** is characterized by repeated measurements of the dependent variable over time with an introduction of the independent variable at a particular point in time. Trends or patterns of behavior are observed both before and after introduction of the independent variable. Consistent with the theme of this chapter, the time-series analysis can be conducted with more than one participant but data analysis is typically focused on individual participants.

Because time-series analysis is characterized by relatively long-term measurements of some dependent variable, you must be careful to consider extraneous variables often associated with repeated measures designs. Such extraneous variables may include history, maturation, attrition, instrumentation, and carryover effects. In some cases, a change in the level of behavior may result from one of these extraneous variables rather than from the introduction of the independent variable.

Time-series analysis is often used to track changes in behavior that occur on a large scale. For example, does a full moon make people more likely to commit crimes? One could track crime statistics on a daily basis over a long period of time and relate those statistics to

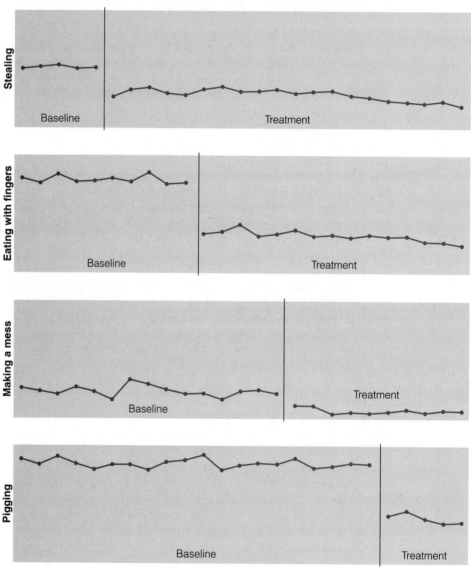

Figure 14.8 An Idealized Graphic Representation of a Successful Effort to Suppress Undesired Behaviors by the Use of Punishment Using the Multiple Baseline Procedure

Note that the treatment effects appear to be relatively independent and that all four undesirable responses were successfully suppressed.

the fullness of the moon. Note that this is not an experimental design because there is no independent variable manipulated by the researcher. Thus, cause–effect conclusions would not be warranted. A time-series analysis in which there is a bit more control would involve the tracking of crime statistics both before and after a new law is passed that increases the punishment for a particular crime. A primary purpose of such a law is to cause a reduction in the incidence of the crime. Even in this example, it is very difficult to verify the effect of the new law because so many other factors that influence crime rate are likely to vary over time (for example, the economy). However, this is not to suggest that time-series analyses of such questions should not take place. In fact, they should. What we do suggest is that we need to evaluate such information with a very critical eye.

CASE ANALYSIS

Some individuals with developmental disabilities exhibit self-injurious behavior; it is one of the most disturbing behaviors for people to observe. Attention can sometimes be an effective treatment for self-injurious behavior (see, for example, Vollmer, Iwata, & Zarcone, 1993). Let's consider the hypothetical case of Mark T. Mark is a 53-year-old male with profound mental retardation. Each morning, Mark engages in head-banging behavior. As a result, he has to wear a protective helmet. You decide to explore the possibility that attention from caregivers could be an effective treatment. The study will take place over a two-week period, with baseline recordings made during the first week and treatment imposed during the second week. During the first week, the number of head-banging incidents is recorded from 7:00 to 9:00 each morning. During the second week, a procedure is implemented during the same two-hour period each morning. Every time a ten-minute interval passes with no head-banging, a caregiver will approach and talk to Mark for two minutes. Thus, Mark is reinforced for behaviors other than head-banging. The data that represent the number of head-banging incidents during each two-hour period are as follows:

Week 1 (Baseline)	Day 1	Day 2	Day 3	Day 4	Day 5	Day 6	Day 7
	6	10	8	13	12	15	16
Week 2 (Treatment)	Day 8	Day 9	Day 10	Day 11	Day 12	Day 13	Day 14
	15	12	10	11	8	8	5

Critical Thinking Questions

1. Which single-subject design was used?

2. Sketch a line graph that shows the number of head-banging incidents across the two-week period.

3. Are you justified in drawing the conclusion that attention was an effective treatment in reducing head-banging behavior? Why or why not?

4. Was an optimal baseline achieved? How would you improve this aspect of the study?

5. Describe how intra- and interparticipant replication could be achieved.

6. What other control procedures should be considered?

GENERAL SUMMARY

Single-subject designs are experimental designs that involve manipulation of an independent variable and careful analysis of the behavior of individual participants. Participants' scores are not grouped together, and inferential statistics are not used to arrive at conclusions. Rather, a single participant's behavior is compared across different treatment conditions, and conclusions are strengthened by intraparticipant replication and interparticipant replication. Intraparticipant replication requires that the experimental conditions be repeated for the same individual. A consistent pattern of behavior differences between baseline and treatment conditions suggests that the independent variable is causing the difference. Intraparticipant replication is difficult when the behavior under investigation is not reversible. In such situations, a multiple baseline procedure may be useful. Interparticipant replication requires that the experimental conditions be repeated with one or more other individuals. Again, a consistent pattern of behavior differences between baseline and treatment conditions that is observed in more than one participant strengthens the argument that the independent variable is causing the difference.

This chapter concludes a series of chapters that described a variety of experimental designs in which cause–effect conclusions could be drawn. Although these experimental designs are powerful tools for answering many research questions, not all questions can, or should, be answered with such techniques. The next chapter will review a variety of nonexperimental methods that can be used to learn more about behavior.

DETAILED SUMMARY

1. The single-subject approach is a method designed to study the behavior of individual organisms. As the method continues to evolve and improve, it has become more popular for both scientific and therapeutic purposes.

2. The single-subject approach is different from the case-study or case-history approach. The latter approach is characterized by lack of experimental control and imprecise measures of behavior.

3. Historically, the introduction of random assignment and statistical analysis to the research world led to a bias to conduct research on relatively large groups of participants. However, there are limitations to what can be learned by studying groups. Single-subject designs, when used properly, can provide valuable information about individual behavior and can elucidate causal relationships between independent and dependent variables.

4. For single-subject designs, the reliability of findings involves actual replications rather than inferential statistics. The two types of replications are intraparticipant replication (replications within an individual participant) and interparticipant replication (replications between individual participants).

5. Advantages of single-subject designs include immediate feedback to the researcher regarding changes in behavior, a focus on individual behavior, and strong conclusions regarding the effect of one variable on another.

6. Limitations of single-subject designs include their unsuitableness for answering actuarial types of questions, for comparing two or more different treatments on the same behavioral measure, for treating an entire group of participants in an identical way, and for "after the fact" studies (ex post facto, correlational, passive observational). Moreover, the single-subject approach makes heavy time demands and often relies on the establishment of stable baselines and reversibility of behavior.

7. Researchers favor the single-subject method for different reasons. Some reasons include interest in individual behavior, the fact that group data can mask individual behavior, unavailability of large groups of participants, and concerns with methods of statistical evaluation.

8. To determine an effect of an independent variable (treatment), the dependent measure should be operationally defined and should exhibit a stable baseline level of occurrence with repeated measurements. An optimal baseline is one that is stable and not subject to floor or ceiling effects.

9. An optimal baseline is achieved by identifying and controlling extraneous sources of variability in the environment.

10. The ABAB design is one of the most powerful design strategies. A baseline is first established (A), then we introduce the treatment for the first time (B). After the criterion of ability is achieved, we then withdraw the treatment and reintroduce the baseline condition (A). Finally, after baseline stability is reestablished, we present the treatment condition (B) for the second time. With this design, the researcher demonstrates the degree of control over behavior in two ways—first by *introducing* the treatment condition, then by *removing* it.

11. Intraparticipant replication demonstrates that the method is reliable, that the treatment effect is real, and that there is control over behavior. Interparticipant replication establishes the generality of the findings.

12. Intraparticipant replication in the ABAB design relies on the reversibility of the behavior to baseline levels after the treatment is withdrawn.

13. The multiple baseline procedure allows the researcher to perform intraparticipant replication with different independent responses rather than the same response.

14. Time-series analysis is characterized by repeated measurements of the dependent variable over time and introduction of the independent variable at a particular point in time. Trends or patterns of behavior are observed both before and after introduction of the independent variable.

KEY TERMS

baseline *(p. 234)*
facilitation *(p. 235)*
interparticipant replication *(p. 242)*
intraparticipant replication *(p. 240)*
irreversible behavior *(p. 242)*
multiple baseline procedure *(p. 243)*

optimal baseline *(p. 235)*
replication *(p. 231)*
reversible behavior *(p. 242)*
suppression *(p. 235)*
time-series design *(p. 245)*

REVIEW QUESTIONS/EXERCISES

1. Construct a hypothetical graph of the results of a single-subject design to evaluate the effects of TV violence on a child. The axes of the graph should be clearly labeled. The graph should illustrate an optimal baseline, reversible behavior, intraparticipant replication, and an effect such that TV violence results in more aggressive behavior.

2. Summarize interparticipant replication and its purpose.

3. In 2002, after much debate, the high school in Conway, Arkansas, implemented a random drug testing program for students involved in any extracurricular activities. The expressed purpose of the program is to reduce drug use among teenagers. Describe how a time-series design might be used to evaluate the effectiveness of the drug testing program.

 ## WEB RESOURCES TO INCREASE LEARNING

The chapter outline, chapter summaries, key terms and definitions, additional chapter questions, chapter exercises, and links to relevant Web sites are available at the course Web site (**http://psychology.wadsworth.com/ lammers_badia1e**).

CHAPTER 15

NONEXPERIMENTAL RESEARCH DESIGNS
CORRELATIONAL DESIGN, EX POST FACTO DESIGN, NATURALISTIC OBSERVATION, AND QUALITATIVE RESEARCH

● Introduction to Nonexperimental Designs

We have said much about true experiments, and we have described their strength in drawing strong, confident conclusions. A word of caution is advisable. An experiment may use random assignment and involve manipulation of the treatment variable and still be essentially worthless as a basis for drawing conclusions. It is essential that rigorous controls, careful execution, planning, and thoughtfulness accompany a valid design. We have also noted the qualities of designs termed quasi-experimental. Recall that these were characterized as designs in which the independent variable was manipulated but the study lacked random assignment of participants to conditions.

As we have seen so far in the book, experimental research is a very powerful tool for generating a scientific database for drawing cause–effect conclusions, for testing hypotheses and evaluating theory, for answering questions and satisfying our intellectual curiosity, for systematic manipulation of variables, and at times, for discovering principles that may be relevant to everyday life. After considerable discussion of the virtues of experimental designs, you might wonder why researchers would use other types of nonexperimental designs. Actually, there are several good reasons to use nonexperimental designs. Many very interesting questions in psychology do not lend themselves to experimental designs. Some of these questions involve independent variables that simply cannot be manipulated by a researcher. If we wish to study the effects on a dependent measure of such naturally occurring variables as gender, ethnic background, intelligence, temperament, or body size, we cannot say to the participants, "For the purposes of this experiment, I am going to declare you a female, or an African-American, or a person with an IQ of 130." In addition, some questions involve independent variables that could theoretically be manipulated by a researcher but are not because the opportunity does not present itself, the financial cost would be too high, or the ethical concerns would be too great. For example, we might ask, "Do individuals who have left hemispheric brain damage show greater verbal impairment than those who have comparable damage to the right hemisphere?" Obviously, it is not possible to randomly assign people to an experimental and control group and then conduct brain surgery to answer this question. If we are to shed any light on the question, we are forced to look into the histories of people who have suffered brain damage as a result of adverse circumstances. Similarly, as we have repeatedly explored the issue of TV violence and aggressive behavior in children, we would certainly be interested in the effects of long-term (in terms of years) exposure to TV violence. I'm sure that you can see the ethical issues involved in randomly assigning a group of children to watch violent television for several years!

Thus, although nonexperimental research designs are not as powerful as experimental designs—that is, they do not rule out as many alternative hypotheses (explanations)—they provide us with options for pursuing interesting and important questions when experimental designs are not available. Figure 15.1 provides an overview of the nonexperimental designs discussed in this chapter. Let's explore some of these options.

● Correlational Design

As noted, there are ethical issues involved in an experimental study to assess the long-term effects of TV violence on aggressive behavior in children. However, we suspect that you can imagine a nonexperimental study that could assess the relationship between these two variables over the time span of several years. Using either a retrospective technique (examine data that already exist) or a prospective technique (collect data across several years), you

Figure 15.1 Overview of Nonexperimental Research Methods

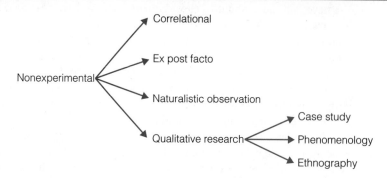

could record the degree of exposure to TV violence and the number of aggressive incidents. **Correlational research** involves collecting data or searching out records of a specified population and ascertaining the relationships among the variables of interest. Such research involves neither random assignment nor manipulation of an experimental variable.

The two research procedures encountered most frequently, and also most sharply contrasted with each other, are the experimental and correlational methods. Again, we repeat the important differences between them. The experimental approach studies the causal relationship between manipulated variables and uses random assignment (or repeated measures), whereas the correlational approach studies the relationship between unmanipulated variables and does not use random assignment. Other examples of the correlational approach would be studies of smoking history and health problems, alcohol use and GPA, and education attained and salary levels. We view these research methods as complementary techniques rather than competing ones. As you will see, they often serve different purposes and provide answers to different questions.

Random assignment of participants and the manipulation of variables are absent in correlational research because the events of interest have already occurred or are naturally occurring. The interest is in determining how measures on one variable are related to measures on another variable. Often, in psychology, the two measures are behavioral measures.

The correlational approach is sometimes referred to as the study of individual differences because emphasis is placed on differences among individuals. For example, assume that we have a distribution of individual scores on one measure (Test 1: Intelligence Test Scores) and a distribution of individual scores on another measure (Test 2: Final Exam Scores). The question asked of these data by a correlational approach is whether differences among individual scores on one variable (Test 1) are related to differences among individual scores on the other variable (Test 2).

A statistical procedure called *correlational analysis* is used to ascertain the extent of the relationship among individual scores on the two variables (tests). This emphasis on individual differences contrasts with an experimental approach, where interest is in comparing the *average* performance of a group in one condition with the *average* performance of a group in another condition (single-subject designs are an exception).

As you may recall from your introductory statistics course, calculating a correlation between two distributions of scores (scores on Test 1 and scores on Test 2) results in a number called a **correlation coefficient.** The strength of the relationship is indicated by the numerical value of the coefficient, and its direction is indicated by a + or − sign. If the individual

Table 15.1	Examples of Some Recent Correlational Research That Found a Relationship Between Variables
Use of ecstasy and memory loss	
Sleep disturbances and posttraumatic stress disorder	
Experiencing child abuse and sensitivity to anger in facial expressions	
Children who have family pets and strength of children's immune systems	
Cholesterol levels and cognitive impairment	
Brain wave activity and drug effectiveness for treating depression	
Anxiety in pregnant women and later emotional/behavioral problems in their children	
Size of the hippocampus and later occurrence of Alzheimer's disease	
Bipolar disorder and creative genius	
Family history of hypertension and maladaptive response to stressful situations	

scores are unrelated (no relationship), the numerical value of the coefficient is 0; if the scores are perfectly related on the two distributions, the numerical value is either −1.0 or +1.0. Thus, the numerical value of the correlation coefficient may range from −1.0 to 0 or from 0 to +1.0, with variations in between. A positive relationship indicates that individuals scoring high on one distribution also tend to score high on the other distribution and that those scoring low on one tend to score low on the other. Put more simply, as individuals' scores on one distribution increase, their scores on the other increase (for example, the more one studies, the higher one's grade point average). If the relationship is negative, then individuals scoring high on one distribution tend to score low on the other and those scoring low on one tend to score high on the other. Again, put simply, as individuals' scores on one distribution increase, their scores on the other decrease (for example, the more one parties, the lower one's grade point average).

Correlational methods are used in virtually every scientific and professional discipline, and they serve many purposes. Correlations between variables are often used to make predictions. When measures on two variables are unrelated (correlation coefficient = 0), knowing an individual's score on one variable is not at all helpful in predicting his or her score on the other variable. As the correlation moves away from 0, the accuracy of predicting the individual's score on one variable, simply by knowing his or her score on the other, increases. And when the correlation is perfect (+1.0 or −1.0), prediction of an individual's score on one variable from knowing his or her score on the other can be made without error.

While we were working on this chapter, a number of articles appeared in newspaper accounts and in popular magazines dealing with correlational research. Some of the correlations found are listed in Table 15.1. This list gives an idea of the variety of problems that can be studied using correlational procedures. We do not describe the results of these reports because we have not read the primary sources from which they came, nor have we evaluated the care with which the studies were conducted. After reading the section on Direction of Control and Third Variable Problems, you may want to return to this table to evaluate the extent to which these two problems might be present in the studies listed in

Table 15.1. You will most likely conclude that many alternative explanations could be offered for the observed relationships.

Although correlational research allows us to discover lawful relationships that can lead to precise predictions, causal statements can be made only with great risk because these methods lack random assignment, active manipulation, and rigorous control over extraneous factors. Such variables as gender, group membership, racial characteristics, birthplace, and age are historical events over which researchers have little control. They are determined before the researcher arrives on the scene. The measures that are correlated are often personality variables or variables related to people's characteristics. These variables generally cannot be manipulated. There are exceptions, of course. Some behavioral measures can be manipulated, but only with great difficulty. As we have seen, a question of ethics often arises, as with cigarette smoking and lung cancer, or cardiovascular disease, exercise, and cardiovascular problems.

Importance of Correlational Research

Stating that a causal relationship cannot be established by correlational research is not intended to devalue the great importance of this type of research. It is often extraordinarily important both in a practical and in a theoretical way. Research with this method has had a marked influence on the lives of many people and on policy formulations of legislatures, decisions of the judiciary, and actions of private enterprise. Here are but a few well-known examples: Correlation of smoking habits with lung cancer led to a warning on cigarette packs. The relation between exercise and lowered rates of cardiovascular problems has stimulated increases in jogging, swimming, tennis, and bicycling. Correlations between socioeconomic conditions and educational proficiency provided a rationale for decisions involving equality in education and school busing. Correlations between particulate matter in the air (pollution) and morbidity rates provided the impetus for clean air legislation.

It is often the case that our interest is in prediction rather than in a cause–effect analysis. After we know the correlation between two measures, we are able to predict one form of behavior from knowledge of the other. For example, there is a correlation between IQ test scores and success, as measured by grades, in school. Over the years, considerable data have been gathered on this relationship, and it is quite well established. With a quantitative measure of the relationship (a correlation coefficient), we can predict with some accuracy success in school simply by knowing a person's score on the IQ test.

Similar examples emphasizing prediction occur when test scores are used as screening devices for selecting those students most likely to succeed in graduate school, medical school, or law school. In this screening process, individuals take examinations over certain specified material; their scores are obtained and prediction formulas then applied. Thus, predictions can be made on large numbers of individuals almost immediately after obtaining their scores. As we have noted, the accuracy of the prediction depends on the strength of the relationship between the two forms of behavior. The stronger (higher) the correlation, the better will be the prediction.

Discovering the relationship between two variables can be very valuable, especially if one behavior that can be easily and inexpensively measured permits us to predict another behavior that is inaccessible or difficult and expensive to measure. Knowing the relationship may also be of great practical value, especially for educational systems. For example, special programs can be instituted to prevent problems from occurring among those in need of help and to enrich those who are in need of challenge.

Another example of correlational research that has proven useful relates to diagnostic purposes. After a disorder is observed, a search can be made for other behaviors or conditions that may vary (correlate) with it. This approach is especially helpful if the disorder is difficult to detect or to diagnose accurately. If the search is successful and the correlation strong, then both the speed and accuracy of identifying the disorder may be substantially increased.

The usefulness and value of a correlational approach are most apparent when studying the effects of events that simply cannot be studied in laboratory settings. This approach may be the only available method when ethical considerations prevent manipulating the phenomena (such as abortion, drug use, sexual practices, serious illness, or suicide), when the phenomena are impossible to manipulate (such as male/female, black/white, temperament), or when studying the effects of natural disasters such as earthquakes, fires, or violent storms.

Direction of Control and Third Variable Problems

Discussion of direction of control and third variable problems will illustrate the difficulties of inferring cause–effect relationships when interpreting correlational data. With correlational research, we usually refer to predictor and criterion variables rather than independent and dependent variables. The measure (or behavior) being predicted is the **criterion variable,** and the measure (or behavior) from which the prediction is made is the **predictor variable.** The use of this terminology emphasizes prediction rather than suggesting a cause–effect relationship. However, there are occasions when individuals, be they scientists, writers, or laypeople, come to cause–effect conclusions based on correlational data. They face a risk of drawing false conclusions when doing so. In effect, they must deal with two different problems: the **direction of control** problem and the **third variable** problem. We will give examples of both.

To infer a cause–effect relationship requires that we specify the direction of control. Assume that variable X and variable Y are highly correlated such that increases in one are associated with increases in the other. Does variable X cause variable Y to vary, or does variable Y cause variable X to vary? With some relationships the answer concerning the direction of control seems obvious, but in other instances it can be difficult to specify. Let's assume that our correlational research on TV violence and aggression showed a positive relationship between these two variables. It would seem to be a natural inference to conclude that exposure to TV violence leads to (causes) more aggressive behavior in children. However, is this necessarily the case? Are there alternative explanations for the observed relationship? Is it not possible that children who are more aggressive, for whatever reason, tend to choose TV shows with more violence?

We will give another example of the direction of control problem. Let us say that a high, positive correlation exists between frequency of drug use (variable X) and difficulties in school (variable Y). We could say that the use of drugs was the cause of experiencing difficulties in school. On the other hand, an equally plausible conclusion is that having difficulties in school caused the individual to use drugs.

The fact that in both of these examples we have a high correlation between variable X and variable Y does not help us at all in determining the direction of control. Our risk of coming to a wrong causal conclusion is not reduced. The only way to reduce the risk is to bring additional information to bear on the issue or, when permitted, to attempt an experimental approach and manipulate the important variables.

The risk of error is even greater when we consider possible third variable problems. In our example with the TV violence study, it is possible that neither of the two variables causes

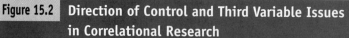

Figure 15.2 Direction of Control and Third Variable Issues in Correlational Research

Direction of Control Problem

Drug use → Poor performance in school

Poor performance in school → Drug use

Third Variable Problem

Conflict within the home → Drug use

Conflict within the home → Poor performance in school

the other. Rather, some other (third) variable may actually cause changes in the two variables that were measured. After giving this some thought, we are sure that you can come up with a potential third variable. In our example involving drug use, instead of drug use causing school problems, or school problems causing drug use, a third (or fourth or fifth) factor could have caused increases in both drug use and school problems. For example, anxiety, depression, low self-esteem, or conflict within the home could give rise to both drug use and school problems. In this case, then, variables X and Y are related only through some third variable. Figure 15.2 illustrates both direction of control and third variable issues.

It is sometimes difficult to avoid a causal conclusion and to maintain the proper perspective when viewing correlational data. The consistent, highly publicized, positive correlation between cigarette smoking and cancer seems causal. The more cigarettes smoked, the higher is the incidence of cancer. This relationship seems to suggest that the smoking of cigarettes controls whether or not cancer will occur. Yet, strictly speaking, we cannot say this based on human research. A third factor may be involved. It is possible that only certain people with this factor smoke and that these people would contract the disease whether or not they smoked. The more of this factor present, the more they would smoke and the greater would be the likelihood of their contracting cancer. If this were so, then increases in both smoking and cancer would result from this unspecified third factor. This causal chain is very unlikely, and the few experimental studies that have recently been done suggest that certain ingredients in tobacco may in fact cause cancer. Nonetheless, third variable problems are sometimes very difficult to detect and to deal with. Further, you can never be sure that they are absent when using correlational designs. However, some techniques are available for addressing the problem.

Addressing Directionality and Third Variable Problems

Several methods are available to attempt to deal with the problems of directionality and third variables. Although these methods are sometimes useful, they do not solve the problems; each has its shortcomings. A full description of these methods is beyond the scope of this text, but we mention them here for those of you who would like to pursue the problems further. A procedure that is sometimes useful for addressing the directionality problem is a *time-lagged correlational design,* also referred to as *cross-lagged panel correlation.* This procedure involves determining a correlation between two variables at Time 1 and again later at Time 2. A procedure referred to as *partial correlation* is sometimes used to address the third variable problem. If a third variable is thought to be a factor affecting the correlation between variables X and Y, the partial correlation technique can be used to eliminate its effects. The result of this procedure is a correlation between X and Y uninfluenced by the third variable. Information regarding these procedures can be found in more advanced research design/statistics textbooks. Another procedure that is sometimes used to eliminate the third variable problem is **matching.** In this case, only data from participants matched (who are the same) on the third variable are analyzed.

For example, if we suspect that parenting style is a third variable that affects both the amount of TV violence that children watch and the children's aggressiveness, we may want to include in the study only those children who have parents with similar parenting styles. At first glance, matching as a technique for ruling out third variable interpretations seems like an attractive solution. That is, if only individuals who were the same or highly similar on these third variables were assessed, and if the relationship between the two variables of interest still existed, then the third variable considerations could be dispensed with. The thought is a good one, but in practice problems remain. One problem is that researchers cannot be sure they have considered the relevant third variables. Other variables may be involved that have not been considered. Also, matching can be difficult to achieve. Moreover, matching on one variable can sometimes unmatch individuals on other variables. Thus, researchers face a more serious problem when they attempt to match on several variables (such as intelligence, education, motivation, and class). The problem is simply getting a sufficiently large sample that has the necessary characteristics.

Correlational Ruling Out Factors

The correlation between cigarette smoking and cancer (and heart disease) can be used to illustrate an important aspect of correlational research. Had no relationship been found, we could have ruled out causal factors, and there would be little interest in pursuing the problem further. Therefore, an important contribution of correlational methods may be a negative one: In the absence of a relationship, there is no need to devote time to an experimental analysis of the problem to identify the controlling or causal factor.

Perhaps an example contrasting the correlational method with the experimental method would be helpful in illustrating why a causal relationship can be established with an experimental approach and not a correlational one. As noted, in a correlational study involving cigarette consumption and incidence of cancer, a positive relationship was found. Although most people of sound mind would be alerted to a possible causal link between the two, a strong relationship regarding cause has not been established. We indicated that it is possible that a third factor may be the cause—for example, that people susceptible to cancer also smoke, but the disease would have occurred whether or not they smoked. Or we could argue that individuals who smoke also engage in other activities that may be related to cancer and that smoking is not the problem. Or we could suggest that individuals with certain dietary habits are susceptible to both smoking and cancer, and so on.

The tobacco industry today argues that a causal link has not been clearly established in humans. To decide the question, an experiment is necessary. It would not be difficult to design a research project to answer the question of smoking as a cause for illness. However, serious problems of ethics and practicality prevent its implementation. We would randomly select a large number of 12- to 14-year-old male and female students from different geographic areas. We could then randomly assign them to conditions A, B, C, D, and E— corresponding to levels 0, 1/2, 1, 2, and 3 packs of cigarettes a day. We would then follow up over the years with annual physical examinations and also record specific measures known to be related to tissue problems. We could then determine whether there was a systematic relationship between our independent variable (smoking) and our dependent variable (measures of illness or tissue abnormality). Obviously, the study cannot and should not be done. However, experimental studies have been conducted with nonhuman species.

Mice, rats, and dogs have been used to study the relationship between exposure to tobacco ingredients and cancer. A variety of procedures have been used, such as placing the substances in tobacco on the skin, confining the animals to enclosed rooms where controlled amounts of cigarette smoke can be dispersed, and teaching animals to smoke. These studies have established that tobacco is hazardous to a laboratory animal's health. We have stated several times that it is improper to draw cause–effect conclusions from correlational data. To say this is not to say that such a relationship does not exist; in fact, it may. To determine its existence, however, requires other research strategies.

There are many examples of correlational studies reported in the media that falsely suggest a cause–effect relationship. You are probably familiar with reports of a link between the phase of the moon and "strange" behavior. The box "Thinking Critically About Everyday Information" focuses on one such report.

Interpretation of Correlational Data

Now that we understand the nature and value of correlational research, let's explore a specific example and discuss some of the issues involved in the interpretation of correlational data. We'll return to a research idea mentioned earlier in this chapter—namely, the long-term effect of TV violence on aggressive behavior in children. As we noted, random assignment of children to groups that view specific levels of TV violence for several years is not ethical. However, we could conduct a correlational study in which children (with assistance from parents) maintain a weekly log of TV shows watched from the time that they are 10 years old until they are 15 years old. Based on these logs, we calculate the mean number of hours of TV violence viewed per week. For the variable that measures aggressive behavior, we obtain the number of disciplinary incidents recorded at their school for the same five-year period. Hypothetical data from 20 students are shown in Table 15.2.

Glancing through the pairs of scores in Table 15.2, whether there is any systematic pattern in the data is difficult to detect, although the one participant with 25 hours/week and 30 incidents does stand out. With correlational data, it is not only helpful, but critical, that the data be graphed in a **scatterplot**. Figure 15.3 is a scatterplot of the data; each point on the graph represents one pair of scores. Because the values on the x-axis increase from left to right and the values on the y-axis increase from bottom to top, it is now easy to detect a general pattern in the data: As the mean hours of TV violence per week increase, the number of disciplinary incidents at school also increases. The presence of the one outlier is also clear on the graph. Because our data are measured on a ratio scale and because our graph suggests a linear relationship, we can calculate a Pearson r correlation coefficient to quantify the relationship (see Figure 10.10 to review the decision tree for measures of relationship). The calculation results in $r = .88$, a significant positive correlation.

It is important to be aware that in correlational research, outliers in the data can have dramatic effects on the value of the correlation coefficient and, therefore, the conclusions

Thinking Critically About Everyday Information

Does the Full Moon Make You Crazy?

The following report was obtained from the online edition of *Weekly World News*. The title of the report is "Research Proves Full Moon Really Does Make You Crazy!" The report reads:

Amazing research proves that the full moon really does drive people loony. And it can even make them kill! Scientific tests confirm that murder rates triple around the time the moon is full. And suicide rates also peak during the full moon of spring—and the new moon in autumn and winter. "Human biological tides respond to the moon's pull much as the sea does and for a very similar reason," Dr. Arnold L. Lieber, author of *The Lunar Effect* (Anchor Press), told a reporter. "I found that in my studies of violent behavior in U.S. cities, instances of murder, aggravated assault, suicide, psychiatric emergencies and fatal auto accidents all went up during the full moon." Dr. Lieber first noticed the curious lunar effect when he was a medical student working in the Jackson Memorial Hospital in Miami and realized that mental patients became highly disturbed during the first few days of each month. And when he approached senior doctors about the phenomena, they told him that patients suffered more epileptic seizures and bleeding ulcers during the full moon. Then police confirmed that criminal behavior was also affected—producing graphs showing that violence and arson increased during the full moon. But Florida police aren't the only ones who have noticed the strange effect of the lunar cycle on criminal behavior. Officers with just about every police department around the globe can tell stories about "mooners," the weirdos who misbehave when the moon is full. And occultists refer to the period of waning lunar phases as a "sacrificial moon," researchers point out. The first vic-

tims of serial killer Ted Bundy are known to have been murdered in Washington state during the waning phases of the moon—always under Taurus, Scorpio or Pisces. DeWitt Clinton Cook became known as "The Moon Maniac" after attacking numerous women and committing 300 burglaries—all while there was a full moon. Cook was executed at California's San Quentin Prison in 1941 for the murder of a college coed. And Robert Louis Stevenson's classic study, *Dr. Jekyll and Mr. Hyde,* was patterned after the true story of a lunatic who committed horrible crimes during the full moon.

Consider the following questions:

- Although some of the evidence cited in the article is anecdotal, some is based on actual crime statistics. Do these latter analyses represent experimental or nonexperimental designs?

- The article suggests that the moon phases cause a change in our biology. For the relationship between moon phase and criminal behavior, could there be a direction of control problem?

- For the relationship between moon phase and criminal behavior, could there be a third variable problem? If so, what is a possible third variable that would explain the relationship?

- The title of the article states that "Research Proves. . . ." What is wrong with this?

- The article clearly states that there is a causal link between moon phase and "crazy" behavior. How would you respond?

SOURCE: "Research Proves Full Moon Really Does Make You Crazy," by C. Linedecker, July 31, 2001. *Weekly World News.* American Media, Inc. Reprinted with permission.

drawn. For example, if we remove the one outlier point from our hypothetical data, the r value shifts from .88 to .62. Thus, that one participant dramatically increased the strength of the relationship between the two variables. In other cases, the outlier can be such that it dramatically decreases the strength of the relationship. In either case, researchers should always carefully inspect the data that produced outliers to be sure that no errors were made in

	Table 15.2	Hypothetical Data to Study the Correlation Between TV Violence and Aggressive Behavior	

PARTICIPANT	MEAN HOURS OF TV VIOLENCE PER WEEK	TOTAL NUMBER OF DISCIPLINARY INCIDENTS
1	3	4
2	4	3
3	2	0
4	3	2
5	7	2
6	5	3
7	8	2
8	1	0
9	6	6
10	0	1
11	25	30
12	4	0
13	9	7
14	13	7
15	4	2
16	7	3
17	5	5
18	11	2
19	4	4
20	9	6

observations or calculations. Even without errors, in some cases there is something unique about that participant that may warrant his or her removal from the data set. If data are removed from the data set, the rationale must be clear and must be reported. A researcher should never remove data simply because they are different from other data or because they work against the hypothesis of the study.

A few other issues that deserve mention are restriction of range, curvilinear relationships, and sample size. Restriction of range refers to the fact that when the range of scores on one or both of your variables is small or nonexistent, you have not adequately addressed the research question and you will almost certainly obtain a nonsignificant value for the correlation coefficient. For example, if all 20 participants in our hypothetical study had watched a mean of 2 hours of TV violence per week, the correlation coefficient would be 0.00 (re-

Figure 15.3 Scatterplot That Depicts the Hypothetical Data in Table 15.2

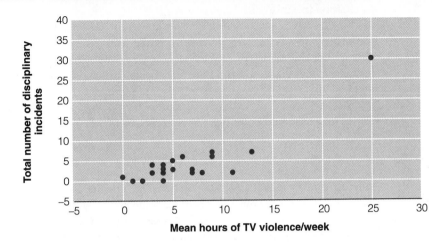

gardless of the values for the number of disciplinary incidents). We would not have addressed the research question. Therefore, when you select variables for correlational research, it is imperative that the measurement of those variables result in a relatively wide range of values from the participants.

It is also important to examine the nature of the relationship between the two variables to determine the most appropriate correlation coefficient. In our analysis of the hypothetical data in Table 15.2, the scatterplot suggested a linear relationship. That is, the best-fitting line through the points on the scatterplot was a straight line. In some situations, the relationship between two variables may be monotonic but curvilinear; that is, the best-fitting line through the points on the scatterplot is a curved line. Consider the scatterplot shown in Figure 15.4. You would probably agree that there is a relationship between mean hours of TV violence per week and number of disciplinary incidents. However, it is a curvilinear

Figure 15.4 Scatterplot That Illustrates a Curvilinear Relationship

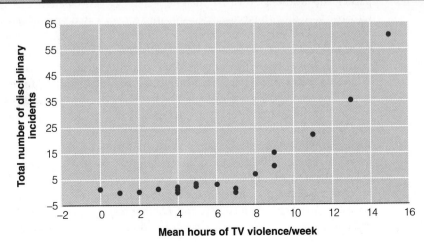

relationship rather than a linear relationship. Thus, the Spearman correlation coefficient, rather than the Pearson correlation coefficient, would be the proper statistic (again, refer to the decision tree in Figure 10.10).

Finally, sample size is an issue to consider in correlational research. The power of a correlational analysis is increased by increasing the sample size. With extremely large samples, weak relationships with correlations of .1 or .2 may be statistically significant but not practically meaningful. On the other hand, with a small sample size, a meaningful relationship might go undetected. The concept of power is an important one (see Chapter 10).

Although correlational research represents a powerful nonexperimental design, it is time to turn to several other types of nonexperimental designs.

Ex Post Facto Design

At times, caution must be exercised in deciding whether a study is nonexperimental or experimental. If the determination is not made, an erroneous conclusion may result. A type of study that can masquerade as a genuine experiment is the **ex post facto design**. Although it appears to be a true experiment because of the way groups are separated and the way the analysis is performed, it is still nonexperimental research and subject to the same limitations discussed earlier with respect to correlational research. It derives its name from the fact that the assignment of participants to levels of the independent variable is based on events that occurred in the past (after the fact). It mimics an experiment in that comparisons are made between two or more groups of individuals with similar backgrounds who were exposed to different conditions as a result of their natural histories. We then measure the participants on a dependent variable of interest to determine whether or not statistically meaningful differences exist between the experimental groups. If reliable differences are found, should we conclude that they were due to the historical differences we found in the past records? The answer is no.

Note that the ex post facto design uses neither random assignment nor active manipulation of the independent variable. The intent of this type of research is precisely that of a true experiment, but the problems encountered in drawing conclusions are very different. A few examples will illustrate our point.

In Chapter 11, we considered an experimental design in which we, as the researchers, determined which levels of TV violence would be studied and randomly assigned research participants to these levels. We then measured aggressive behavior. A nonexperimental alternative would be to place participants into groups based on how much TV violence they just watched (of their own choosing) and then to measure aggressive behavior. Notice that these two research designs are similar in that the aggressive behavior of groups of participants is being compared and the groups differed in terms of exposure to TV violence. We should also mention that the statistical analysis would be similar. However, notice the differences. The second design is an ex post facto design because participants were not randomly assigned to the groups—that is, the independent variable was not manipulated by the researcher. Because we lack the control of an experimental design, we must be very cautious about the nature of the conclusion that we draw from the ex post facto design. As with correlational research, direction of control and third variable issues need to be considered. Let's examine another example.

An instructor in a college math course believes that a relationship exists between performance in college math courses and whether students had the "old math" or "new math" techniques in grade school. She decides to do a study to determine whether her observations are indeed accurate. She looks up the grade school records of a large number of college students taking her college math course. On the basis of these records, she selects 50 students who received "new math" and another 50 students who received "old math" techniques. She then gathers the two groups of students together and gives them a college math proficiency test. Her experimental design would look no different from that of a true experiment.

We have what appears to be a "treatment" condition (new math) and a comparison or control group (old math)—both of which, in this case, have already occurred. The comparison between treatment and control groups appears to be the same type of comparison as in a true experiment. But any conclusions drawn from our example must be guarded and weak. Why? Obviously, our participants cannot be assigned randomly (nor can we manipulate the conditions because we have already selected students). Their assignment to the levels of the independent variable was based on past records.

The groups may be biased in different and unknown ways. It is quite possible that those who received new math in grade school are very different from those who received the old math. They may have been chosen for that program because of their skills (or lack of skills) in mathematics. It is also possible that new math programs were offered only by wealthy and progressive school districts. Thus, it is quite possible that differences existed in the student populations from which the treatment groups were drawn. Perhaps only urban/industrialized communities had new math programs, but rural/suburban communities did not. The point is that this is all idle speculation. We simply do not know the many reasons that some students received new math and some old math. Because we could not randomly assign our students to the two groups, systematic participant bias is a distinct possibility. Our two student groups could have differed in their average math proficiency score for any number of reasons other than "new" or "old" math. (A true experiment would require that we had previously randomly assigned a number of students from the same school district to new math and an approximately equal number to old math classes, holding other factors constant. Then, years later, we would administer a math proficiency test in college.)

Asking two questions will enable you to identify quickly and accurately whether the experiment is an ex post facto one. (1) Did the researcher have control over the random assignment of participants? That is, did the researcher assign participants randomly to groups? If random assignment was not used, then it was not a true experiment. (2) Did the researcher actively manipulate the independent variable, or had it already occurred? Now the choice is deciding between a quasi-experiment or an ex post facto one. If a variable was not actively manipulated at the time of the research, then the experiment is an ex post facto one, and the conclusion is much weaker. Keep in mind that in ex post facto research, membership in the groups in itself constitutes the "treatment." There is no treatment other than membership in a group—for example, male versus female, heavy versus thin, tall versus short, joggers versus nonjoggers, dogmatic versus nondogmatic, or smokers versus nonsmokers. A quasi-experiment lacks random assignment, but it does have control over levels of the IV.

Another example of an ex post facto experiment will help you to discriminate between it and experiments in which the independent variable is, in fact, manipulated. In this example, we are interested in the reactions of anxious and nonanxious participants to a loud noise. Do not confuse the loud noise with the "treatment" condition. It is not a treatment or independent variable, because both groups receive it. It is simply a task to which all participants respond. The reaction to the noise is our dependent variable—the task that all participants perform. The treatment consists of membership in a group based on whatever characteristics the researcher may be interested in. In the present example, this characteristic is level of anxiety (anxious versus nonanxious participants). Let's get on with the example.

We could give a personality test (such as the Taylor Manifest Anxiety Scale) to a large population of students and then select participants on the basis of their scores. We might select ten students who score very high and ten students who score very low on the anxiety scale. Since high-anxiety and low-anxiety participants are our focus of interest and, as it were, our treatment, they cannot be randomly assigned to different groups. Therefore, our independent variable is high versus low anxiety. Our dependent variable is the magnitude of the startle reaction to loud noise. Assume that we find that our high-anxiety participants respond to noise more strongly than do our low-anxiety participants. Can we conclude that they did so because of anxiety? No, we cannot. We are again plagued by the third variable problem. Because we could not employ random assignment—that is, our groups were preexisting groups—it is possible that our participant groups differ in many ways other than anxiety. Their responses could be related to how well they sleep. It may be that high-anxiety participants sleep less well than others and that any participant, regardless of anxiety, who did not get adequate sleep would perform like high-anxiety participants. Perhaps it is the case that high-anxiety participants drink much more coffee than do low-anxiety participants. If we assume that coffee affects the startle response, then any participants who drink much coffee, anxious or nonanxious, would perform in similar ways. This ex post facto design permits any number of other alternative interpretations that would not be possible if the research were either a quasi or a true experiment.

Naturalistic Observation

Naturalistic observation takes place under natural conditions or under real-life conditions without any intervention on the part of the researcher. Such observations contrast with those in experimental settings, where considerable prior control is possible, events can be manipulated, and the observations may be repeated. When using naturalistic observation, we observe nature without imposing change. However, the observations are carefully planned and systematized. Consequently, the data can be organized in a meaningful way to permit analysis and interpretation. However, the interpretation issues already discussed in this chapter must be considered.

Naturalistic observation is the oldest method for the study of behavior or other phenomena. One of the most accurate sciences (in terms of prediction) is astronomy, and it is restricted largely to observation. Ethologists are people who study animal behavior under natural conditions and use natural observation almost exclusively. Jane Goodall's work with primates in Africa has resulted in some fascinating observations regarding their social interactions. Development and personality psychologists have published extremely informative observational studies of children interacting under natural conditions. Jean Piaget's theory of cognitive development in children was based on naturalistic observation. We have been able to identify migration patterns in fish, fowl, and mammals by tagging studies. Naturalistic observation of primitive cultures has given us insight into the range of variation in human institutions. It must be emphasized that natural observation is not anecdotal and casual but, instead, systematic and carefully planned. The observer must be sufficiently skilled to distinguish between an observation and an interpretation. Many of the principles of good observation were discussed in Chapter 6.

Qualitative Research

All of the research designs discussed so far have involved measurement of variables and a subsequent statistical analysis of the values recorded. The application of mathematics to the process of drawing research conclusions lends a degree of objectivity to the decision-making process. Although there can be differences of opinion regarding the most appropriate statistical analysis, for the most part, a given set of data would lead different researchers to the same conclusion. There is value to this quantitative approach, but there is also value to **qualitative research**, in which the researcher gains insights from more informal and nonnumerical observations. In fact, conclusions drawn from such informal observations are often a first step that leads to more rigorous experimental studies to clarify relationships among variables. A good researcher understands that the various types of experimental and nonexperimental designs complement one another when a particular area of behavioral research is studied.

Case Study

In a **case study,** one or more individuals are carefully examined over time. Biographical data, interviews, or psychological tests may be components of a case study. Some case studies are prepared by reconstructing the individual's biography from memory and records (retrospective). On occasion, a case study may be prospective. Rather than relying on memory or records, the researcher takes measurements at planned intervals.

There are two important considerations in a case study approach. One is to search for some regularity or patterning to behavior that might suggest some principle around which it is organized. The second involves additional case studies to confirm the previously observed regularity or pattern. Such information may permit generalization to other situations or persons.

Case studies are often used when it is impossible or unethical to conduct an experiment. At other times, they are closely related to naturalistic observation. Freud's insights into behavior problems were largely based on case studies of his patients. Piaget's theory of intellectual development stems from his intensive observations of his own three children. Case studies of individuals suffering brain damage have been undertaken to assess the extent to which functions are regained.

Phenomenology

How did surviving New York City firefighters process the events that happened at the World Trade Center on September 11, 2001? Understanding their experiences may provide insight into how people deal with traumatic events. An appropriate research design would involve a phenomenological approach. With **phenomenology,** the researcher seeks an in-depth interview with an individual or a group of individuals to understand their experience. The experience may relate to some traumatic event (September 11, death, natural disaster), a joyous event (wedding, birth, winning a sports championship), or any other distinguishing event. The research participants are asked to introspect—to describe their feelings and how they explain the event and their actions. Based on the interview(s), the researcher attempts to discern some underlying principle, conclusion, or generality. There is, of course, a degree of subjectivity and interpretation on the part of both the participants and the researcher. However, it would be rather difficult to study this aspect of the human experience with other research designs.

Ethnography

What could motivate the Al Qaeda terrorists to commit such a violent act as the September 11 attack? To answer this question, one needs to fully understand the way of thinking and the way of life of a group of people. **Ethnography** is an approach designed to understand a group of people that form a culture. The culture to be studied may be quite large (such as African Americans) or quite small (such as an African tribe or an inner-city gang).

Information for an ethnographic study can be gathered in several ways. As in the phenomenological approach, members of the culture can be interviewed. In addition, artifacts produced by the culture (books, art, music, photographs) can be analyzed. Finally, the researcher may simply observe the culture. As discussed in Chapter 6, such observation may involve being a participant observer (observe from the inside) or a nonparticipant observer (observe from the outside), and the observations may or may not be known to the members of the culture. As with all qualitative research, a certain degree of subjectivity and interpretation is inherent in the ethnographic approach.

CASE ANALYSIS

In 1998, the *Psi Chi Journal of Undergraduate Research* published a study titled "The Effects of Extracurricular Activities on Self-Esteem, Academic Achievement, and Aggression in College Students" (Bleeker, Evans, Fisher, & Miller, 1998). The researchers administered a set of questionnaires to 113 undergraduate students and concluded "the scores on these inventories were related to the students' extracurricular involvement and their cumulative grade point averages (GPAs). Women involved in social clubs had significantly higher self-esteem scores than women involved in athletics and women not involved in activities. Men participating in social clubs had significantly higher hostile aggression scores than did women involved in social clubs. Thus, for women, self-esteem is positively related to extracurricular activities, whereas for men, the relationship is less clear." Let's assume that the Director of Student Services on your campus uses these findings to suggest that women should get involved in social clubs to increase their self-esteem.

Critical Thinking Questions

1. What type of nonexperimental research design was used in this study?

2. What is wrong with the suggestion by the Director of Student Services? Why is it wrong?

3. Is direction of control a potential issue in this study? Explain.

4. Is there a potential third variable issue in this study? If so, provide an example.

5. Look again at the title of the article. There is something wrong with it. Rewrite the title so that it better conforms to the type of research design that was used.

GENERAL SUMMARY

In addition to experimental and quasi-experimental research designs, nonexperimental designs offer valuable techniques for better understanding human behavior. As a category, nonexperimental designs are characterized by a low level of experimental control, lack of cause–effect conclusions, and an increased likelihood that the data were obtained from "real-world" settings. Correlational research assesses the nature of the relationship between predictor and criterion variables; ex post facto research assesses the differences between preexisting groups on some dependent variable. Conclusions should be drawn only after careful consideration of direction of control and third variable issues. Naturalistic observation is a method in which observations occur in a natural setting without any interference by the researcher. In addition to research designs that are based on quantitative measurements, qualitative techniques can provide important information. Case studies involve a careful analysis of an individual or small group of individuals over time; phenomenological studies rely on in-depth interviews to better understand the subjective experience of individuals; ethnographic studies seek to better understand the behavior of individuals who are part of a particular culture.

Now that we have explored a variety of experimental and nonexperimental designs, we turn in the next chapter to methods by which we share our research with the public.

DETAILED SUMMARY

1. Nonexperimental designs are characterized by the researcher's lack of control over the independent variable.

2. Although experimental designs are quite powerful, there are several good reasons to use nonexperimental designs. For many interesting research questions, the researcher cannot manipulate or control the independent variable for practical, ethical, or financial reasons.

3. Correlational research involves collecting data or searching out records of a specified population and ascertaining the relationships among the variables of interest. Such research involves neither random assignment nor manipulation of an experimental variable.

4. Experimental designs study the causal relationship between manipulated variables and use random assignment (or repeated measures), whereas correlational designs study the relationship between unmanipulated variables and do not use random assignment.

5. The degree of relationship between variables in a correlational design is measured by calculating a correlation coefficient.

6. Correlation coefficients have values that range from −1.0 to +1.0. Positive correlations indicate that as values for one variable increase, values for the other variable also increase. Negative correlations indicate that as values for one variable increase, values for the other variable decrease. Zero correlations indicate no relationship between the variables.

7. Correlations are used to make predictions regarding behavior. Such predictions can be used to make decisions about who gets selected for a job, a special program, or admission to college. Correlations are also used to assess the reliability of testing instruments and observers. Other uses include assessment of test validity, development of diagnostic criteria, and theory evaluation.

8. The issues of direction of control and third variables are two reasons why cause–effect conclusions are unwarranted in correlational research.

9. Even if two variables are correlated, the correlational analysis does not reveal which variable is causing changes in the other variable. This is the direction of control problem.

10. When two variables are correlated, it is possible that some third, unmeasured variable is responsible for the relationship because that third variable is simultaneously causing changes in the original two variables. This is the third variable problem.

11. A procedure that is sometimes useful for addressing the directionality problem is a time-lagged correlational design. This procedure involves determining a correlation between two variables at Time 1 and again later at Time 2.

12. A procedure known as partial correlation is sometimes used to address the third variable problem. If a third variable is thought to be a factor affecting the correlation between variables X and Y, the partial correlation technique can be used to eliminate its effects. Another procedure that is sometimes used to eliminate the third variable problem is matching. In this case, only data from participants matched on the third variable are analyzed.

13. Although correlation does not imply causation, the absence of a correlation does imply the absence of a causal relationship.

14. The interpretation of data from correlational research requires a scatterplot to determine the form of the relationship (linear versus curvilinear), to detect the presence of outliers, and to evaluate variables for restriction of range. The form of the relationship determines the appropriate correlation coefficient; outliers or a restricted range can have a dramatic effect on the value of the correlation coefficient and the interpretation of the relationship.

15. The ex post facto research design mimics an experiment in that comparisons are made between two or more groups of individuals who were exposed to different conditions as a result of their natural histories. We then measure the participants on a dependent variable of interest to determine whether or not statistically meaningful differences exist between the experimental groups.

16. Because the ex post facto design uses neither random assignment nor active manipulation of the independent variable, causal conclusions are not warranted.

17. When observations are made in a real-world setting, we refer to these studies as naturalistic observations.

18. Qualitative research occurs when the researcher gains insights from more informal and nonnumerical observations.

19. A case study involves the systematic collection of information about one or a few individuals either as historical data (retrospective) or as data collected over time (prospective).

20. With phenomenology, the researcher seeks an in-depth interview with an individual or a group of individuals to understand their experience.

21. Ethnography is an approach designed to understand a group of people that form a culture through interviews, artifacts, and direct observation.

KEY TERMS

case study *(p. 265)*

correlation coefficient *(p. 252)*

correlational research *(p. 252)*

criterion variable *(p. 255)*

direction of control *(p. 255)*

ethnography *(p. 266)*

ex post facto design *(p. 262)*

matching *(p. 257)*

naturalistic observation *(p. 264)*

phenomenology *(p. 265)*

predictor variable *(p. 255)*

scatterplot *(p. 258)*

qualitative research *(p. 265)*

third variable *(p. 255)*

REVIEW QUESTIONS/EXERCISES

1. In this chapter, we have suggested several research questions that would be appropriate for each of the nonexperimental designs. Develop your own research question for a correlational design, an ex post facto design, a naturalistic observation, a case study, a phenomenological study, and an ethnographic study. Briefly describe the methodology for each.

2. Summarize the distinctions between experimental and nonexperimental research and also between quantitative research and qualitative research.

3. There has been considerable concern about whether the scholastic performance of public school children has declined. Schools have changed, and there is some evidence that structure, discipline, and supervision have decreased in the public school system. Some educators have argued that these changes account for the decline in academic performance. To support this view, they undertook a study comparing the scholastic performance of students in parochial schools (with

documented high levels of supervision, discipline, structure) with those in public schools. Their beliefs were confirmed. The data revealed that students from parochial schools significantly outperformed students from public schools on each measure of performance. Based on these data, they made a concerted effort to increase discipline, structure, and supervision in the public school system. What type of research design was used? Why would you be critical of their response to the study?

4. Alcohol is the drug of choice on most college campuses. Studies show that students who drink more alcohol per week have lower grade point averages. Many educators and student personnel administrators have argued that since alcohol consumption causes lower GPAs, anti-drinking programs should be immediately instituted to enhance education. What is wrong with their reasoning? (Include a discussion of third variables in your answer.)

LABORATORY EXERCISES

 In Chapter 11, we suggested a laboratory exercise from Chapter 3 of *Research Methods Laboratory Manual for Psychology* (Langston, 2005) that related to pet ownership and health. Consider conducting one of the projects that uses a correlational design (for example, measure some aspect of pet ownership that is a continuous variable).

In Chapter 6, we suggested a laboratory exercise from Chapter 1 of Langston's manual that discusses observations of territoriality in parking lots and suggests several related projects. If you have not done so already, consider conducting one of these yourself.

WEB RESOURCES TO INCREASE LEARNING

The chapter outline, chapter summaries, key terms and definitions, additional chapter questions, chapter exercises, and links to relevant Web sites are available at the course Web site (**http://psychology.wadsworth.com/** **lammers_badia1e**). Explore the interactive workshops "Bivariate Scatterplots," "Correlation," and "Nonexperimental Approaches."

CHAPTER **16**

FUNDAMENTALS OF DISSEMINATING RESEARCH

● Introduction

I (Lammers) will never forget the first time that I presented research to a public audience. It was my first year in graduate school, and several of us in the psychophysiology laboratory at Bowling Green State University were invited to travel to an Industrial/Organizational Psychology conference at the University of Tennessee–Knoxville to present research on the role of circadian rhythms in adjustment to shift work schedules. The image of the presentation room lingers in my mind as I write this. I was well prepared but very nervous, and secretly hoping that few would decide to hear our presentation. As the presentation time arrived, my initial hopes were confirmed; only a handful of people were in the audience. My presentation went well. I felt a distinct sense of accomplishment and actually wished that there had been a large audience to hear it. I felt that same sense of accomplishment when my master's thesis was finally accepted for publication in a scientific journal. What a feeling it was to receive my copy of the journal in the mail and to see my article in among those with authors who were well known in the field and whom I greatly admired.

One of the hallmarks of scientific research is that the information is made public and is thus subject to scrutiny and review by the public. Three of the most common means for disseminating research are discussed in this chapter: manuscript preparation for a journal article (research report), oral presentation, and poster presentation. You are undoubtedly familiar with journal articles. You may not be as familiar with presentations. If you get the chance to attend a scientific conference, we strongly encourage you to go. Conference programs are almost entirely composed of oral presentations and poster presentations. These are excellent ways to learn about the most recent research in psychology. In addition, nearly all conferences encourage presentations by students.

Chances are that the course for which you are using this textbook requires one or more assignments that relate to the methods of disseminating research or presenting a research proposal. We suspect that this assignment is a source of significant anxiety. This is understandable. Describing your research to another person or persons in a coherent and concise fashion is not easy. But it is an essential part of the research enterprise. We hope that the information presented in this chapter will guide you through the process.

● Writing a Research Report

Overview

We will preface our description of the components of a manuscript with some important comments regarding scholarship. Then we will describe in detail the different sections found in scientific reports. We will also talk a little about writing style and ways to avoid sexism in your writing. Other instructions and helpful suggestions for preparing a manuscript appear in the *Publication Manual of the American Psychological Association* (2001). The manual is more extensive and more detailed than our comments in this chapter, which deal only with the most frequent problems undergraduates experience when beginning to write scientific reports. You will want to consult the APA manual for questions not treated here.

A good research report is a mixture of scholarship and craftsmanship in writing. Both require time to develop, along with considerable practice and feedback from your instructors. Whether one writes well or poorly reflects one's developmental history in the acquisition of writing skills. Although good writing is an essential requirement for effective communication, it is not sufficient in itself. Good writing must be buttressed by good scholarship. The term *scholarship* implies such characteristics as accuracy, thoroughness, and objectivity. In addition, the writer must have the highest regard for presenting important aspects of a topic in a precise, unbiased, and fair manner. Special care must be taken to acknowledge and cite the ideas and works of other writers if their material is used in the report. Failure to do so, or to imply that their work is your own when it is not, is plagiarism. It is unethical and can also be illegal. Keep in mind that the author of a written report is responsible for all aspects of its contents. From the inception of the research idea, through the literature search, data acquisition, statistical analysis, and the final written report, great care must be taken to be honest, accurate, precise, and thorough.

Original Sources

One way to avoid error and to ensure the accuracy and thoroughness of a report is to read the original sources of the information about which you are writing. Relying on secondary sources can result in problems that range from minor inaccuracies to major misstatements of fact. When a writer makes assertions regarding the work of another writer, it is your responsibility to verify their factual basis before citing them in your report. The only way to do this is to read the original source. There are many instances in science where a secondary source misstated or misinterpreted the primary source material. Other researchers, reading the secondary source, perpetuate the errors in their writing. When continued by third- and fourth-generation writers, the errors become so deeply ingrained in the literature that they take on the qualities of a myth. At this point, they become exceedingly difficult to refute.

Sections of a Research Report

The behavioral science community has developed a standard format for preparing a research report. This format includes discrete sections that address different aspects of the research. As we discuss each section, we suggest that you continually refer to the sample research report in Appendix B. This will help you to visualize the layout and to better understand the nature of the content. Because many of you will be asked to write a research proposal for this course, we have also included a sample research proposal in Appendix C. The format and guidelines are very similar to those for a research report. A research proposal will not have an Abstract section or a Discussion section. In addition, the Method and proposed Results sections are written in future tense rather than in past tense.

Title Page   The title page consists of a header, running head, title, authorship, and author affiliation. The header is right-justified within the top margin of every page and includes the first few words of the title and the page number. Word processing programs have a method for creating a header that will appear within the top margin and will automatically update the page numbers. The running head is an abbreviated title that will ultimately appear on every page of the published article.

When you consider a title for your paper, remember that most psychologists do not pick up a journal and read it cover to cover. They read what interests them. When they receive their scientific journal (or any magazine), they scan the table of contents for articles of interest. If the title of an article is uninformative or misleading, it may not attract readers to the research. Short and informative titles are preferred, limited to not more than 15 words. Within these 15 words, you should clearly state the dependent and independent variables or the theoretical issues with which the article deals. The title should be a statement of content so that it alone can be used by various information retrieval systems. Abbreviations should be avoided. If the title is adequate, it will be referenced appropriately, thereby increasing the probability that it will gain the attention of its intended audience. Clever titles are permissible if they convey the necessary information and are understandable. Writers with established reputations sometimes use clever titles containing very little information, but their works read routinely because of past contributions to the literature. When working out a title, avoid redundant information. You do not have to include the words *investigation* or *experiment* in the title; that is already understood. Often, authors first state the title in a long and fully descriptive way and then begin to shorten it to the essentials. For example, the title "An Investigation of the Choice Behavior of Subjects for Either Predictable or Unpredictable Events" could be reduced to "Choosing Between Predictable and Unpredictable Events." The new title tells us as much as the old one in a more appealing and specific way and with fewer words (14 versus 6).

When only one person is responsible for the research project, authorship for the manuscript is not a problem. However, deciding the authorship of a manuscript when several people have been involved can be a delicate issue. Only individuals judged to have made a substantial contribution to the research should be authors. The first author of a manuscript is usually the individual who took the primary responsibility for initiating the research and supervising its completion. Subsequent authorship is assigned in terms of the amount of responsibility taken by each author. Usually, the first author also takes the major responsibility for writing the manuscript. When order of authorship cannot be resolved, some writers have relied on a coin toss for a decision. Whatever the order of authorship, the professional reputation and responsibility for the content of the manuscript are shared equally.

In addition to the authors, others may have made some contributions along the way (such as performing the statistical analysis or reviewing a draft of the manuscript). It is appropriate to acknowledge their contribution in a footnote.

Abstract The abstract is an important part of the manuscript, and considerable effort should be devoted to writing it. Like the title, it serves indexing and information retrieval systems. If the title is sufficiently informative and interesting, the next step for the journal reader is to go to the abstract. Some readers whose major research interests are in other areas may go no further than the abstract. Clearly, the abstract should inform them as fully as possible about the contents of the article so that an informed decision can be made. Other researchers, more directly interested in the topic, will read the abstract both for its content and to determine if the manuscript warrants the commitment of the time necessary to reading and understanding it. Whatever the case, the abstract allows the reader to quickly survey the material.

Because the abstract is usually written after the entire manuscript is completed, the flow of the abstract follows that of the manuscript. You can look upon the abstract as a compressed version of the manuscript. It should contain in very brief form all of the important information, such as the statement of the problem, participant sample and characteristics, design, procedure, summary of results, statistical analyses, and conclusions. The abstract may vary in length, but the APA *Publication Manual* recommends that it be not more than 120 words. No material or information should appear in the abstract that is not in the manuscript. Usually, the first several drafts of the abstract are well beyond the 120-word limit. This forces the writer to make decisions concerning the relative importance of the information—then eliminate material considered less important. The number of words can also be reduced by carefully going over the structure of each sentence and saying things more concisely. Eliminating articles and prepositions also reduces the number of words. References are typically not included in the abstract.

Introduction   No heading is required because, in effect, the manuscript begins here. A difficult decision involves judging the level at which the manuscript should be written. Should you assume a highly sophisticated, knowledgeable audience or one that is naive? The answer is neither. Instead, assume a generally informed individual who is not specifically familiar with your topic. How long should the introduction be? It should be long enough to provide sufficient information so that the reader can comprehend the content of your paper. Therefore, for some papers, only a few paragraphs are necessary. For others, the introduction may be considerably longer.

Your first paragraph should prepare the reader for what is to come. It should broadly identify the problem or question that your research addresses. In fact, the very first sentence could be used to introduce the general topic of your paper—what the paper is about, the general thesis. The last sentence of the introductory paragraph could identify the problem or question more specifically. Sentences between the first and last may be devoted to a brief general rationale leading to the question with which your research deals. You do not state specifically what your independent and dependent variables are, the logic leading to the question, the hypothesis, your expectations, or the procedure that you will use. The first paragraph simply sets up the reader for what will follow.

Intermediate paragraphs should relate to both the preceding paragraph and the paragraph that follows. They are tied together by transition sentences. Transition sentences allow the reader to move smoothly without unexpected changes from one paragraph to the next. A transition sentence may be the first sentence of a new paragraph or it may simply include a word or idea that ended the last paragraph. For example, after describing one approach to a problem, you then state either at the end of one paragraph or the beginning of the other, "Badia suggested a different approach to the problem." Words such as *therefore, nevertheless, however, of course* are often used with transitions. An outline containing main ideas, literature survey, and so on, may help you write a smoothly flowing introduction. Also, read carefully the section on writing style in Chapter 2 of the APA manual.

These intermediate paragraphs should be used to develop a logical argument and rationale for your research, the origin of the problem, and a summary of the present state of knowledge. The directly relevant research is reviewed in these paragraphs. This background literature is not intended to be exhaustive. You simply summarize the major points of directly relevant literature. If exhaustive general reviews of the literature are available, you can refer the reader to them. In these paragraphs, you acknowledge the work of others that relates to your research and also any theoretical development that you wish to undertake. A critique of previous research may be given if it relates to the purposes of your study. Whatever your interest, it is important that you develop a rationale (a logical argument) for your research—that is, how did your study evolve?

To help you organize the sequence of material in these intermediate paragraphs, you might think about a funnel. Start off broad and gradually narrow your topics and ideas as they become more directly related to the hypothesis and methodology of your study. A good introduction should lead the reader to the hypothesis in your final paragraph. In fact, a very good introduction will result in the reader's being able to anticipate your study and your hypothesis even before reading about it in the final introductory paragraph.

In the final introductory paragraph, you summarize for the reader what you have been saying in preceding paragraphs. You restate your problem, summarize your arguments, and present your rationale or logic. You make it clear for the reader what the specific purpose of your research is and indicate how you intend to provide an answer. It is important that you be specific about your hypothesis, your expectations, or your predictions. Your rationale must follow logically. To be specific means that you will have to identify your dependent and independent variables, describe in general terms the procedure used to test your hypothesis, and articulate what you expect to find.

Method The method must be appropriate for the problem or question under investigation. How did you go about answering the research question? This section must be sufficiently descriptive to allow a reader to evaluate how well this was done. It must be sufficiently complete to allow others to replicate your method. For some aspects of the study, considerable detail will be necessary; others will require less detail. You must make this decision. Too much detail concerning relatively unimportant information may be more confusing than helpful. Keep two things in mind when deciding on details: (1) Are they important to the outcome of the study? (2) Are they necessary for understanding or for replicating the study? The method section is usually divided into subsections that include *participants, apparatus* or *materials, procedure,* and in some cases, *design.* This division is for the reader's convenience when questions arise regarding specific information about the method. The method section should be written while you are conducting the experiment. Trying to reconstruct it at a later time may be difficult, and some important details may be omitted.

The first subsection of the Method section is *Participants.* Here we include details regarding the participants of the study. Who were they? How many? Their sex? Age or age range? How were they selected? Were they paid? Volunteers? Was participation a class requirement? Geographic area? Did any participants fail to complete the study? Why? Were the data from any participant discarded? Why? Were participants informed of the hypothesis being tested?

Different details are necessary when animals are used. We must specify the genus, species, and strain. In addition, the vendor from whom the animals were purchased must be specified. It is also necessary to give their sex, age or age range, and weight. How were they housed and maintained? Was any special treatment given?

The second subsection of the Method section is *Materials/Apparatus.* This section should not be confused with the following *Procedure* section. It is sometimes difficult not to do so. Include in this section the apparatus and materials used in the experiment. In some cases, only testing material will be used. If so, important information regarding the tests must be given. Under this circumstance, the title of this section might be changed to *Materials* or *Tests.* When commercial laboratory equipment is used, identify the model number and the company. Custom-built equipment that was central to the research should be described in sufficient detail to allow others to build it. In this case, a drawing or photograph may also be helpful.

The third subsection of the Method section is *Procedure.* Detail is necessary in this section. The questions that must be clearly answered are "What did you do, and how did you do it?" State precisely what treatment was given to each participant. If different groups received different treatments, be sure that your description identifies these differences. Independent, dependent, and control variables must be clearly identified for the reader. Identify experimental and control groups, and indicate how they were formed. Time intervals, durations, and sequences of important events should be described. Instructions should be summarized or paraphrased. If instructions themselves are studied as an independent variable, then they should be presented verbatim. If counterbalancing or randomization is used, describe how this was accomplished.

Some Method sections include a *Design* subsection. For some complex experiments, a design section may be appropriate. If so, then this section would include the type of experimental design that was used (such as within subjects, between subjects, or mixed design) along with the treatment conditions and a description of the statistical analyses or model. When a design section is used, some of the material in the procedure section would be placed in this section.

Results The Results section is used to describe the results of the research and to evaluate their reliability. It is sometimes difficult to present your results without also discussing them. In fact, on occasion, some writers do combine the Results and Discussion sections under one heading. However, more often than not, the two sections are kept separate. All data relevant to the purposes of your research should be presented, whether favorable or unfavorable to your views. Different formats, such as tables and figures, can be used to supplement and clarify the verbal description. They are intended as supplements, however, and should not serve as the only source of information regarding results. Avoid presenting the same data in several places. (If data appear in a table, they generally should not appear in a figure, and vice versa.)

Different methods are used to determine whether the obtained results are reliable (significant). When group data are presented, the results are usually analyzed statistically and their reliability (significance level) reported in terms of a t, F, χ^2, or other statistics along with a given p (probability) value. When a single-subject approach is used, data from individual participants are presented and their reliability assessed by intraparticipant and interparticipant replication.

A reasonably standard format is used when reporting tests of significance. A verbal description of the results (data) comes first, followed by the outcome of statistical analyses of these results. For example, after describing the data obtained with Groups A and B under two different conditions, you might then report the following: "The difference between Groups A and B under the first condition was significant, $F(1,21) = 9.01$, $p < .01$, but it was not significant under the second condition, $F(1,21) = 1.55$, $p > .05$." Note the manner in which the statistical test is reported. First, the symbol for the statistic is given (italicized), followed by the degrees of freedom (in parentheses), then an equal sign followed by the value of the statistic, a comma, an italicized lowercase p (probability), followed by a less than (<) or greater than (>) or equal sign, and finally the level of significance. Again, it is important to describe your data first and only then give the outcome of tests of significance.

Discussion If the experiment is a simple one with few findings reported in the Results section, you can begin the discussion with a clear, unambiguous statement of the contribution that your study makes. If a question was raised or a hypothesis stated, you should make a direct statement regarding an answer to the question or whether the hypothesis was or was not supported. When the Results section consists of many findings, it is appropriate to open the discussion with a brief summary of your findings.

The important points raised in the Introduction should be addressed in your Discussion. Also, the major findings of your study should be evaluated and interpreted. In this section, you describe the relationship of your findings to those of others and identify similarities and differences. You may want to emphasize some of your findings while qualifying others. Indicate whether your procedure, subject population, or experimental manipulations restrict or limit the generalizations that can be drawn. Theoretical speculation closely related to your data is appropriate in this section. However, avoid rambling ideas and speculation distant from your data. The practical implications of your data, if any, should be noted here. If you feel that your study has some unusual strengths, then it is appropriate to note them. Any weaknesses should also be identified briefly, with suggestions to correct them. You may want to conclude your discussion by pointing to future research. The insight derived from your study may suggest additional research or even a different direction that should be pursued.

References   Only works cited in the report are included in the References section, ordered alphabetically by the first author's last name. The References format described here is simple and efficient, but it differs from that used by some other professions. Each reference usually has four components: author(s), date, title, and publication. The format differs for journal articles, authored books, edited books, chapters appearing in edited books, electronic sources, unpublished manuscripts, and so on. Because such a wide variety of sources exist, you should consult the APA manual for the proper format for the particular type of source you are referencing. Samples of three of the most common source types follow.

Journal Article
Lammers, W. J., Badia, P., Hughes, R., & Harsh, J. (1991). Temperature, time-of-night of testing, and responsiveness to stimuli presented while sleeping. *Psychophysiology, 28,* 463–467. (Note: In journal titles, unlike article and book titles, the initial letter of each major word is capitalized.)

Authored Book
Ramachandran, V. S., & Blakeslee, S. (1998). *Phantoms in the brain: Probing the mysteries of the human mind.* New York: Morrow.

Chapter in an Edited Book
Lammers, W. J. (1999). Reading, writing, and thinking before each class. In L. T. Benjamin, B. F. Nodine, R. M. Ernst, & C. Blair-Broeker (Eds.), *Activities handbook for the teaching of psychology* (Vol. 4, pp. 28–29). Washington, DC: American Psychological Association.

Tables   Tables are not intended to duplicate the text of a manuscript. They are used to supplement it and to display a large amount of data in a clear and compressed way. Whenever a table is used, it must be referred to in the text. However, it is not necessary to launch into a detailed description of all the data in the table. Only the most important data need be described. Tables are sometimes difficult to construct; they require both thought and trial and error. For helpful suggestions, consult the APA manual. Tables are always referred to by number—Table 1, Table 2, and so on—and they require a brief explanatory heading. Often, headings identify the dependent and independent variables. Tables may also have footnotes immediately below them that provide additional information to make them easier to understand.

Figures   Another way to present considerable data in a clear and compressed way is to use figures. As with tables, each figure must be referred to in the text along with a description of the important data they display. They, too, are used only to supplement the text. Figures are also referred to by number—Figure 1, Figure 2, and so on—and they must be accompanied by a figure caption (title). The caption is usually descriptive and includes the dependent and independent variables that compose the figure. If additional information is needed to identify specific groups or conditions, then a legend is included (for example, open circles = placebo group, closed circles = experimental group). The vertical and horizontal axes must be clearly labeled. Heavy dark lines should be used when drawing these axes. The dependent variable is plotted along the vertical axis, and the independent variable is plotted along the horizontal axis. Usually no more than four curves should be plotted on any figure. Careful consideration should be given to the scale that is used on the vertical axis. It is possible to distort the visual display of the findings by using different scale values. Decimal values—such as .1, .2, and so on—may exaggerate the obtained differences, whereas a scale value in units of 10 (10, 20, and so on) might minimize the obtained differences.

Appendixes   The most common reason for including an appendix is to present detailed information about the experimental method that would be too cumbersome to include in the Method section of the paper. This supplementary material might include examples of the visual stimuli presented (such as word lists or pictures) or a questionnaire that was used. As the author, you can simply refer the reader to the appendix at the appropriate place in the paper (for example, "Photos of people with different body types were presented to participants for five seconds each. The appendix illustrates the actual photos that were used.").

Arrangement of the Manuscript

The APA *Publication Manual* specifies a precise arrangement of the manuscript. This arrangement is necessary when submitting a manuscript to a journal for publication. It differs in a number of ways from the appearance of the published article. Many instructors request that the report be submitted in a form similar to the published article. In particular, they ask that tables and figures be placed in the Results section where the data are described. The APA manual suggests the following arrangement:

1. Title page (separate page)—includes running head, title, authors, affiliation.
2. Abstract (starts on separate page)—the word "Abstract" centered at top of page; no title, author affiliation, or paragraph indentation.
3. Main text (starts on separate page)—title at top of page but no author or affiliation noted. Do not start a new page because of a heading (Method, Results, Discussion) until References.
4. References (starts on separate page).
5. Footnotes (starts on separate page).
6. Tables (each on a separate page).
7. Figure captions (starts on separate page).
8. Figures (each on a separate page).
9. Appendixes (each on a separate page).

Headings

Written reports usually have three levels of headings: main headings, side headings, and paragraph headings. Short papers may need only one or two levels of headings.

Main Headings

Main headings are the principal headings. They are centered on the page, the first letter of each main word is capitalized, and no period is placed at the end. With all headings, use of bold font to highlight the text is recommended.

Side Headings

The second level of headings is referred to as side headings. These headings are typed at the side of the page flush with the margin. Again, the first letter of each main word is capitalized. All words are italicized, and no period is placed at the end.

Paragraph headings. The third level of headings is referred to as a paragraph heading. These headings are typed with the paragraph indentation as here. Only the first letter of the first word is capitalized. The heading is italicized, the last word is followed by a period, and one space later the text begins.

Writing Style

The APA *Publication Manual* provides some very helpful guidelines regarding writing style. As noted earlier, Chapter 2 of the manual is particularly helpful. Besides working on improving your writing style, you need to develop skill in using language that is not biased by gender, sexual orientation, race, disabilities, or age. These issues are also addressed in Chapter 2 of the manual.

Writing the Manuscript

For many, the most difficult part of doing the research is writing the report. Writing is a solitary activity; it is not compatible with socializing. To write a concise, coherent report requires planning, persistence, skill, and concentration. It is easy to put off writing until the deadline is upon you. For many, simply getting started writing is a very difficult task. Other tasks are suddenly given higher priority or become more urgent. One major reason for procrastinating is that the task of writing the report seems overwhelming. You are probably thinking of going from the beginning to the final copy—from "start" to "finish"—in one marathon session. You are concerned about getting all the ideas into the report and expressing the ideas adequately.

Let's look at some procedures that should be helpful in writing your report. Perhaps the single most important consideration is to allow sufficient time to complete the report. Don't hobble yourself with added stress of fighting a course deadline. Consider the advantages and benefits that you will derive from finishing early. Set a realistic deadline earlier than the one set by the instructor. Perhaps you can use some self-control techniques, such as rewarding yourself for progress and punishing yourself for falling behind.

To make the task of writing the report more manageable, consider doing one section at a time. You do not have to start with the introduction and proceed through each section in their given order. There are no binding rules concerning which section should be written first. Begin with the section that is of greatest importance to you. Once this decision is made, then develop an outline that will organize what you want to say. If your notes and references are on cards (3×5 or 5×7), you can arrange them in the order you plan to write as an alternative to the outline.

After the outline is arranged, then start to write. Let your ideas flow. Do not worry about revising and restructuring your sentences. Writing and revising are two different tasks requiring two different mental sets. Revising requires more intense effort and concentration on a single sentence. Writing requires that the ideas and thoughts simply be expressed. After the ideas are out, some reorganization can take place, and sentences can be refined or restructured. Your first draft will be and should be "rough."

Upon completion of the first draft, begin the task of revising it. Is the organization reasonable? Correct errors in spelling, grammar, and logic. Look at your sentences and word structure. Are there any ambiguous expressions or awkward sentences? Again, do not attempt to compose a final polished report. After this second revision is complete, put the report aside for a few days. Putting the report aside is important for several reasons. It allows you to do other things that may be beginning to distract you. Setting the report aside also allows you to return to it with a different perspective. Errors become more glaring, cumbersome sentences stand out, needed revisions become more obvious. Also, new insights may occur during the period the report was set aside. During that period, you may want to have a fellow student read the report simply for clarity. Often a fresh reader can detect unclear or confusing statements that you may have repeatedly missed.

In completing the final draft, do not be satisfied with anything less than your best efforts. You should also be your own severest critic. If you would like a standard with which to compare your writing, ask your instructor to name a few excellent writers whose published works you can read. It is sometimes helpful to observe their writing style when trying to improve your own. You can develop your own distinctive style after you have mastered some of the basic skills.

As another aid to writing a research report, Table 16.1 presents the guidelines that one of your authors uses when he grades student research reports. It is likely that your course instructor uses similar criteria.

Making an Oral Presentation

Purpose of an Oral Presentation

The bulk of any scientific conference consists of oral presentations. In most cases, these presentations represent the researcher's most recent findings. Thus, it is an important way for researchers to stay abreast of new developments in the field. It also provides an opportunity for the researcher to receive feedback from others through both formal and informal question/answer sessions at the conference.

Typically, a conference will put out a call for submissions several months before the conference. Researchers then submit an abstract of their proposed presentation, which is reviewed and then either accepted for the program or rejected. The level of peer review is much less stringent than that for publication. Opportunities exist for student researchers to present at their own university, at regional conferences, and at national conferences.

Sections of the Presentation

The organization of the presentation is at the discretion of the presenter. However, an oral presentation of research findings typically follows a format similar to that of manuscripts. It includes an introduction, a description of the methods, a presentation of the results, and a discussion of the findings.

Working From Notes

In some cases, the researcher makes an oral presentation by simply reading a written manuscript. In many cases, student researchers make their first presentation by reading a written research report. We do not recommend this! How much do you enjoy having a professor lecture by reading his/her notes from a lectern? Such presentations can be good but are more often boring. You should know your research project well enough to simply talk about it, using an outline or note cards to remind you of important points that you want to make. Another useful strategy is to let your visual aids serve as your outline and notes.

Table 16.1 **Grading Form: Research Report**

Section	Does Not Apply	Unsatisfactory	Satisfactory	Good	Very Good	Points Possible	Points Awarded
Abstract						10	
Purpose of study							
Summary of methods							
Summary of results							
Introduction						20	
Introduction to the area							
Literature review							
Statement of purpose/ hypotheses							
Method						20	
Description of participants							
Description of materials							
Description of procedures							
Results						20	
Presentation of descriptive statistics							
Presentation of inferential statistics							
Use and format of figures/tables							
Description of results							
Discussion						20	
Summary of findings							
Relationship to hypotheses							
Relationship to theory/ literature							
Comment on shortcomings							
Practical applications							
Ideas for future research							
Other						10	
Title page							
References							
Adherence to APA format							
Writing style							
TOTAL						100	

Table 16.2	Quick Tips for an Effective Oral Presentation
1. Develop sections similar to that of a manuscript.	
2. Present from notes; do not read your presentation.	
3. Use visual aids (outlines, figures, tables, pictures, videos, Web sites).	
4. Relax.	
5. Make eye contact with the audience.	
6. Speak slowly.	
7. Avoid ums and uhs.	
8. Be enthusiastic.	
9. Practice, practice, practice.	

Visual Aids

Visual aids may take the form of written outlines, pictures, tables, figures, and more recently, Web sites on the Internet. They can provide organization for your presentation, help describe your experimental design, help describe your results, and help summarize your major points. Overhead transparencies are still a very popular method of displaying information to an audience. Electronic presentations (such as PowerPoint or Corel) are becoming popular and offer new opportunities for video clips and linking to sites on the Internet. It is wise to remember that technology does not always function properly, so you should have overhead transparencies as a backup. Visual aids should have a minimal amount of text, and the text presented should be large enough for easy reading. Another nice feature of many presentations is the use of a laser pointer. With this device, you can direct the viewers' attention to a particular part of the visual display (such as a particular data point on a graph).

Speaking Tips

As many of you know firsthand, public speaking can cause anxiety. Often, it is this anxiety that leads to behaviors during public speaking that make the presentation less effective. As a speaker, you should make eye contact with the audience and shift your gaze around the room. This requires that you not read a set of written notes or the text projected on a screen. You should also avoid the danger of speaking too fast. Your audience needs time to process the information that you are presenting. This is especially true when presenting information in a table or figure. You must remember that although you are very familiar with the data, this is the first time that your audience has viewed this information. Try to avoid ums and uhs. Be sure to practice your presentation several times and to deliver it with enthusiasm. As noted at the beginning of the chapter, making a high-quality presentation takes much effort but also results in a very rewarding sense of accomplishment.

Table 16.2 summarizes these suggestions for an effective oral presentation.

● Making a Poster Presentation

Purpose of Poster Sessions

Poster sessions provide yet another way for researchers to disseminate information and are a common feature at scientific conferences. Normally, poster sessions last about one hour, and there may be 50 other posters set up in the same room. At least one of the authors remains with the poster during the session. Attendees will often peruse the poster titles and stop at those that arouse interest. Because at least one author is present, poster sessions provide a wonderful opportunity to meet and talk with the researcher.

Sections of the Poster

Although APA guidelines do not apply to posters, the sections are often the same as in a research report. The organization hosting the conference will typically provide submission guidelines with specific details regarding poster size and format. Most posters include introduction, method, results, and discussion sections. Because space is limited and because an author is available to fill in details, the text in each section is much more concise. In addition, posters lend themselves to visual depictions of data in the form of figures and tables.

Layout of the Poster

The layout of the poster should be user friendly and should maintain a professional appearance. The title should be clearly visible from a distance and should be descriptive. The poster should include the authors' names and affiliations, section headings, and visual aids. The main text should be in a large font size (16–18 pt.) so that it is readable from a distance of three feet. Each section should be positioned on the poster so that there is a clear flow from the left side of the poster to the right side. Figure 16.1 provides a sample layout.

Figure 16.1 Sample Layout for a Poster Presentation

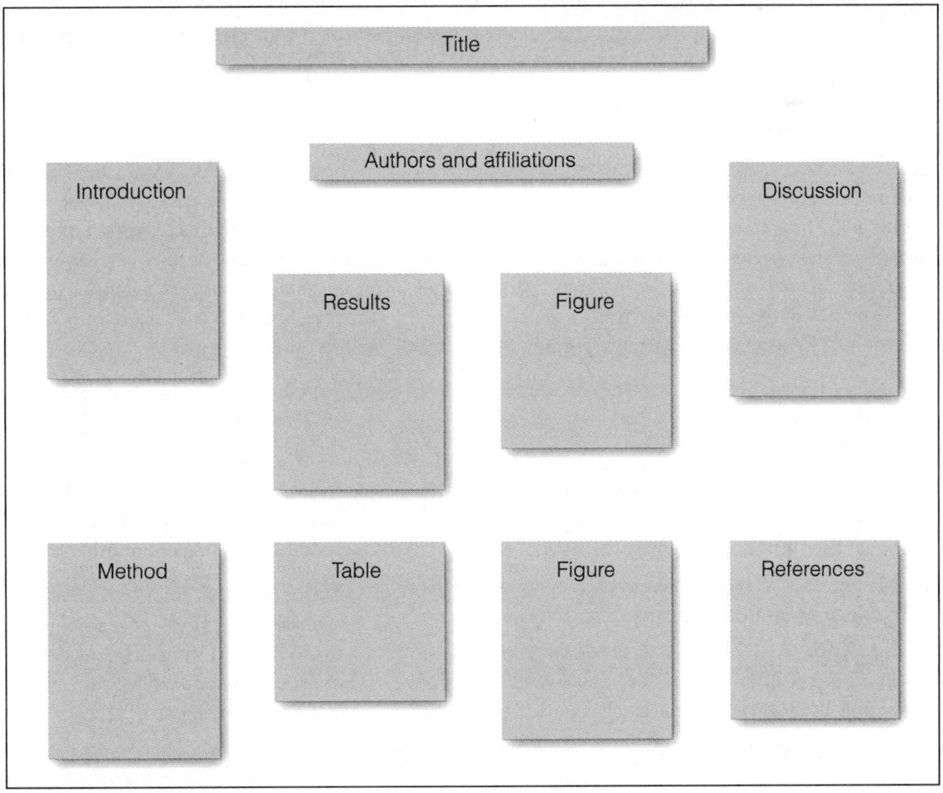

Table 16.3	Quick Tips for an Effective Poster Presentation
1. Provide a descriptive title.	
2. Clearly label all sections of the poster.	
3. Use a large font size (16–18 pt.).	
4. Make the text concise.	
5. Use graphs and tables to show results.	
6. Use a professional look.	
7. Have handouts available.	
8. Be prepared to summarize your study.	
9. Be prepared to discuss your study with others.	

Researcher's Role During the Session

As mentioned above, at least one of the researchers should stand with the poster. When someone approaches the poster, the researcher should introduce him/herself, offer to provide a summary, offer to provide a handout, and offer to answer any questions. This is a more proactive approach than most presenters take, but we believe that it makes a positive impression and encourages interaction among researchers.

Table 16.3 summarizes these suggestions for an effective poster presentation.

GENERAL SUMMARY

Behavioral research is most often disseminated via published research reports, oral presentations, and poster presentations. This is an essential part of the scientific process, and researchers should learn to do it well. The *Publication Manual of the American Psychological Association* provides guidelines for writing research reports. This manual describes the content, organization, and style of a manuscript. Oral presentations and poster presentations are important components of many scientific conferences. Both presentation types should include clear and concise information, professionalism in materials, professionalism in speaking, much preparation, and much practice. Research is valuable only if it is communicated well to others.

DETAILED SUMMARY

1. An important component of scientific research is the dissemination of information to the public and subsequent scrutiny and review by the public.

2. Written research reports are the most common means by which scientific information is shared with others.

3. The *Publication Manual of the American Psychological Association* (2001) provides extensive guidelines for writing and formatting a research report.

4. A quality research paper is clearly written, concise, thorough, objective, precise, and unbiased, and acknowledges the ideas of others.

5. Accuracy and thoroughness depend on obtaining information from original sources rather than secondary sources. Relying on secondary sources can result in problems that range from minor inaccuracies to major misstatements of fact.

6. The behavioral science community has developed a standard format for preparing a research report that includes title page, abstract, introduction, method, results, discussion, references, tables, figures, and appendixes.

7. The title page consists of a header, running head, title, authorship, and author affiliation. It is particularly important that the title be both brief and descriptive.

8. The abstract is a brief summary of the entire research paper.

9. The Introduction section provides a broad introduction to the topic, a review of the relevant literature, a basis and rationale for the study, and a precise statement of the research hypothesis.

10. The Method section describes the participants, apparatus/materials, and procedures in sufficient detail to enable someone else to replicate the study.

11. The Results section provides both descriptive and inferential statistics to evaluate the data. Presentation of data in tables and figures can be a useful way to summarize and describe data.

12. The Discussion section summarizes the findings, relates the findings to the hypothesis, relates the findings to what other researchers have found, notes advantages and limitations of the study, and discusses possible future research in the area.

13. Writing is not easy. Writers should allow sufficient time before deadlines, have someone else read the paper and provide feedback, and revise the writing until it is the best that can be achieved.

14. Much of the most recent research is presented orally by researchers at scientific conferences.

15. Effective oral presentations require that the presenter organize the talk, present from notes, use visual aids, relax, make eye contact, speak slowly, be enthusiastic, and practice.

16. Poster presentations are very popular at conferences. They provide an informal method for sharing research and discussing the research with the author.

17. Effective posters provide a descriptive title, clearly label all sections of the poster, use a large font size, use concise text, use graphs and tables, and look professional. An effective presenter has handouts available, is prepared to summarize the study to visitors, and is prepared to discuss the study with visitors.

 ## WEB RESOURCES TO INCREASE LEARNING

For many tips on good writing style, visit the classic reference book *Elements of Style* by William Strunk, Jr., online at http://www.bartleby.com/141/index.html.

The chapter outline, chapter summaries, key terms and definitions, additional chapter questions, chapter exercises, and links to relevant Web sites are available at the course Web site (**http://psychology.wadsworth.com/lammers_badia1e**). Explore the interactive workshop "APA Style."

CHAPTER 17

SUMMARY OF BEHAVIORAL RESEARCH

The Research Enterprise

Your Skills as a Researcher

Your Skills as a Critical Consumer of Research and Research-Related Information

A Final Word

The Research Enterprise

We learn about our world in many different ways. Much of what each of us knows is the result of personal experiences, our everyday interaction with the world. However, there is also much we know that we have not experienced directly. People, particularly authority figures (such as parents, teachers, and ministers), share information with us. At other times, we learn through a rationalist approach, in that we take pieces of existing knowledge and, often using logic, derive new ideas about the world. Finally, much of what we know about our world is based on empiricism. The empirical approach emphasizes the importance of testing ideas or hypotheses by making systematic observations. Although we use this approach informally during our normal course of experiencing the world, the research enterprise provides a more formal, systematic, and objective prescription for learning about our world. This scientific approach to obtaining knowledge is not perfect, and there is value in all approaches. However, it is a very powerful method that leads to much confidence in the conclusions that we draw.

As you know, the scientific approach can be applied to many disciplines of study, including biology, astronomy, physics, geology, and so on. The use of the scientific method to better understand human behavior is both valuable and fascinating. It is one thing to be able to predict the movement of a planet; it is another to predict the behavior of a person. Human behavior is so complex, with so many variables interacting to result in even a simple act or a simple thought. Other ways of knowing (personal experience, authority, rationalism) can provide only so much understanding about human behavior. In fact, other ways of knowing often provide misunderstanding and misconceptions about human behavior. An empirical approach using the scientific method is designed to avoid misunderstanding and is truly the foundation of the discipline we call psychology. It is particularly fascinating that we, as behavioral scientists, have used our thoughts and behaviors to develop methods for better understanding our thoughts and behaviors. We are using the very processes that we seek to understand.

As we embark on behavioral research to better understand ourselves, there are limits to what we can do. We must always consider how research participants are treated. Attention to ethical issues is amplified by some research in the past that was improper. The Tuskegee Syphilis Study involved studying men with a disease without their being fully informed and later withholding treatment. The Milgram shock studies put participants in a position where they believed that they were delivering harmful shocks to another person. The Zimbardo Prison Study resulted in a situation in which participants who assumed the role of prison guards exhibited degrading treatment of other participants who assumed the role of prisoners.

The field of behavioral research has learned much about ethical treatment from these studies and others. The American Psychological Association now has very clear ethical guidelines for the treatment of both human and nonhuman research participants. For human research, the guidelines emphasize proper informed consent of participants, deception only when necessary, and the general guide that no participants should feel degraded or mistreated in any way. For animal research, the guidelines emphasize proper care of animals, proper housing, and the use of methods to reduce any pain and suffering. The use of animals in research will continue to be a hotly debated issue. We each have our own position on this issue, and we should each have a right to have our own position. However, each of us should be responsible enough to be informed regarding the arguments on all sides of the issue so that our position is an informed one and not a position guided by misconceptions.

Your Skills as a Researcher

In this book, you have been introduced to the fundamentals of behavioral research. These fundamentals begin with asking research questions. We get interested in a particular area of psychology, we learn about that area and what other researchers have done, and we develop testable questions that we believe will add to the existing knowledge. These questions can be answered using either experimental, quasi-experimental, or nonexperimental research designs.

As you have seen, experimental designs are the most powerful in that they lead to cause–effect conclusions. Experimental designs begin with the expression of research questions as hypotheses. These hypotheses make predictions about how people (or animals) should behave given a particular set of circumstances and clearly identify the variables to be studied. The independent variable is the one that is manipulated by the researcher, and the dependent variable is the one that is observed for possible changes. As you would expect with the scientific method, these variables must be measured. Numbers must be assigned to different levels of each variable. These numbers exist on a particular scale of measurement (nominal, ordinal, interval, or ratio) and, as such, provide different types of information about the variable. For many variables, measurement requires observation of behavior.

Measurement and observation are particularly important issues in psychological research because we are often dealing with fuzzy concepts such as aggression, intelligence, memory, or love. Observations can be made in different ways. The researcher may be a participant observer or a nonparticipant observer; each approach has its advantages and disadvantages. Observations often occur on a particular schedule and can involve measures of frequency, duration, and/or intervals. Measurements made by equipment (such as computers) are often very reliable as long as you ensure that the equipment is calibrated and working properly. However, measurements made by human observers are susceptible to differences in criteria and the presence of bias. Thus, human observations should be assessed for reliability by using multiple observers and calculating interobserver agreement. This technique provides some level of confidence that you are indeed observing and measuring what you believe you are observing and measuring.

As you realize by now, many of the research questions that we ask in psychology involve questions about a very large number of individuals (for example, all children, everyone with depression, all humans). It is not possible to collect data from all of those individuals, but we would like to generalize our findings to them. Thus, we must collect data from samples of the population. We strive for samples that are representative of the population, and we have learned about sampling techniques that help achieve this goal. The advantages of random sampling were emphasized, and the methods of stratified random sampling, convenience sampling, and quota sampling were also discussed.

When we examine the data collected from samples, we are interested in the nature of the variability in the scores obtained. We predict that some of this variability in scores will be systematic variance due to manipulation of the independent variable. But we also understand that some of the variability in scores is likely the result of systematic error (confounding variables) and random error. These sources of variance are due to extraneous variables in the research and originate from the participants, the experimenters, and/or the method used. The presence of extraneous variables makes it more difficult for us to see any effects of the independent variable on our dependent variable. Thus, one of our major goals in conducting behavioral research is to design and control the experimental situation in ways that reduce extraneous variability. By doing this, we increase both the internal and external validity of our research.

The use of these control techniques is the hallmark of experimental research. The good researcher knows that extraneous variables can creep in at every step of the research process. Researchers can control extraneous variables through the experiment setting, consent, instructions, sampling techniques, assignment techniques, observation techniques, measurement techniques, interactions with participants, and the use of research designs with proper control groups. The research design may involve independent samples, correlated samples, designs with more than one independent variable, or designs that study a single participant over time. The use of the experimental techniques permits the researcher to test cause–effect hypotheses and to draw cause–effect conclusions. To be able to understand whether one variable causes changes in another variable is the most powerful type of information that we can learn in behavioral research.

Although not as powerful, quasi-experimental and nonexperimental research designs also provide valuable information that increases our understanding of psychology. Quasi-experiments are nearly identical to true experiments with the exception that participants are not randomly assigned to the experimental conditions. Because of this, the potential presence of extraneous variables makes cause–effect conclusions risky. Nonexperimental designs can include correlational designs, ex post facto designs, naturalistic observation, and qualitative research. Nonexperimental designs are usually selected when the independent variable cannot be manipulated by the researcher or should not be manipulated for ethical reasons. Correlational designs simply measure different variables to determine whether any relationship, either positive or negative, exists between or among them. Ex post facto designs focus on potential differences between groups in which the independent variable is not manipulated by the researcher and the different groups already exist. Naturalistic observation provides real-world descriptions of behavior in situations where the researcher has little or no control over the environment. Qualitative research is based on the insights that psychologists gain by interacting with individuals. Each of these research methods can be used to add important information as we continue on our journey to better understand ourselves.

Equipped with these tools, you may decide to go into a research-related field. University professors conduct both basic and applied research. The federal government hires researchers to evaluate federal programs and to conduct behavioral research, both basic and applied. State governments also hire researchers to evaluate state programs. Businesses and large corporations hire researchers to address issues such as personnel selection, employee satisfaction, management structure, effective advertising/marketing of products, and characteristics of consumers. In fact, there are some companies whose mission is to conduct research (for example, companies that conduct surveys and polls for clients).

Even if you do not enter a career that is research related, you may be able to apply research techniques to a career that normally does not take advantage of research to provide important information. For example, you may own or work for a business that is trying to decide whether advertising for customers in the local paper is cost effective. Is the extra income generated greater than the advertising costs? Instead of a subjective assessment or a poorly designed assessment with data, you could use a time-series design. For example, you could record advertising expenses and income over a four-month period, during which you advertise only during Months 2 and 4. You could then plot your income (minus advertising expenses) across the four months to determine whether adjusted income is higher during months when you advertise. This is just one example out of many possibilities for using research methods to increase the effectiveness of decision making. You now have the fundamental skills to do this. When you market yourself to potential employers, make sure that they know you have these skills.

Your Skills as a Critical Consumer of Research and Research-Related Information

No matter what you do in life, you will be constantly exposed to research-related information. This type of information is pervasive. You experience it in college classes, in business meetings, in the newspaper, in all types of magazines, on the nightly news, on a variety of other television programs, on the radio, on Internet sites, and in conversations. Much of this information is good, some is mediocre, and much of it is just crap! To become a more educated and informed citizen, you need to be a critical consumer of this type of information. The "Thinking Critically About Everyday Information" box in each chapter of this book provided you with examples of everyday information that required critical evaluation. You now have the fundamental skills to ask the right questions and do your own evaluations. We hope and expect that you will.

A Final Word

We know that research design concepts are a challenge to learn and may not be as interesting as learning about people with psychological disorders. We understand that a course in research design is often the second least anticipated course in the psychology curriculum (we know which is first—Statistics!). Therefore, we congratulate you on your completion of this course.

We hope that we have presented the concepts clearly, provided interesting and informative examples, increased your appreciation of behavioral research, helped you become a more critical consumer of information, and perhaps increased your interest in conducting research in the future. You have learned many truly important concepts and skills in this book. We wish you the best of luck in the future.

APPENDIX A

STATISTICAL TABLES

Table A.1	Random Numbers							
	1	**2**	**3**	**4**	**5**	**6**	**7**	**8**	**9**
1	32942	95416	42339	59045	26693	49057	87496	20624	14819
2	07410	99859	83828	21409	29094	65114	36701	25762	12827
3	59981	68155	45673	76210	58219	45738	29550	24736	09574
4	46251	25437	69654	99716	11563	08803	86027	51867	12116
5	65558	51904	93123	27887	53138	21488	09095	78777	71240
6	99187	19258	86421	16401	19397	83297	40111	49326	81686
7	35641	00301	16096	34775	21562	97983	45040	19200	16383
8	14031	00936	81518	48440	02218	04756	19506	60695	88494
9	60677	15076	92554	26042	23472	69869	62877	19584	39576
10	66314	05212	67859	89356	20056	30648	87349	20389	53805
11	20416	87410	75646	64176	82752	63606	37011	57346	69512
12	28701	56992	70423	62415	40807	98086	58850	28968	45297
13	74579	33844	33426	07570	00728	07079	19322	56325	84819
14	62615	52342	82968	75540	80045	53069	20665	21282	07768
15	93945	06293	22879	08161	01442	75071	21427	94842	26210
16	75689	76131	96837	67450	44511	50424	82848	41975	71663
17	02921	16919	35424	93209	52133	87327	95897	65171	20376
18	14295	34969	14216	03191	61647	30296	66667	10101	63203
19	05303	91109	82403	40312	62191	67023	90073	83205	71344
20	57071	90357	12901	08899	91039	67251	28701	03846	94589
21	78471	57741	13599	84390	32146	00871	09354	22745	65806
22	89242	79337	59293	47481	07740	43345	25716	70020	54005
23	14955	59592	97035	80430	87220	06392	79028	57123	52872
24	42446	41880	37415	47472	04513	49494	08860	08038	43624
25	18534	22346	54556	17558	73689	14894	05030	19561	56517
26	39284	33737	42512	86411	23753	29690	26096	81361	93099
27	33922	37329	89911	55876	28379	81031	22058	21487	54613
28	78355	54013	50774	30666	61205	42574	47773	36027	27174
29	08845	99145	94316	88974	29828	97069	90327	61842	29604
30	01769	71825	55957	98271	02784	66731	40311	88495	18821
31	17639	38284	59478	90409	21997	56199	30068	82800	69692
32	05851	58653	99949	63505	40409	85551	90729	64938	52403
33	42396	40112	11469	03476	03328	84238	26570	51790	42122
34	13318	14192	98167	75631	74141	22369	36757	89117	54998
35	60571	54786	26281	01855	30706	66578	32019	65884	58485
36	09531	81853	59334	70929	03544	18510	89541	13555	21168
37	72865	16829	86542	00396	20363	13010	69645	49608	54738
38	56324	31093	77924	28622	83543	28912	15059	80192	83964
39	78192	21626	91399	07235	07104	73652	64425	85149	75409
40	64666	34767	97298	92708	01994	53188	78476	07804	62404
41	82201	75694	02808	65983	74373	66693	13094	74183	73020
42	15360	73776	40914	85190	54278	99054	62944	47351	89098
43	68142	67957	70896	37983	20487	95350	16371	03426	13895
44	19138	31200	30616	14639	44406	44236	57360	81644	94761
45	28155	03521	36415	78452	92359	81091	56513	88321	97910
46	87971	29031	51780	27376	81056	86155	55488	50590	74514
47	58147	68841	53625	02059	75223	16783	19272	61994	71090
48	18875	52809	70594	41649	32935	26430	82096	01605	65846
49	75109	56474	74111	31966	29969	70093	98901	84550	25769
50	35983	03742	76822	12073	59463	84420	15868	99505	11426

Table A.2 The Normal Distribution

Column A gives the positive
z score.

Column B gives the area
between the mean and z.
Because the curve is symmet-
rical, areas for negative z
scores are the same as for
positive ones.

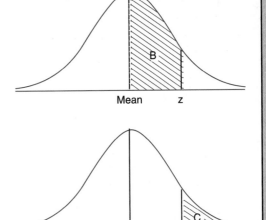

Column C gives the area that
is beyond z.

How to Use Table A.2: The values in this table represent the proportion of areas in the
standard normal curve, which has a mean of 0, a standard deviation of 1.00, and a total
area equal to 1.00. The raw scores must first be transformed into a z score. Column A
represents this z score, Column B represents the distance between the mean of the
standard normal distribution (0) and the z score, and Column C represents the
proportion of the area beyond a given z.

(continued)

Table A.2 The Normal Distribution (continued)

(A) z	(B) Area Between Mean and z	(C) Area Beyond z	(A) z	(B) Area Between Mean and z	(C) Area Beyond z	(A) z	(B) Area Between Mean and z	(C) Area Beyond z
0.00	.0000	.5000	0.45	.1736	.3264	0.90	.3159	.1841
0.01	.0040	.4960	0.46	.1772	.3228	0.91	.3186	.1814
0.02	.0080	.4920	0.47	.1808	.3192	0.92	.3212	.1788
0.03	.0120	.4880	0.48	.1844	.3156	0.93	.3238	.1762
0.04	.0160	.4840	0.49	.1879	.3121	0.94	.3264	.1736
0.05	.0199	.4801	0.50	.1915	.3085	0.95	.3289	.1711
0.06	.0239	.4761	0.51	.1950	.3050	0.96	.3315	.1685
0.07	.0279	.4721	0.52	.1985	.3015	0.97	.3340	.1660
0.08	.0319	.4681	0.53	.2019	.2981	0.98	.3365	.1635
0.09	.0359	.4641	0.54	.2054	.2946	0.99	.3389	.1611
0.10	.0398	.4602	0.55	.2088	.2912	1.00	.3413	.1587
0.11	.0438	.4562	0.56	.2123	.2877	1.01	.3438	.1562
0.12	.0478	.4522	0.57	.2157	.2843	1.02	.3461	.1539
0.13	.0517	.4483	0.58	.2190	.2810	1.03	.3485	.1515
0.14	.0557	.4443	0.59	.2224	.2776	1.04	.3508	.1492
0.15	.0596	.4404	0.60	.2257	.2743	1.05	.3531	.1469
0.16	.0636	.4364	0.61	.2291	.2709	1.06	.3554	.1446
0.17	.0675	.4325	0.62	.2324	.2676	1.07	.3577	.1423
0.18	.0714	.4286	0.63	.2357	.2643	1.08	.3599	.1401
0.19	.0753	.4247	0.64	.2389	.2611	1.09	.3621	.1379
0.20	.0793	.4207	0.65	.2422	.2578	1.10	.3643	.1357
0.21	.0832	.4168	0.66	.2454	.2546	1.11	.3665	.1335
0.22	.0871	.4129	0.67	.2486	.2514	1.12	.3686	.1314
0.23	.0910	.4090	0.68	.2517	.2483	1.13	.3708	.1292
0.24	.0948	.4052	0.69	.2549	.2451	1.14	.3729	.1271
0.25	.0987	.4013	0.70	.2580	.2420	1.15	.3749	.1251
0.26	.1026	.3974	0.71	.2611	.2389	1.16	.3770	.1230
0.27	.1064	.3936	0.72	.2642	.2358	1.17	.3790	.1210
0.28	.1103	.3897	0.73	.2673	.2327	1.18	.3810	.1190
0.29	.1141	.3859	0.74	.2704	.2296	1.19	.3830	.1170
0.30	.1179	.3821	0.75	.2734	.2266	1.20	.3849	.1151
0.31	.1217	.3783	0.76	.2764	.2236	1.21	.3869	.1131
0.32	.1255	.3745	0.77	.2794	.2206	1.22	.3888	.1112
0.33	.1293	.3707	0.78	.2823	.2177	1.23	.3907	.1093
0.34	.1331	.3669	0.79	.2852	.2148	1.24	.3925	.1075
0.35	.1368	.3632	0.80	.2881	.2119	1.25	.3944	.1056
0.36	.1406	.3594	0.81	.2910	.2090	1.26	.3962	.1038
0.37	.1443	.3557	0.82	.2939	.2061	1.27	.3980	.1020
0.38	.1480	.3520	0.83	.2967	.2033	1.28	.3997	.1003
0.39	.1517	.3483	0.84	.2995	.2005	1.29	.4015	.0985
0.40	.1554	.3446	0.85	.3023	.1977	1.30	.4032	.0968
0.41	.1591	.3409	0.86	.3051	.1949	1.31	.4049	.0951
0.42	.1628	.3372	0.87	.3078	.1922	1.32	.4066	.0934
0.43	.1664	.3336	0.88	.3106	.1894	1.33	.4082	.0918
0.44	.1700	.3300	0.89	.3133	.1867	1.34	.4099	.0901

(continued)

| Table A.2 | The Normal Distribution *(continued)* |

(A) z	(B) Area Between Mean and z	(C) Area Beyond z	(A) z	(B) Area Between Mean and z	(C) Area Beyond z	(A) z	(B) Area Between Mean and z	(C) Area Beyond z
1.35	.4115	.0885	1.80	.4641	.0359	2.25	.4878	.0122
1.36	.4131	.0869	1.81	.4649	.0351	2.26	.4881	.0119
1.37	.4147	.0853	1.82	.4656	.0344	2.27	.4884	.0116
1.38	.4162	.0838	1.83	.4664	.0336	2.28	.4887	.0113
1.39	.4177	.0823	1.84	.4671	.0329	2.29	.4890	.0110
1.40	.4192	.0808	1.85	.4678	.0322	2.30	.4893	.0107
1.41	.4207	.0793	1.86	.4686	.0314	2.31	.4896	.0104
1.42	.4222	.0778	1.87	.4693	.0307	2.32	.4898	.0102
1.43	.4236	.0764	1.88	.4699	.0301	2.33	.4901	.0099
1.44	.4251	.0749	1.89	.4706	.0294	2.34	.4904	.0096
1.45	.4265	.0735	1.90	.4713	.0287	2.35	.4906	.0094
1.46	.4279	.0721	1.91	.4719	.0281	2.36	.4909	.0091
1.47	.4292	.0708	1.92	.4726	.0274	2.37	.4911	.0089
1.48	.4306	.0694	1.93	.4732	.0268	2.38	.4913	.0087
1.49	.4319	.0681	1.94	.4738	.0262	2.39	.4916	.0084
1.50	.4332	.0668	1.95	.4744	.0256	2.40	.4918	.0082
1.51	.4345	.0655	1.96	.4750	.0250	2.41	.4920	.0080
1.52	.4357	.0643	1.97	.4756	.0244	2.42	.4922	.0078
1.53	.4370	.0630	1.98	.4761	.0239	2.43	.4925	.0075
1.54	.4382	.0618	1.99	.4767	.0233	2.44	.4927	.0073
1.55	.4394	.0606	2.00	.4772	.0228	2.45	.4929	.0071
1.56	.4406	.0594	2.01	.4778	.0222	2.46	.4931	.0069
1.57	.4418	.0582	2.02	.4783	.0217	2.47	.4932	.0068
1.58	.4429	.0571	2.03	.4788	.0212	2.48	.4934	.0066
1.59	.4441	.0559	2.04	.4793	.0207	2.49	.4936	.0064
1.60	.4452	.0548	2.05	.4798	.0202	2.50	.4938	.0062
1.61	.4463	.0537	2.06	.4803	.0197	2.51	.4940	.0060
1.62	.4474	.0526	2.07	.4808	.0192	2.52	.4941	.0059
1.63	.4484	.0516	2.08	.4812	.0188	2.53	.4943	.0057
1.64	.4495	.0505	2.09	.4817	.0183	2.54	.4945	.0055
1.65	.4505	.0495	2.10	.4821	.0179	2.55	.4946	.0054
1.66	.4515	.0485	2.11	.4826	.0174	2.56	.4948	.0052
1.67	.4525	.0475	2.12	.4830	.0170	2.47	.4949	.0051
1.68	.4535	.0465	2.13	.4834	.0166	2.58	.4951	.0049
1.69	.4545	.0455	2.14	.4838	.0162	2.59	.4952	.0048
1.70	.4554	.0446	2.15	.4842	.0158	2.60	.4953	.0047
1.71	.4564	.0436	2.16	.4846	.0154	2.61	.4955	.0045
1.72	.4573	.0427	2.17	.4850	.0150	2.62	.4956	.0044
1.73	.4582	.0418	2.18	.4854	.0146	2.63	.4957	.0043
1.74	.4591	.0409	2.19	.4857	.0143	2.64	.4959	.0041
1.75	.4599	.0401	2.20	.4861	.0139	2.65	.4960	.0040
1.76	.4608	.0392	2.21	.4864	.0136	2.66	.4961	.0039
1.77	.4616	.0384	2.22	.4868	.0132	2.67	.4962	.0038
1.78	.4625	.0375	2.23	.4871	.0129	2.68	.4963	.0037
1.79	.4633	.0367	2.24	.4875	.0125	2.69	.4964	.0036

(continued)

Table A.2   The Normal Distribution *(continued)*

(A) z	(B) Area Between Mean and z	(C) Area Beyond z	(A) z	(B) Area Between Mean and z	(C) Area Beyond z	(A) z	(B) Area Between Mean and z	(C) Area Beyond z
2.70	.4965	.0035	2.95	.4984	.0016	3.20	.4993	.0007
2.71	.4966	.0034	2.96	.4985	.0015	3.21	.4993	.0007
2.72	.4967	.0033	2.97	.4985	.0015	3.22	.4994	.0006
2.73	.4968	.0032	2.98	.4986	.0014	3.23	.4994	.0006
2.74	.4969	.0031	2.99	.4986	.0014	3.24	.4994	.0006
2.75	.4970	.0030	3.00	.4987	.0013	3.25	.4994	.0006
2.76	.4971	.0029	3.01	.4987	.0013	3.30	.4995	.0005
2.77	.4972	.0028	3.02	.4987	.0013	3.35	.4996	.0004
2.78	.4973	.0027	3.03	.4988	.0012	3.40	.4997	.0003
2.79	.4974	.0026	3.04	.4988	.0012	3.45	.4997	.0003
2.80	.4974	.0026	3.05	.4989	.0011	3.50	.4998	.0002
2.81	.4975	.0025	3.06	.4989	.0011	3.60	.4998	.0002
2.82	.4976	.0024	3.07	.4989	.0011	3.70	.4999	.0001
2.83	.4977	.0023	3.08	.4990	.0010	3.80	.4999	.0001
2.84	.4977	.0023	3.09	.4990	.0010	3.90	.49995	.00005
2.85	.4978	.0022	3.10	.4990	.0010	4.00	.49997	.00003
2.86	.4979	.0021	3.11	.4991	.0009			
2.87	.4979	.0021	3.12	.4991	.0009			
2.88	.4980	.0020	3.13	.4991	.0009			
2.89	.4981	.0019	3.14	.4992	.0008			
2.90	.4981	.0019	3.15	.4992	.0008			
2.91	.4982	.0018	3.16	.4992	.0008			
2.92	.4982	.0018	3.17	.4992	.0008			
2.93	.4983	.0017	3.18	.4993	.0007			
2.94	.4984	.0016	3.19	.4993	.0007			

SAMPLE RESEARCH REPORT

Running head: SELF-PRESENTATION AND HINDSIGHT BIAS

Relationship Between Self-Presentation and Hindsight Bias

Student's Name

University of Central Arkansas

Abstract

Hindsight bias is a tendency for people to believe that they would have known the answer to a question once the answer is revealed. This study examined the effect of increased social pressure on hindsight bias. Participants were randomly assigned to one of four groups. Group 1 received the answers to the questions and believed that their "knowledge" score would be shared with other participants (Answer/Share), Group 2 was Answer/No Share, Group 3 was No Answer/Share, and Group 4 was No Answer/No Share. As expected, groups that received the answers demonstrated greater hindsight bias. However, participants in groups that believed their score would be shared demonstrated reduced hindsight bias.

Relationship Between Self-Presentation and Hindsight Bias

By claiming to have known something after the fact, people exhibit the social phenomenon identified as hindsight bias. It is formally defined by social psychologists as the tendency to judge events as more predictable when the outcome information is known (Myers, 1999). It is commonly referred to as the "I knew it all along" phenomenon. In addition to claiming to have known something, people often have a need to self-present themselves in a positive manner. This enables people to protect their self-concepts (Myers, 1999). There have been extensive investigations regarding these two social psychological theories.

Hindsight bias has a strong, comprehensive foundation in people's interactions. It is a phenomenon that is not restricted to certain disciplines or matters of life (Szalanski & Willham, 1991). Hindsight has been used as an explanation for having known about layoffs, the fate of the stock market, medical diagnoses, and answers to test questions (Melvin & Mellor, 1991; Szanlanski & Willham, 1991). In two studies by Pohl and Hell (1996), people clung to the hindsight bias after having been informed of the bias and after being previously informed of the study's design. Studies have uncovered several factors that produce this effect.

Hindsight bias is influenced by several factors. It is greater when the subject matter has positive self-relevance (Melvin & Mellor, 1991), when outcome is important to the situation, when the situation is unambiguous, and when less time is given to respond (Creyer & Ross, 1993). However, it has been reported that if the subject matter's outcome is either surprising or not relevant to the person making the judgment, the bias will be reduced (Melvin & Mellor, 1991; Ofir & Mazursky, 1997).

Self-presentation, also widely utilized by people, has similar factors affecting it. People are more likely to self-present when the social context is of importance, self-relevant, beneficial, related to attractive skills, believable, and will be publicly known (Schlenker, Weigold, & Hallam, 1990). In addition, Friedrich (1996) found that self-serving and self-presentation were high when socially desirable circumstances were at an above average level. In this study, it was found that people falsely saw themselves as better than others at performing socially desirable tasks. However, the study by Schlenker et al. (1990) found that low self-esteem decreased self-presentation.

Knowing that there are many factors that affect the self-serving bias, Campbell and Sedickedes (1999) put together a meta-analytic study of 14 factors that contribute to the bias. The 14 factors were (1) role of actor or observer, (2) task importance, (3) self-esteem, (4) achievement motivation, (5) self-focused attention, (6) choice in participation, (7) outcome expectancies, (8) perceived difficulty, (9) competitive versus noncompetitive, (10) equal or unequal status between people, (11) positive or negative affect, (12) locus of control, (13) gender, and (14) task type. The combination of these factors was renamed self-threat. The study found that when people's favorable views of themselves were questioned, mocked, or challenged, the person was motivated to present more self-serving bias.

Along with all the research pertaining to hindsight bias, several theories have been formed. One of the first theories is that memory has been impaired (Stahlberg, Eller, Maass, & Frey, 1995). This theory states that hindsight bias occurs because new knowledge becomes integrated with previous knowledge and this leads to a permanent modification. Another, more recent theory is that using the hindsight bias is necessary for memory in that it updates the base of knowledge for that particular situation involving hindsight bias (Hoffrage, Hertwig, & Gigerenzer, 2000). A view that directly relates to this study is the self-presentational explanation. Stahlberg et al. (1995) explain that the hindsight bias can be driven by the motivation to self-present. This enables people to maintain high self-esteem. Stahlberg's study did not find confirmation for this explanation, but it did focus on hindsight biases between groups. Another study also found that although hindsight bias was prevalent, it was not affected by self-presentation (Pohl, Stahlberg, & Frey, 1999). This study did not concentrate on the manipulation in creating motivation for self-presentation.

The current study seeks to find the effects of self-presentation in the social tendency to report hindsight bias. It is proposed that hindsight bias will occur more when outcomes are given than when they not and that it will be increased when pressure to self-present exists. By controlling for factors that elicit hindsight bias and self-presentation, this study proposes to find these results. It is unsure what the results will be for groups who do not know the outcome but will self-present and for those who do know the outcome and will not self-present.

Method

Participants

Participants were students recruited as volunteers from the university's General Psychology classes. There were a total of 67 students. Forty-six were women and 21 were men. Some of the students were awarded extra credit points for their participation.

Relationship Between 6

Materials

The materials used for this study included the Superlab software program (Cedrus Corp.) on personal computers. The program presented a series of 30 general knowledge questions. The questions were devised to be at a level of difficulty that gave the researchers confidence that the participants had at some point been exposed to the questions and would also have been familiar with the answers.

Procedure

Participants arrived at the experimental lab and signed in. They were instructed to sit at a computer station, to read and sign a written consent form, then wait for further instructions. The consent form included statements describing the purpose of the study and how the data would be collected. The exact purpose of the study was not disclosed to the participants. Instead, they were told they would be reviewing questions that average college students can answer correctly. This statement was used in order for participants to be motivated to work in an environment likely to induce hindsight bias and self-presentation. The motivation comes from feeling that the purpose of the study was believable, relevant to their self-esteem, and that the skills needed to succeed were desirable. After all participants completed the forms, they were directed to begin the session. Participants began the session by reading the instructions on the computer screen and then continued to answer the questions by following the prompts given on-screen.

Participants were randomly placed into one of four groups, with an equal number of participants in each group. There were four experimental sessions, with each session addressing one of four conditions. The four conditions were created as follows: Half the participants were placed in groups that reviewed each question followed by its answer (Answer groups); the other half reviewed just the questions (No Answer groups). Questions were shown for ten seconds and answers shown for four seconds. Upon reading either the question and answer or just the question, participants were asked, "If you had to answer the question, would you have answered it correctly? Press Y for yes and N for no." Both the Answer and No Answer groups were divided in half according to whether they were to believe that the number of "yes" responses would be shared with the other participants or kept confidential. This division created the four final groups. They are as follows: Answer/Share, Answer/No Share, No Answer/Share, and No Answer/No Share.

In summary, the Answer/Share group was created to measure hindsight bias and its relationship with self-presentation. The Answer/No Share group was created to measure hindsight bias only. The No Answer/Share measured self-presentation only, and the No Answer/No Share group served as the control. The following figure represents the design:

		Share Answers	
		Yes	No
Get Answers	Yes	Answer/Share (hindsight & self-presentation)	Answer/No Share (hindsight only)
	No	No Answer/Share (self-presentation only)	No Answer/No Share (control)

After completing all 30 questions, all participants were told that the experiment was completed and they would be sent a letter by e-mail discussing the purpose and results of the research. This was done to prevent participants from discussing the study with potential participants.

Results

Participants responded to each question by answering either "yes" or "no." The dependent variable was the number of "yes" responses. Only comparison of the number of "yes" responses (score) was needed to determine whether hindsight bias and self-presentation occurred.

It was believed that the groups who received the answers would demonstrate more hindsight bias by giving more "yes" responses than those who were not given the answers. Due to self-presentation, groups that were told that their answers would be shared were also expected to respond "yes" more often than groups who expected their answers to be kept private.

Table 1 shows means and standard deviations for each group. Figure 1 shows the comparison of mean scores between groups. The table and figure show that participants who received the answers scored higher in the number of "yes" responses than those who did not receive the answers. However, it can be seen that groups who did not believe their responses would be shared responded "yes" more often than the groups who were told their responses would be shared.

A 2×2 between-subjects ANOVA was used to assess the main effects and interaction. Participants who received the answers scored significantly higher than participants who did not, $F(1,65) = 8.409$, $p = .005$. Also, participants who believed their scores would be shared scored significantly lower than the participants who did not believe they would be sharing scores, $F(1,63) = 4.813$, $p = .032$. No interaction occurred between the answer and sharing groups, $F(1,63) = 1.004$, $p = .32$.

Discussion

This research found that when participants were given answers to the questions, they reported that they would have known the answer had they been asked. Participants who were not given the answers reported significantly fewer questions they would have answered correctly. Participants who believed they would share their answers reported that they would have known fewer answers than those who did not believe they would share.

As hypothesized, participants displayed hindsight bias. This was seen in the greater number or "yes" responses when answers were given, as compared to when no answers were given. This finding corresponds to the numerous research studies that have demonstrated the use of hindsight bias (Creyer & Ross, 1993; Melvin & Mellor, 1991; Szalanski & Willham, 1991). It also adds to the list of subject areas of Pohl and Hell's (1996) meta-analysis study in which hindsight occurs.

When participants believed they were going to share their scores, they reported they would not have known the answers more often than did those who believed their scores would not be shared. This finding does not correspond to the prediction of this study. Research used to conduct this study reported that people use self-presentational styles that make themselves look good to their peers. Research has reported that people tend to want to impress others by displaying positive qualities (Stahlberg et al., 1995).

Relationship Between 10

This opposing finding may be due to several factors. One reason may be that participants did not want to look overconfident. They may have anticipated that others would not know as much as they did and feared that they would look foolish for knowing too much. It is also likely that participants were not aware of how they were going to share their answers. If they did not think they were going to share them out loud and be identified with their score, they may have been more honest instead of wanting to self-present. A third explanation may be that participants did not regard the task as important or competitive. Research by Campbell and Sedikides (1999) states that the factors of the task will be reflected in the amount of self-presentation. A last possibility is that these people had lower self-esteem. Research by Schlenker et al. (1990) showed that people with lower self-esteem self-present less. They are more likely to be modest in how they portray themselves to others.

Even though many studies have been done on both hindsight bias and self-presentation, more studies are needed to understand the interaction between the two. It would be important to look at variables such as self-esteem, competitiveness, and relatedness in regard to the nature of participants and design of the study.

References

Campbell, W., & Sedikides, C. (1999). Self-threat magnifies the self-serving bias: A meta-analytic integration. *Review of General Psychology, 3,* 23–43.

Creyer, E., & Ross, W. (1993). Hindsight bias and inferences in choice: The mediating effect of cognitive effort. *Organizational Behavior and Human Decision Processes, 55,* 61–77.

Friedrich, J. (1996). On seeing oneself as less self-serving than others: The ultimate self-serving bias. *Teaching of Psychology, 23,* 107–109.

Hoffrage, U., Hertwig, R., & Gigerenzer, G. (2000). Hindsight bias: Not just a convenient memory enhancer but an important part of an efficient memory system. *Journal of Experimental Psychology: Learning, Memory and Cognition, 26.* Retrieved February 7, 2001, from http://www.eurekalert.org/releases/ apa-hbn050500.

Melvin, M., & Mellor, S. (1991). Effect of self-relevance of an event on hindsight bias: The foreseeability of a layoff. *Journal of Applied Psychology, 76,* 469–577.

Myers, D. (1999). *Social psychology* (6th ed.). Boston: McGraw-Hill.

Ofir, C., & Mazursky, M. (1997). Does a surprising outcome reinforce or reverse the hindsight bias? *Organizational Behavior and Human Decision Processes, 69,* 51–57.

Pohl, R., & Hell, W. (1996). No reduction in hindsight bias after complete information and repeated testing. *Organizational Behavior and Human Decision Processes, 67,* 49–58.

Pohl, R., Stahlberg, D., & Frey, D. (1999). I'm not trying to impress you, but I surely knew it all along! Self-presentation and hindsight bias. *Sonder Forschungs Bereich, 504,* 99-19.

Schlenker, B., Weigold, M., & Hallam, J. (1990). Self-serving attributions in social context: Effects of self-esteem and social pressure. *Journal of Personality and Social Psychology, 58,* 855–863.

Stahlberg, D., Eller, F., Maass, A., & Frey, D. (1995). We knew it all along: Hindsight bias in groups. *Organizational Behavior and Human Decision Processes, 63,* 46–58.

Szalanski, J., & Willham, D. (1991). The hindsight bias: A meta-analysis. *Organizational Behavior and Human Decision Processes, 48,* 147–168.

Table 1

Comparison of Mean "Yes" Responses Between Groups

Answer Condition	Share Condition	Mean	SD	N
Answer	Share	16.67	4.16	18
	No Share	19.68	2.89	19
No Answer	Share	14.87	3.26	16
	No Share	16.00	4.99	14
Total	Share	15.82	3.82	34
	No Share	18.12	4.27	33

Figure Caption

Figure 1. Mean score of "yes" responses as a comparison between groups.

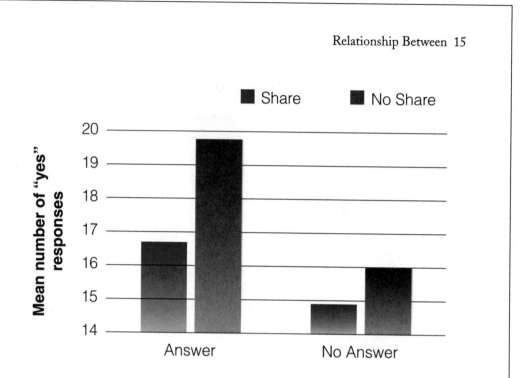

SAMPLE RESEARCH PROPOSAL

Running head: ACETAMINOPHEN IN THE TREATMENT

Acetaminophen in the Treatment of Headache Pain

Student's Name

University of Central Arkansas

Acetaminophen 2

Acetaminophen in the Treatment of Headache Pain

The use of acetaminophen, the main ingredient in Tylenol, has been a controversial issue over the past few decades. The debate concerns how well the drug actually alleviates cephalodynia, or more commonly known as a headache. Many people, mostly the older population, believe that the drug does not relieve the pain of a headache, while the younger generations say they could not live without acetaminophen.

A headache is "a pain in various parts of the head, not confined to the area of distribution of any nerve," according to *Stedman's Concise Medical Dictionary for the Health Professions,* 3rd edition. This definition makes a headache very difficult to measure. In fact, very few studies have been conducted and published concerning acetaminophen's efficacy in the relief of head pain, although the major use of this drug is for treatment of headaches (Fladung, Mehlisch, & Weaver, 1998). Cephalodynia, or headaches, usually occur in an uncontrolled outpatient environment and they are usually sporadic and unpredictable, making them very hard for researchers to observe (Fladung et al., 1998). In most cases, the data collection is dependent upon the patient's/participant's report or subjective account of the pain (Fladung et al., 1998).

Acetaminophen is one of the most common over-the-counter (OTC) analgesics used in the United States for the treatment of headaches (Fladung et al., 1998). When effective, OTC medications offer several advantages over prescription drugs, including easy access, lower cost, and fewer adverse effects (Baggish, Codispoti, Fu, Lipton, & Stewart, 2000).

Fladung et al. (1998) recently conducted an experiment to test if acetaminophen was effective in the treatment of tension headaches. Participants were asked to evaluate the drug over four hours following ingestion of a drug (either acetaminophen, ketoprofen, or placebo). Pain intensity was rated as none, mild, moderate, or severe; all were recorded at different time intervals. The results of the study concluded that acetaminophen proved to be numerically more favorable than placebo, but could not be separated from placebo with statistical significance.

Hamalainen (1998) conducted an experiment to review acetaminophen and placebo in relation to the treatment of migraine headache pain in children. Patients were recruited from headache outpatient clinics. Patients were asked to administer a single dose (15 mg/kg) of acetaminophen at the onset of the headache at home. Figures showed that 54% of the children with severe or moderate migraine attacks were significantly relieved by a single dose of acetaminophen at two hours after taking the drug. The study also concluded that acetaminophen can be very easily swallowed, especially in liquid form.

Baggish et al. (2000) studied the efficacy of acetaminophen in the treatment of migraine headaches. Baggish reports that 19–26% of people in Western countries experience migraine headaches. Of that population, 90% treat their migraines with over-the-counter medications. The United States, in 1998, approved the first OTC agent as a treatment for migraine headaches. Baggish also states that studies previous to his experiment reported acetaminophen as the drug of choice for migraine sufferers. Many reasons for this have been found. One reason is that acetaminophen is not associated with gastrointestinal tract irritation, and it also has only weak anti-inflammatory activity. This study was conducted two hours after dosage with either

Acetaminophen 4

acetaminophen or placebo, and participants were asked to record if they experienced a change in baseline pain intensity from severe or moderate pain to mild or no pain. The study concluded that acetaminophen was highly effective for treating pain; the drug also had an excellent safety profile and was well tolerated by participants.

Although many people use acetaminophen for treatment of different types of headaches, other research needs to be conducted in order to test the validity and reliability of this drug. After reviewing the literature, it is the researchers' hypothesis that there will be statistical significance in acetaminophen's being an effective treatment for headache pain.

Method

Participants

Fifty participants, 25 males and 25 females, who chronically experience headaches will be randomly selected from Conway Regional Medical Center. Participants will range in age from approximately 20 to 60 years of age.

Apparatus/Materials

Several items will be needed for this study. A notebook, a pencil, and a watch are all necessary to record and time the duration and severity of the headache pain. Acetaminophen and placebo in a specially designed pill box are also necessary for the experiment in order to determine if either has an effect on reducing the headache pain.

Procedure

The study will be a single-blind study, in which the participants do not know whether they are taking acetaminophen or placebo. Participants will be randomly assigned to two groups; one will be taking acetaminophen first, and the other group will be taking placebo first. The order of the pills will then rotate back and forth between the two options. The acetaminophen and placebo are the same shape, color, and taste. The pills will be kept in a divided rectangular-shaped box, and the participant has to take the pills in order from left to right. Only the researcher will know which pill the participant has taken.

At the onset of pain (headache), the participant is to record the degree of pain he/she is experiencing. The pain will be scaled on a Likert scale where 0 represents no pain and 5 represents severe pain. The participant is to record the time the pill (either acetaminophen or placebo) is taken, and the participant is also to record the sequence written on the pill. Every hour (for four hours), the participant is to record the degree of pain. Each time the participant experiences a headache, the above process is to be conducted until all ten pills are taken, or until two weeks have elapsed. The data will be collected from each participant after the two-week period. The experimenter will then analyze the data.

Results

It is hypothesized that acetaminophen is an effective treatment for headache pain. To analyze the data, the experimenter must consider the severity of the pain, which has been rated on a Likert scale with 0 representing no pain and 5 representing severe pain. The researcher will summarize the data by using the mean as a measure of central tendency. The mean pain rating for each participant under each condition will be calculated. Also, a mean for each condition across all participants will be calculated. A

Acetaminophen 6

bar graph will then be used to portray the results of the study. The graph will have the dependent variable (Likert scale of pain ratings) along the y-axis and the independent variable (acetaminophen and placebo) along the x-axis. The experimenter will also conduct a correlated groups t test to show whether there is a significant difference between acetaminophen and placebo.

References

Baggish, J., Codispoti, J., Fu, M., Lipton, R., & Stewart, W. (2000). Efficacy and

safety of acetaminophen in the treatment of migraine. *Archives of Internal

Medicine, 160,* 3486–3492.

Fladung, B., Mehlisch, D., & Weaver, M. (1998). Ketoprofen, acetaminophen, and

placebo in the treatment of tension headache. *Headache, 38,* 579–589.

Hamalainen, M. (1998). Attack treatment of migraine in children. *Headache

Quarterly, 9,* 241–244.

GLOSSARY

a priori specific comparison test Inferential statistics used to make specific comparisons among some group means when such comparisons are planned in advance of the data collection.

active control Procedure in which the control participants receive an established treatment with a known degree of effectiveness.

alpha (α) level The probability value at which the experimenter decides to reject the null hypothesis and conclude that the independent variable did have an effect on the dependent variable; the probability of falsely rejecting a true H_0.

alternate form reliability Reliability established by administering two different forms of the same test to the same individuals.

alternative hypothesis (H_1) Hypothesis that the independent variable does have an effect on the dependent variable; sample means come from populations with different means.

attrition Withdrawal of participants that may be focused on a particular group or participants with particular characteristics.

baseline Comparison point established by repeated observations of the natural frequency of the behavior of interest.

basic research Research engaged in for the purpose of increasing knowledge of fundamental processes; may have no immediate goals or applications.

carryover effects Effects that earlier conditions have on later performance.

case study Nonexperimental research technique involving a single individual or a small group of individuals in which observations are made over time (either retrospectively or prospectively).

ceiling effect Measurement of the dependent variable results in many very high or highest scores on the dependent variable, thus masking a potential effect of the independent variable.

census All elements in a population are included in the study.

chaos theory An attempt to understand complex, nonlinear, dynamic systems by using mathematical modeling.

completely randomized factorial design Experimental design with two independent variables in which participants are randomly assigned to the different levels of each independent variable.

concurrent validity Validity established by comparing scores to a similar test instrument.

confidence interval An interval that, with repeated sampling, will include the parameter of interest between its boundaries a specified percentage of the time—for example, the 95% confidence interval.

confirmation bias A general tendency to emphasize positive confirming outcomes rather than negative or disconfirming ones.

confounding variables (confounds) A type of extraneous variable that acts like an independent variable to create differences among group scores.

construct validity An instrument is considered to have construct validity if it assists in understanding and predicting operationally defined behavior.

content validity Measuring material is drawn directly from the content of the course or training program.

convenience sampling The quick, inexpensive, and convenient use of participants who are available at the moment.

correlated samples Experimental design in which scores in the groups are clustered into sets.

correlated samples *t* test An inferential statistic used to analyze an experiment in which natural pairs, matched pairs, or repeated measures were used to place participants into two treatment conditions.

correlation coefficient A number that describes the direction and strength of a relationship between two variables.

correlational research Selecting a population and ascertaining the relationship among variables of interest; does not use random assignment or manipulation of conditions.

counterbalancing Varying the order of treatment conditions among the participants; used in repeated measures designs to equalize carryover effects among conditions.

criterion variable The measure that is predicted by the predictor variable in correlational research.

critical values Values that define the region of rejection of H_0 at various levels of α.

cross-sectional research Research that compares preexisting groups that come from portions of a particular dimension; commonly used by developmental psychologists to study the behavior of individuals from different age groups in order to assess developmental changes.

debriefing A statement to participants at the end of a study that reveals the true purpose of the study.

deception Research participant is not fully informed about the nature of the study and is often provided misleading information.

deductive reasoning The formulation of specific observational predictions based on a general principle or theory.

demand characteristics Implicit and explicit cues in the research setting that suggest to the participant that he/she behave in a certain way.

dependent variable A measure of behavior that is recorded after the independent variable is introduced.

determinism The notion that all events in the universe, including behavior, are the lawful consequence of prior events.

diffusion of treatment Details about specific treatments in the experiment become known to participants before they participate.

direction of control When two variables (X and Y) are related, it is possible that X causes Y, Y causes X, or that some other variable causes both X and Y.

double-blind study When neither the participant nor the experimenter is aware of the conditions in effect.

duration method of observation Observer records the period of time during which the target behavior lasts.

effect size A statistical measure of the size of the effect of one variable on another variable.

element A single member of a population.

empirical referent An object, person, or event of which we are capable of having a direct experience.

empiricism The use of observational experience as the basis for understanding the past and present and predicting the future.

ethnography Nonexperimental research technique to understand the behavior of members of a culture.

evaluation apprehension Participants' concerns and apprehensions about being observed and/or evaluated.

ex post facto design Nonexperimental research technique in which preexisting groups are compared on some dependent variable.

exhaustive list All members of the population appear on the list.

experimenter bias Experimenter's knowledge of the experiment influences observations or is unintentionally communicated to participants.

experimenter characteristics Personality and physical characteristics of the experimenter that influence the behavior of the participants.

experimenter expectancies The behavior desired by the experimenter is unintentionally communicated to the participant.

external validity When the findings may generalize from a small sample to a population, from a specific setting to a broader setting, from specific values of the independent variable to a broader range of values, and from one behavioral measure to another.

face validity A judgment made after the test is constructed about whether the test instrument appears to measure the content of the course.

facilitation An increase of responding when compared to baseline.

field research Research conducted in an environment not designed and controlled by the experimenter.

floor effect Measurement of the dependent variable results in many very low or lowest scores on the dependent variable, thus masking a potential effect of the independent variable.

frequency method of observation Observer counts the number of times that a target behavior occurs within a specified period of time.

functional relationship A relationship in which the value of one variable varies with changes in the values of a second variable.

historical control Procedure in which the effects of a new treatment are compared to past records of patients who were either untreated or received a different treatment.

history Occurrence of a specific event during the course of data collection that influences the behavior of the participants.

homogeneity of variance Equal variability in each treatment condition; a statistical assumption of several parametric statistical analyses.

hypothesis A prediction of what the relationship will be between one variable and another variable.

independent observation When the observations of one observer do not influence the observations of another observer.

independent samples Experimental design in which participants are randomly assigned to the different treatment conditions.

independent samples *t* test An inferential statistic used to analyze an experiment in which random assignment was used to place participants into two treatment groups; can also be used to analyze ex post facto research with two preexisting groups.

independent variable A variable under the control of and administered by the experimenter.

inductive reasoning Formulation of a general principle or theory based on a set of specific observations.

informed consent Individual agrees to be a research participant after being informed of the nature of the study.

Institutional Review Board (IRB) Committee of persons from the institution and from the community that grants ethics approval to research proposals involving human participants.

instructions Information given to participants that enables them to perform the required task; must be clear and consistent to ensure task does not vary.

instrument An established questionnaire that has known validity and reliability.

instrumentation The methods used to record observations; may change or deteriorate over time.

interaction The effect of one variable depends on the level of another variable.

internal validity When the independent variable is responsible for observed variations in the dependent variable.

interobserver agreement The degree to which the data scorings by independent observers of the same target behavior agree.

interparticipant replication Replication with a different participant or participants.

interval method of observation Observer records whether or not a target behavior is occurring at specified equal time intervals.

interval scale A quantitative scale expressing "how much"; does not have a true zero point.

interview One-to-one interaction with a research participant in which questions are prepared but flexibility is available to clarify and enhance data collection.

intraparticipant replication Replication within the same participant.

inventory An established questionnaire that has known validity and reliability.

irreversible behavior When behavior does not return to baseline after treatment is withdrawn.

laboratory research Research conducted in an environment designed and controlled by the experimenter.

longitudinal research Repeated testing of the same individuals over a substantial time span, usually years.

main effect An effect of one variable found over all levels of a second variable.

matched pairs Correlated samples design in which scores in the groups are clustered into sets because the experimenter matches participants on some variable.

matching Pairing participants according to their similarity on a predictor variable.

maturation Changes in the state of participants over time that influence their behavior.

mean Measure of central tendency obtained by summing all the scores and dividing by the number of scores.

measure of central tendency Measure that describes the center of a distribution of scores.

measure of variability Measure that describes the extent of the dispersion of scores.

measurement The process of assigning numbers to objects and events in accordance with a set of rules.

median The middle score in a distribution of scores; half the scores are above the median, and half are below.

meta-analysis A statistical technique that provides an indication of the size of an effect across the results of multiple studies.

mixed factorial design Experimental design with two independent variables in which participants are randomly assigned to different levels of one independent variable and participate in all levels of the other independent variable.

mode The most frequent score in a distribution.

monotonic relationship A consistent relationship between two variables such that as the values of one variable increase, the values of the other variable always increase (or always decrease).

multiple baseline procedure Intraparticipant replication with different and independent (uncorrelated) responses.

natural pairs Correlated samples design in which the scores in the groups are clustered into sets for a natural reason (e.g., twin studies).

naturalistic observation Correlational or ex post facto design that takes place in a "real-world" setting.

nominal scale A scale in which numbers are assigned to objects or events for identification purposes.

nonmonotonic relationship A relationship between two variables such that as the values of one variable increase, the values of the other variable increase at times and decrease at other times.

nonparametric statistics Inferential statistics used with nominal or ordinal data or when certain assumptions for parametric analysis are not met (e.g., Wilcoxon t, Mann–Whitney, chi-square).

nonparticipant observation Investigators do not interact with the participants during times of observation.

nonprobability sampling There is no way of estimating the probability that an element will be included in the sample.

nonreactive measures Observations of behavior made without the person's being aware that he or she is being observed.

null hypothesis (H_0) The hypothesis that the independent variable has no effect on the dependent variable; sample means come from populations with the same mean.

observer drift A gradual shift in the observational criteria during the course of the research.

one-way correlated samples ANOVA An inferential statistic used to analyze an experiment in which natural pairs, matched pairs, or repeated measures were used to place participants into two or more treatment conditions.

one-way independent samples ANOVA An inferential statistic used to analyze an experiment in which random assignment was used to place participants into two or more treatment groups.

operational definition Defining a term or concept by the way in which it is measured—that is, making the term observable.

optimal baseline When the baseline behavior shows little change from session to session.

ordinal scale A scale in which numbers represent rank order (greater than, less than) without equal intervals.

parametric statistics Inferential statistics used with interval or ratio data and when certain assumptions are met (e.g., t test, ANOVA).

participant observation Investigators interact with participants during times of observation.

percentage agreement among observers A method for measuring the reliability of observations.

phenomenology Nonexperimental research technique in which in-depth interviews provide insight into the experiences of an individual or a group of individuals.

placebo control Procedure in which the control participants believe that they receive an effective treatment when in fact they do not.

plagiarism Taking the ideas or words of someone else and representing them as yours.

population All members that meet a specified criterion; all measurements meeting a set of specifications.

post hoc specific comparison test Inferential statistics used to make specific comparisons among group means when there are more than two groups and the ANOVA is significant (e.g., Tukey HSD, Bonferroni test, Scheffé test).

power The probability of correctly rejecting a false null hypothesis.

predictive validity Validity established by how well the test predicts relevant aspects of behavior.

predictor variable The measure that is used to predict the criterion variable in correlational research.

probability sampling A researcher can specify the probability that an element will be included in the sample.

qualitative research Nonexperimental research that describes and interprets observations but does not seek to quantify observations numerically.

qualitative variable A variable that differs in kind rather than in amount.

quantitative variable A variable that differs in quantity or amount.

quasi-experiment Similar to a true experiment except that random assignment of participants is not used.

questionnaire A set of questions designed to measure facts, opinions, and attitudes from a large sample of individuals.

quota sampling When lists are not available, interviewers are assigned a starting point, a specified direction, and a goal of meeting quotas of various subsets of the population.

random assignment Assigning participants to each experimental condition in such a way that any given participant is as likely to be assigned to one condition as another.

random error The operation of extraneous variables in a chance manner to increase variability of scores within groups.

random sampling Selecting samples in such a way that each sample of a given size has the same probability of being selected; each element in the population has an equal chance of being selected.

random sampling error A sample is biased (does not accurately represent the intended population) simply due to chance.

range Measure of variability defined as the difference between the highest and lowest scores in a distribution.

ratio scale A scale with the properties of an interval scale but with a true zero, so that ratios between quantities can be expressed.

rationalism The use of reason and logic as the basis for knowledge.

reactive measures Observations of behavior made with the person aware that he or she is being observed.

reductionist A person who seeks to explain complex phenomena in terms of relatively simple and basic building blocks.

region of rejection Portion of the area under a curve that includes values of a test statistic that lead to a rejection of H_0.

regression to the mean Individuals high or low on one testing are found to be closer to (regress toward) the mean on a subsequent testing.

reliability The consistency of the measuring instrument.

reliability coefficient A statistic that measures the reliability of observations.

repeated measures Correlated samples design in which scores in the groups are clustered into sets because the same participants participate in all conditions.

repeated measures factorial design Experimental design with two independent variables in which the same participants participate in all conditions.

replication An independent repetition of an experimental procedure under as similar conditions as the experimental materials permit.

reversible behavior When behavior returns to baseline after treatment is withdrawn.

sample A subset of a population.

sampling distribution A theoretical probability distribution of possible values of some sample statistic that would occur if we were to draw all possible samples of a fixed size from a given population.

sampling error The fact that samples drawn from the same population will rarely provide identical estimates of the population parameter of interest.

scatterplot A graph of points whose coordinates represent values of two variables under study.

selection Behavioral observations are affected by the particular participants chosen for the study or the particular participants assigned to the treatment conditions.

simple effect An effect of one independent variable is not found over all levels of a second independent variable.

single-blind study Only the participant is unaware of the condition to which he or she is being exposed.

split-half reliability Reliability established by comparing responses to half the questions on a test with responses on the other half of the same test.

standard deviation The square root of the variance; on average, how far scores are from the mean.

stratified random sample Random samples are selected from different strata or subgroups of the population.

suppression A decrease of responding when compared to baseline levels.

survey Using an interview, questionnaire, or inventory in an attempt to estimate opinions, attitudes, and characteristics of a population based on a sample.

systematic error (confounding) Intermixing of effects of extraneous variables with possible effects of the independent variable; variability in scores between groups that is the result of variables other than the independent variable.

systematic observation Observations planned and prepared in advance, including control over conditions under which the observations are made.

systematic sampling error A sample is biased because it was not properly drawn by the researcher.

systematic variance Variability in scores between groups that is the result of the manipulation of the independent variable.

task Behavioral observations are affected if what participants are asked to do is not the same for all groups or conditions.

tautological (circular) reasoning Using a definition as an explanation, thus reasoning in a circle—for example, they are fighting because they are hostile; I know they are hostile because they are fighting.

test–retest reliability Reliability established by administering the same test twice to the same individuals.

testing effects Behavioral observations during subsequent testing are affected by prior testing or observational experiences in the study.

theory A system of ideas or a set of principles, often dealing with mechanisms or underlying reasons for behavior, that help us organize and assimilate the empirical relationships (observations) that we discover.

third variable The variable that actually causes changes in two variables (X and Y) and that explains the relationship between X and Y.

time-series design Repeated measurements of the dependent variable over time with an introduction of the independent variable at a particular point in time.

transient effects Short-term effects of prior conditions, such as fatigue or boredom.

Type I error An error made when H_0 is true but is mistakenly rejected.

Type II error An error made when H_0 is actually false but is not rejected.

unobtrusive measures Measures recorded from individuals without their awareness.

validity A valid instrument measures what it purports to measure.

variable A condition that can vary or change in quantity or quality.

variance Measure of variability based on the squared deviations of scores from the mean.

yoked control Procedure in which two participants are simultaneously exposed to the same condition but the behavior of only one participant determines exposure to the treatment.

REFERENCES

American Psychological Association. (2001). *Publication manual of the American Psychological Association* (5th ed.). Washington, DC: Author.

Appel, L. J., Champagne, C. M., Harsha, D. W., Cooper, L. S., Obarzanek, E., Elmer, P. J., Stevens, V. J., Vollmer, W. M., Lin, P., Svetkey, L. P., & Young, D. R. (2003). Effects of comprehensive lifestyle modification on blood pressure control: Main results of the PREMIER clinical trial. *JAMA: Journal of the American Medical Association, 289,* 2083–2093.

Asch, S. E. (1956). Studies of independence and conformity: A minority of one against a unanimous majority. *Psychological Monographs, 70,* 416.

Barnes, M. L., & Rosenthal, R. (1985). Interpersonal effects of experimenter attractiveness, attire, and gender. *Journal of Personality and Social Psychology, 48,* 435–446.

Barton, E. S., Guess, D., Garcia, E., & Baer, D. M. (1970). Improvement of retardates' mealtime behaviors by timeout procedures using multiple baseline techniques. *Journal of Applied Behavioral Analysis, 3,* 77–84.

Bellon, M. L., Ogletree, B. T., & Harn, W. E. (2000). Repeated storybook reading as a language intervention for children with autism: A case study on the application of scaffolding. *Focus on Autism and Other Developmental Disabilities, 15,* 52–58.

Binder, A., McConnell, D., & Sjoholm, N. A. (1957). Verbal conditioning as a function of experimenter characteristics. *Journal of Abnormal and Social Psychology, 55,* 309–314.

Bleeker, M. M., Evans, S. C., Fisher, M. N., & Miller, K. A. (1998). The effects of extracurricular activities on self-esteem, academic achievement, and aggression in college students. *Psi Chi Journal of Undergraduate Research, 3,* 34–38.

Brady, J. V. (1958). Ulcers in "executive" monkeys. *Scientific American, 199,* 95–104.

Bryant, J. A., Mealey, L., & Herzog, E. A. (2001). Paradoxical effect of surveyor's conservative versus provocative clothing on rape myth acceptance of males and females. *Journal of Psychology and Human Sexuality, 13,* 55–66.

Callaway, J. W., Nowicki, S., & Duke, M. P. (1980). Overt expression of experimenter expectancies, interaction with subject expectancies, and performance on a psychomotor task. *Journal of Research in Personality, 14,* 27–39.

Cohen, J. (1960). A coefficient of agreement for nominal scales. *Psychological Measurement, 20,* 37–46.

Cohen, J. (1977). *Statistical power analysis for the behavioral sciences* (rev. ed.). New York: Academic Press.

Davis, M. K., & Gidycz, C. A. (2000). Child sexual abuse prevention programs: A meta-analysis. *Journal of Clinical Child Psychology, 29,* 257–265.

Ehrlich, J. S., & Riesman, D. (1961). Age and authority in the interview. *Opinion Quarterly, 25,* 39–56.

Fisher, J. D., Fisher, W. A., & Bryan, A. D. (2002). Information-motivation-behavioral skills model–based HIV risk behavior change intervention for inner-city high school youth. *Health Psychology, 21,* 177–186.

Fleishhacker, W. W., & Marksteiner, J. (2000). Future perspectives in antipsychotic drug development. In M. S. Lidow (Ed.), *Neurotransmitter receptors in actions of antipsychotic medications* (pp. 243–246). Boca Raton, FL: CRC Press.

Friedman, N., Kurland, D., & Rosenthal, R. (1965). Experimenter behavior as an unintended determinant of experimental results. *Journal of Projective Techniques and Personality Assessment, 29,* 479–490.

Goon, A. R., Teel, S., Fuller, S., & Allen, M. J. (1998). College students' attitudes toward gender equity in intercollegiate sports. *Psi Chi Journal of Undergraduate Research, 3,* 18–23.

Katz, I., Robinson, J. M., & Epps, E. G. (1964). Race of experimenter and instructions in the expression of hostility of Negro boys. *Journal of Social Issues, 20,* 54–60.

Kawas, C. H., Clark, C. M., & Farlow, M. R. (1999). Clinical trials in Alzheimer disease: Debate on the use of placebo controls. *Alzheimer Disease and Associated Disorders, 13,* 124–129.

Khersonskaya, M. Y., & Smith, R. A. (1998). Cross-cultural differences in perception of physical attractiveness. *Psi Chi Journal of Undergraduate Research, 3,* 39–42.

Kolb, K. J., & Jussim, L. (1994). Teacher expectations and underachieving gifted children. *Roeper Review, 17,* 26–30.

Langston, W. (2005). *Research methods laboratory manual for psychology* (2nd ed.). Belmont, CA: Wadsworth.

Leitenberg, H. (1973). The use of single-case methodology in psychotherapy research. *Journal of Abnormal Psychology, 82,* 87–101.

Milgram, S. (1963). Behavioral study of obedience. *Journal of Abnormal and Social Psychology, 67,* 371–378.

Milgram, S. (1965). Some conditions of obedience and disobedience to authority. *Human Relations, 18,* 57–76.

Mitchell, C., Thompson, D., & Burns, R. (1972). Vampire bat control by systemic treatment of livestock with an anticoagulant. *Science, 177,* 806–808.

Moskalenko, S., & Heine, S. J. (2003). Watching your troubles away: Television viewing as a stimulus for subjective self-awareness. *Personality and Social Psychology Bulletin, 29,* 76–85.

National Science Foundation. (1969). TRACES: Basic research links to technology appraised. *Science, 163,* 374–375.

Rosenthal, R., & Jacobsen, L. (1968). *Pygmalion in the classroom.* New York: Rinehart and Winston.

Schaller, G. B. (1963). *The mountain gorilla.* Chicago: University of Chicago Press.

Schulz, S. C., van Kammen, D. P., Balow, J. E., Flye, M. W., & Bunney, W. E., Jr. (1981). Dialysis in schizophrenia: A double blind evaluation. *Science, 211,* 1066–1068.

Seligman, M. E. P. (1998). *Learned optimism: How to change your mind and life.* New York: Simon & Schuster.

Seligman, M. E. P., & Maier, S. F. (1967). Failure to escape traumatic shock. *Journal of Experimental Psychology, 74,* 1–9.

Shapiro, A. K., & Morris, L. A. (1978). The placebo effect in medical and psychological therapies. In S. L. Garfield & A. E. Bergin (Eds.), *Handbook of psychotherapy and behavior change.* New York: Wiley.

Sheets, K. J. (1999). Effects of extraversion and introversion on job interview success. *Journal of Psychological Inquiry, 4,* 7–11.

Sidman, M. (1960). *Tactics of scientific research.* New York: Basic Books.

Solomon, G. B. (2002). Confidence as a source of expectancy information: A follow-up investigation. *International Sports Journal, 6,* 119–127.

Thompson, J. B., & Buchanan, W. (1979). *Analyzing psychological data*. New York: Scribner's.

Vollmer, T. R., Iwata, B. A., & Zarcone, J. R. (1993). The role of attention in the treatment of attention-maintained self-injurious behavior: Noncontingent reinforcement and differential reinforcement of other behavior. *Journal of Applied Behavior Analysis, 26*, 9–21.

Weiss, J. M. (1968). Effects of coping response on stress. *Journal of Comparative and Physiological Psychology, 65*, 251–260.

Weiss, J. M. (1971a). Effects of coping behavior in different warning signal conditions on stress pathology in rats. *Journal of Comparative and Physiological Psychology, 77*, 1–13.

Weiss, J. M. (1971b). Effects of punishing the coping response (conflict) on stress pathology in rats. *Journal of Comparative and Physiological Psychology, 77*, 14–21.

Weiss, J. M. (1971c). Effects of coping behavior with and without a feedback signal on stress pathology in rats. *Journal of Comparative and Physiological Psychology, 77*, 22–30.

Zimbardo, P. G. (1969). The human choice: Individuation, reason, and order versus deindividuation, impulse, and chaos. In W. J. Arnold & D. Levine (Eds.), *Nebraska Symposium on Motivation* (Vol. 17, pp. 237–307). Lincoln: University of Nebraska Press.

NAME INDEX

J

Jacobson, L., 125
Jussim, L., 126

K

Katz, I., 124
Kawas, C. H., 153
Khersonskaya, M. Y., 49
Kinsey, A. C., 91
Kolb, K. J., 126
Kurland, D., 124

L

Lammers, W. J., 2, 23, 69, 271, 277
Langdon, Alf, 92, 103
Langston, W., 98
Leitenberg, H., 243
Levinson, P., 132
Lieber, A. L., 259
Lysenko, T. D., 26

M

Maier, S. F., 70
Marksteiner, J., 154
McConnell, D., 124
Mealey, L., 123
Milgram, S., 7–8
Mitchell, C., 42
Morris, L. A., 153
Moskalenko, S., 52

N

Nodine, B. F., 277
Nowicki, S., 126

O

Ogletree, B. T., 230
Ostertag, L., 111

P

Pavlov, I., 26
Piaget, Jean, 264, 265
Ptolemy, 30

R

Ramachandran, V. S., 277
Rechtschaffen, A., 152
Riesman, D., 124
Robinson, J., 124
Roentgen, W., 40
Roosevelt, Franklin D., 92, 103
Rosenthal, R., 124, 125

S

Sabin, A. B., 40
Salk, J. E., 40
Schulz, G. B., 150
Seligman, M. E. P., 70
Shakespeare, William, 27
Shapiro, A. K., 153
Sheets, K. J., 20, 49
Sidman, M., 237
Sjoholm, N. A., 124
Skinner, B. F., 40, 230
Smith, R. A., 49
Solomon, G. B., 126
Stevenson, Robert Louis, 259

T

Teel, S., 49
Thompson, D., 42
Thompson, J. B., 176
Truman, Harry, 103

V

van Kammen, D. P., 150
Vedantam, S., 16
Vollmer, T. R., 247

W

Weiss, J. M., 152

Z

Zarcone, J. R., 247
Zimbardo, P., 8

SUBJECT INDEX

Experimenter bias
    classes of, 125
    defined, 307
    expectancy and, 125–126
    ruling out, 149
Experimenter characteristics, 124–125, 307
Experimenter expectancies, 125–126, 307
Experimenters, 144
    bias of, 125–126, 149, 307
    characteristics, 124–125, 307
    control and, 144–145
    extraneous variability from, 121, 124–126
Experiments, true
    characteristics of, 138–139
    compared with quasi-experiments, 194
Explanation, as goal of science, 28
Ex post facto design
    defined, 306
    as nonexperimental method, 262–264
    summary of, 289
External validity
    defined, 307
    generalization and, 131–133
    repeated measures and, 203
Extraneous variability. See Variability, extraneous
Extrasensory perception (ESP), 43

F

Face validity, 68–69, 307
Facilitation, 235, 307
Factorial design, 217–228
    case analysis, 226
    characteristics of, 217–218
    completely randomized, 220, 305
    complex, 225–226
    main effects and interactions, 223–225
    mixed, 221, 223, 308
    possible outcomes of 2 × 2 factorial experiment, 218–220
    repeated measures, 220–222, 310
    summary/review, 226–228
    terminology, 227
Faculty, 48
Faith, vs. empiricism, 26
Fatigue, as transient effect, 204
Field research
    defined, 307
    ethics and, 14
    laboratory research compared with, 95–96

Figures (captions)
    descriptive statistics and, 164–165
    in written reports, 277–278
Floor effect, 55–56, 307
Footnotes, written reports, 278
F-ratio, 190, 192, 210
Frequency
    measures, 56
    ratio scale vs. nominal scale, 66
Frequency distribution
    graphing a range of scores, 165
    of sample mean, 169
    of scores in descriptive statistics, 158
Frequency histogram, 165
Frequency method of observation, 82, 307
Frustration, constructive play of children and, 208
Functional relationship, of variables, 51, 307

G

Galaxy search engine, 48
Gallup Poll
    attitude assessment by, 113
    quota sampling, 109
    as survey method, 92
Generalization
    external validity and, 131–133
    of observation, 37–38
Genetics, study linking child abuse to, 16
Glossary, of this book, 321–327
Goals, of science, 28–29, 35
Graduate Record Examination (GRE), 94
Graphs
    measuring variability, 164–165
    scatterplot, 257, 310
Greater than (>), 177
GRE (Graduate Record Examination), 94
Groups
    comparing more than two with one-way correlated samples, 211–212
    comparing more than two with one-way independent samples, 191–192
    comparing two with one-way correlated samples, 208–209
    comparing two with one-way independent samples, 188–189
    in molecular-molar continuum, 38–39
Guilt, operational definition, 62

TO THE OWNER OF THIS BOOK:

We hope that you have found *Fundamentals of Behavioral Research* useful. So that this book can be improved in a future edition, would you take the time to complete this sheet and return it? Thank you.

School and address:___UTK_____

Department:___Psychology_____

Instructor's name:___Saudargas_____

1. What I like most about this book is:_____

_____

_____

2. What I like least about this book is:
   ___I had to pay $120 for it. Hello._____

_____

3. My general reaction to this book is:

_____

_____

4. The name of the course in which I used this book is:
   ___Psych 295 → Statistical Analysis Something___

5. Were all of the chapters of the book assigned for you to read?___Yes_____

   If not, which ones weren't?_____

6. In the space below, or on a separate sheet of paper, please write specific suggestions for improving this book and anything else you'd care to share about your experience in using this book.

_____

_____

DO NOT STAPLE. TAPE HERE. TAPE HERE. DO NOT STAPLE.

FOLD HERE

THOMSON

★

™

WADSWORTH

BUSINESS REPLY MAIL

FIRST-CLASS MAIL   PERMIT NO. 102   MONTEREY CA

POSTAGE WILL BE PAID BY ADDRESSEE

Attn: Vicki Knight, Psychology Editor

Wadsworth/Thomson Learning
60 Garden Ct Ste 205
Monterey CA 93940-9967

FOLD HERE

OPTIONAL:

Your name: _Jim Shu_____ Date: _9|05|04___

May we quote you, either in promotion for *Fundamentals of Behavioral Research* or in future publishing ventures?

Yes: ___/_____   No: _____

Sincerely yours,

William J. Lammers and Pietro Badia